T0328771

MARKET LIQUIDITY

This book presents the theory and evidence on the effect of market liquidity and liquidity risk on asset prices and on overall securities market performance. Illiquidity means incurring high transaction cost, which includes a large price impact when trading and facing a long time to unload a large position. Liquidity risk is higher if a security becomes more illiquid when it needs to be traded in the future, which will raise its trading cost. The analysis in this book shows that higher illiquidity and greater liquidity risk reduce securities prices and raise the expected return that investors require as compensation. Aggregate market liquidity is linked to funding liquidity, which affects the provision of liquidity services. When these become constrained, there is a liquidity crisis, which leads to downward price and liquidity spiral. Overall, this book demonstrates the important role of liquidity in asset pricing.

Yakov Amihud is the Ira Rennert Professor of Finance at the Stern School of Business, New York University. His research focuses on the effects of the liquidity of stocks and bonds on their returns and values, and the design and evaluation of securities markets' trading methods and systems. On these topics, Professor Amihud has advised the New York Stock Exchange, American Stock Exchange, Chicago Board of Options Exchange, Chicago Board of Trade, and other securities markets. He has published more than ninety research articles on economics and finance in professional journals and in books, and has edited and co-edited five books on securities market design, international finance, leveraged buyouts, and bank mergers and acquisitions.

Haim Mendelson is the Kleiner Perkins Caufield & Byers Professor of Electronic Business and Commerce, and Management, at the Graduate School of Business, Stanford University. His research interests include securities markets, electronic markets, information technology, and the information industries. He was elected Distinguished Fellow of the Information Systems Society in recognition of outstanding intellectual contributions to the discipline. Professor Mendelson has published more than one hundred research papers in professional journals and has consulted for high-tech companies, financial institutions, and securities markets including the New York Stock Exchange, American Stock Exchange, Chicago Board of Options Exchange, and Chicago Board of Trade.

Lasse Heje Pedersen is the John A. Paulson Professor of Finance and Alternative Investments at the Stern School of Business, NYU, and a principal at AQR Capital Management. He has been part of the Liquidity Working Group of the Federal Reserve Bank of New York, the New York Fed's Monetary Policy Panel, the Board of Directors of the American Finance Association, the Economic Advisory Boards of NASDAQ and FTSE, and associate editor at the *Journal of Finance, Journal of Economic Theory, Review of Asset Pricing Studies*, and *Quarterly Journal of Economics*. His research explains how crises can arise from liquidity spirals and how market and funding liquidity risks explain equity returns, bond yields, option prices, and currency crashes. Professor Pedersen received the 2011 Bernàcer Prize to the best European Union economist under 40 years of age.

Market Liquidity

Asset Pricing, Risk, and Crises

YAKOV AMIHUD
Stern School of Business, New York University

HAIM MENDELSON
Graduate School of Business, Stanford University

LASSE HEJE PEDERSEN
Stern School of Business, New York University

CAMBRIDGE
UNIVERSITY PRESS

32 Avenue of the Americas, New York NY 10013-2473, USA

Cambridge University Press is part of the University of Cambridge.

It furthers the University's mission by disseminating knowledge in the pursuit of education, learning and research at the highest international levels of excellence.

www.cambridge.org
Information on this title: www.cambridge.org/9780521139656

First published 2013

A catalogue record for this publication is available from the British Library

Library of Congress Cataloguing in Publication data

Market liquidity : asset pricing, risk, and crises / Yakov Amihud, Stern School of Business, New York University, Haim Mendelson, Graduate School of Business, Stanford University, Lasse Heje Pedersen, Stern School of Business, New York University.
pages   cm
Includes bibliographical references and index.
ISBN 978-0-521-19176-0 (hardback) – ISBN 978-0-521-13965-6 (paperback)
1. Liquidity (Economics)   2. Securities – Prices.   I. Amihud, Yakov, 1947–
II. Mendelson, Haim.   III. Pedersen, Lasse Heje.
HG178.M37   2013
332.63′222–dc23   2012010868

ISBN 978-0-521-19176-0 Hardback
ISBN 978-0-521-13965-6 Paperback

Contents

v

Acknowledgments

Acknowledgment is gratefully made to the following co-authors and journals for their permission to reprint the original articles included here:

Yakov Amihud and Haim Mendelson, Asset pricing and the bid–ask spread. *Journal of Financial Economics* 17, 1986

Yakov Amihud and Haim Mendelson, Liquidity, maturity and the yields on U.S. Treasury securities. *Journal of Financial Economics* 46, 1991

Yakov Amihud, Haim Mendelson, and Beni Lauterbach, Market microstructure and securities values: Evidence from the Tel Aviv Stock Exchange. *Journal of Financial Economics* 45, 1997

Yakov Amihud, Illiquidity and stock returns: Cross-section and time-series effects. *Journal of Financial Markets* 5, 2002

Viral V. Acharya and Lasse Heje Pedersen, Asset pricing with liquidity risk. *Journal of Financial Economics* 77, 2005

Markus K. Brunnermeier and Lasse Heje Pedersen, Market liquidity and funding liquidity. *Review of Financial Studies* 22, 2009

Yakov Amihud, Haim Mendelson, and Robert Wood, Liquidity and the 1987 stock market crash. *Journal of Portfolio Management* 16, 1990

Mark Mitchell, Lasse Heje Pedersen, and Todd Pulvino, Slow moving capital. *American Economic Review* 97, 2007

Introduction and Overview
of the Book

This book is about the pricing of *liquidity*. We present theory and evidence on how liquidity affects securities prices, why liquidity varies over time, how a drop in liquidity leads to a decline in prices, and why liquidity crises create liquidity spirals. The analysis has important implications for traders, risk managers, central bankers, performance evaluation, economic policy, regulation of financial markets, management of liquidity crises, and academic research.

Liquidity and its converse, illiquidity, are elusive concepts: You know it when you see it, but it is hard to define. A liquid security is characterized by the ability to buy or sell large amounts of it at low cost. A good example is U.S. Treasury bills, which can be sold in blocks of $20 million dollars instantaneously at the cost of a fraction of a basis point. On the other hand, trading an illiquid security is difficult, time-consuming, and/or costly. Illiquidity is observed when there is a large difference between the offered sale price and the bid (buying) price, if trading of a large quantity of a security moves its price by a lot, or when it takes a long time to unload a position. A recent example of this is collateralized debt obligations, which investment banks have not been able to unload at an acceptable price for a long time.

Liquidity risk is the risk that a security will be more illiquid when its owner needs to sell it in the future, and a *liquidity crisis* is a time when many securities become highly illiquid at the same time. Some liquidity crises are dramatic: investors have a hard time selling the equities they want when prices fall as they submit their sale orders; market makers who are supposed to provide liquidity take their phones off the hook; or currency traders say it will take twenty days to trade out of large positions instead of the usual two days.

Historically, financial economists used to ignore liquidity problems: The theory assumed "frictionless markets," which are perfectly liquid all of the time, and most academics considered this assumption to be innocuous. We believe otherwise. In this book, we argue that illiquidity is a central feature of the securities and financial markets. We present and review central research contributions on liquidity and its effect on asset prices made over the past twenty-five years. Recent events have borne out our thesis: the Global Financial Crisis of 2007–2009 illustrates all too dramatically the importance of liquidity and liquidity risk and their effects on securities prices and on the functioning of financial markets.

The recent crisis is just one of a series of liquidity crises in the history of finance. Traders, regulators, and other market participants have long recognized the central importance of liquidity in financial markets. Securities market regulations aim to enhance the liquidity of the markets as a central goal, and market practitioners know that the cost and time of implementing trades are important determinants of performance. Sophisticated financial institutions are already implementing some of the techniques presented in this book in their trading and pricing models, and their ability to manage liquidity risk in addition to market risk make the difference between success and failure, as pointed out by the Chairman of the Federal Reserve, Ben Bernanke:

Some more-successful firms also consistently embedded market liquidity premiums in their pricing models and valuations. In contrast, less-successful firms did not develop adequate capacity to conduct independent valuations and did not take into account the greater liquidity risks posed by some classes of assets.[1]

Each of this book's three parts addresses a different facet of friction in financial markets: *liquidity, liquidity risk,* and *liquidity crises.* Each part starts with a brief overview that explains the theory and how to apply it, and the evidence that supports it. Each part then presents original articles in that research area and, for each article, gives a short summary of its essential ideas, findings, and later extensions.

Part I introduces the theory of why liquidity is priced and focuses on the effect of the *level* of liquidity on securities' required returns. Across securities, investors are willing to pay lower prices, or demand higher returns, for securities that are more costly to trade. This gives rise to a positive relation between securities' trading costs and expected returns, or a negative relation

---

[1] Bernanke at the Chicago Federal Reserve Annual Conference on Bank Structure and Competition, Chicago, Illinois, May 15, 2008.

between trading costs and prices (for any given cash flow that the security generates). As the liquidity of securities rises, so does their price.

Part II shows that over time, market liquidity shocks translate into shocks in market prices and vice versa. A rise in market illiquidity, which means a greater cost of trading, makes forward-looking investors require higher future yields on their investments for any given cash flows generated by these investments because they expect the illiquidity to persist for a while. This increase in the required return causes securities' prices to fall. The result is a negative relation between market illiquidity changes and changes in market price levels. Therefore, the effect of market liquidity shocks on securities market prices introduces additional risk to market returns beyond the risk that is associated with shocks to expectations about future cash flows.

Faced with the risk of such liquidity and price shocks, risk-averse investors prefer securities whose returns and trading costs are less sensitive to market-wide liquidity shocks and whose trading costs do not rise when market prices fall. In short, investors prefer securities with lower liquidity risk. The higher the *liquidity risk*, the higher the expected return required as compensation.

Part III discusses how *liquidity crises* arise as shocks are amplified many-fold through *liquidity spirals*. It describes how liquidity dries up when its providers – dealers, proprietary traders, and hedge funds – run out of capital and need to reduce their positions. A crash in market prices imposes greater constraints on the traders' resources (i.e., reduces their *funding liquidity*), and consequently traders are less able to provide liquidity to the market. As the ability to fund trading activity declines, so does market liquidity. This generates a vicious cycle that creates liquidity crises: a reduction in market liquidity pushes prices down and worsens the funding problems, which, in turn, reduces market liquidity and increases volatility as market conditions spiral downward.

The liquidity paradigm presented in this book should be viewed in contrast to the traditional economic paradigm. The traditional paradigm assumes that investors are able to trade without transaction costs (friction-less markets), asset prices depend only on their fundamentals (the Law of One Price), corporations' investment decisions are independent of how they finance themselves (the Modigliani-Miller proposition), and derivative prices can be determined using no-arbitrage pricing.

During the recent global financial crisis, these basic pillars of traditional finance and economics were fundamentally shaken as the importance of liquidity risk became more apparent than ever: The Law of One Price broke down in currency markets (the covered interest rate parity failed), credit markets (a price gap opened between corporate bonds and credit default swaps), and other markets (documented by Garleanu and Pedersen 2011). Corporations strapped for cash felt the tightening of liquidity and had to change their investment policy, violating the Modigliani-Miller proposition (Ivashina and Scharfstein 2010). Funding problems in the financial sector and broader liquidity deterioration sent the economy into a severe recession, showing how financial liquidity shocks can affect the business cycle beyond the effect of real economic factors. Central banks scrambled to introduce unconventional forms of monetary policy to improve market and funding liquidity, such as the purchasing of bonds and liquidity facilities targeted at alleviating investors' funding frictions and margin requirements (Ashcraft, Garleanu, and Pedersen 2010).

Paradoxically, not only did financial frictions increase dramatically during the crisis, but policy makers attempted to improve the situation by introducing additional frictions such as short sale bans and transaction taxes, although such initiatives are not supported by the theory presented in this book.

Having seen how liquidity and transaction costs affect asset prices, what can finance professionals glean from the insights presented in this book? Portfolio managers can incorporate liquidity considerations into portfolio construction and management strategies. These strategies should consider the portfolio's current liquidity characteristics and its liquidity risk, just as they incorporate standard market risk into the analysis. The results reported in this book provide a rigorous approach that can be employed in both thinking about portfolio composition and implementing portfolio strategies through trades.

Traders in financial markets are probably aware of the importance of transaction costs. This book provides a structured approach for quantifying their effect and thinking about the implementation of trading strategies that take liquidity cost considerations into account. Strategies that produce paper profits may fail in implementation because liquidity costs offset potential gains that could have been earned had it been feasible to execute trades at observed market prices. Therefore, traders should perform an analysis of their own transaction costs, either in-house or through a professional transaction cost analysis provider.

The effect of liquidity on prices also presents opportunities for investors. Investors with long horizons or superior trading technology can earn the liquidity premium by buying illiquid securities. Further, since the liquidity premium varies over time, the returns to buying illiquid securities are expected to be the highest after times of crises when capital pursuing such strategies is scarce.

Corporate financial managers should not take the liquidity of their company's publicly traded claims – stocks and bonds – as exogenously given. They can employ corporate policies that enhance the liquidity of their company's claims.[2] The evidence presented in this book shows that such policies can reduce the corporate cost of capital and raise the company's market value. Liquidity-enhancing policies include greater transparency and better information disclosure practices that reduce informational asymmetry and thus improve liquidity. Liquidity also increases when the company's investor base is broadened and there is greater dispersion of ownership among investors who are likely to trade the stock. Means to achieve that include improved investor relations, advertising, and facilitating trades in small stock units. Multiple types of securities lead to fragmentation of the company's investor base, which can reduce liquidity and value. Therefore, having fewer types of claims, each with a larger float, contributes to greater liquidity. Capital structure and leverage policies may also affect liquidity to the extent that they affect the liquidity of the company's stocks and bonds. Also, when deciding to distribute cash to shareholders, stock buybacks may be preferred only if they do not hamper stock liquidity.

Policy makers and regulators should incorporate liquidity considerations into policy decisions on financial markets. For example, regulations that increase disclosure and reduce information asymmetry – such as Regulation Fair Disclosure and mandating the prompt release of pertinent information, as well as the prohibition of insider trading – contribute to increase market liquidity. Major market reforms, such as the reduction in the minimum tick (price change) from $1/8$ to $1/16$ and finally to $0.01 reduced the cost of trading for many stocks, especially the frequently traded stocks that constitute most of the value in the stock market. Also, while information technology can be a double-edged sword, it can often increase liquidity and reduce transaction costs: the dramatic increase in stock liquidity since the 1980s is no doubt due in large part to improvements in computing and communications technologies.

The implications for public policy go beyond financial market structure issues per se. For example, every few years, policy makers in the United States and Europe propose to impose a securities transaction tax. As of the

---

[2] An analysis of liquidity-enhancing corporate policies appears in Amihud and Mendelson (1988, 2012).

writing of this book, bills have been introduced in the U.S. Congress to place a tax of up 0.25% on the value of stock trades (and a lower rate on other financial instruments), and the European Commission has proposed a tax of up to 0.10% on trading in stocks, bonds, and financial derivatives. Such a tax naturally reduces market liquidity by increasing the cost of trading. Eventually, investors will reduce their valuation of stocks by the present value of the stream of taxes that they would have to pay. By the estimation method presented in Chapter 1 to gauge the effect of transaction costs on asset values, a tax of 0.25% on stock trading in the United States would lead to a reduction of about 10% in the values of stocks. Put differently, as Chapter 1 demonstrates, the tax will raise the required expected return on investment in companies' stocks. This means that the corporate cost of capital will rise and the hurdle rate for new investments will be higher. The result will be a reduction in real corporate investment. In this way, a liquidity-reducing securities transaction tax will have negative effects on the real economy.

Liquidity considerations also become important for central bankers during crises when financial stability is at risk, as Part III discusses. At such times, central bankers often seek to improve the funding in the financial system such that liquidity providers can continue to operate and market liquidity is restored.

In summary, this book is about the effects of liquidity and liquidity risk on financial markets. It presents and reviews central research in this area and demonstrates how the liquidity theory provides a unified explanation of asset price determination, market price dynamics, and severe market breakdowns such as the recent global financial crisis. Liquidity problems always lurk in the market, and this crisis highlights the importance of liquidity and the price investors are willing to pay for it in dire economic situations.

PART I

THE EFFECT OF LIQUIDITY COSTS ON SECURITIES PRICES AND RETURNS

Introduction and Overview

We begin by considering the *direct* effects of trading costs on the values of financial assets. Investors require compensation for the trading costs they pay when they buy or sell securities. If two assets generate the same cash flows over time but one of them is less liquid (has higher trading costs), rational investors will pay less for the less liquid asset, which costs more to trade. Consequently, the less liquid asset will have a lower value and a higher required (expected) return. Overall, we should observe that the returns on financial assets are increasing in asset illiquidity or transaction costs. Just as risk-averse investors require a higher return to compensate for a higher asset risk, we propose that investors require a higher return to compensate for greater asset illiquidity or transaction costs. The following chapters study these relations.

First, we address the meaning of illiquidity or trading costs. Stated simply, trading costs are the direct and indirect costs associated with trading a security. The most easily measured component of trading costs is the direct costs: brokerage fees, transaction taxes, and other trade-processing fees. In addition, there are search and delay costs that arise because the buyers and sellers of a security are not continuously available to transact, so a seller needs to search for buyers, especially if he or she needs to liquidate a large-size position and, similarly, a buyer needs to find sellers at the time he or she wants to buy. Another component of trading costs is the bid–ask spread. In securities markets with quoted bid and offer (ask) prices, which are the buying and selling prices, the buy transaction is naturally executed at a higher price than the sell transaction, resulting in a bid–ask spread. However, the bid and ask prices apply only to limited trade quantities. Larger transactions have a greater impact on the transaction price: They raise the buying price and lower the selling price, resulting in a market impact cost. The market impact cost is greater for larger-size transactions, when there is greater information asymmetry between the two parties in the transaction, and when there is greater friction in accessing the market by traders willing to trade.

The nature of trading costs depends on the structure of the market where the security is traded. Most financial markets include market makers, intermediaries who buy or sell securities for their own accounts to close or narrow down the time gaps between purchases and sales. These market makers may be "official" market makers, such as the New York Stock Exchange (NYSE) specialists or Nasdaq market makers, or they may be traders who submit limit orders to the market and thus stand ready to buy and sell on demand. Market makers are willing to take a long or short position in the security so they will, for example, buy the security when a sell order arrives, hoping to sell it shortly thereafter at a profit.[1] As this happens, market makers accept inventory risk for which they expect to be compensated. As their inventory position (short or long) increases, their risk further increases, which means that the compensation they demand for each additional unit they trade increases as well. Therefore, market makers quote bid and ask prices at which they are willing to sell or buy limited quantities of the security, but beyond that limited quantity they further increase the price at which they are willing to sell or reduce the price at which they are willing to buy, depending on the quantities involved.

This is further exacerbated by adverse selection, which results from the fact that there is asymmetric information between traders about the value of the asset being traded. Adverse selection arises when a trader sells a security because he has private information that the security is overpriced. An uninformed market maker or trader on the other side of the transaction will try to protect himself by offering the seller a lower price. Similarly, a purchase may indicate positive information that buyers have about the security's price, and this will induce uninformed market makers and traders to ask for a higher selling price.[2] The greater the extent of asymmetric information, the lower will be the selling price and the higher will be the buying price. Because uninformed sellers and buyers are viewed as being possibly informed ones – other traders and market makers cannot

---

[1] See Amihud and Mendelson (1980) for a formal model of market making. In the NYSE, in addition to trading by market making, there was trading by auction. Amihud and Mendelson (1987) analyze the effects of the two trading methods – auction and market making – on stock return behavior. Mendelosn (1982) models securities price behavior in an auction market.

[2] See Glosten and Milgrom (1985) and Kyle (1985) for formal models.

distinguish between informed and uninformed sellers and buyers – they have to bear a price discount when selling and pay a premium when buying. These discounts and premia constitute illiquidity costs for these uninformed traders.

The result of these effects is that the trading cost of buying from or selling to a liquidity provider, such as market maker, has a fixed component and a variable component. The "round-trip" fixed component of the trading cost is given by the bid–ask spread (the difference between the ask and bid prices), which is the cost of buying and selling a small quantity of the security (for a single transaction, the fixed component is taken to be half the bid–ask spread). The variable component of trading costs is given by the market impact cost: the more the investor buys or sells, the greater the trading cost per unit he is trading.

The trading cost of traded stock often amounts to less than a percent of its value. Data provided by the Investment Technology Group (ITG) for the twenty-five quarters ending in the fourth quarter of 2011 show that the average trading cost of stocks in the United States was 0.52% of stock value (including commissions), ranging between a low of 0.33% in the third quarter of 2007 and a high of 0.94% in the last quarter of 2008. Average U.S. equity trading costs ranged from 0.43% for large-cap stocks to 1.01% for small-cap stocks. In fact, large stocks are more liquid. In the United Kingdom and Japan, ITG estimates 2011 trading costs to be slightly above 0.5%.[3]

Although trading costs of the order of 0.5% may seem small, their value effect is large because they are incurred *repeatedly* each time the security is traded. Therefore, we need to consider the cumulative effect of trading costs throughout the security's life. Consider, for example, an asset that pays out a riskless annual dividend of $4 in perpetuity and suppose the risk-free annual rate is 4%. Absent trading costs, the asset price is $100. However, if the asset incurs a trading cost of $0.50 (0.5% of its value) and is traded once a year, the cash flow stream associated with the trading costs has a net present value of $12.5 of the asset's value, meaning that the price of the asset drops to $100 – $12.5 = $87.5. Said differently, while a transaction cost of 0.5% is a small fraction of the asset's value, it should really be compared to the 4% dividend yield, because both dividends and transaction costs are "flows" that are incurred repeatedly. Since the transaction cost is one-eighth of the dividend yield, its present value is one-eighth of the present value of dividends ($12.5/$100 = 1/8). Furthermore, if the asset is traded every half-year, then after accounting for transaction costs, the asset's value will be about $75, a discount of $25. The value discount is translated to a return premium. The $4 dividend constitutes a 5.3% return on the asset whose price is $75, which means a return premium of 1.3% due to transaction cost of 0.5% compared to the return on the perfectly liquid asset with the same cash flow.

A similar analysis can be applied to any asset whose cash payments grow over time and whose trading costs are proportional to its price. Consider a stock whose next-period cash dividend, D, grows at a rate of g, and its required return is $r > g$. Absent transaction costs, its price (the present value of its cash payments), is given by what is known as Gordon's growth formula $P_0 = D/(r - g)$. If transaction costs in the stock are a fraction c of its price, they increase at the same rate as the stock price, namely g. Assume that transaction costs are incurred at the same frequency for which r and g apply. The present value of the transaction costs is thus $cP/(r - g)$, and because $g = r - D/P$, where D/P is the dividend yield, we obtain that the relative price discount is simply $c/(D/P)$. In this context, $1/(D/P)$ is the *transaction cost multiplier* which, when applied to the transaction cost c, gives the price discount. The dividend yield D/P on the S&P 500 stocks has recently been about 2%, corresponding to a transaction cost multiplier of $1/(D/P) = 50$. With this dividend yield, a transaction cost of $c = \frac{1}{2}\%$ translates into a price discount of 25% (if the stock trades once a year). Therefore, we observe that a small trading cost brings about a large (fifty-fold in this example) decline in the stock's price. Securities with higher trading costs will have lower values and they will have to generate higher returns to become attractive to investors. This implies a higher cost of capital for firms whose securities have higher trading costs. Trading costs thus significantly affect firms' ability to raise capital for investments, the capital allocation process, and the real economy.

Higher trading costs can be better borne by long-term investors who trade less frequently and, therefore, can depreciate them over a longer investment horizon. Frequently trading investors are willing to pay more for assets with low transaction costs. In equilibrium, there will be *liquidity clienteles:* Other things being equal, fewer liquid assets will be held by investors with a longer expected holding period. Therefore, while expected return is an increasing function of trading costs, it should be concave (increasing at a decreasing rate), reflecting the mitigating effect of long-term holding periods on the sensitivity of return to transaction costs.

The following chapters show, both theoretically and empirically, that differences in trading costs explain differences in securities values and returns across stocks and bonds. Furthermore, when stock liquidity improves, its value rises, as the theory predicts. The first article by Amihud and Mendelson

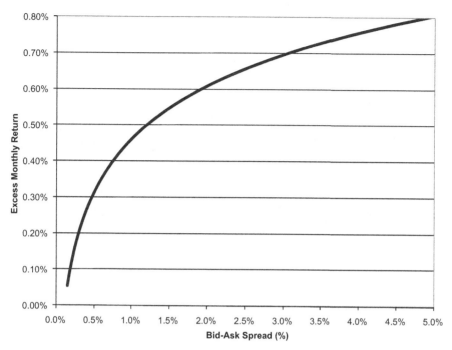

Figure PI.1. Relation between excess monthly return on NYSE stocks and their bid–ask spread, 1961–1980.

(1986) lays the theoretical foundations for the relation between asset returns and trading costs and shows empirically that this relation is economically and statistically significant across stocks that are traded on the NYSE and American Stock Exchange (AMEX). Figure PI.1 shows the estimated relation between excess monthly returns and stocks' bid–ask spreads. As suggested by the theory, the relation is increasing and concave.

    Amihud and Mendelson (1986) measure stock illiquidity by the quoted bid–ask spread, a measure of trading costs that was available in the 1980s. A decade later, trade-by-trade data became available, which enabled Brennan and Subrahmanyam (1996) to estimate stock illiquidity using both the market impact cost and the bid–ask spread. The authors find that illiquidity increases the required return on stocks. Silber (1991) examines the effect of illiquidity on stock prices in the context of stocks whose trading is restricted. Consistent with the theory, the author finds that trading restrictions lower stock prices.

    The finding that less liquid stocks generate higher (risk-adjusted) returns is supported in a recent paper by Amihud, Mendelson, and Goyenko (2010),

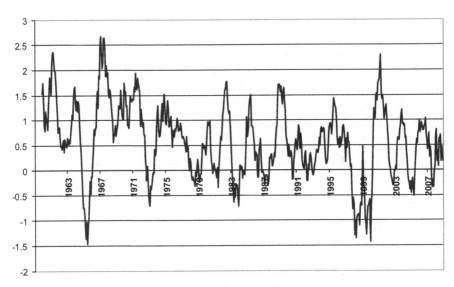

Figure PI.2. Twelve-month moving averages of monthly risk-adjusted liquidity premia (HMLI) for NYSE- and AMEX-traded stocks, 1960–2009 (in %). *Source:* Amihud, Mendelson and Goyenko (2010).

who study the return-liquidity relation over the past fifty years (1960–2009). Stocks on the NYSE and AMEX are sorted each month by their past illiquidity, using the illiquidity measure of Amihud (2002), conditional on their past volatility, and ranked into five equally sized portfolios. The monthly return on the high-minus-low illiquidity portfolios ([HMLI], top and bottom quintiles), measures the liquidity premium given by the excess return on illiquid stocks relative to liquid ones. The average HMLI liquidity premium over the fifty-year sample period is significantly positive. Adjusting for risk by a regression of HMLI on the four common risk factors of Fama and French (1993) and Carhart (1997) generates an alpha of 0.5% per month that is significantly positive. This means that in the past fifty years, the average risk-adjusted excess return of the HMLI portfolio is about 6% annually.

Figure PI.2 plots the twelve-month moving averages of the monthly risk-adjusted liquidity premia HMLI, given by the sum of the alpha coefficient and the residuals from the above regression of HMLI on the four risk factors. Figure PI.2 shows that while the risk-adjusted liquidity premium fluctuates over time, it is mostly positive. Although it becomes negative during the 1997–2000 period, it reverts to being positive during the last decade, including the period surrounding the recent financial crisis.

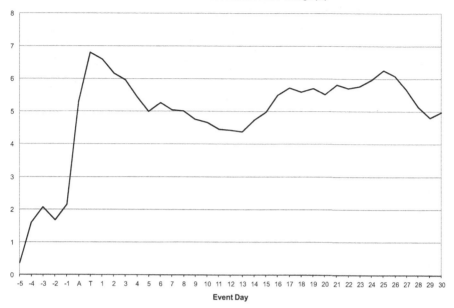

Figure PI.3. Cumulative price appreciation (net of market) for stocks transferred to a more liquid trading venue (in %). Day A is the day of the announcement on the stock being transferred to the new and more liquid trading venue; day T is the day the stock started trading in the more liquid trading venue.

The positive relation between asset expected returns and transaction costs also holds for fixed income securities. Amihud and Mendelson (1991; Chapter 2 in this book) study this relation for Treasury Bills and Notes. This work was extended by Chen, Lesmond, and Wei (2007) to the case of corporate bonds. For bonds, the tests examine the effects of liquidity on the yields to maturity. After controlling for risk and duration, both studies show that the yield to maturity is higher for less liquid bonds, as the theory predicts.

So far, this review has considered the cross-sectional relation between trading costs and securities returns (and values). A further step is taken by Amihud, Mendelson, and Lauterbach (1997; Chapter 3 in this book), who examine the effects of a *change* in stock liquidity of a given financial asset over time, showing that increased stock liquidity due to an improved trading system significantly raises stock prices. Whereas studies on the effect of liquidity on asset prices require controlling for other factors that affect asset returns, in this study the stocks and their underlying cash flows remained the same. Their liquidity, however, increased due to their transfer to a new venue and trading method. Importantly, the change in trading venue was exogenous and did not convey information about the stocks, because the decisions were made by the management of the stock exchange, without any company discretion. This comes as close as possible to a controlled experiment on the effects of changing liquidity on stock prices, where everything else remains unchanged. The stocks that were transferred to the more liquid trading venue enjoy a sharp and permanent price increase of nearly 6% on average. The evolution of stock prices around the time of the transfer to the new and more liquid trading venue is depicted in Figure PI.3.

CHAPTER 1

Asset Pricing and the Bid–Ask Spread

Summary and Implications

This article establishes the theory on the effect of liquidity on asset values and provides estimations of the relation between expected returns and liquidity across different stocks. The Amihud–Mendelson model gives rise to two major empirical predictions that are discussed in this chapter's introduction: expected asset returns increase in the assets' trading costs and the return–trading cost relation is concave. The first prediction results from the fact that investors demand a higher compensation for bearing higher trading costs. The second is due to the clientele effect: because less liquid assets are held in equilibrium by investors with longer holding periods, the additional compensation they require for an increase in trading costs is lower.

The Amihud–Mendelson model shows that, in equilibrium, the return on an asset whose trading is costly is equal to the return that would be earned on a similar-risk asset that is perfectly liquid (entailing zero trading costs) plus a return premium that compensates investors for the transaction costs they bear. That return premium is an increasing function of the expected trading cost per unit of time, which is the product of the asset's transaction cost by the frequency of asset sales. Consequently, higher trading costs lower asset prices because when discounting an asset's cash flow (dividend) at a higher rate of return due to higher trading costs, its value is lower. That is, higher trading costs produce an asset price discount.

Amihud and Mendelson show that there is a *clientele effect* whereby long-term investors tend to invest in assets that are less liquid (yielding higher returns) and short-term investors tend to invest in assets that are more liquid. Because of this specialization, the higher the trading costs, the smaller the effect of a marginal increase in these costs on the return required by investors. As a result, the required return on assets is not only an increasing function of transaction costs but also concave (increasing at a decreasing rate). Long-term investors can effectively depreciate their trading costs over a longer holding period, and thus require a smaller compensation in terms of per-period additional return than short-term investors.

Further, the Amihud–Mendelson model shows that the price discount due to trading costs consists of two components. The first component is the expected present value of all trading costs in the asset over its lifetime (for stocks, this is calculated by discounting the infinite stream of transaction cost cash flows). The second component reflects an additional discount in value that is needed to induce long-term investors to hold the less liquid assets. While all investors prefer assets with lower trading costs, long-term investors can outbid short-term investors on assets with any trading costs because long-term investors bear these costs less frequently. Long-term investors will not hold the less liquid assets unless offered more than a mere compensation for their higher expected transaction costs. To induce these investors to hold the less-liquid assets, their price net of expected trading costs must be lower than the net price of the more liquid assets. As a result, even after subtracting the present value of all trading costs, low-liquidity assets are still cheaper for their investors than liquid assets. Thus, the *net* return on assets, after subtracting the expected per-period cost of trading, is higher for assets with higher transaction costs.

Amihud and Mendelson test these predictions on the return–trading cost relation using data on stocks traded on the NYSE and AMEX over the period 1961–1980. Their measure of trading cost is the relative bid–ask spread, that is, the ratio of the dollar difference between the bid and ask prices to the stock price. The analysis groups stocks in each year into 49 (7 × 7) portfolios sorted on the previous year's relative spread and, within that, on past systematic risk (beta). The average bid–ask spreads on the lowest and highest spread portfolios are 0.49% and 3.2%, respectively, with the median-spread portfolio having an average bid–ask spread of 1.1%. The test procedure estimates a regression of the monthly return of each portfolio on the portfolio's bid–ask spread and beta. To test the clientele effect, the estimation allows the return–spread relation to be piecewise linear. Specifically, the estimation regresses the portfolio return in each year on dummy variables for each portfolio. The coefficients of these dummy variables provide the average return for each spread group and each beta risk group. The model also includes bid–ask spreads adjusted for the spread groups' mean, alowing a different coefficient for each of the seven spread groups, as well as the beta. The two research questions that are examined are (i) whether the average portfolio returns are higher for portfolios with higher bid–ask spreads and (ii) whether the return–spread sensitivity is lower for high-spread stocks than for low-spread stocks.

The results support the predictions of the theoretical model. First, portfolio returns increase with the level of the bid–ask spread, showing that investors ask in equilibrium to be compensated for higher trading costs. For example, the risk-adjusted excess return on the highest-spread portfolio is higher by 0.68% per month (more than 8% per annum) than on the lowest-spread portfolio (among the seven spread portfolios considered). Second, as the theory predicts, the slope of the return–spread relation declines for higher bid–ask spreads. This is a result of the clientele effect, by which stocks with higher spreads are chosen by investors who trade less frequently, incur lower average trading costs and, as a result, require a lower marginal compensation (excess return) for trading costs. For example, when moving from the lowest-spread portfolio to the median-spread portfolio, the stock return increases by about 0.4% for a 1% increase in the bid–ask spread, whereas moving from the median-spread to the highest-spread portfolio raises the return by about 0.2% for a 1% increase in the bid–ask spread (these returns are monthly in excess of the risk-adjusted level).

A simple way to summarize the results is to estimate the spread effect in logarithmic form. This makes sense because the logarithm is a concave function, consistent with the clientele effect. Amihud and Mendelson (1986a) find that the logarithmic regression is

$$R_j = 0.0065 + 0.001\beta_j + 0.0021 ln(S_j),$$

where R_j is the monthly return on the stock portfolio in excess of the 90-day Treasury Bill rate, β_j is the systematic risk estimated from data in the preceding periods, and S_j is the relative bid–ask spread in the preceding year. By this estimation, the return difference between a stock with a 0.5% spread and a stock with a 1% spread (and the same systematic risk) is 0.15% per month, or roughly 1.8% per year. However, when moving from a 1% to a 1.5% spread, the return rises by less, only 0.09%, or 1% per annum.

The effect of the bid–ask spread on stock prices is as follows. Consider a stock with a bid–ask spread of 1% and a price/earnings (P/E) multiple of 12. Another stock with the same earnings, risk, and growth rate but with a bid–ask spread of 0.5% will have a P/E ratio of about 15. That is, the decline of 0.5% in trading costs raises the stock price by about 25%, holding everything else equal. In this case, the value change is 50-fold the change in the bid–ask spread (25%/0.5%).

The conclusion is that liquidity is priced: stocks with a higher bid–ask spread have a higher cost of capital or lower price for any given cash flow that these stocks generate.

Trading data that became available in the 1990s enabled estimation of trading costs that are finer than the bid–ask spread. Brennan and Subrahmanyam (1996) use data on intra-day trades and quotes to estimate two parts of trading costs: a fixed component that is independent of trade size and a variable component that increases with trade size. The fixed component reflects the bid–ask spread, as well as any other market maker compensation that does not increase with trade size. The variable component is equal to the market impact cost coefficient λ (in dollars per share) times the trade size q (number of shares traded). The market impact cost coefficient λ in Kyle's (1985) model shows by how much the purchase of one share raises (or the sale of one unit decreases) the stock's market price.

To estimate these coefficients, Brennan and Subrahmanyam regress the trade-by-trade price change, Δp_t, on the independent variables that include (i) the signed transaction size, q_t, and (ii) $D_t - D_{t-1}$, where $D_t = 1$ for a buyer-induced transaction and $D_t = -1$ for a sell transaction. The slope coefficient of q_t from this regression is λ, an estimate of the market impact cost, and the coefficient ψ of $(D_t - D_{t-1})$ reflects the fixed component of trading costs that is unrelated to trade size. Brennan and Subrahmanyam then use as trading costs the average of the marginal cost of trading, $C_q = \lambda q/P$, where q and P are the monthly averages of trade size and price, respectively (or $C_n = \lambda n/P$, where n is the monthly average of number of shares outstanding), and the relative fixed cost of trading, ψ/P.

Having estimated these measures of trading costs for the years 1984 and 1988, Brennan and Subrahmanyam form for each of the years 1984–1991, 25 (5 × 5) annual stock portfolios by sorting the stocks traded on the NYSE into five size groups and, within each size group, five market impact groups based on the stocks' estimated market impact coefficients λ. Pooling the resulting portfolio data, they estimate the relations between the monthly portfolio returns over the period 1984–1991 and their two measures of trading costs, adjusting for common risk factors that are suggested by Fama and French (1993).

The results support the positive return–trading costs relation. Brennan and Subrahmanyam find that the coefficients are positive and significant for both the fixed and variable components of trading costs, implying that trading costs entail a considerable risk-adjusted return premium. Their study also provides a robust methodology for calculating the components of trading costs using transaction and quote data, and for estimating their effects on the return premium.

A number of later studies support the existence of cross-section positive relation between trading costs and stock returns.[1] Datar, Naik, and Radcliffe (1998) use an alternative measure of stock liquidity: the stock turnover rate (the ratio of trading volume to shares outstanding), which roughly indicates the stock's trading frequency. By Amihud–Mendelson's model, more liquid stocks are held in equilibrium by investors who trade them more frequently. Therefore, if stock liquidity cannot be fully observed, it can be inferred from the trading frequency. Stocks with higher turnover rates have higher liquidity, and Datar et al. (1998) find that such stocks have lower expected returns, as the theory predicts. The authors find that, on average, a drop of 10% in the turnover rate is associated with a higher return of about 0.4% per month, after controlling for firm size, book-to-market ratio, and the *beta* risk.

While realized average returns are unbiased estimates of expected returns under rational expectations, they are clearly very noisy estimates. Loderer and Roth (2005) employ a different approach, directly examining the effect of stocks' trading costs on the stock P/E ratio. Using data from both the Swiss Stock Exchange and NASDAQ for the years 1995–2001, these researchers regress the stock's P/E ratio on trading costs (measured by the relative bid–ask spread), controlling for projected earnings growth obtained from analysts' estimates, dividend payout ratio, systematic (*beta*) risk and size. Their results show that the P/E ratio is significantly lower for stocks with a higher bid–ask spread. The effect is economically significant, with the median-spread stock having a 13% P/E discount compared to a zero-spread stock in their Swiss Stock Exchange sample, and 27% P/E discount for their NASDAQ sample. The relation between the P/E ratio and liquidity is similar when using trading volume as a measure of liquidity.

Fang, Noe, and Tice (2009) test the Amihud-Mendelson prediction that the stock bid–ask spread has negative effect on stock value by examining the effect of the spread on the firm's market-to-book ratio (the Q ratio). The authors find that across firms, higher bid–ask spread leads to lower firm's market-to-book ratio, controlling for firm characteristics such as risk, age and size. The authors also find that the decline in the bid–ask spread, brought about by the price decimalization of stock trading in 2001,

---

[1] See Amihud, Mendelson, and Pedersen (2005) for a survey of the literature.

raised the market-to-book ratio of firms in proportion to the improvement in their stock liquidity.

Garleanu and Pedersen (2004) show how illiquidity arising from investors' private information affects asset allocations and prices, and Easley and O'Hara (2004) propose that asymmetric information exposes uninformed investors to the risk of being unable to infer information from prices. Therefore, they are disadvantaged because they are unable to shift their portfolio to incorporate new information. As a result, this information risk affects asset expected returns. Easley, Hvidkjaer, and O'Hara (2002) test this hypothesis on the cross-section of stock returns, employing the probability of informed trading, denoted *PIN*: an estimate of the fraction of information-based orders, derived from the imbalance between buy and sell trades. Using data for NYSE stocks over the years 1983–1998, they find that across stocks, *PIN* has a positive and significant effect on return after controlling for other risk factors. However, Duarte and Lance (2009) find that the effect of *PIN* becomes statistically insignificant when a direct measure of stock illiquidity is included in the estimation. They conclude that the relation between *PIN* and the cross-section of expected returns can be explained by illiquidity effects unrelated to information asymmetry.

Liu (2006) introduces an illiquidity measure, a function of the proportion of trading days with zero trading volume and the reciprocal of monthly trading turnover. He then sorts U.S. stocks on this measure into ten portfolios ranked by their illiquidity and calculates the time series of differential monthly return between the portfolios with the least liquid and the most liquid stocks. This differential monthly return is positive and highly significant. It is estimated to be 0.7% per month after controlling for the return factors of Fama and French (1993), which account for excess returns due to market risk, size and book-to-market. Liu then adds the high-minus-low illiquidity return factor to the standard factor of market excess return, creating a two-factor model, and estimates the stocks' *beta* coefficients on these two factors. His estimations show that stocks with high illiquidity *beta* have higher excess return. [This follows the liquidity-adjusted CAPM of Acharya and Pedersen (2005).]

The aforementioned papers consider cross-sectional comparisons between stocks with different levels of trading costs and find a statistically significant relation between a stock's level of trading cost and its expected return. Therefore, across stocks, higher trading costs command a higher return premium. A different way to examine whether trading costs affect securities values is to perform a controlled experiment involving two versions of the *same* security with different levels of trading costs. If the two versions are identical in all relevant respects except their trading costs, will the price of the less liquid security be significantly discounted?

Such a controlled experiment is provided by Silber (1991), who compares the prices of publicly traded stocks and a restricted version of the *same* stocks. These stocks are identical in their cash flow and control rights but differ in their liquidity. Restricted or "letter" shares of stock, which are issued by firms under U.S. Securities and Exchange Commission (SEC) Rule 144, are not registered with the SEC and cannot be sold in the public market for a period of time after they have been acquired.[2] There is, however, a record of the selling price of these sharers at their private placement. Comparing the prices of these shares to those of the publicly traded shares of the same stock at the same time provides a controlled experiment that enables us to discern the effect of liquidity on stock prices. Using a sample of sixty-nine transactions during the period 1981–1988, Silber finds an average price discount of 34% on restricted stocks. This sizable discount highlights the considerable effect of liquidity on stock prices.

The value discount of an asset for lack of marketability can be modeled as the value of the option to divest the asset should the investor's information suggest doing so. Longstaff (1995) considers a hypothetical investor with perfect market timing ability who holds an asset whose sale is restricted. Therefore, this investor foregoes the highest value attained by the asset during the restriction period. The foregone value is calculated in the framework of a lookback option and provides an upper bound on the cost to the investor due to the restriction. Within this framework, the foregone value increases in the length of the restriction and in the volatility of the asset value, as observed in practice.

The importance of transaction costs in investment decisions is shown by Amihud and Mendelson to depend on the investors' expected holding period. They propose that in equilibrium there is *liquidity clientele* by which investors with longer expected holding period invest in less liquid assets and earn higher return net of transaction cost. This is the evidence presented by Anginer (2010) in a study of 66,000 households from a large U.S. discount broker. The author finds that investors with longer investment horizons hold more illiquid securities, and that households with longer holding periods earn significantly higher returns after amortized transaction costs. Similar results are found by Dias and Ferreira (2004) and Naes and Odegaard (2009) for the Portuguese market and for the Oslo Stock Exchange: the investor

---

[2] This may be the case, for example, when a public company raises private capital, when a company goes public and its founders or board members are not allowed to sell their stock in the public market for a period of time, or as part of an acquisition.

holding period is positively related to the bid–ask spreads of the stocks that they hold. For the NYSE, Atkins and Dyl (1997) find that stocks with lower bid–ask spreads trade more frequently (have higher turnover) after controlling for risk.

Liquidity is particularly important in high frequency trading (HFT), which greatly expanded in the last decade. Naturally, trading strategies that generate paper profit may become unprofitable after transaction costs, and this is particularly so for HFT. By the Amihud-Mendelson clientele effect, high frequency traders are more sensitive to transaction costs, hence liquid assets are more valuable for HFT traders. Bowen, Hutchison, and O'Sullivan (2010), who analyzed HFT trades in the FTSE100 constituents stocks, find that while HFT strategy returns are almost unrelated to risk factors, they are extremely sensitive to transaction costs. For example, for a range of transaction costs from zero to fifteen basis points, the excess returns of the strategy vary from 15.2% to 7.0%. And, a slight extension of the waiting period for execution altogether eliminates the excess returns. Thus, delay in execution is an aspect of illiquidity and, as we point out in the Introduction, there is a tradeoff between direct monetary transaction costs and the opportunity cost of delayed execution.

HFT is practiced by hedge funds and "quants" who employ forms of program trading based on quantitative models, which require fast execution to take advantage of pricing disparities. This has made liquidity a more important consideration in investment strategies. By the Amihud–Mendelson (1986) model, frequent traders opt for more liquid securities. Therefore, as the weight of the HFT traders rises, the value of liquidity increases. Market observers have commented that securities that seem "cheap" are shunned by quant funds because of their low liquidity.[3] For example, Renaissance Medallion, a large and highly successful hedge fund, is prevented from making large trades because of liquidity constraints (see Mallaby 2010). Ziemba and Ziemba (2007) point out that the choice of stocks in executing trading strategy depends on stock liquidity. For example, in executing a strategy to exploit the January effect (higher returns on small stocks), traders prefer stock indexes that provide greater liquidity. The rise in importance of HFT may raise the value of liquid stocks that are more amenable to HFT and strengthen the positive illiquidity-expected return relation.

---

[3] For example, a hedge fund consultant is quoted as saying: "Once you try and sell a low-liquidity stock, by definition there is no one to buy it." See Richard Teitelbaum, "The Code Breakers," *Bloomberg*, January 2008. Amihud and Mendelson (1987a) discuss the upward bias in performance evaluation of trading strategies based on market prices, ignoring the effects of illiquidity.

Strategies employed in HFT often consume liquidity, sometimes aggressively so (as in the Flash Crash of May 6, 2010; see Kirilenko, Kyle, Samadi, and Tuzum, 2011). At the same time, quants that use HFT also often provide liquidity. They use computer algorithms that effectively make markets in a similar way to traditional market makers, just more systematically and across many markets simultaneously. HFT is a recent stage in a process by which trading frequency increases, market access broadens, and liquidity providers proliferate all over the world. Trading in most stock markets around the world was initially done in periodic call auctions. These markets later moved to continuous floor trading, which was then replaced by automated electronic trading, or they moved directly from call to automated trading. The consequences of these changes are analyzed by Amihud, Mendelson, and Lauterbach (1997; Chapter 3 in this book) for the Israeli market, and then studied for markets in 120 countries by Jain (1995). The studies show that the feasibility of higher trading frequency increases liquidity and raises securities prices. This is consistent with the positive price-liquidity relation, suggested by the Amihud–Mendelson model, because reduced delay in execution through faster trading systems increases liquidity.

Finally, there is strong evidence that liquidity is priced in stock markets around the world. Amihud, Hameed, Kang, and Zhang (2011) estimate the liquidity premium for stock markets in forty-five countries, nineteen of which are classified as emerging markets. The liquidity return premium is the return differential on the high-minus-low illiquidity portfolio (HMLI), constructed in a similar methodology to that presented in this chapter's introduction. After adjusting the HMLI return for the common stock return factors of Fama and French (1993) – both at a global and regional level (having altogether six factors) – they obtain the *alpha* coefficient, which measures the excess return attributed to illiquidity. The average *alpha* coefficient estimated over the period 1990–2010 is positive and significant. It is higher for emerging markets, whose stock markets are less liquid, and lower for stock markets in developed countries. These results provide robust support for the theory advanced in this book of a positive relation between illiquidity and expected return. In fact, the existence of a liquidity premium is a global phenomenon.

Asset Pricing and the Bid–Ask Spread*
Yakov Amihud and Haim Mendelson
Journal of Financial Economics 17, 1986

1. Introduction

Liquidity, marketability or trading costs are among the primary attributes of many investment plans and financial instruments. In the securities industry, portfolio managers and investment consultants tailor portfolios to fit their clients' investment horizons and liquidity objectives. But despite its evident importance in practice, the role of liquidity in capital markets is hardly reflected in academic research. This paper attempts to narrow this gap by examining the effects of illiquidity on asset pricing.

Illiquidity can be measured by the cost of immediate execution. An investor willing to transact faces a tradeoff: He may either wait to transact at a favorable price or insist on immediate execution at the current bid or ask price. The quoted ask (offer) price includes a premium for immediate buying, and the bid price similarly reflects a concession required for immediate sale. Thus, a natural measure of illiquidity is the spread between the bid and ask prices, which is the sum of the buying premium and the selling concession.[1] Indeed; the relative spread on stocks has been found

---

[1] Demsetz (1968) first related the spread to the cost of transacting. See also Amihud and Mendelson (1980, 1982), Phillips and Smith (1982), Ho and Stoll (1981, 1983), Copeland and Galai (1983), and West and Tinic (1971). For an analysis of transaction costs in the context of a fixed investment horizon, see Chen, Kim and Kon (1975), Levy (1978), Milne and Smith (1980), and Treynor (1980).

* We wish to thank Hans Stoll and Robert Whaley for furnishing the spread data, and Manny Pai for excellent programming assistance. We acknowledge helpful comments by the Editor, Clifford W. Smith, by an anonymous referee, by Harry DeAngelo, Linda DeAngelo, Michael C. Jensen, Krishna Ramaswamy and Jerry Zimmerman, and especially by John Long and G. William Schwert. Partial financial support by the Managerial Economics Research Center of the University of Rochester, the Salomon Brothers Center for the Study of Financial Markets, and the Israel Institute for Business Research is acknowledged.

to be negatively correlated with liquidity characteristics such as the trading volume, the number of shareholders, the number of market makers trading the stock, and the stock price continuity.[2]

This paper suggests that expected asset returns are increasing in the (relative) bid–ask spread. We first model the effects of the spread on asset returns. Our model predicts that higher-spread assets yield higher expected returns, and that there is a clientele effect whereby investors with longer holding periods select assets with higher spreads. The resulting testable hypothesis is that asset returns are an increasing and concave function of the spread. The model also predicts that expected returns net of trading costs increase with the holding period, and consequently higher-spread assets yield higher net returns to their holders. Hence, an investor expecting a long holding period can gain by holding high-spread assets.

We test the predicted spread-return relation using data for the period 1961–1980, and find that our hypotheses are consistent with the evidence: Average portfolio risk-adjusted returns increase with their bid–ask spread, and the slope of the return–spread relationship decreases with the spread. Finally, we verify that the spread effect persists when firm size is added as an explanatory variable in the regression equations. We emphasize that the spread effect is by no means an anomaly or an indication of market inefficiency; rather, it represents a rational response by an efficient market to the existence of the spread.

This study highlights the importance of securities market microstructure in determining asset returns, and provides a link between this area and mainstream research on capital markets. Our results suggest that liquidity-increasing financial policies can reduce the firm's opportunity cost of capital, and provide measures for the value of improvements in the trading and exchange process.[3] In the area of portfolio selection, our findings may guide investors in balancing expected trading costs against expected returns. In sum, we demonstrate the importance of market-microstructure factors as determinants of stock returns.

In the following section we present a model of the return–spread relation and form the hypotheses for our empirical tests. In section 3 we test the predicted relationship, and in section 4 we relate our findings to the firm size anomaly. Our concluding remarks are offered in section 5.

---

[2] See, e.g., Garbade (1982) and Stoll (1985).

[3] See, e.g., Mendelson (1982, 1985, 1986, 1987), Amihud and Mendelson (1985, 1986) for the interaction between market characteristics, trading organization, and liquidity.

2. A Model of the Return-Spread Relation

In this section we model the role of the bid–ask spread in determining asset returns. We consider M investor types numbered by $i = 1, 2, \ldots, M$, and $N + 1$ capital assets indexed by $j = 0, 1, 2, \ldots, N$. Each asset j generates a perpetual cash flow of $\$d_j$ per unit time ($d_j > 0$) and has a relative spread of S_j, reflecting its trading costs. Asset 0 is a zero-spread asset ($S_0 = 0$) having unlimited supply. Assets are perfectly divisible, and one unit of each positive-spread asset j ($j = 1, 2, \ldots, N$) is available.

Trading is performed via competitive market makers who quote assets' bid and ask prices and stand ready to trade at these prices. The market makers bridge the time gaps between the arrivals of buyers and sellers to the market, absorb transitory excess demand or supply in their inventory positions, and are compensated by the spread, which is competitively set. Thus, they quote for each asset j an ask price V_j and a bid price $V_j(1 - S_j)$, giving rise to two price vectors: an ask price vector $(V_0, V_1, \ldots, V_N)$ and a bid price vector $(V_0, V_1(1 - S_1), \ldots, V_N(1 - S_N))$.[4]

A type-i investor enters the market with wealth W_i used to purchase capital assets (at the quoted ask prices). He holds these assets for a random, exponentially distributed time T_i with mean $E[T_i] = 1/\mu_i$, liquidates his portfolio by selling it to the market makers at the bid prices, and leaves the market. We number investor types by increasing expected holding periods, $\mu_1^{-1} \leq \mu_2^{-1} \leq \cdots \leq \mu_M^{-1}$, and assets by increasing relative spreads, $0 = S_0 \leq S_1 \leq \cdots \leq S_N < 1$. Finally, we assume that the arrivals of type-i investors to the market follow a Poisson process with rate λ_i, with the interarrival times and holding periods being stochastically independent.

In statistical equilibrium, the number of type-i investors with portfolio holdings in the market has a Poisson distribution with mean $m_i = \lambda_i/\mu_i$ [cf. Ross (1970, ch. 2)]. The market makers' inventories fluctuate over time to accommodate transitory excess demand or supply disturbances, but their *expected* inventory positions are zero, i.e., market makers are 'seeking out the market price that equilibrates buying and selling pressures' [Bagehot (1971, p. 14); see also Garman (1976)]. This implies that the expected sum of investors' holdings in each positive-spread asset is equal to its available supply of one unit.

Consider now the portfolio decision of a type-i investor facing a given set of bid and ask prices, whose objective is to maximize the expected discounted

---

[4] Competition among market makers drives the spread to the level S_j of trading costs. In a different scenario, V_j may be viewed as the sum of the market price and the buying transaction cost, and $V_j(1 - S_j)$ as the price net of the cost of a sell transaction.

net cash flows received over his planning horizon. The discount rate ρ is the spread-free, risk-adjusted rate of return on the zero-spread asset. Let x_{ij} be the quantity of asset j acquired by the type-i investor. We call the vector $\{x_{ij}, j = 0, 1, 2, \ldots, N\}$ 'portfolio i'. The expected present value of holding portfolio i is the sum of the expected discounted value of the continuous cash stream received over its holding period and the expected discounted liquidation revenue. This sum is given by

$$
\mathrm{E}_{T_i} \left\{ \int_0^{T_i} e^{-\rho y} \left[\sum_{j=0}^{N} x_{ij} d_j \right] \mathrm{d}y \right\} + \mathrm{E}_{T_i} \left\{ e^{-\rho T_i} \sum_{j=0}^{N} x_{ij} V_j (1 - S_j) \right\}
$$

$$
= (\mu_i + \rho)^{-1} \sum_{j=0}^{N} x_{ij} \left[d_j + \mu_i V_j (1 - S_j) \right].
$$

Thus, for *given* vectors of bid and ask prices, a type-i investor solves the problem

$$
\max \sum_{j=0}^{N} x_{ij} \left[d_j + \mu_i V_j (1 - S_j) \right], \tag{1}
$$

subject to

$$
\sum_{j=0}^{N} x_{ij} V_j \leq W_i \quad \text{and} \quad x_{ij} \geq 0 \quad \text{for all} \quad j = 0, 1, 2, \ldots, N, \tag{2}
$$

where condition (2) expresses the wealth constraint and the exclusion of investors' short positions.[5] Under our specification, the usual market clearing, conditions read

$$
\sum_{i=1}^{M} m_i x_{ij} = 1, \quad j = 0, 1, 2, \ldots, N, \tag{3}
$$

(recall that m_i is the expected number of type-i investors in the market).

When an $M \times (N + 1)$ matrix X^* and an $(N + 1)$-dimensional vector V^* solve the M optimization problems (1)–(2) such that (3) is satisfied, we call X^* an equilibrium allocation matrix and V^* – an equilibrium ask price

---

[5] In our context, the use of short sales cannot eliminate the spread effect, since short sales by themselves entail additional transaction costs. Note that a constraint on short positions is necessary in models of tax clienteles [cf. Miller (1977), Litzenberger and Ramaswamy (1980)]. Clearly, market makers are allowed to have transitory long or short positions, but.are constrained to have zero expected inventory positions [cf. Garman (1976)].

vector [the corresponding bid price vector is $(V_0^*, V_1^*(1 - S_1), \ldots, V_N^*(1 - S_N)]$. The above model may be viewed as a special case of the linear exchange model [cf. Gale (1960)], which is known to have an equilibrium allocation and a unique equilibrium price vector. Our model enables us to derive and interpret the resulting equilibrium in a straightforward and intuitive way as follows.

We define the expected *spread-adjusted return* of asset *j* to investor-type *i* as the difference between the gross market return on asset *j* and its expected liquidation cost per unit time:

$$r_{ij} = d_j/V_j - \mu_i S_j, \tag{4}$$

where d_j/V_j is the gross return on security *j*, and $\mu_i S_j$ is the *spread-adjustment*, or expected liquidation cost (per unit time), equal to the product of the liquidation probability per unit time by the percentage spread. Note that the spread-adjusted return depends on *both* the asset *j* and the investor-type *i* (through the expected holding period).

For a given price vector *V*, investor *i* selects for his portfolio the assets *j* which provide him the highest spread-adjusted return, given by

$$r_i^* = \max_{j=0,1,2,\ldots,N} r_{ij}, \tag{5}$$

with $r_1^* \le r_2^* \le r_3^* \le \cdots \le r_M^*$, since, by (4), r_{ij} is a non-decreasing function of *i* for all *j*. These inequalities state that the spread-adjusted return on a portfolio increases with the expected holding period. That is, investors with longer expected holding periods will earn higher returns *net* of transaction costs.[6]

The *gross* return required by investor *i* on asset *j* is given by $r_i^* + \mu_i S_j$, which reflects both the required spread-adjusted return r_i^* and the expected liquidation cost $\mu_i S_j$. The equilibrium gross (market-observed) return on asset *j* is determined by its highest-valued use, which is in the portfolio *i* with the minimal required return, implying that

$$d_j/V_j^* = \min_{i=1,2,\ldots,M} \left\{ r_i^* + \mu_i S_j \right\}. \tag{6}$$

---

[6] This is consistent with the suggestions that while the illiquidity of investments such as real estate [Fogler (1984)] coins [Kane (1984)] and stamps [Taylor (1983)] excludes them from short-term investment portfolios, they are expected to provide superior performance when held over a long investment horizon (the same may apply to stock-exchange seats) [Schwert (1977)]. See also Day, Stoll and Whaley (1985) on the clientele of small firms, and Elton and Gruber (1978) on tax clienteles.

Eq. (6) can also be written in the form

$$V_j^* = \max_{i=1,2,\ldots,M} \left\{ d_j / (r_i^* + \mu_i S_j) \right\}, \tag{7}$$

implying that the equilibrium value of asset j, V_j^*, is equal to the present value of its perpetual cash flow, discounted at the gross return $(r_i^* + \mu_i S_j)$. Alternatively, V_j^* can be written as the difference between (i) the present value of the perpetual cash stream d_j and (ii) the present value of the expected trading costs for all the present and future holders of asset j, where both are discounted at the spread-adjusted return of the holding investor. To see this, assume that the available quantity of asset j is held by type-i investors; then (7) can be written as

$$V_j^* = d_j / r_i^* - \mu_i V_j^* S_j / r_i^*,$$

where the first term is, obviously, (i). As for the second, the expected quantity of asset j sold per unit time by type-i investors is μ_i, and each sale incurs a transaction cost of $V_j^* S_j$; thus, $\mu_i V_j^* S_j / r_i^*$ is the expected present value (discounted at r_i^*) of the transaction-cost cash flow.

The implications of the above equilibrium on the relation between returns, spreads and holding periods are summarized by the following propositions.

Proposition 1 (clientele effect). *Assets with higher spreads are allocated in equilibrium to portfolios with (the same or) longer expected holding periods.*

Proof: Consider two assets, j and k, such that in equilibrium asset j is in portfolio i and asset k is in portfolio $i + 1$ (recall that $\mu_i \geq \mu_{i+1}$). Applying (5), we obtain $r_{ij} \geq r_{ik}$ and $r_{i+1,k} \geq r_{i+1,j}$; thus, substituting from (4), $d_j / V_j^* - \mu_i S_j \geq d_k / V_k^* - \mu_i S_k$ and $d_k / V_k^* - \mu_{i+1} S_k \geq d_j / V_j^* - \mu_{i+1} S_j$, implying that $(\mu_i - \mu_{i+1})(S_k - S_j) \geq 0$. It follows that if $\mu_i > \mu_{i+1}$, we must have $S_k \geq S_j$. The case of non-consecutive portfolios immediately follows.   Q.E.D.

Proposition 2 (spread–return relationship). *In equilibrium, the observed market (gross) return is an increasing and concave piecewise-linear function of the (relative) spread.*

Proof: Let $f_i(S) = r_i^* + \mu_i S$. By (6), the market return on an asset with relative spread S is given by $f(S) \equiv \min_{i=1,2,\ldots,M} f_i(S)$. Now, the proposition follows from the fact that monotonicity and concavity are preserved by the minimum operator, and that the minimum of a finite collection of linear functions is piecewise-linear. Q.E.D.

Proposition 2 is the main testable implication of our model. Intuitively, the positive association between return and spread reflects the compensation required by investors for their trading costs, and its concavity results from the clientele effect (Proposition 1). To see this, recall that transaction costs are amortized over the investor's holding period. The longer this period, the smaller the compensation required for a given increase in the spread. Since in equilibrium higher-spread securities are acquired by investors with longer horizons, the added return required for a given increase in spread gets smaller. In terms of our model, longer-holding-period portfolios contain higher-spread assets and have a lower slope μ_i for the return–spread relation.

A simple numerical example can illustrate the spread–return relation. Assume $N = 9$ positive-spread assets and $M = 4$ investor types whose expected holding periods are $1/\mu_1 = 1/12$, $1/\mu_2 = 1/2$, $1/\mu_3 = 1$, and $1/\mu_4 = 5$. For simplicity, we set $\lambda_i = \mu_i$, implying that the expected number of investors of each type i is $m_i = 1$. Assets yield $d_j = \$1$ per period, and all investors have equal wealth. The relative spread of asset j is $S_j = 0.005j$, $j = 0, 1, 2, \ldots, 9$; thus, asset percentage spreads range from zero to 4.5%.

Using this data, we solve (1)–(3) and obtain the results in Table 1.1 and Figures 1.1 and 1.2. Note that the additional excess return per unit of spread goes down from $\mu_1 = 12$ in portfolio 1 to $\mu_2 = 2$ for portfolio 2, then to $\mu_3 = 1$ in portfolio 3, and finally to $\mu_4 = 0.2$ in portfolio 4. The behavior of the excess market return as a function of the spread is shown in Figure 1.1, which demonstrates both the positive compensation for higher spread and the clientele effect which moderates the excess returns, especially for the high-spread assets. This figure summarizes the main testable implications of our model: The observed market return should be an increasing and concave function of the relative spread. The piecewise-linear functional form suggested by our model provides a specific and detailed set of hypotheses tested in the next section. The effect of the spread on asset values (or prices) is demonstrated in Figure 1.2: the equilibrium values are decreasing and convex in the spread.

While the above model provides a lucid demonstration of the spread–return (or spread–price) relation, our main results do not hinge on its specific form, and hold as well under different specifications. Consider $(N + 1)$ assets, each generating the same stochastic (gross) cash flow given by the

Table 1.1. *An example of the equilibrium relation between asset bid–ask spreads, returns and values (see section 2). There are 10 assets (j), each generating $1 per period, with relative bid–ask spreads S_j (= dollar spread divided by asset value) ranging from 0 to 0.045 (column 2), and 4 investor types (i) with expected holding periods, μ_i^{-1}, of 1/12, 1/2, 1, and 5 periods.[a] The return on the zero-spread asset is ρ; all returns are measured in excess of ρ. A type-i investor chooses the assets j which maximize his spread-adjusted return, r_{ij}; given by the difference between the gross market return on asset j and its expected liquidation cost per unit time. The equilibrium solution gives the excess spread-adjusted returns, $r_{ij} - \rho$, in columns 3–6, where the boxes highlight the assets with the highest excess spread-adjusted return for each investor-type. The equilibrium portfolio for each investor-type is composed of the boxed assets. Column 7 shows the assets' equilibrium excess gross returns observed in the market, which include the expected liquidation cost to their holders. Column 8 shows the resulting asset values, obtained by discounting the perpetuity by the respective equilibrium market return, as a fraction of the value of the zero-spread asset*

Asset, j (1)	Relative bid–ask spread, S_j (2)	Investor type, i				Market return in excess of ρ, the return on the zero-spread asset (7)	Value of asset j relative to that of the zero-spread asset, V_j/V_0 (8)
		1	2	3	4		
		5					
		Length of holding period, μ_i^{-1}					
		1/12	1/2	1			
		(3)	(4)	(5)	(6)		
		Excess spread-adjusted return, $r_{ij} - \rho$					
0	0	0	0	0	0	0	1
1	0.005	0	0.05	0.055	0.059	0.06	0.943
2	0.01	0	0.10	0.11	0.118	0.12	0.893
3	0.015	−0.05	0.10	0.115	0.127	0.13	0.885
4	0.02	−0.10	0.10	0.12	0.136	0.14	0.877
5	0.025	−0.155	0.095	0.12	0.140	0.145	0.873
6	0.03	−0.21	0.09	0.12	0.144	0.15	0.870
7	0.035	−0.265	0.085	0.12	0.148	0.155	0.866
8	0.04	−0.324	0.076	0.116	0.148	0.156	0.865
9	0.045	−0.383	0.067	0.112	0.148	0.157	0.864

[a] Investors have the same wealth, and the expected number of investors of each type is 1.

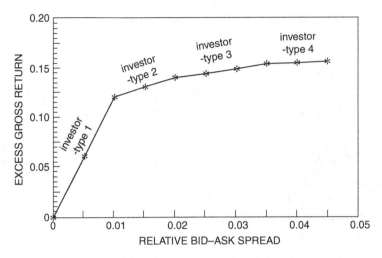

Figure 1.1. An illustration of the relation between observed market return in excess of the return on the zero-spread asset (the excess gross return) and the relative bid–ask spread (see the numerical example of Section 2 and Table 1.1, column 7). There are 10 assets, each generating $1 per period, with relative bid–ask spreads (= dollar spread divided by asset value) ranging from 0 to 0.045, and 4 investor types with expected holding periods ranging from 1/12 to 5 periods. Investors have equal wealth, and the expected number of investors of each type is 1.

The relation between asset returns and bid–ask spreads is piecewise-linear, increasing and concave, with each linear section corresponding to the portfolio of a different investor type.

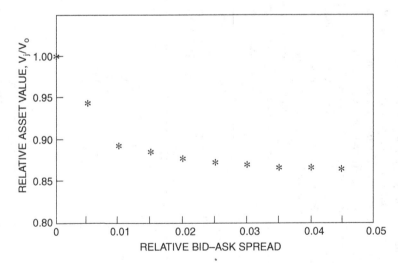

Figure 1.2. The relation between asset values and bid–ask spreads for the numerical example of section 2 (see Table 1.1, column 8, and Figure 1.1). The figure depicts the value of each asset j relative to the value of the zero-spread asset, V_j/V_0 as a function of the bid–ask spread relative to the asset's value. Asset values are a decreasing function of the spread.

26

process $\{X(t), \ t \geq 0\}$. Assume that each transaction in asset j entails a cost of $\$c_j$, with $0 = c_0 < c_1 < c_2 < \cdots < c_N$ (asset 0 having zero spread). There are M investor types numbered by $i = 1, 2, \ldots, M$, and the transaction epochs of type-i investors follow a renewal process with given parameters (depending on i).[7] Denote the highest price a type-i investor will pay for asset j by V_{ij}. When the price of each asset j is determined by its highest-valued use, we have $V_j = \max_{i=1,2,\ldots,M} V_{ij}$ with $V_{ij} = V_{i0} - c_j \theta_i$, where θ_i is the value (for investor-type i) of \$1 at each transaction epoch. Letting $f_i(c) = V_{i0} - c\theta_i$, and following the arguments of Proposition 2, we obtain that the price [given by $\max_{i=1,2,\ldots,M} f_i(c)$] is decreasing and convex in c. Further, it can be shown that the price is a decreasing and convex function of the relative transaction cost, thus demonstrating the robustness of our results. Qualitatively, similar results will hold as long as a longer investment horizon mitigates the burden of transaction costs by enabling their amortization over a longer holding period.

The next section presents empirical tests of our main testable hypotheses (Proposition 2).

3. Empirical Tests

This section presents an empirical examination of the relation between expected returns and bid–ask spreads of NYSE stocks, focusing on the particular functional relationship predicted by our model. Specifically, our hypothesis is that expected return is an increasing and concave function of the spread.

3.1. The Data and the Derivation of the Variables

Our data consist of monthly securities returns provided by the Center for Research in Security Prices and relative bid–ask spreads collected for NYSE stocks from *Fitch's Stock Quotations on the NYSE*. The relative spread is the dollar spread divided by the average of the bid and ask prices at year end. The actual spread variable used, S, is the average of the beginning and end-of-year relative spreads for each of the years 1960–1979 [the data is the same as in Stoll and Whaley (1983)].

---

[7] An investor could be viewed as owning a number of portfolios with different liquidation. horizons, without changing the results.

The relationship between stock returns, relative risk[8] (β), and spread[9] is tested over the period 1961–1980. Following the methodology developed by Black, Jensen, and Scholes (1972), Fama and MacBeth (1973) and Black and Scholes (1974), we first formed portfolios by grouping stocks according to their spread and relative risk, and then tested our hypotheses by examining the cross-sectional relation between average excess return, spread, and relative risk over time. We divided the data into twenty overlapping periods of eleven years each, consisting of a five-year β estimation period E_n, a five-year portfolio formation period F_n, and a one-year cross-section test period T_n ($n = 1, 2, \ldots, 20$).[10] The three subperiods of each eleven-year period are now considered in detail:

(i) *The beta estimation period E* was used to estimate the β coefficients from the market model regressions

$$R^e_{jt} = \alpha_j + \beta_j R^e_{mt} + \varepsilon_{jt}, \quad t = 1, \ldots, 60,$$

where R^e_{jt} and R^e_{mt} are the month-t excess returns (over the 90-day T-bill rates) on stock j and on the market,[11] respectively, and β_j is the estimate of the relative risk[12] of stock j.

(ii) *The portfolio formation period F_n* was used to form the test portfolios and estimate their β and spread parameters. All stocks traded through the entire eleven-year period n and for which the spread was available for the last year of F_n were ranked by that spread and divided into seven equal groups. Within each of the seven spread groups, stocks were ranked by their β coefficients, obtained from E_n, and divided into seven equal subgroups. This yields 49 (7×7) equal-sized portfolios,[13] with significant variability of the spreads as well as the betas within the spread groups. Then, we estimated

---

[8] By the CAPM, the β risk is the major determinant of asset returns. Our analysis in section 2 dealt with certainty-equivalent rates of return.

[9] The cost of transacting also includes brokerage commissions. In Stoll and Whaley (1983), the correlation between portfolio spreads and brokerage fees was 0.996, hence we omitted the latter.

[10] To illustrate, $E_1 = 1951$–1955, $F_1 = 1956$–1960, $T_1 = 1961$; $E_2 = 1952$–1956, $F_2 = 1957$–1961, $T_2 = 1962; \ldots E_{20} = 1970$–1974, $F_{20} = 1975$–1979, $T_{20} = 1980$.

[11] Throughout this study, R_m and the test portfolios are equally weighted. See Black, Jensen and Scholes (1972), Fama and MacBeth (1973) and Stoll and Whaley (1983, p. 71).

[12] Jensen (1968) has shown that the measure of relative risk, β_j, may be used for a holding period of any length (p. 189).

[13] The long trading-period requirement might have eliminated from our sample the riskier and higher-spread stocks, thus reducing the variability of the data. Throughout, 'equal' portfolios may differ from one another by one security due to indivisibility.

β for each portfolio from the market model regression over the months of F_n,

$$R^e_{pt} = \alpha_p + \beta_p R^e_{mt} + \varepsilon_{pt}, \quad t = 1, \ldots, 60, \quad p = 1, \ldots, 49,$$

where R^e_{pt} is the average[14] excess return of the securities included in portfolio p in month t. Finally, we calculated the portfolio spread S_{pn} by averaging the spreads (of the last year of F_n) across the stocks in portfolio p. Each portfolio p in period n is thus characterized by the pair (β_{pn}, S_{pn}) ($p = 1, 2, \ldots, 49$, $n = 1, 2, \ldots, 20$). Altogether, we have 980 (= 49 × 20) portfolios.

(iii) *The cross-section test period T_n* was used to test the relation between R^e_{pn}, β_{pn}, and S_{pn} across portfolios, where R^e_{pn} is the average monthly excess return on the stocks in portfolio p in T_n, the last year of period n.[15]

Table 1.2 presents summary statistics for the 49 portfolio groups, classified by spread and β. Note that both β and the excess return increase with the spread. The correlation coefficients between the portfolio excess returns R^e_p, the portfolio betas β_p and the spreads S_p, presented in Table 1.3, show that both β_p and S_p are positively correlated with excess returns; the correlation between R^e_p and the spread over the twenty-year period is about twice as high as that between R^e_p and β. Also, note the high positive correlation between β and the spread.

3.2. Test Methodology

We now turn to test the major hypothesis of model, namely, that expected return is an increasing and concave function of the relative spread. This is a classical case of covariance analysis and pooling of cross-section and time-series data [see Kmenta (1971, ch. 12-2), Maddala (1977, ch. 14), Judge et al. (1980, ch. 8)], where the estimation model has to allow for differences over cross-sectional units (portfolios) and over time. This is done by employing two sets of dummy variables: The first set consists of 48 portfolio dummy variables, defined by $DP_{ij} = 1$ if the portfolio is in group (i, j) and zero otherwise; $i = 1, 2, \ldots, 7$ is the spread-group index and $j = 1, 2, \ldots, 7$ is the β-group index, with $DP_{7,7} \equiv 0$. By construction, the spread increases in i, and β increases in j. A second set of dummy variables, defined by $DY_n = 1$

---

[14] Throughout, averaging means arithmetic averaging.

[15] Note that our test is predictive in nature, using estimates of risk and spread which are available at the beginning of the test period. See Fama (1976, 349–351).

Table 1.2. *Average relative bid–ask spread, monthly excess return, relative risk (β) and firm size for die 49 portfolios for the 20 test-period years 1961–1980. Portfolios are indexed by the spread group i (i = 1 for the smallest spread) and by the beta group j (j = 1 for the smallest beta). Portfolio composition changes every year and the sample size ranges between 619 and 900 stocks.*

The relative bid–ask spread of a stock is its dollar spread divided by the average of the bid and ask prices at year end.
The portfolio spread is the average relative spread of stocks in the portfolio.

The portfolio (monthly) excess return is the 12-month arithmetic average of the monthly average returns on the stocks in the portfolio in excess of that month's Treasury-Bill rate.

The portfolio beta is the average relative risk (β) coefficient for the stocks in the portfolio, estimated over the 5 years preceding the test period. Size is the market value of the firm's equity in millions of dollars at the end of the year preceding the test period, averaged over the firms included in the portfolio

Spread group, i		Beta group, j							Mean
		1	2	3	4	5	6	7	
1	Spread	0.004765	0.004850	0.004860	0.004789	0.004878	0.004891	0.004980	0.00486
	Excess return	0.002706	0.001306	0.003380	0.004409	0.003427	0.005416	0.003781	0.00349
	Beta	0.54001	0.67797	0.75890	0.77867	0.83231	0.91651	1.08973	0.799
	Size	4089.8	3245.5	3231.9	2317.3	1430.0	1418.8	595.7	2333
2	Spread	0.007435	0.007445	0.007463	0.007414	0.007508	0.007412	0.007452	0.00745
	Excess return	0.003174	0.003543	0.003549	0.004995	0.003050	0.006424	0.011061	0.00511
	Beta	0.55369	0.71874	0.81652	0.84596	0.90668	1.02999	1.21992	0.870
	Size	780.2	880.3	741.5	707.6	656.1	605.9	282.7	665
3	Spread	0.009392	0.009386	0.009400	0.009375	0.009339	0.009350	0.009425	0.00939
	Excess return	0.001838	0.003165	0.006707	0.002619	0.004473	0.006133	0.005063	0.00429
	Beta	0.56069	0.67271	0.79543	0.89866	1.00357	1.04518	1.20940	0.884
	Size	476.2	502.1	695.9	370.1	363.9	293.3	227.1	418

4	Spread	0.011470	0.011473	0.011411	0.011464	0.011449	0.011487	0.011411	0.01145
	Excess return	0.003217	0.002447	0.005296	0.004521	0.008505	0.008033	0.009178	0.00589
	Beta	0.58821	0.69158	0.84828	0.92208	0.99515	1.07535	1.26739	0.913
	Size	331.9	362.7	370.6	248.4	250.5	192.4	174.5	276
5	Spread	0.014015	0.013913	0.013955	0.013998	6.013883	0.013969	0.013988	0.01396
	Excess return	0.002583	0.004340	0.003318	0.006763	0.008076	0.011460	0.010266	0.00669
	Beta	0.60153	0.71197	0.82031	0.92906	1.04923	1.12224	1.28927	0.932
	Size	243.1	257.3	213.6	166.3	149.2	146.2	111.3	184
6	Spread	0.017662	0.017513	0.017699	0.017759	0.017789	0.017763	0.017967	0.01774
	Excess return	0.003637	0.006937	0.007209	0.007415	0.011254	0.010877	0.012516	0.00855
	Beta	0.65522	0.73861	0.87193	0.94479	1.07714	1.16769	1.33498	0.970
	Size	135.6	131.1	127.1	113.1	91.2	89.9	72.8	109
7	Spread	0.032890	0.029385	0.031614	0.031472	0.031647	0.033169	0.034385	0.03208
	Excess return	0.006683	0.008876	0.008044	0.007405	0.012335	0.013384	0.014929	0.01024
	Beta	0.76132	0.88340	0.99811	1.12656	1.23899	1.33249	1.46259	1.115
	Size	75.2	67.8	57.5	54.7	44.0	47.8	37.3	55
Mean	Spread	0.013947	0.013424	0.013772	0.013753	0.013792	0.014006	0.014230	0.01385
	Excess return	0.003405	0.004373	0.005357	0.005447	0.007303	0.008818	0.009542	0.00632
	Beta	0.60867	0.72785	0.84421	0.92083	1.01472	1.09849	1.26761	0.926
	Size	876	778	777	568	426	399	214	577

Table 1.3. *Correlation coefficients between the annual average portfolio spread S_p, excess return R_p^e and beta β_p for the entire sample period 1961–1980 and for its two 10-year subperiods, 1961–1970 and 1971–1980. Portfolio spread is the average bid–ask spread as a fraction of the year-end average of the bid and ask prices for all securities in the portfolio. Excess returns are the average monthly returns in excess of the monthly T-Bill rate*

| | Correlation coefficient between | | | Number of |
Period	R_p^e and S_p	R_p^e and β_p	β_p and S_p	observations
1961–80	0.239	0.123	0.361	980
1961–70	0.179	0.132	0.163	490
1971–80	0.285	0.118	0.540	490

in year n $(n = 1, 2, \ldots, 19)$ and zero otherwise, accounts for differences in returns between years.

An important implication of our model is that the slope of the return–spread relation declines as we move to higher-spread groups. To allow for different slope coefficients across spread groups, we decomposed the spread variable S_{pn} into seven variables S_{pn}^i $(i = 1, 2, \ldots, 7)$ defined by $S_{pn}^i = S_{pn}$ if in spread group i $(i = 1, 2, \ldots, 7)$ and zero otherwise. Due to the high correlation between S_{pn}^i and $\sum_{j=1}^{7} DP_{ij}$, we constructed the mean-adjusted spread variables, $\hat{S}_{pn}^i = S_{pn}^i - \overline{S}^i$ if portfolio (p, n) is in group i and zero otherwise where $\overline{S}^i$ is the mean spread for the ith spread group. The means of $\hat{S}_{pn}^i$ are zero and their correlations with $\sum_{j=1}^{7} DP_{ij}$ are zero. Replacing S_{pn}^i by the mean-adjusted variables thus leads to a separation between the level effects among groups (captured by DP_{ij}) and the slope effects within spread groups (captured by $\hat{S}_{pn}^i$).

Using the above variables, we carried out the pooled cross-section and time-series estimation of our model:

$$R_{pn}^e = a_0 + a_1\beta_{pn} + \sum_{i=1}^{7} b_i\hat{S}_{pn}^i + \sum_{i=1}^{7}\sum_{j=1}^{7} c_{ij}DP_{ij} + \sum_{n=1}^{19} d_nDY_n + \varepsilon_{pn}, \quad (8)$$

where a_0, a_1, b_i, c_{ij}, and d_n are coefficients and the ε_{pn} are the residuals. The slope coefficients b_i measure the response of stock returns to increasing the spread *within* spread group i, and the dummy coefficients c_{ij} measure the difference between the mean return on portfolio (i, j) and that of portfolio $(7, 7)$ which corresponds to the highest spread and β group.

The sums $\sum_{i=1}^{7} c_{ij}$ measure the differences in mean returns between β groups j, while $\sum_{j=1}^{7} c_{ij}$ measure the differences in mean returns between spread groups i. Thus, for any given β, model (8) represents a piecewise-linear functional form of the return–spread relation. This follows the Malinvaud (1970, pp. 317–318) and Kmenta (1971, pp. 468–469) methodology for estimating non-linear relationships, which groups the data based on the values of the explanatory variable, and fits a piecewise linear curve using two sets of variables: group dummies to capture differences between group means, and products of the explanatory variable by the group dummies to allow for the different slopes.

Estimation of the pooled model (8) using OLS is problematic due to the possibility of cross-sectional heteroskedasticity and cross-sectional correlations among residuals across portfolio groups. While the estimated OLS coefficients are unbiased and consistent, their estimated variances are not, leading to biased test statistics. This calls for a generalized least squares (GLS) estimation procedure. Given that the variance–covariance matrix of the residuals in (8) is $\sigma^2 V$, where σ^2 is a scalar and V is a symmetric positive-definite matrix, the GLS procedure uses a matrix Q satisfying $Q'Q = V^{-1}$ to transform all the regression variables by pre-multiplication. The variance–covariance matrix V was assumed to be block diagonal (reflecting independence between years), where the diagonal blocks consist of twenty identical 49×49 positive definite matrices U. Then, $V = I \otimes U$, where I is the 20×20 identity matrix and $\otimes$ denotes the Kronecker product. To obtain the 49×49 matrix U, we first estimated model (8) by OLS and then used the data month by month to obtain the residuals $\hat{\varepsilon}_{pm}$ ($p = 1, 2, \ldots, 49$) for each month m ($m = 1, 2, \ldots, 240$). Then, we estimated U by averaging the resulting 240 monthly variance–covariance matrices – the resulting estimate of the variance–covariance matrix V is known to be consistent [cf. Kmenta (1971, ch. 12)]. The transformation matrix Q was calculated using the Choleski decomposition method. The variables of model (8) were then pre-multiplied by the transformation matrix Q, and the transformed version of model (8) was estimated to provide the GLS results.

3.3. The Results

We first ran a simple OLS regression of the excess returns on β, the spread and the nineteen-year dummy variables:

$$R^e_{pn} = 0.0040 + \underset{(9.17)}{0.00947\beta_{pn}} + \sum_{n=1}^{19} d_n DY_n + e_{pn},$$

and

$$R^e_{pn} = 0.0036 + \underset{(6.18)}{0.00672\beta_{pn}} + \underset{(6.83)}{0.2111\,S_{pn}} + \sum_{n=1}^{19} d_n DY_n + e_{pn}.$$

(t-statistics are in parentheses.) The results show that excess returns are increasing in both β and the spread. The coefficient of S_{pn} implies that a 1% increase in the spread is associated with a 0.211% increase in the monthly risk-adjusted excess return. The coefficient of β declines when the spread variable is added to the equation, indicating that part of the effect which could be attributed to β may, in fact, be due to the spread.[16] The coefficient of β is 0.00672, very close to 0.00671, which is the average monthly excess return on common stocks for this period.

Next, we estimated the detailed model (8) using both OLS and GLS. The slope coefficients of the spread variables are presented in Table 1.4, and the coefficients of DP_{ij} are given in Table 1.5. To estimate the pattern of the dummy coefficients, we employed the model

$$c_{ij} = \alpha + \sum_{i=1}^{6} \gamma_i DS_i + \sum_{j=1}^{6} \delta_j DB_j + e_{ij}, \tag{9}$$

where the spread dummy DS_i ($i = 1, \ldots, 6$) is one if the portfolio is in spread group i and zero otherwise, and the β dummy DB_j ($j = 1, \ldots, 6$) is one if the portfolio is in β group j and zero otherwise. Thus, the coefficients γ_i in (9) measure the difference between the average return of spread group i and that of the seventh (highest) spread group, and the coefficients δ_j measure the corresponding differences between β groups.

The estimates of (8)–(9) presented in Tables 1.4 and 1.6 support our two hypotheses:

(i) The coefficients γ_i of DS_i in model (9) are negative and generally increasing in i, implying that risk-adjusted excess returns increase with the spread. The difference in the monthly mean excess return between the two extreme spread groups is 0.857% when estimated by OLS and 0.681% when estimated by GLS.

(ii) The slope coefficients of the spreads, b_i, are positive and generally decreasing as we move to higher spread groups. This is consistent with the hypothesized concavity of the return–spread relation, reflecting the lower sensitivity of long-term portfolios to the spread.

The effect of the relative risk is measured in model (8) by both β and the dummy variables and is further summarized by the DB_j coefficients of model (9). The emerging pattern is that (spread-adjusted) excess returns increase with β as depicted by the significant negative and increasing coefficients δ_j.

---

[16]　Given the strong positive correlation between S_{pn} and β_{pn}, the omission of S_{pn} from the regression equation which tests the CAPM results in an upward bias in the estimated coefficient of β; see Kmenta (1971, p. 392).

Table 1.4. *Estimated regressions of the portfolio monthly excess returns, R^e, on the mean-adjusted spread variables $\hat{S}^i$ and relative risk, β, for the years 1961–1980, using ordinary least squares and generalized least squares estimation methods. The regression model (8)[a] applies pooled cross-section and time-series estimation. The coefficient of $\hat{S}^i$ reflects the response of stock returns to an increase in the bid–ask spread within spread group i, where $i = 1$ corresponds to the lowest-spread group. (t-values are in parentheses)*

Independent variable	Ordinary least squares coefficients	Generalized least squares coefficients		
	Entire period 1961–1980	Entire period 1961–1980	Subperiod 1961–1970	Subperiod 1971–1980
$\hat{S}_1$	3.641	1.310	0.080	2.303
	(2.76)	(1.16)	(0.05)	(1.27)
$\hat{S}_2$	3.242	1.747	0.975	2.505
	(3.50)	(2.56)	(0.91)	(2.41)
$\hat{S}_3$	2.854	1.660	0.934	2.27
	(3.93)	(3.01)	(1.10)	(2.80)
$\hat{S}_4$	1.657	0.482	−0.149	0.983
	(3.06)	(1.16)	(0.21)	(1.69)
$\hat{S}_5$	2.224	1.206	0.922	1.500
	(5.69)	(3.84)	(1.67)	(3.47)
$\hat{S}_6$	1.365	0.650	0.838	0.475
	(5.28)	(2.96)	(2.21)	(1.50)
$\hat{S}_7$	0.605	0.256	0.176	0.489
	(5.28)	(2.56)	(1.49)	(2.49)
β	−0.0058	−0.000	−0.002	−0.003
	(2.53)	(0.10)	(0.47)	(0.72)

[a] The regression model is

$$R^e_{pn} = a_0 + a_1\beta_{pn} + \sum_{i=1}^{7} b_i \hat{S}^l_{pn} + \sum_{i=1}^{7}\sum_{j=1}^{7} c_{ij} DP_{ij} + \sum_{n=1}^{19} d_n DY_n + \varepsilon_{pn}, \qquad (8)$$

where R^e_{pn} is the average excess return for portfolio p in year n, β_{pn} is the average portfolio relative risk, $\hat{S}^l_{pn}$ is the mean-adjusted spread within spread group i (= the deviation of the spread of portfolio p in year n from the mean spread of its spread group, i), DP_{ij} are the portfolio-group dummy variables (= 1 in portfolio group (i, j), zero otherwise), DY_n are the year dummy variables (= 1 in year n, 0 otherwise), and ε_{pn} are the residuals. The GLS estimated coefficients of the portfolio-group dummies DP_{ij} arc reported in Table 1.5.

The effect of β is captured mainly through the dummies rather than the coefficient a_1, which is highly insignificant in the GLS estimation. Finally, we estimated models (8)–(9) for the two ten-year subperiods, with generally the same pattern of results.

Table 1.5. *Generalized least squares estimates of the difference between the mean monthly excess return of the portfolio with the highest spread and beta – portfolio (7,7), the 49th portfolio – and the mean monthly excess returns of each of the other 48 portfolios. These are the estimated coefficients of die 48 portfolio dummy variables DP_{ij} in the pooled cross-section and time-series regression model (8), using GLS, over the entire period 1961–1980. t-statistics for all unmarked table entries are greater than 1.96, implying that the estimated coefficient is significant at better than the 2.5% level (one-tail test)*

Spread group, i	Beta group, j							
	1 (low)	2	3	4	5	6	7 (high)	Mean
1 (low)	−0.0117	−0.0132	−0.0111	−0.0100	−0.0111	−0.0091	−0.0108	−0.0110
2	−0.0113	−0.0109	−0.0109	−0.0094	−0.0115	−0.0079	−0.0033[b]	−0.0093
3	−0.0127	−0.0113	−0.0078[a]	−0.0118	−0.0100	−0.0082	−0.0094	−0.0102
4	−0.0113	−0.0120	−0.0091	−0.0099	−0.0059[a]	−0.0064	−0.0052[b]	−0.0085
5	−0.0120	−0.0101	−0.0111	−0.0077	−0.0062[a]	−0.0030[b]	−0.0041[b]	−0.0077
6	−0.0108	−0.0074[a]	−0.0072	−0.0070	−0.0032[b]	−0.0035[b]	−0.0020[b]	−0.0059
7 (high)	−0.0080	−0.0049[b]	−0.0063	−0.0068	−0.0019[b]	−0.0013[b]	0.0000	−0.0042
Mean	−0.0111	−0.0100	−0.0091	−0.0089	−0.0071	−0.0056	−0.0050	

[a] $1.645 < t < 1.96$, implying significance at better than the 5% level (one-tail test).
[b] $t < 1.645$, insignificant at the 5% level (one-tail test).

Table 1.6. *Regression estimates of the difference between the mean return of the spread and beta groups and the mean return of the highest-spread and highest-beta portfolio. The estimation model is*

$$c_{ij} = \alpha + \sum_{i=1}^{6} \gamma_i DS_i + \sum_{j=1}^{6} \delta_j DB_j + e_{ij}, \qquad (9)$$

where c_{ij} are the dummy coefficients estimated from model (8) (Table 1.5); $DS_t = 1$ for the ith spread group and zero otherwise; and $DB_j = 1$ for the jth beta group and zero otherwise. Spreads are increasing in i, and betas are increasing in j.
(t-statistics are in parentheses)

	Estimated regression coefficients			
	Entire 1961–1980 period		Subperiods	
Independent variable	From OLS regression	From GLS regression	1961–1970 GLS	1971–1980 GLS
DS_1	−0.00857 (9.05)	−0.00681 (7.74)	−0.00730 (7.46)	−0.00397 (3.33)
DS_2	−0.00654 (6.90)	−0.00517 (5.88)	−0.00578 (5.91)	−0.00267 (2.24)
DS_3	−0.00729 (7.70)	−0.00599 (6.82)	−0.00556 (5.69)	−0.00483 (4.05)
DS_4	−0.00552 (5.83)	−0.00439 (4.99)	−0.00446 (4.56)	−0.00301 (2.53)
DS_5	−0.00461 (4.86)	−0.00359 (4.08)	−0.00335 (3.42)	−0.00272 (2.28)
DS_6	−0.00252 (2.66)	−0.00172 (1.95)	−0.00246 (2.52)	0.00051 (0.42)
DB_1	−0.00964 (10.18)	−0.00614 (6.98)	−0.00669 (6.84)	−0.00454 (3.81)
DB_2	−0.00767 (8.10)	−0.00500 (5.68)	−0.00495 (5.06)	−0.00421 (3.53)
DB_3	−0.00626 (6.61)	−0.00411 (4.67)	−0.00325 (3.32)	−0.00434 (3.64)
DB_4	−0.00568 (6.00)	−0.00398 (4.53)	−0.00260 (2.66)	−0.00485 (4.07)
DB_5	−0.00336 (3.55)	−0.00214 (2.43)	−0.00098 (1.00)	−0.00293 (2.46)
DB_6	−0.00147 (1.56)	−0.00065 (0.74)	0.00017 (0.18)	−0.00121 (1.01)

Detailed tests of our main hypotheses are presented in Table 1.7. In 7(B), we test the significance of the spread effect by omitting all spread-related variables and examine the resulting increase in the unexplained variance. In 7(C), we test whether the mean excess returns of all spread groups are equal by eliminating all spread-related dummy variables. The significance of the non-linearities was tested in two ways: First, we replaced all the spread-related variables (eliminating the $\hat{S}^i_{pn}$ and replacing the DP_{ij} with six β dummies) by the original spread variable S_{pn} [see 7(D)]. Then, we tested the equality of the slope coefficients across spread groups by re-estimating model (8), replacing the variables $\hat{S}^1$ through $\hat{S}^7$ by their sum [see 7(E)]. In all four cases, the F-tests for the changes in the sum of squared residuals reject the null hypotheses at better than the 0.01 level. Thus, our hypotheses are fully supported by the data.

4. Firm Size, Spread and Return

The well-known negative relationship between spread and firm size suggests that our findings may bear on the 'small-firm anomaly': Banz (1981) and Reinganum (1981a, b) found a negative relation between risk-adjusted mean returns on stocks and their market value, indicating either a misspecification of the CAPM or evidence of market inefficiency [see Schwert (1983) for a comprehensive review]. Thus, it is instructive to estimate the effects of a firm-size variable and to test its significance vis-a-vis our variables.

We re-estimated our models adding a new explanatory variable – *SIZE*, the market value of the firm's equity in millions of dollars at the end of the year just preceding the test period. As seen in Table 1.2, there is a negative relationship between *SIZE* and both spread and β. The effect of firm size on stock returns was tested by incorporating *SIZE* in all our models, but its estimated effect was negligible and highly insignificant.

To allow for a possible non-linear effect (as other studies do), we replaced *SIZE* by its natural logarithm and examined the impact of adding $\log(SIZE)$ to our regression equations. First, we estimated the simple linear model

$$R^e_{pn} = 0.0082 + 0.0060\beta_{pn} + 0.158\,S_{pn} + 0.0006\,\log(SIZE)_{pn}$$
$$(5.05) \qquad\quad (3.44) \qquad\quad (1.56)$$

$$+ \sum_{n=1}^{19} d_n DY_n + e_{pn}.$$

The results indicate that the risk and spread effects prevail, whereas the size effect is insignificant. We then re-estimated our detailed model (8)

Table 1.7. *Tests of hypotheses on the return–spread relation. All regressions are estimated by GLS*

Model[a]	Degrees of freedom of the model	SSR, sum of squared residuals	Difference from model (A)[b]			F-statistic
			DF	SSR	MS	
(A)	75	76.7877	–	–	–	–
(B)	26	85.5489	49	8.7612	0.1788	2.10
(Q)	33	83.3506	42	6.5629	0.1563	1.84
(D)	27	84.7339	48	7.9462	0.1655	1.95
(E)	69	78.4249	6	1.6372	0.2729	3.21

[a] The regression models are as follows.

Model (A) – the full model:

$$R^e_{pn} = a_0 + a_1\beta_{pn} + \sum_{i=1}^{7} b_i \hat{S}^i_{pn} + \sum_{i=1}^{7}\sum_{j=1}^{7} c_{ij} DP_{ij} + \sum_{n=1}^{19} d_n DY_n + \varepsilon_{pn}, \qquad (8)$$

where $p = 1, 2, \ldots, 49$, $n = 1, 2, \ldots, 20$, and $DP_{Ti} = 0$.

Model (B) – a restricted model for testing the existence of any spread effect:

$$R^e_{pn} = a_0 + a_1\beta_{pn} + \sum_{j=1}^{6} \gamma_i DB_j + \sum_{n=1}^{19} d_n DY_n + \varepsilon_{pn}.$$

Model (C) – a restricted model for testing the equality of mean excess returns across spread groups:

$$R^e_{pn} = a_0 + a_1\beta_{pn} + \sum_{i=1}^{7} b_i \hat{S}^i_{pn} + \sum_{j=1}^{6} \gamma_j DB_j + \sum_{n=1}^{19} d_n DY_n + \varepsilon_{pn}.$$

Model (D) – a restricted model for testing the non-linearity of the return-spread relation:

$$R^e_{pn} = a_0 + a_1\beta_{pn} + a_2 S_{pn} + \sum_{j=1}^{6} \gamma_j DB_j + \sum_{n=1}^{19} d_n DY_n + \varepsilon_{pn}.$$

Model (E) – a restricted model testing the equality of the slope coefficients across spread groups:

$$R^e_{pn} = a_0 + a_1\beta_{pn} + a_2 \left(\sum_{i=1}^{7} \hat{S}^i_{pn} \right) + \sum_{i=1}^{7}\sum_{j=1}^{7} c_{ij} DP_{ij} + \sum_{n=1}^{19} d_n DY_n + \varepsilon_{pn}.$$

The regression variables are:

R^e_{pn} = average portfolio excess return (the dependent variable) for portfolio p in year n,

β_{pn} = average portfolio relative (β) risk,

S_{pn} = average portfolio relative spread,

S^i_{pn} = mean-adjusted spread (the deviation of the spread S_{pn} of portfolio p in year n from the mean spread of its spread group, i),

DP_{ij} = portfolio group dummy; one in portfolio group (i, j), zero otherwise,

DY_n = year dummy; one in year n, zero otherwise,

DB_j = β group dummy; one in β group j, zero otherwise. $DB_j = \sum_{i=1}^{7} DP_{ij} (j = 1, 2, \ldots, 6)$.

[b] Data for the F-test on each of the restricted models:

DF = difference in the number of degrees of freedom between the full and restricted model,

SSR = difference in the sum of squares between the full and restricted model,

MS = SSR/DF, the mean square.

Table 1.8. *Effects of firm size on portfolio returns, controlling for the effects of the bid–ask spread, over the period 1961–1980 and its two 10-year subperiods*

Model[a]	Sample period	Definition of size variable	Estimates for the size variable		Spread variables included in the regression equation
			Coefficient	t-value	
(A)	1961–80	SIZE	-0.23×10^{-6}	0.74	all[b]
(B)	1961–80	log(SIZE)	-0.000650	1.52	all[b]
(B)	1961–70	log(SIZE)	-0.000916	1.46	all[b]
(B)	1971–80	log(SIZE)	-0.000216	0.34	all[b]
(C)	1961–80	log(SIZE)	-0.00032	1.08	S ($a_2 = 0.153$, $t = 2.51$)
(D)	1961–80	log(SIZE).	-0.00057	2.0	none

[a] The models used are as follows.
Model (A) is obtained by adding SIZE to (8), i.e.,

$$R^e_{pn} = a_0 + a_1 \beta_{pn} + \sum_{i=1}^{7} b_i \hat{S}^i_{pn} + \sum_{i=1}^{7} \sum_{j=1}^{7} c_{ij} DP_{ij} + \psi \cdot SIZE_{pn} + \sum_{n=1}^{19} d_n DY_n + \varepsilon_{pn}.$$

Model (B) is obtained by adding log(SIZE) to (8), i.e., replacing $SIZE_{pn}$ in (A) by log($SIZE_{pn}$).
Model (C) includes log(SIZE) and the spread variable S_{pn}:

$$R^e_{pn} = a_0 + a_1 \beta_{pn} + a_2 S_{pn} + \sum_{j=1}^{6} \gamma_j DB_j + \eta \cdot \log(SIZE_{pn}) + \sum_{j=1}^{19} d_n DY_n + \varepsilon_{pn}.$$

Model (D) is obtained by omitting S_{pn} from model (C).
The regression variables are:
R^e_{pn} = average excess return for portfolio p in year n (the dependent variable),
β_{pn} = average portfolio relative (β) risk,
S_{pn} = average portfolio relative spread,
S^i_{pn} = mean-adjusted spread (the deviation of the spread S_{pn} of portfolio p in year n from the mean spread of its spread group, i),
DP_{ij} = portfolio group dummy; one in portfolio group (i, j), zero otherwise,
DB_j = β-group dummy; one in β-group j, zero otherwise.
DB_j = $\sum_{i=1}^{7} DP_{ij}$ (j = 1, 2, ..., 6).
DY_n = year dummy; one in year n, zero otherwise,
$SIZE_{pn}$ = average market value of the equity of firms in portfolio p in the year just preceding n, in millions of dollars.
[b] Results obtained by adding the size variable to the full model (8).

with the added variable log(SIZE) using GLS over the entire sample period and its two ten-year subperiods. The results in Table 1.8(B) suggest that the size effect is insignificant, and it remains insignificant when the only spread variable appearing in the regression equation is S_{pn} [see 8(C)]. The coefficient of log(SIZE) becomes significant only when all the spread-related variables are altogether omitted [Table 1.8(D)]. Finally, we performed an F-test for the significance of our set of spread variables given log(SIZE). The test produced $F = 2.02$, significant at better than the 0.01 level. Thus, while our spread variables render the size effect insignificant, they remain highly significant even with log(*SIZE*) in the regression equation. In sum, our results on the return-spread relation cannot be explained by a 'size effect' even if the latter exists. In fact, any 'size effect' may be a consequence of a spread effect, with firm size serving as a proxy for liquidity. And, rather than suggesting an 'anomaly' or an indication of market inefficiency, our return–spread relation represents a rational response by an efficient market to the existence of the spread.

A number of studies have attempted to explain the size effect in terms of the bid–ask spread. Stoll and Whaley (1983) suggested that investors' valuations are based on returns net of transaction costs, and observed that the costs of transacting in small-firm stocks are relatively higher. They thus subtracted these costs from the measured returns and tested for a small-firm effect. Using an interesting empirical procedure based on arbitrage portfolios, they found that if round-trip transactions occurred every three months, the size effect was eliminated. They thus concluded that the CAPM, applied to after-transaction-cost returns over an appropriately chosen holding period, cannot be rejected.

This conclusion was challenged by Schultz (1983), who claimed that transaction costs do not completely explain the size effect. Extending Stoll and Whaley's sample to smaller AMEX firms, Schultz found that small firms earn positive excess returns after transaction costs for holding periods of one year. He thus concluded that transaction costs cannot explain the violations of the CAPM. This criticism, however, hardly settles the issue, and in fact highlights a basic problem. Given the higher returns and higher spreads of small firms' stocks, it is always possible to find an investment horizon which nullifies the abnormal return after transaction costs. But then, finding that a horizon of one year does not eliminate the size effect is insufficient to determine whether or not transaction costs are the proper explanation.

Our examination of the relation between stock returns and bid–ask spreads is based on a theory which produces well-specified hypotheses. In the context of our model, the after-transaction-cost return, as defined in the above studies, is not meaningful. Stoll–Whaley and Schultz consider this key variable to be a property of the security, and calculate it by subtracting the transaction cost from the gross return, implicitly assuming the same holding period for all stocks. By our model, the spread-adjusted return depends not only on the stock's return and spread, but also on the holding horizon of its specific clientele [see (4)]. Thus, their method is inapplicable to test our hypotheses on the return–spread relation.

The different objective guiding our empirical study has shaped its different methodology and structure. Stoll–Whaley and Schultz aim at explaining the 'small firm' anomaly through the bid–ask spread, hence their portfolio construction and test procedure are governed by firm size.[17] We start from a theoretical specification of the return–spread relation, and the objective of our empirical study is to test the explicit functional form predicted by our model. Thus, our empirical results are disciplined by the theory and in fact the test procedure is called for by the theory.

A second issue raised by Schultz (1983) is the seasonal behavior of the size effect, which is particularly pronounced in the month of January.[18] In the context of our study, there is a question whether liquidity has a seasonal. A test of this hypothesis requires data on monthly bid–ask spreads which was unavailable to us. Given our data of a single spread observation per year, we are unable to carry out a powerful test incorporating seasonality, a topic which is worthy of further research.

An empirical issue in the computation of returns on small firms is the possible upward bias due to the bid–ask spread, suggested by Blume and Stambaugh (1983), Roll (1983) and Fisher and Weaver (1985). Blume and Stambaugh estimate the bias to be $\frac{1}{4}S^2$, where S is the relative spread. Given the magnitudes of the spreads and the excess returns, this difference is negligible. Indeed, we re-estimated models (8)–(9), applying the Blume–Stambaugh and Fisher–Weaver approach and obtained similar results which uniformly supported our hypotheses.[19]

5. Conclusion

This paper studies the effect of securities' bid–ask spreads on their returns. We model a market where rational traders differ in their expected holding periods and assets have different spreads. The ensuing equilibrium has the following characteristics: (i) market-observed average returns are an increasing function of the spread; (ii) asset returns to their holders, net of trading costs, increase with the spread;[20] (iii) there is a clientele effect, whereby stocks with higher spreads are held by investors with longer holding

---

[17] Stoll–Whaley and Schultz subordinate their study of the bid–ask effect to the small-firm classification, a procedure which is natural for studying the small-firm anomaly. Our portfolio-construction method is motivated by the prediction that stock returns are a function of the bid–ask spread and β, and is designed specifically to test this hypothesis.

[18] Lakonishok and Smidt (1984) found that the small-firm effect prevails at the turn-of-the-year when returns are measured net of transaction costs, using the high and low prices as proxies for the ask and bid prices.

[19] To illustrate, the coefficient of DS_1 in model (9), which reflects the difference in returns between the highest and lowest spread groups, was -0.00765 ($t = 8.15$) by the OLS method and -0.00587 ($t = 6.73$) by GLS.

[20] Recall that, in the context of our model, net returns cannot be defined as stock characteristics, since they depend on both the stock and the owning investor. Our result is that despite their higher spread, the net return on high-spread stocks to their holders is higher.

periods; and (iv) due to the clientele effect, returns on higher-spread stocks are less spread-sensitive, giving rise to a concave return–spread relation. We design a detailed test on the behavior of observed returns, and our results support the theory. The robustness and statistical significance of our results are very encouraging, especially when compared to the Fama–MacBeth (1973) benchmark. These results do not point at an anomaly or market inefficiency; rather, they reflect a rational response by investors in an efficient market when faced with trading friction and transaction costs.

The higher yields required on higher-spread stocks give firms an incentive to increase the liquidity of their securities, thus reducing their opportunity cost of capital. Consequently, liquidity-increasing financial policies may increase the value of the firm. This was demonstrated for our numerical example in Figure 1.2, which depicts the relation between asset values and their bid–ask spreads. Applying our empirical results, consider an asset which yields $1 per month, has a bid–ask spread of 3.2% (as in our high-spread portfolio group) and its proper opportunity cost of capital is 2% per month, yielding a value of $50. If the spread is reduced to 0.486% (as in our low-spread portfolio group), our estimates imply that the value of the asset would increase to $75.8, about a 50% increase, suggesting a strong incentive for the firm to invest in increasing the liquidity of the claims it issues. In particular, phenomena such as 'going public' (compared to private placement), standardization of the contractual forms of securities, limited liability, exchange listing and information disclosures may be construed as investments in increased liquidity. It is of interest to examine to what extent observed corporate financial policies can be explained by the liquidity-increasing motive. Such an investigation could create a link between securities market microstructure and corporate financial policies, and constitutes a natural avenue for further research.

This also suggests that a more comprehensive model of the return–spread relation could consider supply response by firms. Rather than set the spread exogenously, as in our model, firms may engage in a supply adjustment, increasing the liquidity of their securities at a cost. In equilibrium, the marginal increase in value due to improved liquidity will equal the marginal cost of such an improvement. Then, differences in firms' ability to affect liquidity will be reflected in differences in bid–ask spreads and risk-adjusted returns across securities.[21]

We believe that this paper makes a strong case for studying the role of liquidity in asset pricing in a broader context. The generality of our

---

[21] Even if some firms could issue an unlimited supply of zero-spread securities, our results show that there will still be differentials in investors' net yields.

analysis is limited in that we do not consider the difference between marginal liquidity and total liquidity, and the associated relation between liquidation uncertainty and holding period uncertainty. This issue deserves further attention. In our model, all assets are liquidated at the end of the investor's holding period. Thus, there is no distinction between the liquidity of an asset when considered by itself and its liquidity in a portfolio context, nor is it necessary to consider the dispersion of possible holding periods for each asset in the portfolio. In a more general model, each investor may be faced with a sequence of stochastic cash demands occurring at random points in time. The investor would then have to determine the quantities of each security to be liquidated at each point in time. In such a setting, an investor's portfolio is likely to include an array of assets with both low and high spreads, whose proportions will reflect both the distribution of the amounts to be liquidated and the dispersion of his liquidation times. Then, there would be a distinction between the liquidity of an asset and its marginal contribution to the liquidity of an investor's portfolio. A study along these lines should focus on the interrelationship between total and marginal liquidity and its effect on asset pricing.

Further research could also be carried out on the interplay between liquidity and risk, and on the relation between asset returns and a more comprehensive set of liquidity characteristics. And finally, it is of interest to pursue the link between corporate financial theory and the theory of exchange, possibly leading to a unified framework which will enhance our understanding of organizations and markets.

References

Amihud, Yakov and Haim Mendelson, 1980, Dealership market: Market-making with inventory, Journal of Financial Economics 8, 31–53.

Amihud, Yakov and Haim Mendelson, 1982, Asset price behavior in a dealership market, Financial Analysts Journal 29, 50–9.

Amihud, Yakov and Haim Mendelson, 1985, An integrated computerized trading system, in: Y. Amihud, T.S. Ho and R.A. Schwartz, eds., Market making and the changing structure of the securities industry (Lexington Heath, Lexington, MA) 217–35.

Amihud, Yakov and Haim Mendelson, 1986a, Liquidity and stock returns, Financial Analysts Journal 42, 43–8.

Amihud, Yakov and Haim Mendelson, 1986b, Trading mechanisms and stock returns: An empirical investigation, Working paper.

Bagehot, Walter, 1971, The only game in town, Financial Analysts Journal 27, 12–4.

Banz, Rolf W., 1981, The relationship between return and market value of common stocks, Journal of Financial Economics 9, 3–18.

Benston, George and Robert Hagerman, 1974, Determinants of bid–ask spreads in the over-the-counter market, Journal of Financial Economics 1, 353–64.

Black, Fischer, Michael C. Jensen and Myron Scholes, 1972, The capital asset pricing model: Some empirical tests, in: Michael C. Jensen, ed., Studies in the theory of capital markets (Praeger, New York) 79–121.

Black, Fischer and Myron Scholes, 1974, The effects of dividend yield and dividend policy on common stock prices and returns, Journal of Financial Economics 1, 1–22.

Blume, Marshall E. and Robert F. Stambaugh, 1983, Biases in computing returns: An application to the size effect, Journal of Financial Economics 12, 387–404.

Chen, Andrew H., E. Han Kim and Stanley J. Kon, 1975, Cash demand, liquidation costs and capital market equilibrium under uncertainty. Journal of Financial Economics 2, 293–308.

Day, Theodore, E., Hans R. Stoll and Robert E. Whaley, 1985, Taxes, financial policy and small business (Lexington Heath, Lexington, MA) forthcoming.

Demsetz, Harold, 1968, The cost of transacting, Quarterly Journal of Economics 82, 35–53.

Elton, Edwin J. and Martin J. Gruber, 1978, Taxes and portfolio composition, Journal of Financial Economics 6, 399–410.

Fama, Eugene F., 1976, Foundations of finance (Basic Books, New York).

Fama, Eugene F. and James MacBeth, 1973, Risk, return and equilibrium: Empirical tests, Journal of Political Economy 81, 607–36.

Fisher, Lawrence and Daniel G. Weaver, 1985, Improving the measurement of returns of stocks, portfolios, and equally-weighted, indexes: Avoiding or compensating for 'biases' due to bid–ask spread and other transient errors in price, Mimeo.

Fogler, H. Russel, 1984, 20% in real estate: Can theory justify it?, Journal of Portfolio Management 10, 6–13.

Gale, David, 1960, The theory of linear economic models (McGraw-Hill, New York).

Garbade, Kenneth, 1982, Securities markets (McGraw-Hill, New York).

Garman, Mark B., 1976, Market microstructure, Journal of Financial Economics 3, 257–75.

Ho, Thomas and Hans Stoll, 1981, Optimal dealer pricing under transactions and return uncertainty, Journal of Financial Economics 9, 47–73.

Ho, Thomas and Hans Stoll, 1983, The dynamics of dealer markets under competition. Journal of Finance 38, 1053–74.

Jensen, Michael C., 1968, Risk, the pricing of capital assets, and the evaluation of investment portfolios, Journal of Business 42, 167–247.

Judge, George G., William E. Griffiths, R. Carter Hill and Tsoung-Chao Lee, 1980, The theory and practice of econometrics (Wiley, New York).

Kane, Alex, 1984, Coins: Anatomy of a fad asset. Journal of Portfolio Management 10, 44–51.

Kmenta, Jan, 1971, Elements of econometrics (Macmillan, New York).

Lakonishok, Josef and Seymour Smidt, 1984, Volume, price and rate of return for active and inactive stocks with applications to turn-of-the-year behavior, Journal of Financial Economics 13, 435–55.

Levy, Haim, 1978, Equilibrium in an imperfect market: A constraint on the number of securities in a portfolio, American Economic Review 68, 643–58.

Litzenberger, Robert H. and Krishna Ramaswamy, 1980, Dividends, short selling restrictions, tax-induced investor clienteles and market equilibrium, Journal of Finance 35, 469–82.

Maddala, G.S., 1977, Econometrics (McGraw-Hill, New York).

Malinvaud, E., 1970, Statistical methods of econometrics (Elsevier, New York).

Mendelson, Haim, 1982, Market behavior in a clearing house, Econometrica 50, 1505–24.

Mendelson, Haim, 1985, Random competitive exchange: Price distributions and gains from trade, Journal of Economic Theory 37, 254–80.

Mendelson, Haim, 1986, Exchange with random quantities and discrete feasible prices, Working paper (Graduate School of Management, University of Rochester, Rochester, NY).

Mendelson, Haim, 1987, Consolidation, fragmentation and market performance, Journal of Financial and Quantitative Analysis, forthcoming.

Miller, Merton H., 1977, Debt and taxes. Journal of Finance 32, 261–75.

Milne, Frank and Clifford W. Smith, Jr., 1980, Capital asset pricing with proportional transaction costs, Journal of Financial and Quantitative Analysis 15, 253–65.

Phillips, Susan M. and Clifford W. Smith, Jr., 1980, Trading costs for listed options: The implications for market efficiency, Journal of Financial Economics 8, 179–201.

Reinganum, Marc R., 1981a, Misspecification of capital asset pricing: Empirical anomalies based on earnings yields and market values, Journal of Financial Economics 9, 19–46.

Reinganum, Marc R., 1981b, The arbitrage pricing theory: Some empirical evidence, Journal of Finance 36, 313–20.

Roll, Richard, 1983, On computing mean return and the small firm premium, Journal of Financial Economics 12, 371–86.

Ross, S.M., 1970. Applied probability models with optimization applications (Holden-Day, San Francisco, CA).

Schwert, G. William, 1977, Slock exchange seats as capital assets, Journal of Financial Economics 6, 51–78.

Schwert, G. William, 1983, Size and stock exchange, and other empirical regularities, Journal of Financial Economics 12, 3–12.

Schultz, Paul, 1983, Transaction costs and the small firm effect: A comment, Journal of Financial Economics 12, 81–8.

Stoll, Hans R. and Robert E. Whaley, 1983, Transaction costs and the small firm effect. Journal of Financial Economics 12, 57–79.

Stoll, Hans, 1985, Alternative views of market making, in: Y. Amihud, T. Ho and R. Schartz, eds., Market making and the changing structure of the securities industry (Lexington Heath, Lexington, MA) 67–92.

Treynor, Jack, 1980, Liquidity, interest rates and inflation. Unpublished manuscript.

West, Richard R. and Seha M. Tinic, 1971, The economics of the stock market (Praeger, New York).

CHAPTER 2

Liquidity, Maturity, and the Yields on U.S. Treasury Securities

Summary and Implications

This article tests the Amihud–Mendelson (1986; Chapter 1 in this book) theory on the effect of liquidity on asset prices using data on U.S. Treasury securities, which, when held to maturity, are riskless. Therefore, the yield to maturity is the expected return over the remaining life of the bond. If two Treasury securities with the same maturity and cash flow have different yields, the difference must result from differences in their liquidity. This provides a controlled experiment on the effect of liquidity on asset expected returns without the need to control for risk.

Amihud and Mendelson study the return-liquidity relation by examining U.S. Treasury bills and notes with less than 6 months to maturity. U.S. Treasury bills are discount bonds, as are Treasury notes with less than 6 months to maturity (which have only one final payment). Thus, both securities have identical payoffs (a single payment at maturity), and if they have the same maturity, they should have the same price. However, the two instruments are traded in different markets with different trading costs, and this provides the basis for the test of a liquidity effect. Treasury notes are traded actively only during the period following their auction, in which they are purchased by primary dealers and turned around multiple times. During this active period of trading that follows the auction, they are called "on the run" securities.[1] Thereafter, investors absorb the notes in their investment portfolios and, by the time the following auction takes place, trading volumes in the previously auctioned notes dwindle as the primary dealers, followed by other market participants, focus on the next auction, while the notes become "off the run" until their maturity. In contrast, Treasury bills, which are issued frequently and for short maturities, are

---

[1] Active trading in "when issued" securities also takes place during the days preceding the auction.

actively traded until they mature. During the sample period of the study by Amihud and Mendelson, the brokerage fee per $1 million was $12.50–$25 for bills, compared to $78–1/8 for notes. The conventional bid–ask spreads per $100 face value for bills were around $1/128, compared to $1/32 for notes. In addition, the search and delay costs were significantly higher for notes than bills. Altogether, bills were much less costly to trade than notes.

Given that the two Treasury securities have the same cash flows but different trading costs, the liquidity theory predicts that Treasury bills will have lower yields to maturity than notes with the same time to maturity. Amihud and Mendelson test this proposition using the yield differential of 489 pairs of notes and bills with less than 6 months to maturity over 37 trading days during April through November 1987, using actual price quotes. The authors compare each note with Treasury bills whose maturities straddle the note's (the one just before it and the one following it). The average bid–ask spread on the notes is 0.03%, compared to 0.0078% for the bills. Correspondingly, the average note yields 0.43% more than the corresponding bill, a statistically and economically significant difference. The controlled experiment shows that the asset with the higher trading costs has a significantly lower price (higher yield) than an asset that is otherwise identical.

Because the fixed cost of trading notes is higher than that for bills, the yield differential should be larger when maturities are shorter. Accordingly, Amihud and Mendelson find that the yield differential between notes and bills decreases with the time to maturity.[2] The note-bill yield differential also decreases with the note's coupon, reflecting the preference of some institutions for a higher coupon because they can distribute only the interest that they receive.

Given the large yield differential between Treasury notes and bills, why do investors not buy the high-yield note and short a low-yield bill of similar maturity, holding them to maturity and pocketing the difference? And, would such arbitrage not erase the yield differential? To be profitable, such an arbitrage would need to generate profits in excess of the trading costs of executing the arbitrage. Amihud and Mendelson simulate the execution of such an arbitrage, taking into account the associated trading costs: the bid–ask spread, brokerage fees, and the costs of carrying the short position. The authors show that the apparent profit opportunity disappears once trading costs are taken into account. This leads to the insight that the effect

---

[2] The relation is convex, with the yield differential increasing with the reciprocal of the yield to maturity.

of liquidity on the pricing of assets that can be arbitraged is bound by the cost of excuting the arbitrage.

Does the liquidity effect found in U.S. Treasury securities apply to corporate bonds as well? Unlike Treasury securities, which have zero default risk, corporate bonds differ in their default risk, which in turn affects their yield spread (the yield in excess of that of same-maturity Treasury bonds). Naturally, greater default risk and expected loss because of default entails a higher yield spread. However, studies show that the yield spreads exceed the required compensation for default risk and loss. Following Amihud and Mendelson's finding that part of the bond yield reflects a compensation for illiquidity, the yield spread in excess of the default premium can be attributed to bond illiquidity. It then follows that the bond yield spread reflects a premium for both default risk and illiquidity.

Unlike stocks, corporate bonds do not trade in a centralized market, which makes it harder to measure their liquidity. In a study on the effect of corporate bond liquidity on their yields, Chen, Lesmond, and Wei (2007) measure bond illiquidity in three ways. One is the bound around the bond price within which new information (daily change in the 10-year risk-free interest rate and the change in the S&P 500 index, both scaled by the bond's duration) will not trigger a transaction. The bound is estimated from daily data by the limited dependent variable model of Lesmond, Ogden, and Trzcinka (1999), which is referred to hereafter as LOT. Traders refrain from trading if the would-be value change does not exceed transaction costs, and thus the no-trade bound measures unobservable transaction costs. The two other measures of illiquidity are the quoted bid–ask spread and the percentage of days with zero returns within a given year.

Chen et al. (2007) examine a few thousand corporate bonds traded in the U.S. between 1995 and 2003. As might be expected, lower-rated bonds are more illiquid because they are subject to greater information asymmetry, rendering market making in these bonds more costly. For example, the LOT measure of transaction costs on BBB-rated bonds is about five times greater than it is on AAA-rated bonds for short-maturity bonds. Because BBB bonds have greater default risk than AAA bonds, part of the yield spread between AAA and BBB bonds reflects a compensation for illiquidity and the other part reflect the default risk premium.

Next, Chen et al. (2007) estimate the effect of bond illiquidity on yield spreads across bonds, controlling for a number of variables that account for the bond's risk and its characteristics, as well as the issuing firm's characteristics. Their results show a significant positive effect of illiquidity on the yield spread. The positive liquidity effect on bond yields holds for both investment- and speculative-grade bonds, with the illiquidity premium (the coefficient of the illiquidity variables) being larger for speculative-grade bonds. For example, transaction costs (measured by LOT) that are higher by 1 basis point lead to a yield that is higher by 0.21 basis point for investment-grade bonds and by 0.82 basis point for speculative bonds, after controlling for default risk and issuer characteristics. The authors further find that across bonds, a *change* in their transaction costs induces a subsequent change in their yield spread in the same direction; that is, a rise in transaction costs leads to an increase in the yield, with the increase being about five times greater for speculative-grade bonds.

Liquidity is also priced in the international bond market. Studying international corporate bonds and sovereign bonds, Hund and Lesmond (2008) find that an increase of 1 basis point in transaction costs (measured by LOT) is associated with higher yield: 0.26 basis point on international corporate bonds and 0.63 basis point on sovereign bonds, both after controlling for default risk and issuer characteristics.

Similarly, Longstaff, Mithal, and Neid (2005) study the yield-liquidity relation in corporate bonds, controlling for the default component of the yield by using information from credit default swaps. The authors find that the non-default component of the bond yield is an increasing function of bond illiquidity measured by bid–ask spread and maturity, and it declines in the principal amount outstanding, which indicates higher liquidity. Furthermore, the aggregate non-default component of bond yield responds to market-wide liquidity shocks in a predicted way: when market illiquidity rises, bond yields rise as well.

Trading in corporate bonds is sparse compared to trading in stocks with incomplete data on quotes and trades, which makes it hard to measure bond liquidity. Nashikkar, Subrahmanyam, and Mahanti (2011) use *latent liquidity* that weighs the turnover of funds holding the bond by their fractional holdings of the bond. Thus, a bond is assigned the weighted average liquidity of its holders. This is consistent with the proposition of Amihud and Mendelson (1986) on the existence in equilibrium of a liquidity clientele for each security, by which frequent traders opt for liquid bonds while long-term holders invest in less liquid bonds. The idea here is that while the actual bond liquidity is unobserved, the trading frequency of its holder provides a clue as to the bond's liquidity. The authors find that bonds with higher latent liquidity have a significantly lower yield after controlling for the yield component that is due to default (using the CDS premium of the same bond issuer and the USD-LIBOR swap rate as a measure of the riskless rate). One standard deviation increase in the latent liquidity reduces bond annual yields by about 0.1%. There is a 1% difference in the default-adjusted yield between the most and least liquid bond portfolio (there are 10 altogether). Also, bonds with larger issue size, another measure of liquidity, have lower yield while older bonds, which are less liquid than newer bonds, have higher yield, after adjusting for issuer characteristics. In sum, a number of bond-related liquidity measures are shown to have a significant impact on corporate bond yields.

Liquidity, Maturity, and the Yields on U.S. Treasury Securities*

Yakov Amihud and Haim Mendelson

Journal of Finance 46, 1991

This paper studies empirically the effects of the liquidity of capital assets on their prices. Amihud and Mendelson (1986, 1989) proposed that liquidity affects asset prices because investors require a compensation for bearing transaction costs. Transaction costs – paid whenever the asset is traded – form a sequence of cash outflows. The discounted value of this cost stream proxies for the value loss due to illiquidity, which lowers the asset's value for any given cash flow that the asset generates.[1] As a result, the return on assets should be an increasing function of their illiquidity (other things equal). For stocks, the illiquidity effect is expected to be strong because their transaction cost sequence is infinite. Amihud and Mendelson (1986, 1989) demonstrated that common stocks with lower liquidity yielded significantly higher average returns, after controlling for risk and for other factors.

These results on the importance of liquidity in the pricing of stocks raise additional questions: (i) does the liquidity effect depend on the specific controls used by Amihud and Mendelson (1986, 1989)? (ii) does illiquidity have a similarly strong effect on the pricing of bonds, whose maturities are finite?, and (iii) if liquidity affects bond yields, how is this effect related to the bond's time to maturity?

---

[1] The impact of the cost of transacting on price can be illustrated as follows (Amihud and Mendelson (1988a)): consider a stock which is expected to be traded once a year at a cost of 1 cent on the dollar value; discounting the infinite stream of transaction costs, at, say, 8%, gives a present value of 12.5 cents per dollar of value, which is the loss due to transaction costs or the discounted cost of illiquidity.

* Graduate School of Business, New York University, New York, and Faculty of Management, Tel Aviv University, Tel Aviv; and Graduate School of Business, Stanford University, Stanford, CA; respectively. This paper was first drafted while the second author was with The William E. Simon Graduate School of Business Administration, University of Rochester, Rochester, NY. The authors thank Kenneth Garbade, William Silber, and an anonymous referee for valuable suggestions and First Boston Corporation for providing the data.

These questions are answered in this empirical examination of the effects of liquidity on the pricing of U.S. government securities. Specifically, we compare the yields on short-term U.S. Treasury notes and bills with the *same* maturities of 6 months or less. For these maturities, both securities are similar short-term single-payment (discount) instruments generating the same underlying cash flows and having identical risk. Their liquidity, however, is different. This enables us to estimate the effects of liquidity on asset values with no need to control for other factors that affect them. For example, we do not have to assume any capital asset pricing model of the risk-return relation in order to control for risk. Furthermore, unlike the case of stocks that do not have a fixed maturity date, the securities we study here have finite maturities, which enables us to study the interaction between the time to maturity and the yield differential between notes and bills.

In what follows, we briefly describe the features of the U.S. Treasury securities market that are relevant to our study, focusing on the differences in liquidity between securities (Section I). The effects of these liquidity differences are tested on actual dealers' price quotes on bills and notes (Section II). We close with concluding remarks (Section III).

I. Liquidity and the U.S. Government Securities Market

Liquidity in the U.S. government securities market is provided by dealers (or market-makers) and brokers. Dealers trade with retail customers and with each other, standing ready to buy and sell for their own account at their quoted bid and ask prices, respectively. Sellers can execute their orders instantaneously by selling to a dealer at the quoted bid price, and buyers can obtain immediate execution by buying from the dealer at the quoted ask price.[2] Most interdealer trading and much of the retail trading are done through brokers. They have quotation systems which display the dealers' quotes, easing communication and facilitating execution. Dealers and brokers thus provide liquidity services that save investors the costs, risks, and delays of searching for compatible trading partners. As compensation for providing these services, dealers charge investors the spread between the bid and the ask prices, and brokers charge additional fees. Naturally, lower fees and bid–ask spreads are associated with greater liquidity.

---

[2] For a detailed description of the government securities market, see Stigum (1983), Ch. 13. Garbade and Silber (1976) derived the pricing policies of dealers in the government securities market and estimated the determinants of the bid–ask spread. See also Tanner and Kochin (1971) and Garbade and Rosey (1977).

U.S. Treasury notes and bills are distinct fixed-income securities. Bills are short-term discount bonds whereas notes are coupon-bearing bonds with far longer maturities. Within 6 months to maturity, however, notes become short-term single-payment securities like bills. Still, notes and bills remain distinguishable with different procedures for yield calculation, quotation, and trading, and their quotes are transmitted on different systems. Traders usually specialize in one type of these government securities,[3] and there are differences between the two markets.

The market for U.S. Treasury bills is substantially more liquid than the market for notes. While a trade of $100 million in treasury bills can be effected almost instantaneously, the situation is quite different for notes of short maturities. Despite the large size of U.S. treasury note issues (typically two to ten billion dollars in our sample), by the time they approach maturity the notes have already been *locked away* in investors' portfolios, and a large part of each issue is not readily available for trading. Investors who wish to trade a large quantity of notes of short maturities have to go through considerable search in order to arrange the quantity desired, imposing an additional fixed cost of search.[4] The differences in liquidity are evidenced by the differences in the bid–ask spread, the brokerage fees, and the standard size of a transaction. The brokerage fee for bills is between $12.5 and $25 per $1 million, compared with $78,125 per $1 million for notes (paid by the party initiating the transaction),[5] and the typical bid–ask spread on bills is of an order of 1/128 of a point compared with 1/32 on notes (both per $100 face value). It is worth noting that this difference in bid–ask spreads cannot be attributed to the often-assumed problem of asymmetric information about fundamental values faced by market-makers because both instruments are affected by the same information. The difference in the spread represents transaction costs borne by dealers when trading notes because of the associated direct and inventory-related costs. Still, notes are far more liquid than stocks. For example, the spread on the highly-liquid IBM stock is about four times larger than the spread on short-term notes.

Treasury notes and bills with less than 6 months to maturity are thus financial instruments with *identical* underlying cash flows but with *different liquidity*, reflected in differences in their transaction costs. Both the bid–ask

---

[3] Some investors may specialize in treasury bills because of regulation or by their own policies. Yet, there are dealers and investors who can freely choose to invest in either instrument.

[4] Garbade and Silber (1976) analyzed the cost of search as a component of the cost of illiquidity in the government securities market.

[5] Stigum (1983), p. 437; costs might have slightly declined since.

spread and the brokerage fees are higher for notes compared to bills. The question that arises is how these liquidity differences affect the valuation of notes and bills.

The effect of illiquidity costs is that investors are willing to pay less for the less-liquid security to compensate for its higher transaction costs. We thus obtain the following hypothesis:

The bills, which have lower transaction costs, will have a lower yield to maturity than notes.

Empirical tests of the liquidity effects are presented in the next section.

II. Empirical Tests

A. The Data

The data were obtained from the quote sheets of First Boston Corporation, a primary dealer in U.S. government securities, and include bid–ask quotes, maturities, and the notes' coupon rates. The quotes are for standard size transactions as of 3:00 P.M. in each trading day. These are *real* quotes that were *pulled off the screen.*[6] Our sample consists of 37 trading days that represent about 5 days in each month between April and November 1987. We included in our sample only bills and notes with less than 6 months to maturity. For these maturities, notes have only one coupon left to be paid at maturity, and thus they become pure discount securities, just as Treasury bills are. Then, the duration and maturity are the same for both securities, and the tax consequences are also the same.

Consider a note n with maturity date τ_n and annual coupon rate C_n, paid semiannually. The quote sheet for day t includes the ask price on the note, P_{tn}, and the bid price Pb_{tn}, in units of $1/32$. The actual price paid on the settlement date (typically, two business days after the transaction date) includes the interest accrued on the note. Let Δt be the number of days from the last coupon payment to the settlement date, and let H be the number of days in the half-year coupon period in which the settlement takes place. The accrued interest on the note is then given by

$$AC = \frac{C}{2} \cdot \frac{\Delta t}{H},$$

---

[6] Being real rather than *representative* quotes, the bid–ask spreads are often substantially narrower than those reported in the *Wall Street Journal.* There, quotes often represent an indication of the price range (particularly for notes).

and the price actually paid by the buyer is $P + AC$ (we suppress the date and note indices (t, n) whenever they are unambiguous). The time to maturity $T (= T_{tn})$ is the number of days from the settlement date to the maturity date τ. The bid–ask spread on the note relative to the ask price is given by

$$S = \frac{\text{ask price} - \text{bid price}}{\text{ask price} + \text{accrued interest}} = \frac{P - Pb}{P + C\Delta t/2H}.$$

Next consider the bills. The quotes on bills are in terms of discount rates relative to face value, which we converted into price quotes using the formula (Stigum (1983) pp. 46–49)

$$P = 100 \left[1 - \frac{T \cdot D}{360} \right], \tag{1}$$

where P is the price, D is the discount rate, and T is the time to maturity (i.e., the number of days from the settlement date to the maturity date of the bill, τ_B). The bill quotes consist of a bid discount D_b and an ask discount D_a, which we converted into bid and ask prices, Pb and P, using equation (1). Clearly, for bills, $C = AC = 0$.

For each security in our sample, we calculated the (annualized) yield to maturity Y relative to the *ask* price by solving for Y from the following equation:[7]

$$P + AC = \frac{\frac{1}{2}C + 100}{(1 + Y)^{T/365}}. \tag{2}$$

Notes usually mature either in the middle of the month – the 15th – or at month-end – the 30th or 31st (28th or 29th in February). Bills are auctioned every week and have more frequent maturity dates. For each day in our sample, we had a number of notes with maturities of up to 6 months. We matched each note with two bills whose maturity dates immediately straddle the note's. Thus, for each day t in our sample ($t = 1, 2, \ldots, 37$), we assigned to each note N_{tn} with a price quote on that day (n indexes the notes within day t) the two bills $B1_{tn}$ and $B2_{tn}$ with the nearest maturities, satisfying

$$\tau_{B1_{tn}} \leq \tau_{N_{tn}} \leq \tau_{B2_{tn}}.$$

---

[7] The conventional bond yields for notes and equivalent bond yields for bills, included in the quote sheets, are calculated as $\frac{365 \cdot D}{360 - T \cdot D}$ using the *ask* discount and, hence, constitute linear approximations for the actual yield to maturity. Garbade (1983) discussed the bias in this method of yield calculation. We replicated our estimations using these yields, and the results were similar.

Thus, the days to maturity T are related by

$$T_{B1_{tn}} \leq T_{N_{tn}} \leq T_{B2_{tn}}.$$

Finally, we constructed from the pair of bills that match each note the weighted average yield Y_B defined by

$$Y_B = w_1 \cdot Y_{B1} + w_2 \cdot Y_{B2}$$

where $w_1 = (T_{B2} - T_N)/(T_{B2} - T_{B1})$ and $w_2 = 1 - w_1$. In the cases where $T_{B1} = T_{B2}$, $w_1 = w_2 = \frac{1}{2}$. The yield differential between notes and bills is

$$\Delta Y_{tn} = Y_{N_{tn}} - Y_{B_{tn}},$$

with $n = 1, 2, \ldots, M_t$, M_t being the number of notes in day t, and $t = 1, 2, \ldots, 37$. We sometimes had more than one note with the same maturity because they may have been originally issued at different times for different maturities. In these cases, each note was treated as a separate observation. Altogether, we had 489 matched triplets, each consisting of one note and the two straddling bills, with the note maturities stretching from 9 to 182 days.

B. The Liquidity Effect

Table 2.1 presents summary statistics for the number of days to maturity T, the relative bid–ask spread S, and the yield to maturity Y for the 489 matched triplets of notes and bills. Since the yield curve was generally increasing during the period, we have in general $Y_{B1} < Y_{B2}$. Table 2.1 shows two key differences between the bills and the notes:

1) The relative bid–ask spread on notes is greater than that on bills by a factor of about 4. This indicates the lower liquidity of notes compared to bills.
2) The yield to maturity on notes is higher than the yield on bills with the same maturity. On average, $\Delta Y = 0.428\%$ per annum with a standard error of 0.021 and is significantly different from zero.

These observations support the hypothesis that asset returns are a function of liquidity (holding other things constant): the lower the liquidity, the higher the yield measured relative to the ask price.

Given that both instruments also incur different brokerage fees, we recalculated the yields, adding to the ask price the respective costs, viz., $1/128 per $100 of face value for notes and $12.5 per $1,000,000 of face value for bills. These yield calculations are based on buying and holding to maturity

Table 2.1. *Estimated means and standard deviations for the days to maturity T,*
relative bid-ask spread S (in %), and annualized yield to maturity Y (in %), for 489
matched triplets of notes and bills. Each note is matched with two bills whose
maturities straddle the note's

The relative bid-ask spread is defined by $S = \frac{\text{ask price} - \text{bid price}}{\text{ask price} + \text{accrued interest}}$, where the accrued interest for bills is zero. The yield to maturity Y is obtained from the equation

$$\text{Ask Price} + \text{Accrued Interest} = \frac{\frac{1}{2}C + 100}{(1 + Y)^{T/365}},$$

where C is the coupon rate (zero for bills). The differences shown are between the bid-ask spreads S and the yields to maturity Y of notes and the weighted averages of the two matching bills. The data represent 37 days from April to November 1987.

	Days to maturity, T	Spread (%), S	Annual yield (%), Y
Notes (N)			
Mean	97.41	0.0303	6.523
StDev	51.44	0.0004	0.606
Bill 1 ($B1$)			
Mean	94.69	0.00761	6.039
StDev	51.53	0.00547	0.756
Bill 2 ($B2$)			
Mean	100.95	0.00801	6.137
StDev	51.79	0.00664	0.677
Difference (Notes – Bills)			
Mean		0.02252	0.428
StDev		0.00523	0.475

both the note and the bill. The average difference between the resulting yields to maturity was 0.388% per annum (standard error of 0.021, significant at better than 10^{-9}; the yield differential was higher after the October 19, 1987, stock market crash than before it). We thus find that after accounting for both the bid–ask spread and the brokerage fees, the yield to maturity on notes is higher than the yield on bills with the same maturity. This implies that investors are willing to pay a yield concession for the *option* to liquidate their holdings before maturity at lower costs. This is consistent with the results of Amihud and Mendelson (1986, 1989) that the risk-adjusted return on NYSE stocks was an increasing function of the bid–ask spread. But, unlike the case of stocks, no adjustment for risk is necessary here because the two assets we examine have identical underlying cash flows and they differ only in their liquidity. Thus, the yield differential can be traced directly to the liquidity differential.[8]

C. Maturity Effects

Stocks have infinite maturity, and therefore investors must incur transaction costs whenever they liquidate their positions. For finite-maturity securities, investors can receive the redemption value at maturity without incurring liquidation costs. If investors' holding periods – the time until they need to liquidate their investments – were certain and if they could always exactly match the maturity of the notes and bills they buy with their investment horizons, then the yields to maturity on both securities should be the same when calculated from the ask (buying) price and after adjusting the yields for brokerage fees. We found, however, that the yields thus calculated were higher on notes than on bills.

Our evidence thus suggests that there is no perfect matching between investors' planning horizons and securities' maturities. Instead, investors expect that, with a positive probability, a need may arise to sell securities before maturity, at which time they will incur additional transaction costs. It follows that even a finite-maturity security is likely to incur transaction costs through its life, and that these costs could be incurred repeatedly because each buyer has these expectations anew. These transactions costs are higher on notes than they are on bills.

In order to reduce the likelihood of having to sell before maturity and thus save on liquidation costs, an investor could buy a string of short-term securities maturing in sequence. However, this policy makes the investor incur repeated costs of reinvestment (partly fixed) because his horizon is longer than the securities' maturities. Again, these reinvestment costs are higher for notes than they are for bills.

It follows that an investor with an uncertain investment horizon faces a tradeoff between buying short-maturity securities, which may force him to pay transaction costs when reinvesting at their maturity, and long-maturity securities, which may result in the payment of transaction costs when selling before maturity. This tradeoff suggests an interplay between the time to maturity and the yield differential between notes and bills.

To estimate the relation between the time to maturity and the notes' excess yield ΔY_{tn}, we divided the data into eleven groups based on the time

---

[8] A similar observation for notes and bills was made by Garbade (1984).

to maturity, with each 15 days constituting a group. Each group i ($i = 1, \ldots,$ 11) includes the notes and matched bills with $15i < T_{N_{tn}} \leq 15(i+1)$ (the last group includes up to 182 days to maturity).[9] Each maturity group i was assigned a maturity dummy-variable DM_t defined by

$$DM_i = \begin{cases} 1 & \text{if} \quad 15i < T_{N_{tn}} \leq 15(i+1) \\ 0 & \text{otherwise} \end{cases}$$

for $i = 1, 2, \ldots, 11$. The estimation of the relation between the yield differential ΔY and the 11 maturity groups employed the pooled time-series and cross-section model

$$\Delta Y_{tn} = a_0 + \sum_{i=1}^{10} a_i \cdot DM_i + b \cdot C_{tn} + \sum_{t=1}^{36} c_t \cdot DD_t + \epsilon_{tn}. \qquad (3)$$

The coefficients a_i ($i = 1, 2, \ldots, 10$) measure the difference in the yield differential between the ith maturity group and that of group 11, which has the longest maturity (over 165 days). The model includes the note's coupon rate C_{tn} because it may affect the demand for notes. Institutions that are constrained to distribute only accrued interest (but not the principal) on their holdings may prefer notes with higher coupon rates,[10] and such notes should have correspondingly lower yields, implying that $b < 0$. The dummy variables DD_t, defined as

$$DD_t = \begin{cases} 1 & \text{if the data are from day } t, \ t = 1, 2, \ldots, 36, \\ 0 & \text{otherwise,} \end{cases}$$

control for shifts in ΔY for different days in our sample.

The residual series ϵ_{tn} is subject to heteroskedasticity in the pooled time-series and cross-section estimation. In fact, the residual variances differed across the days in the sample (as might be expected) and as a function of the maturity groups and the coupon. Following Judge et al. (1982), pp. 416–420, we assumed that the residual variances σ_{tn}^2 have the following exponential form:[11]

$$E\left[\epsilon_{tn}^2\right] = \sigma_{nt}^2 = \exp\left[k_0 + \sum_{i=1}^{10} k_i \cdot DM_i + l \cdot C_{tn} + \sum_{t=1}^{36} m_t \cdot DD_t\right]. \qquad (4)$$

---

[9] We excluded the notes with up to 15 days to maturity, whose trading is particularly thin (Stigum (1983), pp. 447–449) and thus exhibit erratic behavior. Including this group did not change the essence of the results.

[10] This was suggested to us by Kenneth Garbade.

[11] This form guarantees positive estimated variances (Judge et al. (1982), p. 416).

The corresponding estimation procedure was as follows. We first estimated model (3) and used its residuals to estimate model (4). The estimated variances from this model were then used for a GLS estimation of model (3). A test of the resulting model for serial correlation could not reject the hypothesis of no serial correlation (DW = 1.83, inconclusive).

The estimation results are presented in Table 2.2. In Panel A, the estimation model includes the group-dummy variables (as well as the day-dummies) and excludes the coupon variable.[12] Panel B presents the results for the complete model (3). The results are similar under both specifications. The coefficients a_i, which measure the excess yield in each group i relative to the longest-maturity group (group 11), are decreasing and convex in i. That is, the yield differential ΔY is a decreasing and convex function of the time to maturity. For example, in the third column, the note-bill yield difference (relative to that of group 11, which had over 166 days to maturity) declines from 46.4 basis points for the first maturity group (16–30 days to maturity) to 22.7 basis points for the second maturity group, a fairly steep decline. The decline in the yield differential for higher maturity groups becomes gradually more moderate. The pattern of a_i closely fits the function $1(i + \frac{1}{2})$,[13] with the correlation between them being 0.97. Thus, the yield differential ΔY seems to conform closely to a linear function of the reciprocal of the time to maturity. The coefficient of the coupon variable, -0.014, implies that a 100-basis-point difference in the coupon rate is associated with a 1.4-basis-point difference in the note-bill yield differential.

We then estimated directly the functional relation between the yield differential and the time to maturity, assuming that ΔY is a linear function of the reciprocal of the days to maturity T. The estimation results were as follows:

$$\Delta Y_{tn} = \gamma_0 + \underset{(9.47)}{12.03} \cdot (1/T_{N_{tn}}) - \underset{(3.23)}{0.014} \cdot C_{tn} + \sum_{t=1}^{36} \gamma_t \cdot DD_t + \epsilon_{tn}, \quad (5)$$

(t-values in parentheses; $DW = 1.85$). The estimation employed the GLS procedure used to estimate model (3) with the variance structure (4). By model (5), increasing the time to maturity from 30 days to 150 days reduces the note–bill yield difference by 32.1 basis points. Notably, the coefficient

---

[12] For this model, we had $DW = 1.86$, inconclusive.

[13] Recall that group i corresponds to an average maturity of $15(i + \frac{1}{2})$ days.

Table 2.2. *Coefficients of the maturity dummy variables and of the coupon rate in the pooled time-series and cross-section regression (3) (t-values are in parentheses)*

Panel A:

$$\Delta Y_{tn} = a_0 + \sum_{i=1}^{10} a_i \cdot DM_i + \sum_{t=1}^{36} c_t \cdot DD_t + \epsilon_{tn},$$

where ΔY_{tn} is the yield differential between notes and bills with matched maturities, and DM_i are dummy variables for the 11 maturity groups, defined by

$$DM_i = \begin{cases} 1 & \text{if} \quad 15i < T_{N_{tn}} \leq 15(i+1), \\ 0 & \text{otherwise}, \end{cases}$$

for $i = 1, 2, \ldots, 11$. $T_{N_{tn}}$ is the number of days to maturity for note n on day t. The coefficient a_i ($i = 1, 2, \ldots, 10$) measures the yield differential between maturity group i and the 11th maturity group. DD_t are the 36 day-dummy variables, $DD_t = 1$ if the observation is on day t and 0 otherwise.

Panel B:

$$\Delta Y_{tn} = a_0 + \sum_{i=1}^{10} a_i \cdot DM_i + b \cdot C_{tn} + \sum_{t=1}^{36} c_t \cdot DD_t + \epsilon_{tn},$$

where C_{tn} is the coupon rate (in %) for note n on day t.

The sample includes 466 triplets of notes and bills of matched maturities for 37 days in 1987. All estimations use GLS with the variance function

$$\sigma_{nt}^2 = \exp\left[k_0 + \sum_{i=1}^{10} k_i \cdot DM_i + l \cdot C_{tn} + \sum_{t=1}^{36} m_t \cdot DD_t\right].$$

| | Coefficient estimates | |
Variable	Panel A	Panel B
Constant	0.662	0.765
	(5.30)	(6.33)
DM_1	0.443	0.464
	(6.50)	(6.54)
DM_2	0.253	0.227
	(5.27)	(4.73)
DM_3	0.166	0.141
	(4.19)	(3.43)
DM_4	0.114	0.107
	(3.25)	(3.24)
DM_5	0.075	0.066
	(2.53)	(2.51)
DM_6	0.055	0.058
	(1.49)	(1.90)
DM_7	0.059	0.040
	(1.90)	(1.45)
DM_8	0.123	0.121
	(3.64)	(3.67)
DM_9	0.032	0.051
	(0.87)	(1.63)
DM_{10}	0.049	0.029
	(1.13)	(0.70)
Coupon		−0.014
		(3.20)

of $(1/T_{N_{tn}})$ was greater after the October 1987 crash and smaller before it. The coefficient of the coupon rate remains unchanged.[14]

The estimates of model (5) establish the existence of a relation between the notes' excess yield over bills and their maturity, which is linear in the reciprocal of the time to maturity. This relation can be reasoned as follows. A longer maturity enables investors to depreciate any fixed transaction costs over a longer time period. Therefore, the excess yield that investors require to compensate for this cost will be lower for longer maturities.

The results of model (5) on the yield differential as a function of the time to maturity directly imply that the price differential between bills and notes may also be a function of maturity. The price differential is defined as

$$\Delta P = P_B - 100 \cdot (P_N + AC)/(100 + C/2),$$

where $P_B = w_1 \cdot P_{B_1} + w_2 \cdot P_{B_2}$ is the weighted average of the prices of the bills whose maturities straddle the note's, and the price of the note is adjusted to have a redemption value (= face value plus half the coupon rate) of 100, as is the case for bills. If the yield differential ΔY were independent of the time to maturity, ΔP would be increasing in the time to maturity. However, we found that ΔY decreases in maturity, which raises the question of how ΔP depends on the time to maturity. From model (5), we obtained that the mean of the intercept terms (plus the mean coupon term) was positive, implying that ΔP is an increasing function of T. To test directly the relation between ΔP and T, we estimated model (3), replacing ΔY by ΔP. The estimation (which employs the GLS procedure as for model (3)) showed that ΔP is an increasing function of the time to maturity.[15]

The price differential between bills and notes suggest the possibility of profitable arbitrage opportunities, especially in long maturity bills and notes, where the price differential is larger. This is analyzed in the next section.

[14] We also employed another methodology to estimate the relation between the yield differential and the days to maturity. Instead of a pooled time-series cross-section estimation, we estimated model (5) for each day t, $t = 1, 2, \ldots, 37$, (without the day-dummies) and obtained 37 estimates for the coefficients of $1/T$ and C. The means of these coefficients were similar to those estimated in (5), and they were highly significant.

[15] The coefficients of the maturity dummy-variables a_i were (going from short to long maturities) as follows: $-0.070, -0.056, -0.057, -0.050, -0.043, -0.042, -0.018, -0.013,$ $+0.003, -0.003,$ and $+0.022$, with t-statistics 6.43, 5.91, 5.81, 5.32, 4.95, 4.23, 1.85, 1.18, 0.30, and 1.56, respectively. The coefficients of the maturity-dummy variables are increasing, indicating that ΔP is an increasing function of the time to maturity. The coefficient of the coupon variable was -0.0036 ($t = 3.20$), and $DW = 1.83$.

III. Arbitrage Opportunities

The existence of a yield differential between bills and notes may give rise to arbitrage opportunities. Specifically, an apparent profitable arbitrage is buying a note and selling short a bill of the same maturity and the same redemption value, and then holding this position until maturity, at which time both securities are redeemed. Because of the yield differential, the cost of the long position in the note is lower than the proceeds from shorting a bill of the same maturity. Such arbitrage is *riskless* because the values of both securities at maturity are known with certainty. Hence, in the spirit of our foregoing analysis, it can be evaluated independently of investors' utility functions or specific models of asset pricing.[16]

However, given that the yield differential is created by differences in transaction costs, these costs should be accounted for in evaluating the arbitrage transaction.

First, the note is bought at the ask price, whereas the bill is sold at the bid price, and therefore the cost of transacting should reflect the bid–ask spread.

Second, there are brokerage fees of 1/128 point, or $78.125 per $1 million for notes and brokerage fees between $12.5 and $25 per $1 million for bills (Stigum (1983), p. 437). The fees are paid by the party that initiates the transaction.

Third, shorting the bill entails a cost of borrowing it which typically equals 0.5% per annum (Stigum (1983), p. 288); this cost varies between transactions, but the 0.5% is quite representative.

Clearly, an investor who holds neither security and wishes to take a position in this market can exploit the yield differential by buying a note instead of a bill. In Section II.*B.*, we found that the *net* yield calculated from the ask price (accounting for the difference in brokerage costs) is still higher for notes than for bills; the mean difference in yields was 0.388% (standard error $= 0.021$). Thus, an investor who takes a position in this market and holds it to maturity may expect a gain by buying a note instead of a bill.

Next, an investor who currently holds a bill can make an immediate gain by selling the bill and buying instead a note of the same maturity and the same face value. The profit for this investor is calculated by the following two profit measures. The first is

$$PROFIT1 = Pb_B - 100 \cdot (P_N + AC)/(100 + C/2),$$

[16] An evaluation of risky arbitrage, where unwinding the position occurs before maturity at uncertain prices, requires modeling assumptions such as knowledge of investors' risk aversion or utility functions; see Tuckman and Vila (1990).

where Pb_B is the bill's bid price. *PROFIT1* is the apparent gain from selling a bill at the bid price and buying a note at the ask price in a quantity which would make the note's redemption value equal to 100, the bill's face value. Given the second cost component, the brokerage fees borne by the party initiating the transaction, the gain to the investor who switches from holding a bill to holding a note is given by

$$PROFIT2 = PROFIT1 - (78.125 + 12.5) \cdot 100/1000000.$$

Finally, we calculated the profit to an investor who currently holds neither securities and is constructing a pure arbitrage position:

$$PROFIT3 = PROFIT1 - (78.125 + 12.5) \cdot 100/1000000$$
$$- 0.005 \cdot (T_N/365) \cdot PB_B.$$

This measure accounts for the full transaction costs of the arbitrage, viz., the brokerage fees and the cost of borrowing the bill, in addition to the bid–ask spread effect captured by *PROFIT1*. *PROFIT3* shows the gain made at the time the arbitrage position is constructed. Given the results in Section II.C. on the price differential between bills and notes being increasing in the time to maturity, it seems that there are arbitrage profits which are higher for longer maturities. However, the third cost component – the cost of borrowing the bill – is increasing in the time to maturity and thus counteracts the effect of the positive relation between maturity and price differential.

Table 2.3 presents the three measures of arbitrage profits for the total sample and for the eleven maturity groups. On average, *PROFIT1* has a positive value of 7.8 cents per \$100 redemption value and *PROFIT2* has a positive value of 6.9 cents per \$100 redemption value. This means that switching from an investment in bills to an investment in notes can be profitable, *provided* the investor is certain that he will not have to liquidate the investment before it matures. (In fact, this type of investor mitigates the institutional differences between trading notes and bills, thereby reducing the yield differential between them.) However, this profit becomes negative, −6.2 cents on average, after subtracting the cost of borrowing the bills in order to short them. This pattern applies to all maturities except one (of 16–30 days), where *PROFIT3* is practically zero. These results imply that on average, the yield differential between bills and notes cannot be exploited for profitable arbitrage. Yet, in all maturity groups there were specific cases of apparent opportunities for arbitrage profits, as indicated by the Maximum column under *PROFIT3*. There are a number of possible explanations

Table 2.3. *Arbitrage profits (in dollars) from selling bills and buying notes of the same maturity. Numbers shown are profits (in dollars) per $100 redemption value in each instrument by maturity group*

PROFIT1 = profit from selling the bill at the bid price and buying the note at the ask price.

PROFIT2 = PROFIT1 minus brokerage costs. PROFIT3 = PROFIT2 minus the cost of borrowing the bill.

The sample includes 489 triplets of notes and bills of matched maturities for 37 days in 1987.

	PROFIT 1	PROFIT 2	PROFIT 3		
Maturity (days)	Mean	Mean	Mean	Min	Max
All maturities	0.078	0.069	−0.062	−0.565	0.200
9–15	0.013	0.004	−0.012	−0.071	0.044
16–30	0.043	0.034	0.001	−0.072	0.082
31–45	0.055	0.046	−0.008	−0.070	0.136
46–60	0.056	0.047	−0.027	−0.091	0.079
61–75	0.082	0.073	−0.020	−0.088	0.065
76–90	0.070	0.061	−0.052	−0.101	0.044
91–105	0.061	0.052	−0.080	−0.232	0.064
106–120	0.102	0.093	−0.059	−0.181	0.158
121–135	0.102	0.093	−0.078	−0.398	0.200
136–150	0.081	0.072	−0.119	−0.565	0.045
151–165	0.129	0.120	−0.091	−0.417	0.159
Over 165	0.104	0.095	−0.137	−0.467	0.028

for this. The calculated profit may not have been feasible because of difficulties in constructing the arbitrage. For example, when a particular bill is *special* (e.g., held to hedge against particular periodic payments), the cost of borrowing it may be higher than the assumed 1/2%. Also, our calculations assumed that the short position in the bills can be held to maturity, and thus no additional cost is incurred by prematurely reversing the position. A short position where the lender of the security cannot call it back for a fixed term may sometimes be more costly, because the lender loses liquidity. Alternatively, the cases with positive profit could indicate transitory disturbances in the instruments' prices, which could indeed be profitably exploited by arbitrageurs.[17]

---

[17] Dealers in the government securities market temporarily change their quotes in response to temporary changes in their inventories; see Garbade and Silber (1976).

IV. Concluding Remarks

If liquidity affects the pricing of capital assets, then both financial theory and practice should incorporate the liquidity effect. Investment decisions and portfolio composition should be based on the liquidity of capital assets as well as on their expected return and risk (however measured). In corporate finance, increasing the liquidity of the firm's financial claims should be regarded as a worthwhile objective,[18] and policymakers should assess the impact of regulatory and public policy initiatives by their contribution to market liquidity.[19] Further, trading technology is a major determinant of asset liquidity, and its role should be evaluated in light of its liquidity effect (cf. Amihud and Mendelson (1988b)).[20]

Amihud and Mendelson (1986, 1989) showed that liquidity is an important factor in asset pricing because the expected returns on stocks increase with their illiquidity, measured by the bid–ask spread. The estimated liquidity effect was strong and significant, and it persisted after controlling for systematic (beta) risk, size, and unsystematic risk, controls which depend on the specific theory of the risk-return relation. The question that arises is whether the dependence of expected returns on liquidity is robust (in particular, whether it depends on the specific controls for risk) and whether it applies not only to stocks, where transaction costs are incurred infinitely many times, but also to assets with finite and short maturities.

This study examined the effects of illiquidity on the yields of finite-maturity securities with identical cash flows: U.S. Treasury bills and notes with maturities under 6 months. For these maturities, both securities are effectively discount bonds and should be equivalent. Their liquidity, however, is different: the cost of transacting bills is lower than the cost of transacting notes. This enables us to study the relation between asset yields and liquidity without the need to control for other factors.

We find that (i) the yield to maturity on notes is higher than the yield on bills of the same maturity and (ii) the excess yield on notes over that on bills is a decreasing function of the time to maturity and is approximately linear in the reciprocal of the time to maturity. These results confirm and extend Amihud and Mendelson's (1986, 1989) earlier findings on the existence of a liquidity effect. Here, the matching of cash flows of the two instruments

---

[18] See Amihud and Mendelson (1988a).

[19] A case in point is the recently proposed securities transaction tax that would reduce liquidity and thus increase the yields required by investors. See Amihud and Mendelson (1990) on the effects of such a tax.

[20] Advances in trading technology may naturally affect the liquidity differential between notes and bills and the corresponding yield differential.

makes the results independent of any particular theory of pricing risk. In conclusion, our results show that asset liquidity is an important factor which must be reckoned within asset pricing.

References

Amihud, Yakov and Haim Mendelson, 1986, Asset pricing and the bid-ask spread, *Journal of Financial Economics* 17, 223–49.

_____ and Haim Mendelson, 1988a, Liquidity and asset pricing: Financial management implications, *Financial Management* 17, 5–15.

_____ and Haim Mendelson, 1988b, Liquidity, volatility and exchange automation, *Journal of Accounting, Auditing and Finance* 3, 369–95.

_____ and Haim Mendelson, 1989, The effects of beta, bid-ask spread, residual risk and size on stock returns, *Journal of Finance* 44, 479–86.

_____ and Haim Mendelson, 1990, The effect of a transaction tax on securities returns and values, Working paper, The Mid-America Institute for Public Policy Research.

Garbade, Kenneth, 1983, Invoice prices, cash flows, and yields on treasury bonds, *Topics in Money and Securities Markets*, Bankers Trust Co.

_____, 1984, Analyzing the structure of treasury yields: Duration, coupon and liquidity effects, *Topics in Money and Securities Markets*, Bankers Trust Co.

_____ and William Silber, 1976, Price dispersion in the government securities market, *Journal of Political Economy* 84, 721–40.

_____ and Irene Rosey, 1977, Secular variation in the spread between bid and offer prices on U.S. treasury coupon issues, *Business Economics* 12, 45–9.

Judge, George G., R. Carter Hill, William Griffiths, and Tsoung-Chao Lee, 1982, *Introduction to the Theory and Practice of Econometrics*. (John Wiley & Sons, Somerset, NJ).

Stigum, Marcia, 1983, *The Money Market*, (Dow Jones-Irwin, Homewood, IL).

Tanner, Ernest J. and Levis Kochin, 1971, The determinants of the difference between bid and ask prices on government bonds, *Journal of Business* 44, 375–79.

Tuckman, Bruce and Jean-Luc Vila, 1990, Arbitrage with holding costs: A utility-based approach, Working paper S-90-19, Stern School of Business, New York University.

CHAPTER 3

Market Microstructure and Securities Values: Evidence from the Tel Aviv Stock Exchange

Summary and Implications

Examining liquidity differences between financial assets, the preceding articles show that trading costs or illiquidity affect the prices of financial assets. By the same logic, an increase in the trading costs of a given financial asset should lower its price, and a decline in trading costs should lead to a price increase. For example, if a stock is transferred to a trading venue with better liquidity, which means lower trading costs, its price is expected to rise. However, changes in trading venue, which are usually voluntary, are often associated with changes in information about the asset, asset risk, or other asset attributes.

This difficulty is overcome in the study of Amihud, Mendelson, and Lauterbach by examining the effect of an *exogenous* change in stocks' trading venue. This was the case when the Tel Aviv Stock Exchange (TASE) transferred stocks from a once-a-day call auction trading to a higher-frequency (and more liquid) trading regime.[1] The transfer decisions were made by the management of the TASE without any company discretion and were pure change-of-liquidity events without any information about the stocks' future cash flows. This comes as close as possible to a true controlled experiment on the effects of changing the liquidity of trading on asset values. Here, the liquidity-increasing event is exogenous and clearly identified, and the

---

[1] For example, listing a stock for trading on a stock exchange is a decision made by the company's management, and it may reflect information available to management about the stock's future. The price change may then reflect this information rather than the pure change in the stock's liquidity.

change in the stock value that immediately follows can be directly attributed to this event.

The TASE transferred stocks to the new trading regime in batches at random times during 1987–1994. After the decisions were made, they were announced publicly, and the stocks were transferred to the more liquid marketplace a few days later. Amihud, Mendelson, and Lauterbach find that the trading volumes of stocks that were transferred increased significantly relative to the market, and other measures of stock liquidity improved as well. Importantly, stocks that were transferred to the new trading regime enjoyed a sharp and permanent price increase of more than 5% on average, consistent with the proposition of Amihud and Mendelson (1986; Chapter 1 in this book) that greater liquidity leads to higher prices, *ceteris paribus*. The price increase was larger for stocks that enjoyed a greater increase in liquidity following the transfer. In addition, the increased liquidity is shown to improve price efficiency, defined as the speed with which information is incorporated into the stock price. This means that enhanced liquidity improves the price discovery process in asset markets.

The authors also show the existence of a *liquidity externality*, meaning that an improvement in the liquidity of a security raises not only its own value, but also the values of related securities. This phenomenon is analyzed in the context of 'twin stocks', two different classes of stock of the same company where one was transferred to the more liquid trading system while the other was not. When the TASE announced the transfer of one of these stocks to the new trading regime, not only did its price increase, but so did the price of its twin (albeit by a lesser amount), which was not transferred. Thus, there was a spillover effect of liquidity on the twin stock's value. This result can be generalized to the broader market. Naturally, the extent of liquidity externality depends on the relation between the assets, with the externality expected to be greater for assets that are more closely related to the one whose liquidity changes.

The results documented in this study are robust. Muscarella and Piwowar (2001) find that when the Paris Bourse enabled continuous trading in lieu of call auction trading, stocks that were transferred to the continuous system appreciated in price, especially if their liquidity subsequently improved. Jain (2005), in a study of the consequences of transfers from floor trading to electronic trading systems in 120 countries, finds that these transfers led to greater liquidity and to a positive stock price reaction. He also finds that the introduction of electronic trading lowered the equity return premium, especially in emerging markets.

The results of the study by Amihud, Mendelson, and Lauterbach and those that follow clearly establish a direction of causality, from liquidity to prices. The changes in trading systems that enabled greater market liquidity were *exogenous* and they were followed by price increases. This also suggests that, more broadly, liquidity shocks create an additional source of risk that affects asset valuation. Pricing this liquidity risk is the subject of the next part of the book.

Market Microstructure and Securities Values
Evidence from the Tel Aviv Stock Exchange*
Yakov Amihud, Haim Mendelson, and Beni Lauterbach

Journal of Financial Economics 45, 1997

1. Introduction

Securities markets around the world are making major investments to improve their trading technology. The London Stock Exchange is phasing in an automated, order-driven trading system to improve liquidity and reduce trading costs (see, London Stock Exchange, 1996). The current plan is to implement the system for the FTSE-100 stocks while preserving the traditional quote-driven system for large block trades. Other European stock exchanges (e.g., the French, Italian, Spanish, and Swedish markets) have converted their trading systems from the traditional call market to computer-based continuous trading alternatives. The stock exchanges of Toronto, Montreal, Vancouver, and Alberta have recently changed their trading systems to support decimal pricing 'in a bid to increase liquidity' (Reuters, 1996). In the United States, the Securities and Exchange Commission has introduced new rules requiring market-makers to incorporate in their public quotes both customer limit orders and orders they quote on electronic communication networks such as Instinet and Selectnet. These rules are intended to improve liquidity through increased market transparency and enhanced quality of execution (see, Securities and Exchange Commission, 1996). These reforms were partly triggered by the studies of Christie and Schultz (1994) and Christie et al. (1994), who presented evidence that market makers implicitly colluded to maintain high bid–ask spreads, and

* We thank Steve Brown, Tai Ma and Bill Silber and particularly an anonymous referee for helpful and thorough comments and suggestions, and the Tel Aviv Stock Exchange, Kobi Abramov, the Faculty of Management at Tel Aviv University and Tochna Lainyan for providing the data.

Huang and Stoll (1996), who showed that Nasdaq spreads exceeded NYSE benchmarks. Further, emerging markets are evaluating and implementing new trading systems, and are making considerable investments in improving their microstructure.

A question of interest for both financial economists and practitioners is whether investments in improving the market microstructure have positive value. The answer relates to the raison d'être of market microstructure research, and it can quantify the benefits of improving trading mechanisms. This paper examines the value of an improvement in the market microstructure for selected stocks on the Tel Aviv Stock Exchange (TASE).

In April 1987, the TASE introduced a new trading method, stating: 'The objective of the new method is to create an efficient and well-functioning market for trading securities' (TASE, 1987). The TASE transferred stocks to the new trading method gradually, periodically selecting stocks on the basis of their perceived 'marketability'. Before the transfer, the selected stocks were traded once a day in a call auction. After the transfer, these stocks traded in repeated continuous trading sessions following an opening daily call auction. Continuous trading after the call auction is expected to improve value discovery and trading efficiency and increase stock liquidity (see, Amihud, Mendelson, and Murgia, 1990). Indeed, a TASE study (Tamari and Resnik, 1990; Lauterbach and Ungar, 1992) documented improvements in the market microstructure-related characteristics of volume and volatility under the new trading method. If improvements in market microstructure are valuable, the prices of stocks selected for trading under the new method should increase upon the announcement of the change in their trading mechanism.

Improved liquidity is expected to increase securities values because rational investors discount securities more heavily in the presence of higher trading costs, holding other things equal. This proposition, first made by Amihud and Mendelson (1986), was empirically supported in various studies. Cross-sectionally, risk-adjusted returns on stocks and bonds were found to be increasing in their illiquidity, measured by the bid–ask spread (Amihud and Mendelson, 1986, 1989a, 1991a; Kamara, 1994; Eleswarapu, 1995) or the price impact of trades (Brennan and Subrahmanyam, 1996), or decreasing in their liquidity, measured by volume or turnover ratio (Datar et al., 1996; Haugen and Baker, 1996). Silber (1991) found that, on average, restricted stocks that are not allowed to trade on public exchanges are lower in value by 33.75% on average compared with identical publicly traded stocks. Amihud, Mendelson, and Wood (1990) found that during the stock market crash of 19 October 1987, price declines were greater for stocks whose liquidity suffered most, and price recovery was greater for stocks whose liquidity subsequently improved.

We therefore expect that stocks transferred to the improved trading mechanism should increase in value. The TASE's board of directors announced a list of stocks to be transferred to the new trading method every few months, and the actual transfers took place a day or more after each announcement. We estimated the market-adjusted price changes of the transferred stocks over a test period that begins five days before the TASE announcement and ends 30 days after these stocks started trading by the new method. The cumulative abnormal return on the transferred stocks over the test period averaged about 5.5%. This suggests a significant value gain, especially compared with the moderate cost of the improvement. In December 1995, the market value of the 100 securities traded under the new method was about $26 billion. Assuming that the new trading mechanism gave rise to a permanent price increase of 5.5%, its introduction contributed at least $1.35 billion to the market value of securities traded on the TASE. The cost of this system was estimated at less than $10 million, according to the Chief Executive Officer of the TASE, Mr. Sam Bronfeld. This estimate includes the cost incurred by the brokers and banks using the system. Comparing these costs with the subsequent stock price appreciation demonstrates the value of investments in improving the market microstructure.

The value of the new trading method exceeded the price appreciation of the transferred stocks since trading is characterized by *liquidity externalities* or spillover effects: when the prices of two securities are correlated, an improvement in the liquidity of one should improve the liquidity of the other (Amihud and Mendelson, 1988b, 1990, 1991c). This results in part from the fact that improved value discovery for one security facilitates value discovery for the other (correlated) security. We test this effect using data on 'twin stocks', i.e., two different classes of stock of the same company of which the 'primary stock' was transferred to the new trading method while the 'secondary stock' was not. Liquidity externalities would imply that the price of the secondary stock should increase upon the transfer announcement of the primary stock, but by a smaller magnitude. Our results support this hypothesis.

Our study is related to research on the effects of exchange listing for stocks that previously traded over the counter. Presumably, the motivation for listing is improved liquidity and value (Cooper et al., 1985; Amihud and Mendelson, 1986, 1988a). Indeed, Christie and Huang (1994) found that exchange listings of Nasdaq stocks sharply reduced trading costs, especially for the less liquid stocks. Grammatikos and Papaioannou (1986) and Kadlec and McConnell (1994) found that listing announcements led to price increases which were positively associated with liquidity improvements.

Our paper adds an important dimension not captured by these previous studies. Exchange listing is a voluntary, endogenously-determined decision of a firm, reflecting some optimization by management, and it can be associated with its private information. Companies are not obliged to list on an exchange, and in fact, hundreds of large companies that are eligible to list choose to remain unlisted. Thus, listing reflects an inherent self-selection: we only observe those cases where management expected listing to have a beneficial outcome. It is therefore impossible to examine the general effect that changing the market microstructure has on securities values.

In contrast, the event studied here is *exogenous* to the firm: the transfer decision was made by the TASE's board of directors, not by the firm's management. The TASE's decision was based on its evaluation of the stock's marketability at the time of the decision, and not on any private information about the firm's prospects. Therefore, the price appreciation reflects the value of improved market microstructure rather than any information generated by firms, and there is no self-selection bias. This should not be construed as a criticism of studies on the effects of exchange listing. Rather, we point out that these studies have different objectives and hence they were not designed to examine the issue under study here.

Our study is also related to studies that examined the effects of the announcement of adding stocks to the S&P 500 Index. Harris and Gurel (1986) and Shleifer (1986) found a temporary price increase which, they claimed, reflected a buying pressure by index funds that must invest in these stocks. For the more recent period, Shleifer (1986) and Lynch and Mendenhall (1996) found a permanent price increase, explained by the growing importance of index funds.

Our results cannot be attributed to the demand by index funds. Index funds currently represent only a small portion of the market for stocks transferred to the new trading method. As of December 1995, funds that invested in stocks available through the new trading method constituted only 1.3% of the market value of these stocks. Some of these funds confine their investment to a subset of these stocks. More importantly, these funds were introduced only in the last two years of our sample period. We found that the price appreciation of stocks that were transferred to the new trading method was the same in the earlier and later transfers. We therefore suggest that in both our study and in those on the S&P 500, the price appreciation of stocks included in the S&P 500 index is due to the improvement in their liquidity, following Amihud and Mendelson (1986). This hypothesis was tested and supported by Edmeister and Pirie (1995). The reason that the more recent period shows permanent price appreciation may reflect the recent relative improvement in the liquidity of the S&P 500 stocks, documented by Jones et al. (1991). Our results on liquidity externalities can also explain Dhillon and Johnson's (1991) findings that for firms whose stocks were added to the S&P 500, other traded securities appreciated. They attributed this finding to favorable information; however, the selection for the S&P 500 list is not based on private information. We suggest that the inclusion of a stock in the S&P 500 Index enhances its liquidity and generates spillover effects that favorably affect the other securities of the same firm.

The next section describes trading mechanisms on the TASE and the market microstructure change that occurred when the new trading system was introduced. Section 3 presents our empirical results. We show in Section 3.2 that the value effects due to the new trading mechanism are positive, persistent, and significant. In Section 3.3 we introduce liquidity externalities and examine their impact. In Section 3.4 we demonstrate how the new trading mechanism affected the liquidity and efficiency of the transferred stocks, and Section 4 offers a brief summary of our results and their implications.

2. Trading Mechanisms on the Tel Aviv Stock Exchange

The Tel Aviv Stock Exchange is the only securities market in Israel. As of June 1995, it had 672 listed stocks in addition to other corporate securities (warrants and bonds) and government bonds (TASE, 1995). The market value of the stocks listed on the TASE was about one half of Israel's annual GNP. The stock market became more important in the last decade due to the economic growth that occurred following the country's 1985 anti-inflation program, the liberalization of the Israeli capital market, the intensified privatization of government-owned firms, and the immigration which brought about a sharp increase in investment.

In 1987, the TASE made a fundamental change in its trading system, introducing a new method that enabled continuous trading facilitated by a number of daily trading sessions. We describe below the traditional call method of trading, the new Variable Price trading mechanism, and the process of transferring stocks from the old to the new method.

2.1. The Call Method

Prior to 1987, all stocks listed on the TASE were traded once a day in a call auction (the Call Method or the C-Method). Until 1991, the auction was conducted by a human auctioneer. Limit and market orders were submitted to the TASE by investors before the opening, or were retained by the brokers. Stocks were called in a predetermined sequence by an auctioneer, who first announced the stock's excess demand, positive or negative, at the previous day's closing price and then changed the price based on the direction of excess demand, proceeding at fixed price increments. As the announced price changed, the excess demand decreased (in absolute value) until an equilibrium was reached. If an equilibrium could not be reached at a daily price increase of 10%, the stock was announced as 'buyers only' and the price was set at the previous day's price plus 5% without executing any order. After two days of 'buyers only', the price was allowed to move without bound. Price declines were treated analogously.

The auction process of the C-Method was computerized in 1991. Traders route orders to the TASE which electronically communicates the excess demand at the previous day's closing price. Traders observe the excess demand and have a short time interval during which they can send additional 'offsetting orders' which can be only sell orders when the excess demand is positive, or buy orders when the excess demand is negative. Afterwards, the new excess demand, reflecting the offsetting orders, is announced, and traders can submit offsetting orders again. Following this round, the system computes the new equilibrium prices that are announced simultaneously for all stocks.

There are a number of problems with the C-Method. First, an investor who submits an order for a particular stock does not know its clearing price, nor the prices of related stocks. Once the price information for all stocks is broadcast after the call transaction, investors may want to adjust their trades for a particular stock. However, under the C-Method, such adjustments must be postponed until the following trading day. Second, investors are reluctant to place large orders that could result in significant price impacts. Instead, they may break large orders into smaller ones and trade them over a number of days, thereby bearing the costs of illiquidity, delay and risk. The C-Method can also result in partial executions that may require additional trading on the following day. Finally, traders bear significant inventory risk when taking a position in a security because it can only be unwound on the following day. This diminishes the willingness of traders to provide liquidity by acting as market makers and absorb temporary demand or supply shocks. These shortcomings of the C-Method are particularly important in a thin and highly volatile market such as the TASE.

2.2. The Variable Price Method

In 1987, the TASE started experimenting with a new method of trading securities, called the Variable Price Method (V-Method). The TASE engaged in a process of learning by doing and changed the V-Method during its initial period of operation. The following describes the method as adopted in its final form on 6 December 1987.

Under the V-method, trading is opened by a call auction similar to the C-Method. Continuous trading then commences through a series of sequential trading sessions in an arena which resembles a trading pit. In each session, stocks are announced in a predetermined order, and traders in the arena can execute bilateral trades continuously, until the demand for trading is satisfied (usually within 1–3 minutes). At first, there was a single arena in which all V-Method trades occurred. Due to the increase in the number of stocks traded under this method, there are now three trading arenas operating simultaneously. On a typical day, there are 3–5 rounds of continuous trading, and each stock is traded a number of limes in each round. In 1994, the mean daily number of transactions in the continuous trading stage was 24.4 per stock, and the median was 17.1 (calculated from data in TASE, 1994).

The V-Method was designed to increase liquidity and efficiency. Traders' ability to execute multiple transactions within the day mitigates the price impact of large orders. Traders can also correct pricing errors after observing the transaction prices of the same and similar stocks and after obtaining additional market information. Such correction of pricing errors in response to market-wide information is typical of exchanges that open with a call auction followed by continuous trading (see, Amihud, Mendelson, and Murgia, 1990 for the Milan Stock Exchange; Amihud and Mendelson, 1991b for the Tokyo Stock Exchange). The V-Method thus facilitates the convergence of prices to new information and contributes to a smoother value discovery process. Finally, the ability to take a position and unwind it during the same day reduces the risk of carrying unwanted inventory. This increases traders' willingness to absorb temporary demand shocks into their inventory and increases liquidity (Amihud and Mendelson, 1980; Ho and Stoll, 1981).

Indeed, stocks transferred from the C-Method to the V-Method enjoyed an improvement in efficiency and liquidity and a decline in volatility (see Section 3.4 below). By the first-half of 1995, trading in V-Method securities accounted for 73% of the total equity trading volume on the TASE, including convertibles. About 40% of the volume in V-Method securities was traded at the opening call auction, and 60% in the subsequent rounds of continuous trading (TASE, 1995).

A large proportion of trades are still executed at the open, partly because of a required minimum order size of $3000 (which was increased to $5000 during part of our sample period) in the continuous trading sessions, although brokers may combine small orders with the same limit price into a larger order. Also, on the opening transaction, all orders are executed at a single price, while in the continuous trading that follows there may be a difference between the buying and selling prices, resulting in a higher cost of trading (Amihud and Mendelson, 1985). For some traders, the concentration of trading at the opening enhances liquidity (Mendelson, 1985; Admati and Pfleiderer, 1988), and some are unwilling to delay their trades. As a result, both the opening call and the continuous trading sessions attract significant volume. Thus, the V-Method makes alternative trading methods available on the same stock exchange (as proposed by Amihud and Mendelson, 1985, 1988b), and investors can choose between them.

2.3. Transfer Procedure

Stocks were phased into the new V-Method gradually. A TASE executive committee periodically selected groups of securities for transfer and made a recommendation to the TASE board of directors. Subsequent to this recommendation, and usually within 5 trading days, the TASE board of directors would publicly announce a new list of securities to be transferred. The announcement day in our study is the day of the board's announcement. The actual transfer took place a few days following the public announcement. The V-Method was designed for stocks with 'high marketability' (TASE, 1988), and this constituted the main selection criterion.[1] The number of securities traded under the V-Method grew gradually, and now stands at one hundred securities.

3. Methodology and Empirical Results

Our main hypothesis is that the improved market microstructure under the V-Method had a positive effect on the prices of stocks transferred from the C-Method. We tested this hypothesis by conducting an event study of the transferred stocks. The transfer of stocks to the V-Method is virtually *a pure microstructure event*. Consequently, any price effect of the TASE transfer decision can be attributed entirely to the change in the trading mechanism.

3.1. The Data

Stocks were transferred from the C-method to the V-method in groups, a few stocks at a time. We study all 120 stock transfers that occurred between 6 December 1987, when the TASE implemented the final and current form

---

[1] Christie and Huang (1994) showed, however, that when stocks were transferred from Nasdaq to US stock exchanges, the greatest liquidity benefits accrued to the less marketable stocks.

of the V-Method, and the end of 1994. The 120 stocks were transferred in 17 batches; the average number of stocks in each transfer was 7 and the median was 6. Part of the 120 transferred stocks were dropped at various times. The net effect of these additions and deletions is that 100 securities are currently traded under the V-Method.

Data on the stocks transferred, the TASE announcement dates and the subsequent transfer dates was obtained from 'This Month in the TASE', an official TASE publication. We designated the date of the transfer decision by TASE's board of directors as the announcement day. Announcements were made immediately after the market's closing, and thus affected stock prices on the following day. The transfer date was announced as part of the board's decision; it was between one and seven business days after the announcement day (the median was 3 days). We denote the announcement day by '*A*' and the transfer day by '*T*'. Daily closing prices, adjusted for cash and stock dividends, were obtained from the Israeli financial data services firm Tochna Lainyan and from the database of the Faculty of Management at Tel Aviv University.

3.2. Cumulative Abnormal Returns

We first present descriptive event-study data documenting the Cumulative Abnormal Returns (CAR) (see Brown and Warner, 1980). The event window is from 5 days before the announcement day $(A - 5)$ until 30 days after the transfer day $(T + 30)$. We start from day $A - 5$ to account for possible leaks of the TASE executive committee's recommendation regarding the list of stocks to be transferred, and allow for a long post-event period to examine whether the effect on stock prices was permanent.

We estimated the market model regressions

$$R_{nt} = \alpha_n + \beta_n \mathrm{RM}_t + \varepsilon_{nt}, \tag{1}$$

where R_{nt} is the return on stock n on day t and RM_t is the daily return on the value-weighted TASE index (returns are the logarithms of the relative price changes, presented in percentage points), α_n and β_n are constant coefficients, and ε_{nt} are the residuals. The market model is estimated over days $T + 31$ to $T + 160$, except for the last transfer event which had data available only through day $T + 103$. The estimation of the market model using post-event data was done in order to avoid an ex-post selection bias.[2]

---

[2] Copeland and Mayers (1982) estimated the market model using post-ranking data in their study of the Value-Line enigma to avoid the problem of ex post selection bias. Brown et al.

The selection criteria of the TASE may induce a bias in the estimated market-model parameters if we use pre-event data to estimate the model. This is because the TASE is more likely to select stocks that reached high volume and capitalization, which could imply that they performed unusually well prior to their selection.

We then calculated the abnormal returns

$$AR_{nt} = R_{nt} - (\alpha_n + \beta_n RM_t) \tag{2}$$

for each day t in the event window, days $A - 5$ through $T + 30$, where the parameters α and β are estimated by the market model (1). The cumulative abnormal returns are

$$CAR_{ns} = \sum_{t=A-5}^{s} AR_{nt}, \tag{3}$$

for the event days $s = A - 5, A - 4, \ldots, T + 30$. Then, we averaged the CAR_{ns} across all stocks to obtain CAR_s. The days between the announcement A and the last day before the transfer, $T - 1$ which varied, were combined.[3]

As shown in Figure 3.1, the average cumulative abnormal return rises slightly during days $A - 5$ to $A - 1$, possibly reflecting news leaks or market anticipation. The CAR for days $A - 5$ through $A - 1$ was 2.15%, mostly due to the abnormal return on day $A - 4$, which was 1.235% (SE = 0.211%). It then rises sharply at the announcement and through the transfer day T, where $CAR_T = 6.80\%$. The average CAR then declines slightly and hovers between + 5% and +6% through the end of the event window. These results show that the transfer of stocks into the V-Method generated a permanent price increase of about 5% on average.

The estimated abnormal return around the announcement and transfer days may underestimate the full effect of the transfer to the V-Method. Because the selection criterion was based on the executive committee's assessment of high marketability, the market could partly anticipate which stocks were likely candidates for transfer to the V-Method, and their prices could have risen well before the announcement. While the TASE decision on the specific stocks to be transferred to the V-Method was made within

(1995) discuss biases in event-study results where parameters are estimated from pre-event data while the test is conditional on ex post information. In their study of the effect of listing, Kadlec and McConnell (1995) used post-listing data to estimate the market model.

[3] A similar methodology was used in a takeover study by Asquith (1983), who combined the abnormal return from the announcement day to the outcome day since, as here, the time interval varied for each case in his sample.

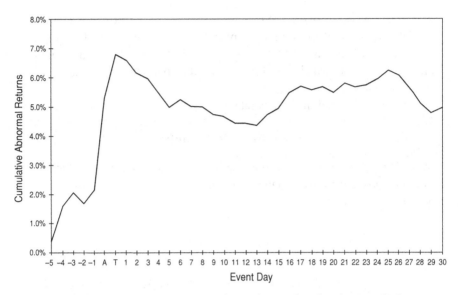

Figure 3.1. Cumulative abnormal returns for stocks transferred to the V-Method. Average cumulative abnormal returns (CAR) for 120 stocks that were transferred from the C-Method to the V-Method of trading on the Tel Aviv Stock Exchange (TASE) between 6 December 1987, and the end of 1994. '*A*' on the event day axis aggregates the time period from the day of the announcement by the TASE of the stocks selected for transfer through the day before the transfer (the number of days in this period varied). '*T*' is the transfer day. The CAR for each stock was estimated over the period $A -$ 5 through $T + 30$. The market model from which the parameters were estimated is $R_{nt} = \alpha_n + \beta_n RM_t + \varepsilon_{nt}$, where R_{nt} is the return on stock n on day t and RM_t is the daily return on the TASE value-weighted index (returns are the logarithm of relative price changes), α_n and β_n are constant coefficients, and ε_{nt} are the residuals. (The market model was estimated over days $T + 31$ through $T + 160$.)

five days before it was announced, there could be earlier speculation regarding the identity of these stocks. The timing of the transfer decisions and the number of stocks in each transfer were unpredictable. For example, *Haaretz* (a leading Israeli newspaper) reported on 20 February 1991, that the TASE was building a new trading arena which would enable trading of 40 additional securities by the V-Method. The report suggested 11 stocks as candidates for the transfer. Two months later, the TASE selected 8 stocks from that list for transfer. We examined the price changes of these 8 stocks. The CAR on the day of the newspaper story and the day that followed was 2.27%. From the story day to day $A - 6$, we had CAR = 6.08%, and from day $A - 5$ to $A + 1$, CAR = 3.90%. This case illustrates our suggestion that the price increase of stocks that were transferred to the V-Method exceeds the CAR estimated by us around the days of the public announcement of the transfer.

For explicitly testing the effect of the transfers to the V-Method, the ordinary event-study test procedure may be inappropriate. Because stocks were transferred in batches, the returns of stocks in the same batch could be cross-sectionally dependent, thereby biasing the variance estimates. We therefore carried out the event study tests for portfolios of stocks transferred in the same batch, referring to these as transfer portfolios. Each of the 17 transfer events i, $i = 1, 2, \ldots, 17$ is identified by its announcement date A_i and transfer date T_i. The following model was estimated for each event i over days $A_i - 5$ through $T_i + 160$:

$$R_{it} = \alpha_i + \beta_i \text{RM}_t + \sum_{j=1}^{3} \gamma_{ij} D_{ijt} + \varepsilon_{it}, \tag{4}$$

where R_{it} is the equally-weighted day-t return on transfer-portfolio i, $i = 1$, $2, \ldots, 17$, RM_t is the daily return on the value-weighted TASE index, and α_i, β_i, and γ_{ij} are constant coefficients. The abnormal return was estimated by using dummy variables, defined as follows:

$$D_{i1t} = \tfrac{1}{5} \text{ on days } A_i - 5 \text{ to } A_i - 1, \tag{5}$$

$$D_{i2t} = \tfrac{1}{2} \text{ on days } A_i \text{ to and } A_i + 1, \tag{6}$$

$$D_{i3t} = 1/k_i \text{ on days } A_i + 2 \text{ to day } T_i + 30, \tag{7}$$

k_i being the number of days during this period (see, Thompson, 1985; Malatesta, 1986; Karafiath, 1988). In the model displayed in Eq. (4), the regression coefficients γ_{ij} measure the cumulative abnormal return over each of the three time intervals associated with the three dummy variables. We also calculated the sum of the dummy-variable coefficients for each event

$$\text{SUM}_i = \gamma_{i1} + \gamma_{i2} + \gamma_{i3}, \tag{8}$$

where SUM_i represents CAR_i over days $A_i - 5$ to $T_i + 30$. For our tests, we calculated the averages of the estimated coefficients across the 17 events, $A\gamma_j = \sum_i \gamma_{ij}/17$, $j = 1, 2, 3$, and the average of SUM_i. The t-statistics are calculated in the ordinary way: $t(A\gamma_j) = A\gamma_j/(\text{SD}\gamma_j/17^{1/2})$, where $\text{SD}\gamma_j$ is the cross-sectional standard deviation of the 17 estimated coefficients γ_{ij}.

The estimation results, presented in Table 3.1, show a highly significant price increase at the announcement of the transfer of stocks to the V-Method. The mean CAR over the pre-announcement period, $A\gamma_1$, and

Table 3.1. *Estimated value effects of stock transfers to the new variable price trading method*

Results for the event-study model $R_{it} = \alpha_i + \beta_i RM_t + \Sigma_{j=1}^{3} \gamma_{ij} D_{ijt} + \varepsilon_{it}$, for 120 TASE stocks that transferred from the call trading method to the variable price method over the period 1988–1994, aggregated in 17 transfer events.

Variable	Mean $(A\gamma_j)$ (t-statistic) (1)	$t(At\gamma_j)$ statistic (2)	Median (3)	Pos:Neg (Binomial Probability) (4)	Weighted Mean (t-statistic) (5)
Intercept	− 0.07 (− 2.19)	− 2.39*	− 0.11	5:12 (0.98)	− 0.07* (− 2.41)
β	1.14** (26.49)	10.64**	1.14	17:0 (0.00)	1.11** (27.82)
D1 $A - 5$ to $A - 1$	2.13* (2.30)	2.34*	0.97	12:5 (0.07)	2.36* (2.61)
D2 A to $A + 1$	3.04** (4.42)	5.36**	3.33	15:2 (0.00)	2.86** (4.48)
D3 $A + 2$ to $T + 30$	0.35 (0.21)	0.56	0.13	9:8 (0.50)	1.10 (0.70)
SUM $A - 5$ to $T + 30$	5.52** (3.05)		6.38	13:4 (0.03)	6.31** (3.95)
SUMT $A - 5$ to T	7.55 (6.95)		7.65	17:0 (0.00)	6.99** (6.16)

* Significant at 0.05.
** Significant at 0.01.

R_{it} is the equally-weighted day-t return on transfer-portfolio, i, $i = 1, 2, \ldots, 17$, RM, is the daily return on the value-weighted TASE market index (returns are in percentage points, with 1% presented as 1) and α_i, β_i and γ_{ij}, $j = 1, 2, 3$ are constant coefficients. The announcement day is denoted by A and the transfer day by T. For each event i, $i = 1, 2, \ldots, 17$, the model was estimated for the portfolio of transferred stocks from day $A_i - 5$ to day $T_i + 160$. The coefficients of the three dummy variables D_{ij} estimate the cumulative abnormal returns (CAR) over three periods, as follows: D_{i1} for day $A_i - 5$ to $A_i - 1$; D_{i2} for day A_i to $A_i + 1$; and D_{i3} for day $A_i + 2$ to $T_i + 30$. $\text{SUM}_i = \gamma_{i1} + \gamma_{i2} + \gamma_{i3}$ is the cumulative abnormal return from day $A - 5$ to $T_i + 30$. The last row documents the results from the event-study model where the dummy variable D_{i2} is for day A to T, D_{i3} for day $T + 1$ to $T + 30$ and $\text{SUMT}_i = \gamma_{i1} + \gamma_{i2}$, the CAR from day $A - 5$ to day T.

(1): average of the estimated coefficients across events (t-statistic in parentheses).

(2): $t(At\gamma_j)$, the t-statistic for the means of the 17 sample $t\gamma_{ij}$ statistics from the regression of the event-study model, $t\gamma_{ij} = \gamma_{ij}/\text{SE}(\gamma_{ij})$. The mean and standard deviation of the 17 t-statistics, $At\gamma_j$ and $\text{SD}t\gamma_j$, are used to calculate the ordinary t-statistic $t(At\gamma_j) = At\gamma_j/(\text{SD}t\gamma_j/17^{1/2})$. The t-tests for α and β are analogous.

(3): medians of the 17 estimated coefficients.

(4): number of positive and negative estimated coefficients. In parentheses: the binomial probability that γ_{ij} is equally likely to be positive or negative, against the alternative hypothesis that it is positive.

(5): weighted average of the estimated coefficients of model (1) over the 17 estimations, the weights being the number of stocks in each transfer portfolio (t-statistics are in parentheses).

over days A to $A + 1$, $A\gamma_2$, are positive and significant, as evidenced by their t-statistics. $A\gamma_3$, the post-announcement CAR, is insignificantly different from zero. SUM, which estimates the CAR over the entire period $A - 5$ to $T + 30$, has a mean of 5.517% which is highly significant. Further tests on the significance of the 17 estimated t-statistics, t_{ij}, which are homoskedastic, confirm the robustness of our results (see Table 3.1, Column (2)).

Given the relatively small number of transfer events, the means could be affected by outliers. Column (3) presents the medians of the estimated regression coefficients of model (4) and of SUM (Eq. (8)). We observe that the key medians are similar in magnitude to the means.

Column (4) of Table 3.1 presents the number of positive and negative coefficients γ_{ij} for each j, and the respective binomial probability of observing the indicated number of negative γ_{ij} under the null hypothesis that the probability is 0.5. The results show that the null is soundly rejected at better than the 0.05 level for γ_{12} and for SUM.

While the improvement in liquidity after the transfer was anticipated on the announcement day, its full benefit could be consummated only in trading that started on the transfer day. Similarly, Christie and Huang (1994) showed that when stocks transfer from Nasdaq to the NYSE, the bid–ask spread narrows only from the day of the transfer. Only then were investors able to exploit the higher liquidity and lower transaction costs, which would induce them to pay more for these stocks. Thus, we also estimated the CAR from day $A - 5$ through (including) the transfer day T, defining the dummy variable D_{i2} t in the event-study model (Eq. (4)) over days A_i to T_i and calculating $SUMT_i = \gamma_{i1} + \gamma_{i2}$. In six of the 17 transfers, day T was day $A + 1$, whereas in 11 cases the transfer occurred after day $A + 1$. The results show that $SUMT_i$ was positive for all 17 events. The mean of $SUMT_i$ was 7.547% ($t = 6.95$) and its median was 7.650%.

Overall, the results strongly support the existence of a positive price effect due to the transfer of stocks to the V-Method. The price increase was permanent, economically meaningful, and statistically significant.

3.3. Liquidity Externalities

Amihud and Mendelson (1988b, 1990, 1991c) postulated that trading is characterized by liquidity externalities, or spillovers, across securities.[4]

---

[4] Liquidity externalities for individual securities were introduced in Mendelson (1985). On the public-good type externality of services provided in the securities markets, see Cohen et al. (1986, ch. 8).

When the values of two securities, A and B, are correlated, an improvement in the trading mechanism for security A will have a positive effect on the liquidity of B. The source of this improvement is that a more efficient trading mechanism improves value-discovery for A, allowing traders in B to use the (improved) observed prices of A to make a more informed inference on the value of B. However, when the returns on A and B are highly correlated, the two securities may serve as partial substitutes in investors' portfolios.

We examine the existence of liquidity externalities as follows. A subsample of TASE companies have two classes of stock with identical claims on capital (including cash distributions and liquidation) but different voting rights.[5] We call such stocks *twin stocks*. The two classes of twin stocks typically have differences in liquidity due to differences in the number of shares outstanding and differences in float. We consider twin stocks where the *primary stock* – usually, the more liquid of the twins – was transferred to the V-Method, while the *secondary stock* continued to be traded by the C-Method. The sample includes twenty-three twin stocks in twelve transfer events.

The null hypothesis is that the transfer of the primary stock to the V-Method had no effect on the corresponding secondary stock. There are two alternative hypotheses:

The liquidity externality hypothesis. Section 3.2 demonstrates that stocks gain when they are transferred to the improved trading mechanism of the V-method. If there are positive liquidity externalities, the secondary stock should also enjoy some of the benefits of the improved trading method for the primary stock, resulting in a price increase for the secondary stock. The hypothesis is thus that at the announcement, (i) the price of the secondary stock increases, but (ii) by less than the price increase of the primary stock.

The substitution hypothesis. If investors' demand for the twin stock is not perfectly elastic (see, Shleifer, 1986), the improved liquidity of the primary stock makes it more attractive relative to the secondary stock, thereby reducing the demand for the secondary stock. Under this hypothesis, the secondary stock's price will decline.

These hypotheses are examined using our subsample of twenty-three twin stocks. Figure 3.2 shows the average CAR over days $A - 5$ through $T + 30$ for both primary and secondary stocks. The CAR for the secondary stocks from day $A - 5$ to day T (transfer) was 3.3% compared with 7.8% for the primary stocks. This result supports both parts of the liquidity externality hypothesis: (i) the prices of secondary stocks increase even though the

---

[5] The ratio of voting rights between the two classes is usually 5:1.

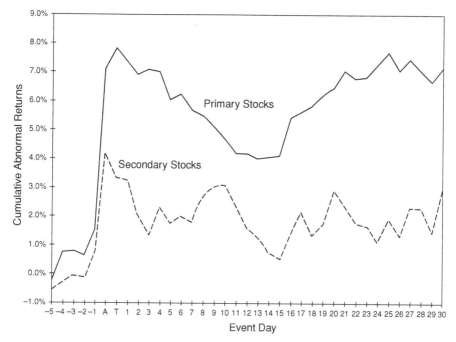

Figure 3.2. Cumulative abnormal returns for twin stocks. Average cumulative abnormal returns (CAR) for twenty-three twin-stock pairs in twelve transfer events on the TASE. In each case, the firm had two classes of stock listed. One class (the 'primary' stock) transferred from the C-Method to the V-Method of trading while the other class (the 'secondary' stock) continued to be traded under the C-Method. See Figure 3.1 for more details regarding the data and estimation. '*A*' on the event day axis aggregates the time period from the day of the announcement by the TASE of the primary stocks selected for transfer to the V-Method through the day before the transfer (the number of days in this period varies). '*T*' is the transfer day.

improved trading method is available only to the primary stocks; and (ii) the price increase is greater for the primary stocks, which directly benefit from the improved trading method.

To test the statistical significance of these results, we estimated the model in Eq. (4) for the secondary stock portfolios, with the dummy variables set to measure the CAR over the period $A - 5$ to T. The secondary stocks' estimation model includes a lagged market return because, being traded on the C-Method, some of these stocks adjust their prices gradually to the market. (See analysis in Section 3.4.2 below.) The mean SUMT was 4.88% ($t = 2.83$) and the median was 4.62%. This supports part (i) of the liquidity externality hypothesis: there was a significant increase in the price of the secondary stocks that continued to trade under the C-Method when their twins were transferred to the V-Method.

To test part (ii) of the liquidity externality hypothesis, we calculated DR_{it}, the difference between the portfolio returns on the primary and secondary stocks in event i on day t. Using DR_{it} as the dependent variable in the event-study model shown in Eq. (4), we found that the cumulative differential return over the period $A - 5$ to T, SUMT, had a mean of 4.25% ($t = 2.34$) and a median of 5.07%. This shows that the price increase of the secondary stocks, which enjoyed a liquidity externality, was significantly lower than the price increase of the primary stocks that directly benefited from higher liquidity under the V-Method.

3.4. Liquidity, Efficiency and the Trading Mechanism

The V-Method was expected to improve market quality compared to the C-Method. Next, we examine how the liquidity and efficiency of trading were affected by the transfer from the C-Method to the V-Method.

3.4.1. Liquidity

Liquidity in the TASE cannot be measured by bid–ask spreads. There are no designated market-makers or specialists who post bid and ask quotes. In trading by the V-Method, brokers and dealers call out prices and quantities and transactions are carried out. While it is theoretically possible to impute a bid–ask spread from the limit prices of the marginal buy and sell orders that could not be executed, these data are unavailable. We therefore use two common measures of liquidity: the stock's trading volume and the stock's liquidity (or Amivest) ratio.

(1) *Trading volume* (*V*): Theoretically, the trading volume or trading frequency of a given security is an increasing function of its liquidity, other things equal (Mendelson, 1982, 1985; Amihud and Mendelson, 1986). Thus, an increase in the trading volume of a stock after its transfer to the V-Method reflects an increase in its liquidity.

We calculated the relative volume of each stock, calculating the stock's volume as a percent of the market volume, for each event-day s, and then averaged the relative volumes across the 120 stocks. The resulting time series are presented in Figure 3.3. Clearly, the transfer of stocks to the V-Method is associated with a dramatic increase in their trading volumes (see also Lauterbach and Ungar, 1992). The upward trend in the relative trading volume of the transferred stocks prior to the announcement is noteworthy.

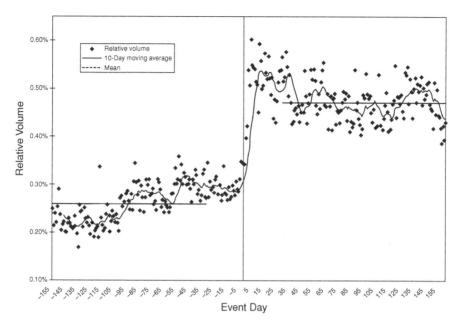

Figure 3.3. Relative volumes before and after stock transfers to the V-Method. Trading volumes are relative to the market volume for the 120 stocks that were transferred from the C-Method to the V-Method on the TASE. For each day t, the daily trading volume of each stock was calculated as a percentage of the market volume on the same day. The results were then averaged over the 120 transferred stocks for each event day. The curved line shows 10-day moving averages for the relative volume time series, and the two steady lines labelled 'mean' represent the mean relative volume before (days $A - 155$ through $A - 31$) and after (days $T + 31$ through $T + 160$) the event period, where A denotes the announcement day and T denotes the transfer day.

This trend probably contributed to the likelihood that these stocks would be selected for transfer to the V-Method.

To test the rise in volume for our sample, we define the change in the relative volume as

$$DV_j = \log(V_j/VM)_{AFTER} - \log(V_j/VM)_{BEFORE}, \tag{9}$$

where V_j and VM are, respectively, the average daily trading volume on stock j and on the market (in monetary units), and the subscripts indicate 'before the announcement' (days $A - 155$ through $A - 31$) and 'after the transfer' ($T + 31$ through $T + 160$). The change in the relative volume, DV_j, was positive for 78% of the transferred stocks; its mean was 0.492% ($t = 7.27$), and the median was 0.421%.

(2) *Liquidity Ratio* (LR): The liquidity ratio, also called the Amivest measure of liquidity, measures the trading volume associated with a unit change in the stock price. A higher LR implies greater market liquidity or depth. The liquidity ratio is defined as

$$LR_j = \sum_t V_{jt} / \sum_t |R_{jt}|, \tag{10}$$

where V_{jt}, and R_{jt} are, respectively, the volume and return on stock j on day t, and the summation is over the days in the estimation period (see, Cooper et al., 1985; Khan and Baker, 1993). The relative change in the liquidity ratio (LR) for stock j is defined by

$$DLR_j = \log(LR_{j,\text{AFTER}} / LR_{j,\text{BEFORE}}), \tag{11}$$

where the subscripts are as defined above. DLR was positive for 85% of the transferred stocks, with a mean of 0.87 ($t = 10.90$) and a median of 0.87. That is, after the transfer to the V-Method, there was an increase in the trading volume that was associated with a change of 1% in the stock price. This means that the market had more depth. In summary, the transfer to the V-Method was associated with a significant increase in liquidity.

The results are thus consistent with our hypothesis on the positive relation between liquidity and stock values: the stocks transferred to the V-Method enjoyed both substantial liquidity gains and significant price increases. Naturally, the impact of the transfer varied across stocks. Thus, a further examination of our hypothesis is provided by estimating the cross-sectional model

$$CAR_j = \delta \cdot DLIQ_j + \sum_{k=1}^{16} \zeta_k \cdot DUMEVENT_{kj} + \kappa_j, \tag{12}$$

where CAR_j is the cumulative abnormal return on stock j from day $A - 5$ to day $T + 30$, DLIQ is the change in liquidity as measured by DV or DLR, and $DUMEVENT_{kj} = 1$ when stock j is in event k (zero otherwise). By our hypothesis, $\delta > 0$.

The estimation results were as follows. For DLIQ defined as DV, $\delta = 5.10$ ($t = 2.03$), and for DLIQ defined as DLR, $\delta = 4.17$ ($t = 1.80$). The standard errors were estimated using White's (1980) method. The estimated coefficient δ is possibly downward biased towards zero due to the problem of errors-in-the-variables. The explanatory variable, DLIQ, is a noisy estimate of the improvement in liquidity of the transferred stocks, and thus its estimated effect is smaller than its true effect. Still, both estimated coefficients are significantly positive at better than 5% (one tail test). This shows that across stocks too, the price increase after the transfer to the V-Method was related to the improvement in liquidity.

3.4.2. Efficiency

Improving market efficiency was a stated objective of the TASE in instituting the V-Method (TASE, 1987). This objective implies an improvement in the value discovery process by which information is incorporated into stock prices. Continuous trading enables investors to obtain information about the value of a stock after having observed both contemporaneous market movements and the transaction prices of the same stock and related (similar) securities. This is consistent with the existence of liquidity externalities, discussed in Section 3.3. Amihud, Mendelson, and Murgia (1990) observed that in the Milan *Borsa*, pricing errors in the call auction were reversed towards the market during the continuous trading session that followed the call. The V-Method should enable investors to incorporate information into the stock price more quickly and with greater precision compared to the C-Method. Therefore, under the V-Method, the pricing errors relative to the contemporaneous market index should be smaller because of both a faster adjustment to changes in the market index, and smaller firm-specific errors given the information available from the observed prices of the same and related stocks. In what follows, we first examine the pricing errors before and after the stock transfer to the V-Method, and then study their sources.

Amihud and Mendelson (1989b, 1991b) introduced the Relative Return Dispersion, based on the variance of returns across securities, as a descriptive measure of the efficiency of a trading mechanism. Christie and Huang (1990, 1995) used the cross-sectional dispersion of equity returns to study the tendency of asset prices to move together over the business cycle and in extreme market moves. The Relative Return Dispersion (RRD) is defined by

$$RRD_s = (1/20) \cdot \sum_{i=1}^{120} \varepsilon_{is}^2, \tag{13}$$

where ε_{is} is the simple market-model residual of stock i on event-day s. The market model was estimated separately before and after the announcement date. The RRD measures, for each day s, the dispersion of the returns on the individual stocks around the market. Since the dispersion of values due to firm-specific information should be independent of the trading

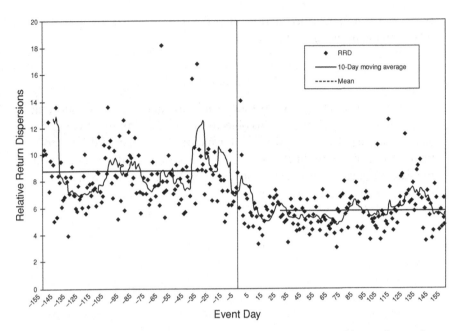

Figure 3.4. Relative Return Dispersions (RRD) before and after stock transfers to the V-Method. Relative Return Dispersions (RRD) of 120 stocks that were transferred from the C-Method to the V-Method on the TASE. The Relative Return Dispersion for event-day s is defined by $RRD_s = (1/20) \cdot \sum_{i=1}^{120} \varepsilon_{is}^2 \cdot \varepsilon_{is}$ is the simple market-model residual of stock i on event-day s, where the market-model was estimated separately before and after the event day. The curved line shows the 10-day moving average of the RRD series, and the two steady lines labelled "mean" represents the mean RRDs before (days $A -$ 155 through $A - 31$) and after (days $T + 31$ through $T + 160$) the event period, where A denotes the announcement day and T denotes the transfer day. On three days, the RRD exceeded 20; the corresponding data points are out of scale (and hence, are not shown in the figure), but they were included in the mean and the moving average calculations.

mechanism, systematic differences in RRD between the 'before' and 'after' periods indicate differences in efficiency.

The behavior of RRD_s, shown in Figure 3.4, is consistent with greater efficiency after the transfer to the V-Method. The average of RRD_s over days $A - 155$ through $A - 31$ was 8.79, compared with 5.79 over the period $T + 31$ through $T + 160$.

We next examine the change in the two factors that may contribute to inefficiency under the C-Method: (a) lagged adjustment to changes in the market index, and (b) high firm-specific noise. We estimated for each stock the lagged market model regression

$$R_{jt} = \alpha_j + \beta_j \cdot RM_t + 1\beta_j \cdot RM_{t-1} + \varepsilon_{jt}, \qquad (14)$$

Table 3.2. *Improvements in efficiency under the variable price trading method*

Estimated parameters of the market model $R_{jt} = \alpha_j + \beta_j \cdot RM_t + 1\beta_j \cdot RM_{t-1} + \varepsilon_{jt}$.

R_{jt} is the daily return on stock j on day t, RM_t is the market daily return and ε_{jt}, is the residual return. β_j and $1\beta_j$ measure the beta coefficients for contemporaneous and lagged RM, and Var(ε) is the estimated residual variance. There are 120 stocks transferred to the V-Method over the 1988–1994 period. The 'before' period is days $A - 155$ through $A - 31$ and the 'after' period is days $T + 31$ to $T + 160$ (A is the announcement day and T is the transfer day).

Period	β	1β	Var(ε)
Before announcement			
Mean	0.929[*1]	0.146[*0]	8.791
(Std. Error)	(0.027)	(0.022)	(0.743)
Median	0.959	0.118	6.251
After transfer			
Mean	1.108[*1]	-0.008[*0]	5.929
(Std. Error)	(0.026)	(0.017)	(0.522)
Median	1.091	-0.020	4.289
Difference			
After-*Before*			
Mean	0.180[*0]	-0.154[*0]	-2.862
(Std. Error)	(0.037)	(0.023)	(0.578)
Median	0.104	-0.130	-2.010
Positive : Negative	77:43[+]	35:85[+]	23:97[+]

[*0], [*1]: The mean is significantly different from 0 or 1, respectively (at the 0.05 level).
[#0], [#1]: The mean is not significantly different from 0 or 1, respectively (at the 0.05 level).
[+] : The proportion of cases which are positive is significantly different from 0.50 (at the 0.05 level).

where R_{jt} is the return on stock j on day i, RM_t is the market return, β_j, and $1\beta_j$ are the coefficients for current and lagged RM, respectively, and ε_{jt} is the residual whose variance is denoted by Var(ε). The model was estimated separately over two periods: before the announcement, days $A - 155$ through $A - 31$, and after the transfer, days $T + 31$ through $T + 160$.

The results, presented in Table 3.2, are consistent with the hypothesis that the V-Method (in particular, the ability to trade throughout the day) improved efficiency.

(a) *Adjustment to market information.* Participants in the V-Method were able to make better adjustments in response to market information. Under the C-Method, there was a significant adjustment lag to the market index:

the mean of 1β was 0.146 and highly significant. After the transfer to the V-Method, 1β declined for most stocks and its mean became practically zero, implying that stock prices adjusted promptly to market information. The coefficient β of the contemporaneous market return correspondingly increased after the transfer so that the mean of $\beta + 1\beta$ remained about the same (1.075 before vs. 1.100 after). Thus, while the fundamental relation between the returns on individual stocks and the market was unaffected by the change, traders' ability to react to market movements on the same day, rather than having to wait for the following day's call, increased market efficiency. While this outcome is directly predictable given the change in the trading mechanism, it is reassuring that the results are strong and statistically significant.

(b) *Firm-specific information.* Continuous trading enables traders to trade on the firm-specific information they have and learn this information from other traders' transactions through the same trading day. Thus, we examined whether the transfer to the V-Method lowered the variance of the residuals from the *lagged* market model (Eq. (14)), which controls for the effects of delayed adjustment to the market. Indeed, the results in Table 3.2 show that after the transfer the residual variance, $\text{Var}(\varepsilon)$, declined for most stocks, and its average was lower by about a third. While the change in market microstructure should not have changed any fundamental information about the stocks (other than the change in their liquidity), it had a favorable effect on the precision with which new firm-specific information was incorporated in stock prices.

3.4.3. The Interaction of Liquidity and Efficiency Improvements

Finally, we propose that the improvements in liquidity and efficiency, brought about by the improvement in market microstructure, are positively correlated (Amihud and Mendelson, 1988b). To test this hypothesis, we used the two measures of change in efficiency, discussed above: the change in the β coefficient of the lagged RM,

$$\mathrm{d}1\beta_j = 1\beta_{j,\text{AFTER}} - 1\beta_{j,\text{BEFORE}}, \tag{15}$$

and the change in the variance of the market model residuals,

$$\mathrm{dVar}(\varepsilon)_j = \log(\text{Var}(\varepsilon)_{j,\text{AFTER}}) - \log(\text{Var}(\varepsilon)_{j,\text{BEFORE}}). \tag{16}$$

Both measures were obtained from the lagged market model regression (Eq. (14)), estimated over both the 'before' and 'after' periods. We then estimated the cross-sectional models

$$d1\beta_j = \eta \cdot DV_j + \sum_{k=1}^{16} \zeta_k \cdot DUMEVENT_{kj} + \kappa_j, \tag{17}$$

and

$$dVar(\varepsilon)_j = \theta \cdot DV_j + \sum_{k=1}^{16} \zeta'_k \cdot DUMEVENT_{kj} + \kappa'_j, \tag{18}$$

where DV_j is the change in volume as defined above, and the dummy variables $DUMEVENT_{kj}$ are as defined in model (2).[6] By our hypothesis on the interaction between liquidity and efficiency changes, we expect $\eta < 0$ and $\theta < 0$. That is, improved liquidity should reduce the lag in price adjustment and the return noise.

The estimated coefficients were $\eta = -0.114$ ($t = 4.05$) and $\theta = -0.062$ ($t = 1.20$). The regression standard errors were estimated using White's (1980) method. Again, the estimated coefficients are possibly biased towards zero due to the problem of errors-in-the-variables (see Section 3.4.1). Both η and θ had the expected sign, although only η was significantly different from zero. In addition, we estimated the relation between the change in β itself and DV, obtaining a regression coefficient of 0.18 with $t = 6.23$, consistent with our hypothesis. This is the mirror image of the results for $d1\beta$, given no change in the fundamentals.

In summary, the results suggest that improvements in liquidity are associated with greater efficiency in the dissemination of information into stock prices.

4. Conclusions

In this paper we showed that improvements in market microstructure are valuable. Specifically, we found that stocks that were transferred to a more efficient trading method in the TASE enjoyed significant and permanent price increases. Since the transfer of stocks was mandated by the TASE and

---

[6] We did not use the liquidity ratio as a measure of liquidity for this test because both DLR and the efficiency measures were generated from the same return data, raising the possibility of a spurious relation between them. Regressions using DLR gave rise to similar results: $\eta = -0.106$ ($t = 3.69$), and $\theta = -0.184$ ($t = 3.90$).

was not a decision made by the companies' managements, it represents a pure market microstructure event: the transfer does not reflect private information of the companies' insiders and the results are not due to self-selection. Rather, the price appreciation found for stocks transferred to the new trading method reflects the value of improved market microstructure that brings about improvement in liquidity.

Stock liquidity improved following the transfer to the new trading method: there was a large and significant increase in both the market-adjusted trading volume and in the liquidity ratio. Across stocks transferred to the new method, the value gains were positively associated with the increase in liquidity. The new method also led to improved efficiency of the value-discovery process. Stock prices adjusted faster to market information, and the noise in stock prices declined. These efficiency gains were positively related to the liquidity improvement across stocks. The greater efficiency made stock prices more informative, and the improved trading system benefitted the market as a whole. We also found that the benefits of the improved trading method generated positive externalities (or spillovers) for related stocks which continued to trade under the old trading method. These stocks, although not directly affected by the more liquid new trading method, also appreciated when their 'twin' stocks were transferred to the new method.

Our results highlight the value of improving the quality of trading mechanisms (Amihud and Mendelson, 1988b). In Israel, the value benefits were a very large multiple of the investment in the improved trading system. Our methodology can be extended to the study of liquidity events in other securities markets that changed their microstructure, such as in Europe and in emerging markets. It would be interesting to define the market-microstructure events for the changes occurring in these markets and to study their impact on securities values.

References

Admati, A., Pfleiderer. P., 1988. A theory of intraday patterns: volume and price variability. Review of Financial Studies 1, 3–40.

Amihud, Y., Mendelson, H., 1980. Dealership market: market making with inventory. Journal of Financial Economics 311–53.

Amihud, Y., Mendelson, H., 1985. An integrated computerized trading system. In: Market Making and the Changing Structure of the Securities Industry. Lexington Books, Lexington, MA, pp. 217–35.

Amihud, Y., Mendelson. H., 1986. Asset pricing and the bid–ask spread. Journal of Financial Economics 17, 223–49.

Amihud, Y., Mendelson, H., 1988a. Liquidity and asset prices: financial management implications. Financial Management 17, 5–15.

Amihud, Y., Mendelson, H., 1988b. Liquidity, volatility and exchange automation. Journal of Accounting, Auditing and Finance 3, 369–95.

Amihud, Y., Mendelson. H., 1989a. The effects of beta, bid–ask spread, residual risk and size on slock returns. Journal of Finance 44, 479–86.

Amihud, Y., Mendelson, H., 1989b. Market microstructure and price discovery on the Tokyo Stock Exchange. Japan and the World Economy 1, 341–70.

Amihud, Y., Mendelson, H., 1990. Option Markets Integration. Paper submitted to the U.S. Securities and Exchange Commission, January.

Amihud, Y., Mendelson, H., 1991a. Liquidity, maturity and the yields on U.S. government securities. Journal of Finance 46, 1411–26.

Amihud, Y., Mendelson, H., 1991b. Volatility, efficiency and trading: evidence from the Japanese stock market. Journal of Finance 46, 1765–89.

Amihud, Y., Mendelson, H., 1991c. How (not) to integrate the European capital markets. In: Giovannini, A., Mayer, C. (Eds.), European Financial Integration. Cambridge University Press, Cambridge, MA, pp. 73–99.

Amihud, Y., Mendelson. H., Murgia. M., 1990. Stock market microstructure and return volatility: evidence from Italy. Journal of Banking and Finance 423–40.

Amihud, Y., Mendelson, H., Wood, R. 1990. Liquidity and the 1987 slock market crash. Journal of Portfolio Management, Spring, 65–9.

Asquith, P., 1983. Merger bids, uncertainty, and stockholders return. Journal of Financial Economics 11, 51–83.

Brennan, M., Subrahmanyam, A., 1996. Market microstructure and asset pricing: on the compensation for illiquidity in stock returns. Journal of Financial Economics 41, 441–64.

Brown, S.J., and Warner, J.B. 1980. Measuring security price performance. Journal of Financial Economics 8, 205–58.

Brown, S.J., Goetzmann, W.N., Ross, S.A., 1995. Survival. Journal of Finance 50, 853–73.

Christie, W.G., Harris J.H., Schultz, P.H., 1994. Why did NASDAQ market makers stop avoiding odd-eighth quotes? The Journal of Finance 49, 1841–60.

Christie, W.G., Huang, RD., 1990. Equity return dispersion: their behavior and relation to business conditions. Working paper, Owen Graduate School of Management, Vanderbilt University, TN.

Christie, W.G., Huang, R.D., 1994. Market structures and liquidity: a transactions data study of exchange listings. Journal of Financial Intermediation 3, 300–26.

Christie, W.G., Huang, R.D., 1995. Following the pied piper: do individual returns herd around the Market? Financial Analysts Journal, 31–7.

Christie, W.G., Schuttz, P.H., 1994. Why do NASDAQ market makers avoid odd-eighth quotes? The Journal of Finance 49, 1813–40.

Cohen, K.J., Maier, S.F., Schwartz, R.A., Whitcomb, D.K., 1986. The Microstructure of Securities Markets. Prentice-Hall, Englewood Cliffs, NJ.

Cooper, S.K., Groth, J.C., Avera, W.E., 1985. Liquidity, exchange listing and common stock performance. Journal of Economics and Business 37, 19–33.

Copeland, T.E., Mayers, D., 1982. The value line enigma. Journal of Financial Economics 10, 289–321.

Datar, V., Naik, N., Radcliffe, R., 1996. The role of trading activity in the cross-section of stock returns. Working paper, London Business School, London, England.

Dhillon, U., Johnson, H., 1991. Changes in the standard and poor's 500 list. Journal of Business 64, 75–85.

Edmeister, R.O., Pirie, W.L., 1995. Trading cost expectations: evidence from S&P 500 index replacement stock announcement. Working paper, University of Mississippi, MS.

Eleswarapu, V.R., 1995. Cost of transacting and expected returns in the NASDAQ market. Working paper, University of Auckland, New Zealand.

Grammatikos, T., Papaionnou, G.J., 1986. Market reaction to NYSE listings: tests of the marketability gains hypothesis. Journal of Financial Research 9, 215–28.

Harris, L., Gurel, E., 1986. Price and volume effects associated with changes in the S&P 500 list: new-evidence for the existence of price pressures. Journal of Finance 41, 815–29.

Haugen, R.A., Baker, N.L., 1996. Commonality in the determinants of expected stock returns. Journal of Financial Economics 41, 401–39.

Ho, T.S., Stoll, H.R., 1981. Optimal dealer pricing under transactions and return uncertainty. Journal of Financial Economics 9, 47–73.

Huang, R.D., Stoll, H.R., 1996. Dealer versus auction markets: a paired comparison of execution costs on NASDAQ and the NYSE. Journal of Financial Economics 41, 313–57.

Jones, J., Lehn, K., Mulherin, J.H., 1991. Institutional ownership of equity: effects on stock market liquidity and corporate long-term investment. In: Sametz, A.W. (Ed.), Institutional Investing. Business One Irwin, Homewood, IL, pp. 115–27.

Kadlec, G.B., McConnell, J.J., 1994. The effect of market segmentation and illiquidity on asset prices: evidence from exchange listings. Journal of Finance 49, 611–36.

Kamara, A., 1994. Liquidity, taxes, and short-term treasury yields. Journal of Financial and Quantitative Analysis 29, 403–16.

Karafiath, I., 1988. Using dummy variables in the event study methodology. Financial Review 23, 351–57.

Khan, V.A., Baker, H.K., 1993. Unlisted trading privileges, liquidity and stock returns. Journal of Financial Research 16, 221–36.

Lauterbach, B., Ungar, M., 1992. The effect of the transfer to the variable trading method on the return behavior and on trading volume. Working paper.

London Stock Exchange, 1996. New Electronic Trading Services. London, UK.

Lynch, A.W., Mendenhall, R.R., 1996. New evidence on stock price effects associated with changes in the S&P 500 index. Journal of Business, forthcoming.

Malatesta, P.H., 1986. Measuring abnormal performance: the event parameter approach using joint generalized least squares. Journal of Financial and Quantitative Analysis 21, 27–38.

Mendelson, H., 1982. Market behavior in a clearing house. Econometrica 50, 1505–24.

Mendelson, H., 1985. Random competitive exchange: price distributions and gains from trade. Journal of Economic Theory 37, 254–80.

Reuters, 1996. Reuters Canadian Financial Market Report, April 15.

Securities and Exchange Commission, 1996. Release No. 34-37619, RIN 3235-AG66, Order Execution Obligations – Final Rules, August 29.

Shleifer, A., 1986. Do demand curves for stocks slope downward? Journal of Finance 41, 579–90.

Silber, W. L., 1991. Discounts on restricted stock: the impact of illiquidity on stock prices. Financial Analysts Journal, 60–4.

Tamari, R., Resnik, I., 1990. The marketability of stocks before and after the transfer to the variable method (In Hebrew). This Month in the Bursa (May), 12–8.

Tel Aviv Stock Exchange, 1987. The trading in variable prices and in multilateral trading (an experiment in a new trading method).

Tel Aviv Stock Exchange, 1988. The trading in variable prices and in multilateral trading. (August).

Tel Aviv Stock Exchange, 1994. Marketability guide 35, 133–5.

Tel Aviv Stock Exchange, 1995. This Month in the Bursa 167.

Thompson, R., 1985. Conditioning the return-generating process on firm-specific events: a discussion of event study methods. Journal of Financial and Quantitative Analysis 20, 151–68.

White, H., 1980. Heteroskedasticity-consistent covariance matrix estimator and a direct test for heteroskedasticity. Econometrica 48, 817–38.

PART II

LIQUIDITY RISK

Introduction and Overview

The Global Financial Crisis of 2007–2009 was associated with severe liquidity shocks in global stock and bond markets. Figure PII.1 shows the variation in trading costs over time as estimated by Investment Technology Group (ITG). It shows that at the height of the recent financial crisis, in the fourth quarter of 2008 (just after Lehman collapsed), average trading costs shot way up reaching 1.5% for small-cap stocks. On the whole, trading costs almost tripled during this quarter, compared to their level in the quarter with the highest liquidity (lowest trading costs), and within the crisis quarter there were days with far higher trading costs. For some securities, such as convertible bonds, the rise in trading costs was significantly higher than depicted in Figure PII.1.

While the Global Financial Crisis of 2007–2009 vividly shows that market liquidity can suddenly deteriorate dramatically, the general point is that liquidity is not constant. Rather, liquidity changes over time for individual securities and for the market overall. Liquidity varies for a number of reasons. First, liquidity depends in part on the transparency of information about a security's value, which can change over time. Second, the number of liquidity providers and their access to capital is an important determinant of liquidity as argued by Brunnermeier and Pedersen (2009; Chapter 6 in this book). When liquidity providers (such as banks, market makers, trading firms, and hedge funds) lose capital and their access to securitized funding is constrained – as happened in 2008 – then they provide less liquidity. As a result, market liquidity drops simultaneously for most securities. Third, increased uncertainty makes the provision of liquidity riskier and increases the reward that liquidity providers demand, that is, the cost of trading increases. Amihud and Mendelson (1980) show that when the long and short positions that market makers can assume become constrained, the bid–ask spread that they charge increases.

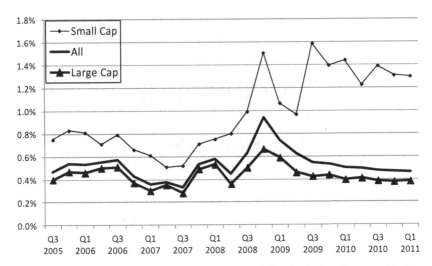

Figure PII.1. Trading costs in the United States as a fraction of stock prices (in %). Shown are the average costs for large-capitalization and small-capitalization (less liquid) stocks, as well as for all stocks. Based on data from Investment Technology Group (ITG).

Liquidity can suddenly dry up because of the *liquidity externality*. The willingness to trade on one side of the market facilitates trading for investors on the other side of the market, whereas avoiding trading by some investors reduces market liquidity for others and exacerbates the liquidity shortfall in the market.[1] This negative external effect is ignored by any individual investor, but it adds up, affecting the liquidity of the entire market. Conversely, when more investors wish to engage in trading, they provide liquidity to each other and draw more traders into the market, augmenting the rise in market liquidity. The withdrawal of investors from the market can thus create, at least temporarily, a downward spiral that leads to deterioration in liquidity, consequently affecting asset prices.

Liquidity shocks represent *changes* in overall market liquidity relative to expectations. If these changes are persistent, the new level of liquidity will affect aggregate asset prices. For example, if the market liquidity deteriorates and trading costs rise, these costs are expected to stay higher for a while and, as a result, stock prices fall. This is because forward-looking investors demand higher expected returns on traded securities to compensate for higher trading costs. That is, investors discount future corporate cash flows

[1] Mendelson (1985) provides a formal analysis of the liquidity externality.

at higher rates, and this leads to lower stock prices, holding everything else equal. Similarly, if the liquidity of bonds declines while their cash flows (principal and coupon) are unaffected, the required yield to maturity will rise and bond prices will consequently fall. This insight is proposed by Amihud (2002; Chapter 4 in this book) and modeled by Acharya and Pedersen (2005; Chapter 5 in this book).

Market-wide liquidity shocks thus generate shocks to asset prices and contribute to uncertainty about asset returns. Hence, these market liquidity shocks are a source of systematic risk that should be priced by risk-averse investors. The transmission of market-wide liquidity shocks to price shocks differs across securities. In fact, securities differ in the relation (or covariance) between returns and liquidity shocks. Risk-averse investors would then require higher expected returns for securities whose returns have greater covariance with market-wide liquidity shocks. Pastor and Stambaugh (2003) and Acharya and Pedersen (2005) provide empirical support for the idea that exposure to liquidity shocks is priced.

By the classic capital asset pricing model (CAPM), well-diversified, risk-averse investors price securities' systematic risk, or the securities' *beta*, which measures the exposure of a security return to the market-wide return. In a world with trading costs, there is an additional source of systematic risk resulting from the covariance of both the security trading costs with shocks in market-wide trading costs, and of trading costs with market return. These covariances constitute components of liquidity-related systematic risk for which investors want to be compensated by higher expected returns. The chapter by Acharya and Pedersen provides a unified, CAPM-based theory of liquidity risk and shows how it affects stock prices. Their analysis demonstrates, both theoretically and empirically, that systematic liquidity risk is priced.

In the Acharya–Pedersen liquidity-adjusted CAPM, the effect of *liquidity risk* on asset prices augments the effect of the *level of liquidity* on asset prices. To understand the liquidity-adjusted CAPM, consider two assets with the same cash flows and *average* liquidity, but one asset has much more liquidity risk, in the sense that its transaction costs rise sharply and its price declines more during liquidity crises. If these assets had the same price, investors would avoid the one with high liquidity risk, because they would fear bearing greater losses if they needed to sell it in a liquidity crisis – when being able to sell is especially important and difficult. Therefore, the price of the asset with greater liquidity risk must drop to a level that compensates investors for the extra liquidity risk.

For stocks and bonds, evidence shows that there is a close connection between the average level of liquidity and the liquidity risk: For example, small-cap stocks and low-grade bonds both have lower average levels of liquidity and higher exposure to market-wide liquidity shocks. For these reasons, liquidity constitutes an important part in their pricing.

CHAPTER 4

Illiquidity and Stock Returns: Cross-Section and Time-Series Effects

Summary and Implications

This article analyzes the effects over time of illiquidity *shocks* on stock prices or returns. The building blocks of the analysis are the following: (i) The expected stock return for period $t + 1$ is an increasing function of expected illiquidity for $t + 1$, given the information in period t. This follows from the theory of Amihud and Mendelson (1986; Chapter 1 in this book) on the positive relation between expected stock returns and expected stock illiquidity. (ii) Illiquidity is highly persistent. Therefore, an unexpected rise in current illiquidity means that illiquidity is likely to be high in the following period.

Consquently, an unexpected rise in illiquidity induces a fall in stock prices so that the expected return rises as required by investors facing the prospect of higher future illiquidity.[1] This produces a negative contemporaneous relation between illiquidity shocks and realized stock returns.

Testing this theory requires time series of stock market illiquidity, which are difficult to obtain over a long period of time. Therefore, the study uses daily data on stock prices and trading volume to develop a measure of illiquidity of a stock (or any security) for a given period,

$$ILLIQ = \text{average of daily } \frac{|R|}{VOLD},$$

where R is the stock return and $VOLD$ is volume in dollars (the product of the number of shares traded by the price). The intuition is that a stock is less liquid if a given trading volume generates a greater move in its price. Thus,

---

[1] This assumes that stock market liquidity shocks do not have a meaningful effect on corporate future cash flows. Some more detailed conditions apply. See Proposition 4 of Section 2.4 in Acharya and Pedersen (2005).

ILLIQ may be viewed as a coarse measure of the λ coefficient of Kyle (1985), whose estimation necessitates intraday data on quotes and trades (see the review in the introduction to Amihud and Mendelson, 1986). *ILLIQ* requires only daily data on prices and trading volume. Indeed, *ILLIQ* is found by Hasbrouck (2009) to be highly correlated with Kyle's (1985) λ, as well as with other measures of illiquidity, such as the bid–ask spread. In general, *ILLIQ* can be viewed as a measure of market impact.

The individual stock *ILLIQ* affects the cross section of stock return, consistent with the theory and evidence of Amihud and Mendelson (1986). The estimation is done for stocks traded on the NYSE over the years 1963–1997. Stocks with higher *ILLIQ*, measured over one year, have higher return in the following year, after controlling for the stock systematic risk, the stock total risk, capitalization, dividend yield, and past returns. The positive effect of *ILLIQ* on stock returns is higher in the month of January, but it is also present (and it is highly significant) in the non-January months. The effect of *ILLIQ* on stock return is also consistently positive and significant in the earlier and later half of the sample period.

A time series of market illiquidity is constructed by averaging all individual stock *ILLIQ* values for each month across stocks. This produces *AILLIQ*, the market monthly illiquidity measure for NYSE stocks during the period 1962–1997. From this series, a series of unexpected liquidity shocks, $AILLIQ_t^U$, is constructed as the (adjusted) residuals from an autoregressive model of $AILLIQ_t$. Finally, the relationship between stock return and illiquidity shocks as well as expected illiquidity is estimated by a regression of the stock return (in excess of the risk-free rate) in period t on the contemporaneous unexpected illiquidity shocks, $AILLIQ_t^U$, and on lagged illiquidity, $AILLIQ_{t-1}$, which is a proxy for expected illiquidity for period t. A rise in current illiquidity (a positive $AILLIQ_t^U$) and, consequently, in expected illiquidity should cause a subsequent rise in expected return, and therefore current stock prices must fall. This implies a negative coefficient of $AILLIQ_t^U$, that is, a negative return-illiquidity shock relation, while the coefficient of lagged illiquidity is positive.

The estimation results are consistent with these predictions. The analysis employs ten portfolios of stocks aggregated by their market capitalization, which is a proxy for their liquidity. The results show that illiquidity shocks have a significant negative effect on stock returns for all ten stock portfolios. The effect is stronger – the coefficient of $AILLIQ_t^U$ is more negative – for the least liquid stocks, those with low market capitalization. For the largest-capitalization stocks, which are the most liquid, the negative effect of illiquidity shocks is the weakest. The weaker effect on large liquid stocks may reflect "flight to liquidity": Liquid stocks become more attractive when liquidity worsens, which mitigates the negative effects of increases in expected illiquidity for these stocks. In summary, less liquid stocks are more sensitive or have greater exposure to marketwide illiquidity shocks, that is, they have greater liquidity risk than larger and more liquid stocks.

Bekaert, Harvey, and Lundblad (2007) test the return–illiquidity shocks relation for 19 emerging markets and the United States (which proxies for the world index). These authors also find that this relation is negative. The market illiquidity measure in this study is the average over all stocks of the relative number of zero-return days in each stock. The study further finds that the return–illiquidity shocks relation is stronger in markets that are less open to foreign investors.

The negative relation between stock return and illiquidity shocks is shown to vary over time. Watanabe and Watanabe (2008) employ a regime-switching model where the regime is based on a detrended aggregate share turnover. They find that illiquidity shocks affect returns more negatively in periods that are characterized by heavy trading and high volatility, and it is in these periods that the liquidity premium is higher.[2] This is consistent with theory (Brunnermeier and Pedersen 2009; Chapter 6 in this book) that the return–illiquidity relation, and consequently the price of illiquidity, varies over time, being higher in times of economic and financial distress. Whereas in 'good times' investors do not heed illiquidity, they do so in times of macroeconomic and financial stress. This was evident during the crisis that began in 2007 and culminated at the fourth quarter of 2008 and the first quarter of 2009, at which time stock market illiquidity was the highest. As presented by Brunnermeier and Pedersen (2009), a decline in the capital available to traders and dealers – that is, lower funding liquidity – causes lower securities market liquidity.[3] Further, when traders have less capital, they are closer to their capital constraints, liquidity provision to the

[2] For analysis of investment and pricing in the context of switch regimes, see Geyer and Ziemba (2008) who study investment strategies in a scenario with three regimes: 'extreme' (or 'crash') periods, 'highly volatile' periods and 'normal' periods, differentiated by stock return volatility.

[3] See also Acharya and Viswanathan (2011) who model the phenomenon that capital is withdrawn from the market because it is realized that the decline in securities values induces moral hazard behavior by levered money managers, who act as the investors' agents. This leads to reduction in overall market liquidity following sharp market price declines.

market declines, and then additional shocks have larger effects on prices. Consistent with this theory, the evidence shows that in times of financial stress, market liquidity shocks are most pronounced in terms of their effect on asset prices.

The negative return-illiquidity shocks relation is also present in corporate bonds. DeJong and Driessen (2007) estimate the effect of shocks in stocks and bonds liquidity on returns of corporate bonds, controlling for the market return. Illiquidity on stocks is estimated by *ILLIQ*, and illiquidity on bonds is measured by the bid–ask spread on Government bonds. The corporate bonds are aggregated into portfolios by credit rating and by maturity. The authors find that bond returns respond negatively to shocks in both these illiquidity measures. The return-illiquidity shocks relation is more negative for longer-maturity bonds and for bonds with lower rating (higher default risk).

However, the extent of the impact of liquidity shocks on bond prices is conditional on the state of the economy. Employing a regime-switching model, Acharya, Amihud, and Bharath (2010) find that in periods of economic and financial stress, an unexpected rise in illiquidity of bonds and stocks strongly lowers the prices of junk bonds while prices of the more liquid investment-grade bonds rise, all relative to the change in overall bond market prices, which react negatively to illiquidity shocks. This is because in times of economic stress, liquidity becomes more valuable and there is flight to liquidity. In benign economic times, there is a much smaller difference between the impacts of illiquidity shocks on the two classes of bonds. A similar pattern is observed for portfolios of stocks differentiated by their book-to-market ratio, which indicates solvency and profitability. In times of economic stress, an unexpected increase in stock market illiquidity causes greater price decline for high book-to-market stocks compared to low book-to-market stocks, whereas there is no such difference in price reaction to illiquidity shocks in time of normal economic conditions. These results are consistent with the model of Brunnermeier and Pedersen (2009) on the changing value of liquidity over time.

Kessler and Scherer (2011) study the exposure to liquidity shocks of returns on nine hedge fund indices that cover various strategies and categories between 2003–2009. The liquidity factor combines six liquidity measures of equities, government bonds, corporate bonds, foreign exchange and commodities. The authors find that for all nine hedge fund indexes, illiquidity shocks have significant negative impact on hedge fund returns. This effect prevails after controlling for the potential effects of eleven risk factors. For the majority of hedge fund indices, the liquidity effect explains the losses that they endured during the month of September 2008, when Lehman collapsed. Given that liquidity risk is priced, as shown by Acharya and Pedersen (2005), these results support the proposition that part of hedge fund excess return is in fact liquidity risk premium. This issue is discussed in Part III.

Illiquidity and Stock Returns
Cross-Section and Time-Series Effects*

Yakov Amihud

Journal of Financial Markets 5, 2002

1. Introduction

The hypothesis on the relationship between stock return and stock liquidity is that return increases in illiquidity, as proposed by Amihud and Mendelson (1986). The positive return–illiquidity relationship has been examined across stocks in a number of studies. This study examines this relationship over time. It proposes that *over time, the ex ante stock excess return is increasing in the expected illiquidity of the stock market.*

The illiquidity measure employed here, called *ILLIQ*, is the daily ratio of absolute stock return to its dollar volume, averaged over some period. It can be interpreted as the daily price response associated with one dollar of trading volume, thus serving as a rough measure of price impact. There are finer and better measures of illiquidity, such as the bid–ask spread (quoted or effective), transaction-by-transaction market impact, or the probability of information-based trading. These measures, however, require a lot of microstructure data that are not available in many stock markets. And, even when available, the data do not cover very long periods of time. The measure used here enables to construct long time series of illiquidity that are necessary to test the effects over time of illiquidity on ex ante and contemporaneous stock excess return. This would be very hard to do with the finer microstructure measures of illiquidity.

The results show that both across stocks and over time, expected stock returns are an increasing function of expected illiquidity. Across NYSE stocks during 1964–1997, *ILLIQ* has a positive and highly significant effect on expected return. The new tests here are on the effects over time of

---

* I thank Haim Mendelson for valuable suggestions and Viral Acharya for competent research assistance and comments. Helpful comments were received from Michael Brennan, Martin Gruber, Richard Roll, two anonymous referees, and Avanidhar Subrahmanyam (the editor).

market illiquidity on market excess return (stock return in excess of the Treasury bill rate). Stock excess return, traditionally called "risk premium", has been considered a compensation for risk. This paper proposes that *expected stock excess return also reflects compensation for expected market illiquidity*, and is thus an increasing function of *expected* market illiquidity. The results are consistent with this hypothesis. In addition, *unexpected* market illiquidity lowers contemporaneous stock prices. This is because higher realized illiquidity raises expected illiquidity that in turn raises stock expected returns and lowers stock prices (assuming no relation between corporate cash flows and market liquidity). This hypothesis too is supported by the results. These illiquidity effects are shown to be stronger for small firms' stocks. This suggests that variations over time in the "size effect" – the excess return on small firms' stocks – are related to changes in market liquidity over time.

The paper proceeds as follows. Section 2 introduces the illiquidity measure used in this study and employs it in cross-section estimates of expected stock returns as a function of stock illiquidity and other variables. Section 3 presents the time-series tests of the effect of the same measure of illiquidity on ex ante stock excess returns. The section includes tests of the effect of expected and unexpected illiquidity, the effects of these variables for different firm-size portfolios and the effects of expected illiquidity together with the effects of other variables – bonds' term and default yield premiums – that predict stock returns. Section 4 offers concluding remarks.

2. Cross-Section Relationship Between Illiquidity and Stock Return

2.1. Measures of Illiquidity

Liquidity is an elusive concept. It is not observed directly but rather has a number of aspects that cannot be captured in a single measure.[1] Illiquidity reflects the impact of order flow on price – the discount that a seller concedes or the premium that a buyer pays when executing a market order – that results from adverse selection costs and inventory costs (Amihud and Mendelson, 1980; Glosten and Milgrom, 1985). For standard-size transactions, the price impact is the bid–ask spread, whereas larger excess demand induces a greater impact on prices (Kraus and Stoll, 1972; Keim and Madhavan, 1996), reflecting a likely action of informed traders (see Easley

---

[1] See discussion in Amihud and Mendelson (1991b).

and O'Hara, 1987). Kyle (1985) proposed that because market makers cannot distinguish between order flow that is generated by informed traders and by liquidity (noise) traders, they set prices that are an increasing function of the imbalance in the order flow which may indicate informed trading. This creates a positive relationship between the order flow or transaction volume and price change, commonly called the price impact.

These measures of illiquidity are employed in studies that examine the cross-section effect of illiquidity on expected stock returns. Amihud and Mendelson (1986) and Eleswarapu (1997) found a significant positive effect of quoted bid–ask spreads on stock returns (risk-adjusted).[2] Chalmers and Kadlec (1998) used the amortized effective spread as a measure of liquidity, obtained from quotes and subsequent transactions, and found that it positively affects stock returns.[3] Brennan and Subrahmanyam (1996) measured stock illiquidity by price impact, measured as the price response to signed order flow (order size), and by the fixed cost of trading, using intra-day continuous data on transactions and quotes.[4] They found that these measures of illiquidity positively affect stock returns. Easley et al. (1999) introduced a new measure of microstructure risk, the probability of information-based trading, that reflects the adverse selection cost resulting from asymmetric information between traders, as well as the risk that the stock price can deviate from its full-information value. This measure is estimated from intra-daily transaction data. They found that across stocks, the probability of information-based trading has a large positive and significant effect on stock returns.

These fine measures of illiquidity require for their calculation microstructure data on transactions and quotes that are unavailable in most markets around the world for long time periods of time. In contrast, the illiquidity measure used in this study is calculated from daily data on returns and volume that are readily available over long periods of time for most markets.

---

[2] Amihud and Mendelson (1986) study is on NYSE/AMEX stocks, 1961–1980, and Eleswarapu's (1997) study is on Nasdaq stocks, 1974–1990. Bond yields are also found to be increasing in the bid–ask spread, after controlling for maturity and risk. See Amihud and Mendelson (1991a) and Kamara (1994).

[3] The effective spread is the absolute difference between the mid-point of the quoted bid–ask spread and the transaction price that follows, classified as being a buy or sell transaction. The spread is divided by the stock's holding period, obtained from the turnover rate on the stock, to obtain the amortized spread.

[4] This measure, based on Kyle's (1985) model, is estimated by the methods proposed by Glosten and Harris (1988) and Hasbrouck (1991). Basically, it is the slope coefficient in a regression of transaction-by-transaction price changes on the signed order size, where orders are classified into "buy" or "sell" by the proximity of the transaction price to the preceding bid and ask quotes. Adjustments are made for prior information (on price changes and order size) and fixed order placement costs.

Therefore, while it is more coarse and less accurate, it is readily available for the study of the time series effects of liquidity.

Stock illiquidity is defined here as the average ratio of the daily absolute return to the (dollar) trading volume on that day, $|R_{iyd}|/VOLD_{iyd}$. R_{iyd} is the return on stock i on day d of year y and $VOLD_{iyd}$ is the respective daily volume in dollars. This ratio gives the absolute (percentage) price change per dollar of daily trading volume, or the daily price impact of the order flow. This follows Kyle's concept of illiquidity – the response of price to order flow – and Silber's (1975) measure of thinness, defined as the ratio of absolute price change to absolute excess demand for trading.

The cross-sectional study employs for each stock i the annual average

$$ILLIQ_{iy} = 1/D_{iy} \sum_{i=1}^{Diy} |R_{iyd}|/VOLD_{ivyd}, \tag{1}$$

where D_{iy} is the number of days for which data are available for stock i in year y. This illiquidity measure is strongly related to the liquidity ratio known as the Amivest measure, the ratio of the sum of the daily volume to the sum of the absolute return (e.g., Cooper et al., 1985; Khan and Baker, 1993). Amihud et al. (1997) and Berkman and Eleswarapu (1998) used the liquidity ratio to study the effect of changes in liquidity on the values of stocks that were subject to changes in their trading methods. The liquidity ratio, however, does not have the intuitive interpretation of measuring the average daily association between a unit of volume and the price change, as does $ILLIQ$.[5]

$ILLIQ$ should be positively related to variables that measure illiquidity from microstructure data. Brennan and Subrahmanyam (1996) used two measures of illiquidity, obtained from data on inraday transactions and quotes: Kyle's (1985) λ, the price impact measure, and ψ, the fixed-cost component related to the bid–ask spread. The estimates are done by the method of Glosten and Harris (1988). Using estimates[6] of these variables for 1984, the following cross-sectional regression was estimated:

$$ILLIQ_i = -292 + 247.9\lambda_i + 49.2\psi_i$$
$$(t =) \quad (12.25) \quad (13.78) \quad (17.33) \quad R^2 = 0.30.$$

[5] Another interpretation of $ILLIQ$ is related to disagreement between traders about new information, following Harris and Raviv (1993). When investors agree about the implication of news, the stock price changes without trading while disagreement induces increase in trading volume. Thus, $ILLIQ$ can also be interpreted as a measure of consensus belief among investors about new information.

[6] I thank M. Bennan and Avanidhar Subrahmnaym for kindly providing these estimates. The estimated variables are multiplied here by 10^3. Outliers at the upper and lower 1% tails of these variables and of $ILLIQ$ are discarded (see Brennan and Subrahmanyam, 1996).

These results show that *ILLIQ* is positively and strongly related to micro-structure estimates of illiquidity.

Size, or the market value of the stock, is also related to liquidity since a larger stock issue has smaller price impact for a given order flow and a smaller bid–ask spread. Stock expected returns are negatively related to size (Banz, 1981; Reinganum, 1981; Fama and French, 1992), which is consistent with it being a proxy for liquidity (Amihud and Mendelson, 1986).[7] The negative return-size relationship may also result from the size variable being related to a function of the reciprocal of expected return (Berk, 1995).

There are other measures of liquidity that use data on volume. Brennan et al. (1998) found that the stock (dollar) volume has a significant negative effect on the cross-section of stock returns and it subsumes the negative effect of size. Another related measure is turnover, the ratio of trading volume to the number of shares outstanding. By Amihud and Mendelson (1986), turnover is negatively related to illiquidity costs, and Atkins and Dyl (1997) found a strong positive relationship across stocks between the bid–ask spread and the reciprocal of the turnover ratio that measures holding period. A number of studies find that cross-sectionally, stock returns are decreasing in stock turnover, which is consistent with a negative relationship between liquidity and expected return (Haugen and Baker, 1996; Datar et al., 1998; Hu, 1997a; Rouwenhorst, 1998; Chordia et al., 2001).

These measures of liquidity as well as the illiquidity measure presented in this study can be regarded as empirical proxies that measure different aspects of illiquidity. It is doubtful that there is one single measure that captures all its aspects.

2.2. Empirical Methodology

The effect of illiquidity on stock return is examined for stocks traded in the New York Stock Exchange (NYSE) in the years 1963–1997, using data from daily and monthly databases of CRSP (Center for Research of Securities Prices of the University of Chicago). Tests are confined to NYSE-traded stocks to avoid the effects of differences in market microstructures.[8] The

---

[7] Barry and Brown (1984) propose that the higher return on small firms' stock is compensation for less information available on small firms that have been listed for a shorter period of time. This is consistent with the illiquidity explanation of the small firm effect since illiquidity costs are increasing in the asymmetry of information between traders (see Glosten and Milgrom, 1985; Kyle, 1985).

[8] See Reinganum (1990) on the effects of the differences in microstructure between the NASDAQ and the NYSE on stock returns, after adjusting for size and risk. In addition, volume figures on the NASDAQ have a different meaning than those on the NYSE, because

test procedure follows the usual Fama and MacBeth (1973) method. A cross-section model is estimated for each month $m = 1, 2, \ldots, 12$ in year y, $y =$ 1964, 1965, $\ldots$, 1997 (a total of 408 months), where monthly stock returns are a function of stock characteristics:

$$R_{imy} = k_{omy} + \sum_{j=1}^{J} k_{jmy} X_{ji,y-1} + U_{imy}. \tag{2}$$

R_{imy} is the return on stock i in month m of year y, with returns being adjusted for stock delistings to avoid survivorship bias, following Shumway (1997).[9] $X_{ji,y-1}$ is characteristic j of stock i, estimated from data in year $y - 1$ and known to investors at the beginning of year y, during which they make their investment decisions. The coefficients k_{jmy} measure the effects of stock characteristics on expected return, and U_{imy} are the residuals. The monthly regressions of model (2) over the period 1964–1997 produce 408 estimates of each coefficient k_{jmy}, $j = 0, 1, 2, \ldots, J$. These monthly estimates are averaged and tests of statistical significance are performed.

Stocks are admitted to the cross-sectional estimation procedure in month m of year y if they have a return for that month and they satisfy the following criteria:

(i) The stock has return and volume data for more than 200 days during year $y - 1$. This makes the estimated parameters more reliable. Also, the stock must be listed at the end of year $y - 1$.

(ii) The stock price is greater than \$5 at the end of year $y - 1$. Returns on low-price stocks are greatly affected by the minimum tick of \$1/8, which adds noise to the estimations.[10]

(iii) The stock has data on market capitalization at the end of year $y - 1$ in the CRSP database. This excludes derivative securities like ADRs of foreign stocks and scores and primes.

---

trading on the NASDAQ is done almost entirely through market makers, whereas on the NYSE most trading is done directly between buying and selling investors. This results in artificially higher volume figures on NASDAQ.

[9] Specifically, the last return used is either the last return available on CRSP, or the delisting return, if available. Naturally, a last return for the stock of – 100% is included in the study. A return of −30% is assigned if the deletion reason is coded by 500 (reason unavailable), 520 (went to OTC), 551–573 and 580 (various reasons), 574 (bankruptcy) and 584 (does not meet exchange financial guidelines). Shumway (1997) obtains that −30% is the average delisting return, examining the OTC returns of delisted stocks.

[10] See discussion on the minimum tick and its effects in Harris (1994). The benchmark of \$5 was used in 1992 by the NYSE when it reduced the minimum tick. Also, the conventional term of "penny stocks" applies to stocks whose price is below \$5.

(iv) Outliers are eliminated – stocks whose estimated $ILLIQ_{iy}$ in year $y - 1$ is at the highest or lowest 1% tails of the distribution (after satisfying criteria (i)–(iii)).

There are between 1061 and 2291 stocks that satisfy these four conditions and are included in the cross-section estimations.

2.3. Stock Characteristics

2.3.1. Liquidity Variables

The measure of liquidity is $ILLIQ_{iy}$ that is calculated for each stock i in year y from daily data as in (1) above (multiplied by 10^6). The average market illiquidity across stocks in each year is calculated as

$$AILLIQ_y = 1/N_y \sum_{t=1}^{N_y} ILLIQ_{iy}, \tag{3}$$

where N_y is the number of stocks in year y. (The stocks that are used to calculate the average illiquidity are those that satisfy conditions (i)–(iv) above.) Since average illiquidity varies considerably over the years, $ILLIQ_{iy}$ is replaced in the estimation of the cross-section model (2) by its mean-adjusted value

$$ILLIQMA_{iy} = ILLIQ_{iy}/AILLIQ_y. \tag{4}$$

The cross-sectional model (2) also includes $SIZE_{jy}$, the market value of stock i at the end of year y, as given by CRSP. As discussed above, $SIZE$ may also be a proxy for liquidity. Table 4.1 presents estimated statistics $ILLIQ$ and $SIZE$. In each year, the annual mean, standard deviation across stocks and skewness are calculated for stocks admitted to the sample, and then these annual statistics are averaged over the 34 years. The correlations between the variables are calculated in each year across stocks and then the yearly correlation coefficients are averaged over the years. As expected, $ILLIQ_{iy}$ is negatively correlated with size: $Corr(ILLIQ_{iy}, \ln SIZE_{iy}) = -0.614$.

2.3.2. Risk Variables

Model (2) includes $BETA_{iy}$ as a measure of risk, calculated as follows. At the end of each year y, stocks are ranked by their size (capitalization) and divided into ten equal portfolios. (Size serves here as an instrument.) Next, the portfolio return R_{pty} is calculated as the equally-weighted average of

Table 4.1. *Statistics on variables*

The illiquidity measure, $ILLIQ_{iy}$, is the average for year y of the daily ratio of absolute return to the dollar volume of stock i in year y. $SIZE_{iy}$ is the market capitalization of the stock at the end of the year given by CRSP, $DIVYLD_{iy}$, the dividend yield, is the sum of the annual cash dividend divided by the end-of-year price, $SDRET_{iy}$ is the standard deviation of the stock daily return. Stocks admitted in each year y have more than 200 days of data for the calculation of the characteristics and their end-of-year price exceeds $5. Excluded are stocks whose $ILLIQ_{iy}$ is at the extreme 1% upper and lower tails of the distribution.

Each variable is calculated for each stock in each year across stocks admitted to the sample in that year, and then the mean, standard deviation and skewness are calculated across stocks in each year. The table presents the means over the 34 years of the annual means, standard deviations and skewness and the medians of the annual means, as well as the maximum and minimum annual means. Data include NYSE stocks, 1963–1996.

Variable	Mean of annual means	Mean of annual S.D.	Median of annual means	Mean of annual skewness	Min. annual mean	Max. annual mean
ILLIQ	0.337	0.512	0.308	3.095	0.056	0.967
SIZE ($ miliion)	792.6	1,611.5	538.3	5.417	263.1	2,195.2
DIVYLD (%)	4.14	5.48	4.16	5.385	2.43	6.68
SDRET	2.08	0.75	2.07	1.026	1.58	2.83

stock returns in portfolio p on day t in year y. Then, the market model is estimated for each portfolio p, $p - 1, 2, \ldots, 10$,

$$R_{pty} = a_{py} + BETA_{py} \cdot RM_{ty} + e_{pty}. \tag{5}$$

RM_{iy} is the equally-weighted market return and $BETA_{py}$ is the slope co-efficient, estimated by the Scholes and Williams (1977) method. The beta assigned to stock i, $BETA_{iy}$, is $BETA_{py}$ of the portfolio in which stock i is included. Fama and French (1992), who used similar methodology, suggested that the precision of the estimated portfolio beta more than makes up for the fact that not all stocks in the size portfolio have the same beta.[11]

The stock total risk is $SDRET_{iy}$, the standard deviation of the daily return on stock i in year y (multiplied by 10^2). By the asset pricing models of Levy (1978) and Merton (1987), $SDRET$ is priced since investors' portfolios

---

[11] The models were re-estimated using betas of individual stocks in lieu of betas of size portfolios. These betas have an insignificant effect in the cross-section regressions. The results on *ILLIQ* remained the same. Also, omitting *BETA* altogether from the cross-section regression has very little effect on the results.

are constrained and therefore not well diversified. However, the tax trading option (due to Constantinides and Scholes, 1980) suggests that stocks with higher volatility should have lower expected return. Also, $SDRET_{iy}$ is included in the model since $ILLIQ_{iy}$ may be construed as a measure of the stock's risk, given that its numerator is the absolute return (which is related to $SDRET_{iy}$), although the correlation between $ILLIQ$ and $SDRET$ is low, 0.278. Theoretically, risk and illiquidity are positively related. Stoll (1978) proposed that the stock illiquidity is positively related to the stock's risk since the bid–ask spread set by a risk-averse market maker is increasing in the stock's risk. Copeland and Galai (1983) modeled the bid–ask spread as a pair of options offered by the market maker, thus it increases with volatility. Constantinides (1986) proposed that the stock variance positively affects the return that investors require on the stock, since it imposes higher trading costs on them due to the need to engage more frequently in portfolio rebalancing.

2.3.3. Additional Variables

The cross-sectional model (2) includes the dividend yield for stock i in year y, $DIVYLD_{iy}$, calculated as the sum of the dividends during year y divided by the end-of-year price (following Brennan et al., 1998). $DIVYLD$ should have a positive effect on stock return if investors require to be compensated for the higher tax rate on dividends compared to the tax on capital gains. However, $DIVYLD$ may have a negative effect on return across stocks if it is negatively correlated with an unobserved risk factor, that is, stocks with higher dividend are less risky. The coefficient of $DIVYLD$ may also be negative following Redding's (1997) suggestion that large investors prefer companies with high liquidity and also prefer receiving dividends.[12]

Finally, past stock returns were shown to affect their expected returns (see Brennan et al., 1998). Therefore, the cross-sectional model (2) includes two variables: $R100_{iy}$, the return on stock i during the last 100 days of year y, and $R100YR_{iy}$, the return on stock i over the rest of the period, between the beginning of the year and 100 days before its end.

The model does not include the ratio of book-to-market equity, BE/ME, which was used by Fama and French (1992) in cross-section asset pricing estimation. This study employs only NYSE stocks for which BE/ME was found to have no significant effect (Easley et al., 1999; Loughran,

---

[12] Higher dividend yield may be perceived by investors to provide greater liquidity (ignoring tax consequences). This is analogous to the findings of Amihud and Mendelson (1991a) that Treasury notes with higher coupon provide lower yield to maturity.

1997).[13] Also, Berk (1995) suggested that an estimated relation between expected return and BE/ME is obtained due to the functional relation between expected return and the market value of equity.

2.4. Cross-Section Estimation Results

In the cross-sectional model (2), stock returns in each month of the year are regressed on stock characteristics that are estimated from data in the previous year (following the Fama and MacBeth (1973) method). The model is estimated for 408 months (34 years), generating 408 sets of coefficients k_{jmy}, $m = 1, 2, \ldots, 12$, and $y = 1964, 1965, \ldots, 1997$. The mean and standard error of the 408 estimated coefficients k_{jmy} are calculated for each stock characteristic j, followed by a t-test of the null hypothesis of zero mean. Tests are also performed for the means that exclude the January coefficients since by some studies, excluding January makes the effects of beta, size, and the bid–ask spread insignificant (e.g., Keim, 1983; Tinic and West, 1986; Eleswarapu and Reinganum, 1993). Finally, to examine the stability over time of the effects of the stock characteristics, tests are done separately for two equal subperiods of 204 months (17 years) each.

The results, presented in Table 4.2, strongly support the hypothesis that illiquidity is priced, consistent with similar results in earlier studies. The coefficient of $ILLIQMA_{iy}$, denoted $K_{ILLIQmy}$, has a mean of 0.162 that is statistically significant ($t = 6.55$) and its median is 0.135, close to the mean. Of the estimated coefficients, 63.4% (259 of the 408) are positive, a proportion that is significantly different from $1/2$ (the chance proportion). The serial correlation of the series $k_{ILLIQmy}$ is quite negligible (0.08).

The illiquidity effect remains positive and highly significant when January is excluded: the mean of $k_{ILLIQmy}$ is 0.126 with $t = 5.30$. The illiquidity effect is positive and significant in each of the two subperiods of 17 years.

The effect of *BETA* is positive, as expected, and significant (the statistical significance is lower when January is excluded). However, it becomes insignificant when *SIZE* is included in the model, since beta is calculated for size-based portfolios. Past returns – *R100* and *R100 YR* – both have positive and significant coefficients.

Table 4.2 also presents estimation results of a model that includes additional variables. The coefficient of *ILLIQMA* remains positive and significant for the entire period, for the non-January months and for each of the two

---

[13] Loughran (1997) finds that when the month of January is excluded, the effect of BE/ME becomes insignificant.

Table 4.2. *Cross-section regressions of stock return on illiquidity and other stock characteristics*[a]

The table presents the means of the coefficients from the monthly cross-sectional regression of stock return on the respective variables. In each month of year y, $y = 1964, 1965, \ldots, 1997$, stock returns are regressed cross-sectionally on stock characteristics that are calculated from data in year $y - 1$. *BETA* is the slope coefficient from an annual time-series regression of daily return on one of 10 size portfolios on the market return (equally weighted), using the Scholes and Williams (1977) method. The stock's *BETA* is the beta of the size portfolio to which it belongs. The illiquidity measure *ILLIQ* is the average over the year of the daily ratio of the stock's absolute return to its dollar trading volume. *ILLIQ* is averaged every year across stocks, and *ILLIQMA* is the respective mean-adjusted variables, calculated as the ratio of the variable to its annual mean across stocks (thus the means of all years are 1). In *SIZE* is the logarithm of the market capitalization of the stock at the end of the year, *SDRET* is the standard deviation of the stock daily return during the year, and *DIVYLD* is the dividend yield, the sum of the annual cash dividend divided by the end-of-year price. *R100* is the stock return over the last 100 days and *R100YR* is the return during the period between the beginning of the year and 100 days before its end.

The data include 408 months over 34 years, 1964–1997, (the stock characteristics are calculated for the years 1963–1996). Stocks admitted have more than 200 days of data for the calculation of the characteristics in year $y - 1$ and their end-of-year price exceeds $5. Excluded are stocks whose *ILLIQ* is at the extreme 1% upper and lower tails of the respective distribution for the year.

Variable	All months	Excl. January	1964–1980	1981–1997	All months	Excl. January	1964–1980	1981–1997
Constant	−0.364	−0.235	−0.904	0.177	1.922	1.568	2.074	1.770
	(0.76)	(0.50)	(1.39)	(0.25)	(4.06)	(3.32)	(2.63)	(3.35)
BETA	1.183	0.816	1.450	0.917	0.217	0.260	0.297	0.137
	(2.45)	(1.75)	(1.83)	(1.66)	(0.64)	(0.79)	(0.59)	(0.30)
ILLIQMA	0.162	0.126	0.216	0.108	0.112	0.103	0.135	0.088
	(6.55)	(5.30)	(4.87)	(5.05)	(5.39)	(4.91)	(3.69)	(4.56)
R100	1.023	1.514	0.974	1.082	0.888	1.335	0.813	0.962
	(3.83)	(6.17)	(2.47)	(2.96)	(3.70)	(6.19)	(2.33)	(2.92)
R100YR	0.382	0.475	0.485	0.279	0.359	0.439	0.324	0.395
	(2.98)	(3.70)	(2.55)	(1.59)	(3.40)	(4.27)	(2.04)	(2.82)
Ln *SIZE*					−0.134	−0.073	−0.217	−0.051
					(3.50)	(2.00)	(3.51)	(1.14)
SDRET					−0.179	−0.274	−0.136	−0.223
					(1.90)	(2.89)	(0.96)	(1.77)
DIVYLD					−0.048	−0.063	−0.075	−0.021
					(3.36)	(4.28)	(2.81)	(2.11)

[a] *t*-statistics in parentheses.

120

subperiods. In addition, the coefficient of ln *SIZE* is negative and significant, although its magnitude and significance is lower in the second subperiod. Size may be a proxy for liquidity, but its negative coefficient may also be due to it being a proxy for the reciprocal of expected return (Berk, 1995). The risk variable *SDRET* has a negative coefficient (as in Amihud and Mendelson, 1989), perhaps accounting for the value of the tax trading option. The negative coefficient of *DIVYLD* may reflect the effect of an unobserved risk factor that is negatively correlated with *DIVYLD* across stocks (less risky companies may choose to have higher dividend yield). The negative coefficient of *DIVYLD* is also consistent with the hypothesis of Redding (1997) about dividend preference by some types of investors. These effects could offset the positive effect of *DIVYLD* that results from the higher personal tax on dividends.

The cross-sectional models are also estimated by the weighted least squares method to account for hetersokedasticity in the residuals of model (2). The results[14] are qualitatively similar to those using the OLS method. In all models, the coefficient of *ILLIQMA* is positive and significant for the entire sample, when January is excluded and for each of the two subperiods.

3. The Effect Over Time of Market Illiquidity on Expected Stock Excess Return

The proposition here is that over time, expected market illiquidity positively affects expected stock excess return (the stock return in excess of Treasury bill rate). This is consistent with the positive cross-sectional relationship between stock return and illiquidity. If investors anticipate higher market illiquidity, they will price stocks so that they generate higher expected return. This suggests that *stock excess return, traditionally interpreted as "risk premium," includes a premium for illiquidity.* Indeed, stocks are not only riskier, but are also less liquid than short-term Treasury securities. First, both the bid–ask spread and the brokerage fees are much higher on stocks than they are on Treasury securities.[15] That is, illiquidity costs are greater for

---

[14] The results are available from the author upon request.

[15] The bid–ask spread on Treasury securities was about $1/128 per $100 of face value of bills (0.008%), $1/32 on short-term notes (0.031%) and $2/32 on long-term Treasury bonds (0.0625%) (see Amihud and Mendelson, 1991a). In recent estimates, the trade-weighted mean of the bid–ask spread of Government bonds is 0.081% (Chakravarti and Sarkar, 1999). For stocks, the bid–ask spread was much higher. The most liquid stocks had a bid–ask spread of $1/8 dollar or 0.25% for a stock with a price of $50. The average bid–ask spread on NYSE stocks during 1960–1979 was 0.71% (value weighted) or 1.43% (equally weighted; see Stoll and Whaley, 1983). In addition, brokerage fees are much lower for

stocks. Second, the size of transactions in the Treasury securities market is greater: investors can trade very large amounts (tens of millions of dollars) of bills and notes without price impact, but block transactions in stocks result in price impact that implies high illiquidity costs.[16] It thus stands to reason that the expected return on stocks in excess of the yield on Treasury securities should be considered as compensation for illiquidity, in addition to its standard interpretation as compensation for risk.

The relationship between market liquidity and market return was studied by Amihud et al. (1990) for the October 19, 1987 stock market crash. They showed that the crash was associated with a rise in market illiquidity and that the price recovery by October 30 was associated with improvement in stock liquidity.

The proposition tested here is that expected stock excess return is an increasing function of expected market illiquidity. The tests follow the methodology of French et al. (1987) who tested the effect of risk on stock excess return. Expected illiquidity is estimated by an autoregressive model, and this estimate is employed to test two hypotheses:

(i) ex ante stock excess return is an increasing function of expected illiquidity, and
(ii) unexpected illiquidity has a negative effect on contemporaneous unexpected stock return.

3.1. Estimation Procedure and Results

The ex ante effect of market illiquidity on stock excess return is described by the model

$$E\left(RM_y - Rf_y | \ln AILLIQ_y^E\right) = f_0 + f_1 \ln AILLIQ_y^E. \tag{6}$$

RM_y is the annual market return for year y, Rf_y is the risk-free annual yield, and $\ln AILLIQ_y^E$ is the expected market illiquidity for year y based on information in $y - 1$. The hypothesis is that $f_1 > 0$.

Treasury securities than they are for stocks. The fee was \$12.5 (or \$25) per million dollar for institutions trading T-bills and \$78,125 per million for notes, that is, 0.00125% and 0.00781%, respectively (Stigum, 1983, p. 437). For stocks, brokerage fees for institutions were no less than 6–10 cents per share, 0.12–0.20% for a \$50 stock. Fees for individuals were of the order of magnitude of the bid–ask spreads (Stoll and Whaley, 1983).

[16] See Chakravarti and Sarkar (1999) on the bond market and Kraus and Stoll (1972) and Keim and Madhavan (1996) on the stock market.

Market illiquidity is measured by $AILLIQ_y$ (see (3)), the average across all stocks in each year y of stock illiquidity, $ILLIQ_{iy}$ (defined in (1)), excluding stocks whose $ILLIQ_{iy}$ is in the upper 1 % tail of the distribution for the year. There are 34 annual values of $AILLIQ_y$ for the years 1963–1996. $AILLIQ_y$ peaked in the mid-1970s and rose again in 1990. It had low values in 1968, the mid-1980s and in 1996. The tests use the logarithmic transformation $\ln AILLIQ_y$.

Investors are assumed to predict illiquidity for year y based on information available in year $y-1$, and then use this prediction to set prices that will generate the desired expected return in year y. Market illiquidity is assumed to follow the autoregressive model

$$\ln AILLIQ_y = c_0 + c_1 \ln AILLIQ_{y-1} + v_y, \tag{7}$$

where c_0 and c_1 are coefficients and v_y is the residual. It is reasonable to expect $c_1 > 0$.

At the beginning of year y, investors determine the expected illiquidity for the coming year, $\ln AILLIQ_y^E$, based on information in year $y-1$ that has just ended:

$$\ln AILLIQ_y^E = c_0 + c_1 \ln AILLIQ_{y-1}. \tag{8}$$

Then, they set market prices at the beginning of year y that will generate the expected return for the year. The assumed model is

$$\begin{aligned}(RM - Rf)_y &= f_0 + f_1 \ln AILLIQ_y^E + u_y \\ &= g_0 + g_1 \ln AILLIQ_{y-1} + u_y,\end{aligned} \tag{9}$$

where $g_0 = f_0 + f_1 c_0$ and $g_1 = f_1 c_1$. Unexpected excess return is denoted by the residual u_y. The hypothesis is that $g_1 > 0$: higher expected market illiquidity leads to higher ex ante stock excess return.

The effect of *un*expected market illiquidity on contemporaneous unexpected stock return should be *negative*. This is because $c_1 > 0$ (in (8)) means that higher illiquidity in one year raises expected illiquidity for the following year. If higher expected illiquidity causes ex ante stock returns to rise, stock prices should *fall* when illiquidity unexpectedly rises. (This assumes that corporate cash flows are unaffected by market illiquidity.) As a result, there should be a negative relationship between unexpected illiquidity and contemporaneous stock return.

The two hypotheses discussed above are tested in the model

$$(RM - Rf)_y = g_0 + g_1 \ln AILLIQ_{y-1} + g_2 \ln AILLIQ_y^U + w_y, \quad (10)$$

where $\ln AILLIQ_y^U$ is the *un*expected illiquidity in year y, $\ln AILLIQ_y^U = v_y$, the residual from (7). The hypotheses therefore imply two predictions:

$$\text{H-1:} \quad g_1 > 0, \text{ and}$$
$$\text{H-2:} \quad g_2 < 0.$$

In estimating model (7) from finite samples, the estimated coefficient $\hat{c}_1$ is biased downward. Kendall's (1954) proposed a bias correction approximation procedure by which the estimated coefficient $\hat{c}_1$ is augmented by the term $(1 + 3\hat{c}_1)/T$, where T is the sample size.[17] This procedure is applied here to adjust the estimated coefficient c_1.

The estimation of model (7) provides the following results:

$$\ln AILLIQ_y = -0.200 + 0.768 \quad \ln AILLIQ_{y-1} + residual_y$$
$$(t =) \qquad (1.70) \quad (5.89) \qquad R^2 = 0.53, \; D - W = 1.57. \qquad (7a)$$

By applying Kendall's (1954) bias correction method, the bias-corrected estimated slope coefficient c_1 is 0.869 (the intercept is adjusted accordingly). The estimated parameters of the model are found to be stable over time, as indicated by the Chow test. It is therefore reasonable to proceed with the coefficients that are estimated using the entire data.[18]

The structure of models (7) and (9) resembles the structure analyzed by Stambaugh (1999). Since by hypothesis H-2 it is expected that $Cov(u_y, v_y)$ < 0, it follows from Stambaugh's (1999) analysis that in estimating (9), the estimated coefficient g_1 is biased upward. This bias can be eliminated by including in model (9) the residual v_y, as in model (10).[19] The procedure first calculates the residual v_y from model (7) after its coefficients are adjusted by Kendall's (1954) bias-correction method, and then it is used in model (10) as $\ln AILLIQ_y^U$ to estimate g_1 and g_2. In model (10), RM_y is the annual return on the equally weighted market portfolio for NYSE stocks (*source*: CRSP), and Rf is the one-year Treasury bill yield as of the beginning of year y (*source*: Federal Reserve Bank).

---

[17] Sawa (1978) suggests that "Kendall's approximation is virtually accurate in spite of its simplicity" (p. 164).

[18] This approach is similar to that in French et al. (1987).

[19] Simulation results of this bias-correction methodology using the actual sample parameters show that the bias in g_1 is about 4% of its value. Simulation results are available from the author upon request.

Table 4.3. *The effect of market illiquidity on expected stock excess return –*
annual data[a]

Estimates of the models:

$$(RM - Rf)_y = g_0 + g_1 \ln AILLIQ_{y-1} + g_2 \ln AILLIQ_y^U + w_y, \qquad (10)$$

RMy is the annual equally-weighted market return and Rf is the one-year Treasury
bill yield as of the beginning of year y. $\ln AILLIQ_y$ is market illiquidity, the logarithm
of the average across stocks of the daily absolute stock return divided by the daily
dollar volume of the stock (averaged over the year). $\ln AILLIQ_y^U$ is the unexpected
market illiquidity, the residual from an autoregressive model of $\ln AILLIQ_y$.

The table also presents regression results of the excess returns on five size-based
portfolios as a function of expected and unexpected illiquidity. The estimated model
is

$$(RSZi - Rf)_y = g_0 + g_1^i \ln AILLIQ_{y-1} + g_2^i \ln AILLIQ_y^U + w_{iy}, \qquad (10sz)$$

RSZ_i, $i = 2, 4, 6, 8$, and 10, are the annual returns on CRSP size-portfolio i (the
smaller number indicates smaller size).

Period of estimation: 1964–1996.

		Excess returns on size-based portfolios				
	$RM - Rf$	$RSZ_2 - Rf$	$RSZ_4 - Rf$	$RSZ_6 - Rf$	$RSZ_8 - Rf$	$RSZ_{10} - Rf$
Constant	14.740	19.532	17.268	14.521	12.028	4.686
	(4.29)	(4.53)	(4.16)	(4.02)	(3.78)	(1.55)
	[4.37]	[5.12]	[5.04]	[4.32]	[3.55]	[1.58]
Ln $AILLIQ_{y-1}$	10.226	15.230	11.609	9.631	7.014	− 0.447
	(2.68)	(3.18)	(2.52)	(2.40)	(1.98)	(0.13)
	[2.74]	[3.92]	[3.31]	[2.74]	[1.84]	[0.14]
Ln $AILLIQ_y^U$	− 23.567	− 28.021	− 24.397	− 20.780	− 18.549	− 14.416
	(4.52)	(4.29)	(3.88)	(3.80)	(3.84)	(3.14)
	(4.11)	[3.91]	[3.63]	[3.41]	[3.50]	[3.39]
R^2	0.512	0.523	0.450	0.435	0.413	0.249
$D - W$	2.55	2.42	2.64	2.47	2.39	2.28

[a] *t*-statistics. [*t*-statistics calculated from standard errors that are robust to heteroskedasticity and
autocorrelation, using the method of Newey and West, 1987.]

The estimation results of model (10), presented in Table 4.3, strongly
support both hypotheses:

H-1: The coefficient g_1 is positive and significant, suggesting that *expected
stock excess return is an increasing function of expected market illiquidity.*
H-2: The coefficient g_2 is negative and significant, suggesting that *unexpected* market illiquidity has a *negative* effect on stock prices. This
result is consistent with the findings of Amihud et al. (1990).[20]

[20] The model is tested for stability and the results show that it is stable over time.

3.2. Market Illiquidity and Excess Returns on Size-Based Portfolios

The effect of market illiquidity on stock return over time varies between stocks by their level of liquidity. In an extreme case of a rise in illiquidity during the October 1987 crash there was a "flight to liquidity": that were more liquid stocks declined less in value, after controlling for the market effect and the stocks' *beta* coefficients (see Amihud et al., 1990). This suggests the existence of two effects on stock return when expected market illiquidity rises:

(a) A decline in stock price and a rise in expected return, common to all stocks.
(b) Substitution from less liquid to more liquid stocks ("flight to liquidity").

For low-liquidity stocks the two effects are complementary, both affecting stock returns in the same direction. However, for liquid stocks the two effects work in *opposite* directions. Unexpected rise in market illiquidity, which negatively affects stock prices, also increases the relative demand for liquid stocks and mitigates their price decline. And, while higher expected market illiquidity makes investors demand higher expected return on stocks, it makes liquid stocks relatively more attractive, thus weakening the effect of expected illiquidity on their expected return.

As a result, small, illiquid stocks should experience stronger effects of market illiquidity – a greater positive effect of expected illiquidity on ex ante return and a more negative effect of unexpected illiquidity on contemporaneous return. For large, liquid stocks both effects should be weaker, because these stocks become relatively more attractive in times of dire liquidity.

This hypothesis is tested by estimating model (10) using returns on size-based portfolios, where RSZ_i is the return on the portfolio of size-decile i:

$$(RSZ_i - Rf)_y = g_0^i + g_1^i \ln AILLIQ_{y-1} + g_2^i \ln AILLIQ_y^U + w_{iy}. \quad (10sz)$$

The estimation is carried out on size portfolios $i = 2, 4, 6, 8,$ and 10 (size increases in i).[21] The proposition that the illiquidity effect is stronger for

---

[21] The results are qualitatively similar when using the odd-numbered portfolios 1, 3, 5, 7, and 9.

small illiquid stocks implies two hypotheses:

(SZ1) The coefficients g_1 in model (10sz), which are positive, decline in size:

$$g_1^2 > g_1^4 > g_1^6 > g_1^8 > g_1^{10} > 0.$$

(SZ2) The coefficients g_2^i in model (10sz), which are negative, rise in size:

$$g_2^2 < g_2^4 < g_2^6 < g_2^8 < g_2^{10} < 0.$$

The results, presented in Table 4.3, are consistent with both hypotheses (SZ1) and (SZ2). First, the coefficients g_1^i decline monotonically in size. Second, the coefficients g_2^i rise monotonically in size (i.e., the effect of unexpected illiquidity becomes weaker).

The results suggest that the effects of market illiquidity – both expected and unexpected – are stronger for small firm stocks than they are for larger firms. These findings may explain the variation over time in the "small firm effect". Brown et al. (1983) who documented this phenomenon "reject the hypothesis that the ex ante excess return attributable to size is stable over time" (p. 33). The findings here explain why: small and large firms react differently to changes in market illiquidity over time.

The greater sensitivity of small stock returns to market illiquidity – both expected and unexpected – means that they have greater *illiquidity risk*. If this risk is priced in the market, then stocks with greater illiquidity risk should earn higher illiquidity risk premium, as shown by Pastor and Stambaugh (2001). This may explain why small stocks earn, on average, higher expected return. The way that illiquidity affects expected stock returns can be therefore measured either by using illiquidity as a stock characteristic (as done in Amihud and Mendelson (1986) and others since), or by using the stock's sensitivity to an illiquidity factor, which is shown here to vary systematically across stocks by their size or liquidity.

3.3. Monthly Data: The Effect of Illiquidity on Stock Excess Returns

The methodology of the previous two sections is replicated here using monthly data. There are 408 months in the period 1963–1996. Monthly illiquidity, $MILLIQ_m$, is the average across stocks of $|R_{idm}|/VOLD_{idm}$, the illiquidity measure of stock i on day d in month m, and then averaged over the days of month m. An autoregressive model similar to (7) is estimated for the monthly data as follows:

$$\ln MILLIQ_m = 0.313 + 0.945 \ln MILLIQ_{m-1} + residual_m$$
$$(t=) \quad (3.31) \quad (58.36) \quad R^2 = 0.89, \ D - W = 2.34. \tag{7m}$$

Applying Kendall's (1954) bias correction method, the adjusted slope coefficient is 0.954. The estimated parameters are stable over time, as indicated by the Chow test. Next, the monthly unexpected illiquidity is calculated, $MILLIQ_m^U$, the residual from model (7m) after the coefficients are adjusted.

Finally, the monthly version of model (10) is estimated:

$$(RM - Rf)_m = g_0 + g_1 \ln MILLIQ_{m-1} + g_2 \ln MILLIQ_m^U$$
$$+ g_3 JANDUM_m + w_m. \tag{10m}$$

This model adds $JANDUM_m$, a January dummy, that accounts for the well-known January effect. RM_m is the monthly return on the equally weighted market portfolio (for NYSE stocks) and Rf is the one-month Treasury bill rate.

The results for the monthly data, presented in Table 4.4, are qualitatively similar to those using annual data. In particular, $g_1 > 0$ and $g_2 < 0$, both statistically significant.

As a robustness check, the sample of 408 months is divided into six equal subperiods of 68 months each and model (10m) is estimated for each subperiod. The following is a summary of the results:

1. All six coefficients g_1 are positive, with mean 0.871 and median 0.827.
2. All six coefficients g_2 are negative with mean -7.089 and median -5.984.

This shows consistency in the effect of illiquidity.

The differences in the effects of illiquidity on different size-based stock portfolios is tested by estimating model (10m) using excess returns on portfolios corresponding to deciles 2, 4, 6, 8, and 10 (decile 10 contains the largest firms). The results, presented in Table 4.4, are again similar to those for the yearly data: g_1 is decreasing in company size, and g_2 is increasing in company size.

3.4. Illiquidity Effect, Controlling for the Effects of Bond Yield Premiums

Two bond yield premiums are known to have a positive effect on ex ante stock returns over time: the default yield premium (the excess yield on risky corporate bonds) and the term yield premium (long-term minus short-term bond yield) (see Keim and Stambaugh, 1986; Fama and French, 1989;

Table 4.4. *The effect of market illiquidity on expected stock excess return – monthly data*[a]

This table presents regression results of the excess returns on the market return and on five size-based portfolios:

$$(RM - Rf)_m = g_0 + g_1 \ln MILLIQ_{m-1} + g_2 \ln MILLIQ_m^U + g_3 JANDUM_m + w_y. \tag{10m}$$

RM is the monthly equally-weighted market return (NYSE stocks), Rf is the one-month Treasury bill rate, $MILLIQ_m$ is the monthly illiquidity, the average across stocks and over days of the absolute stock return divided by the daily dollar volume of the stock, $MILLIQ_m^U$ is the unexpected illiquidity, the residual from an autoregressive model of $\ln MILLIQ_m$, and $JANDUM_m$ is a dummy variable that equals 1 in the month of January and zero otherwise.

In the size-related model, the dependent variable is $(RSZ_i - Rf)_m$, the monthly excess return on CRSP size-based portfolio i, $i = 2, 4, 6, 8,$ and 10 (size rises with i). The period of estimation is 1964–1996.

		Excess returns on size-based portfolios				
	$RM - Rf$	$RSZ_2 - Rf$	$RSZ_4 - Rf$	$RSZ_6 - Rf$	$RSZ_8 - Rf$	$RSZ_{10} - Rf$
Constant	− 3.876	− 4.864	− 4.335	− 4.060	− 3.660	− 1.553
	(2.33)	(2.54)	(2.45)	(2.42)	(2.27)	(1.12)
	[1.97]	[2.03]	[2.12]	[2.13]	[2.05]	[0.99]
Ln $MILLIQ_{m-1}$	0.712	0.863	0.808	0.761	0.701	0.319
	(2.50)	(2.64)	(2.67)	(2.65)	(2.55)	(1.35)
	[2.12]	[2.11]	[2.33]	[2.36]	[2.30]	[1.18]
ln $MILLIQ_m^U$	− 5.520	− 6.513	− 5.705	− 5.238	− 4.426	− 3.104
	(6.21)	(6.37)	(6.04)	(5.84)	(5.15)	(4.19)
	[4.42]	[4.53]	[4.34]	[4.12]	[4.04]	[3.38]
$JANDUM_m$	5.280	8.067	5.446	4.232	3.000	1.425
	(5.97)	(7.94)	(5.80)	(4.74)	(3.51)	(1.93)
	[4.20]	[5.03]	[4.08]	[3.45]	[2.64]	[1.47]
R^2	0.144	0.188	0.140	0.119	0.089	0.049
$D - W$	1.98	1.99	1.96	1.99	2.03	2.14

[a] t-statistics. [t-statistics calculated from standard errors that are heteroskedastic-consistent, following White, 1980.]

Fama, 1990).[22] The following are tests of the effects of illiquidity on stock excess returns after controlling for the effects of these two yield premiums.

[22] Fama and French (1989) and Fama (1990) study separately the effect of the default premium and the term premium on ex ante excess stock return. Keim and Stambaugh (1986) combine the two in a single measure, the difference between the yield on corporate bonds with rating below BAA and on short-term treasury bills. Boudoukh et al. (1993) study the effect of the term yield on subsequent stock excess return.

The default yield premium is defined as

$$DEF_m = YBAA_m - YAAA_m,$$

where $YBAA_m$ and $YAAA_m$ are, respectively, the yield to maturity on long-term $BAAA$-rated and AAA-rated bonds. DEF_m is naturally positive, reflecting the premium on risky corporate bonds.

The term yield premium is

$$TERM_m = YLONG_m - YTB3_m,$$

where $YLONG_m$ and $YTB3_m$ are, respectively, the yields on long-term Treasury bonds and three-month Treasury bills. The data source is Basic Economics. The correlations between the variables are low: $\mathrm{Corr}(\ln MILLIQ_m, DEF_m) = -0.060$, $\mathrm{Corr}(\ln MILLIQ_m, TERM_m) = 0.021$, and $\mathrm{Corr}(TERM_m, DEF_m) = 0.068$.

The following model tests the effects of illiquidity on stock excess return, controlling for the effects of the default and term yield premiums:

$$(RM - Rf)_m = g_0 + g_1 \ln MILLIQ_{m-1} + g_2 \ln MILLIQ_m^U + g_3 JANDUM_m$$
$$+ a_1 DEF_{m-1} + a_2 TERM_{m-1} + u_m. \tag{11}$$

The model is predictive since lagged illiquidity and bond yields are known to investors at the beginning of month m during which $(RM - Rf)_m$, is observed. The hypothesis that expected illiquidity has a positive effect on ex ante stock excess return implies that $g_1 > 0$ and $g_2 < 0$. In addition, the positive effects of the default and term yield premiums imply $a_1 > 0$ and $a_2 > 0$.

The results, presented in Table 4.5, show that $\ln MILLIQ_{m-1}$ retains its positive and significant effect on ex ante stock excess return after controlling for the default and the term yield premiums. Also, $\ln AILLIQ_m^u$, retains its negative effect on contemporaneous stock seen returns. Consistent with Fama and French (1989), the two yield premiums have a positive effect on ex ante stock excess return.

The differences in the effects of illiquidity on different size-based stock portfolios is tested again here in the following model, controlling for the effects of the bond-yield premiums:

$$(RSZ_i - Rf)_m = g_0^i + g_1^i \ln MILLIQ_{m-1} + g_2^i \ln MILLIQ_m^U$$
$$+ g_3^i JANDUM_m + a_1^i DEF_{m-1} + a_2^i TERM_{m-1} + u_{im},$$
$$\tag{11sz}$$

Table 4.5. *The effects of expected market illiquidity, default yield premium, and term yield premium on expected stock excess return – monthly data*[a]

Estimation results of the model

$$(RM - Rf)_m = g_0 + g_1 \ln MILLIQ_{m-1} + g_2 \ln MILLIQ_m^U + g_3 JANDUM_m + a_1 DEF_{m-1} + a_2 TERM_{m-1} + u_m. \tag{11}$$

$(RM - Rf)_m$, the equally-weighted market return in excess of the one-month treasury bill rate for month m. $\ln MILLIQ_m$ is market illiquidity in month m, calculated as the logarithm of the average across stocks over the days of the month of daily absolute stock return divided by the daily dollar volume of the stock. $\ln MILLIQ_m^U$ is the unexpected market illiquidity, the residual from an autoregressive model of $\ln MILLIQ_m$. $DEF_m = YBAA_m - YAAA_m$, where $YBAA_m$ and $YAAA_m$ are, respectively, the yield to maturity on long term, BAA-rated and AAA-rated corporate bonds. $TERM_m = YLONG_m - YTB3_m$ where $YLONG_m$ and $YTB3_m$ are, respectively, the yields on long-term treasury bonds and three-month Treasury bills. $JANDUM_m$ is a dummy variable that equals 1 in the month of January and zero otherwise.

Also estimated is the following model:

$$(RSZi - Rf)_m = g_0^i + g_1^i \ln MILLIQ_{m-1} + g_2^i \ln MILLIQ_m^U + g_3^i JANDUM_m + a_1^i DEF_{m-1} + a_2^i TERM_{m-1} + u_{im}, \tag{11sz}$$

where $(RSZ_i - Rf)_m$ is the monthly return on CRSP size-portfolio i in excess of the one-month T-bill rate, $i = 2, 4, 6, 8, 10$. The estimation period is 1963–1996.

		Excess returns on size-based portfolios				
	$RM - Rf$	$RSZ_2 - Rf$	$RSZ_4 - Rf$	$RSZ_6 - Rf$	$RSZ_8 - Rf$	$RSZ_{10} - Rf$
Constant	− 5.583	− 6.986	− 6.170	− 6.010	− 5.191	− 2.693
	(3.15)	(3.43)	(3.28)	(3.37)	(3.03)	(1.83)
	[2.63]	12.58]	[2.73]	[2.90]	[2.71]	[1.68]
Ln $MILLIQ_{m-1}$	0.715	0.912	0.846	0.803	0.731	0.332
	(2.53)	(2.80)	(2.82)	(2.82)	(2.67)	(1.41)
	[2.18]	[2.20]	[2.41]	[2.48]	[2.38]	[1.23]
Ln $MILLIQ_m^U$	− 5.374	− 6.281	− 5.492	− 5.014	− 4.242	− 2.940
	(6.08)	(6.18)	(5.84)	(5.63)	(4.95)	(3.99)
	[4.39]	[4.48]	[4.27]	[4.05]	[3.97]	[3.26]
$JANDUM_m$	4.981	7.943	5.351	4.128	2.925	1.395
	(5.67)	(7.86)	(5.73)	(4.66)	(3.44)	(1.91)
	[4.40]	[5.11]	[4.11]	[3.46]	[2.64]	[1.48]
DEF_{m-1}	1.193	1.558	1.293	1.386	1.054	0.663
	(2.35)	(2.66)	(2.39)	(2.70)	(2.14)	(1.56)
	[2.39]	[2.52]	[2.30]	[2.76]	[2.13]	[1.54]
$TERM_{m-1}$	0.281	0.185	0.228	0.227	0.221	0.316
	(1.84)	(1.05)	(1.40)	(1.48)	(1.50)	(2.49)
	[1.70]	[1.00]	[1.31]	[1.39]	[1.36]	[2.30]
R^2	0.161	0.205	0.157	0.141	0.106	0.070
$D - W$	2.00	2.03	1.99	2.03	2.06	2.18

[a] *t*-statistics. [*t*-statistics calculated from standard errors that are heteroskedastic-consistent following White, 1980.]

Yakov Amihud

where $(RSZ_i - Rf)_m$ is the monthly return on CRSP size-portfolio i in excess of the one-month T-bill rate, $i = 2, 4, 6, 8, 10$.

The estimation results in Table 4.5 show the same pattern as before. The coefficient g_1 declines as size increases and the coefficient g_2 increases (becomes less negative) as size increases. That is, the illiquidity effect is stronger for smaller firms.

Interestingly, the effect of the default premium varies systematically with firm size. Since the default premium signifies default risk and future adverse economic conditions, it should have a greater effect on the expected return of smaller firms that are more vulnerable to adverse conditions. This is indeed the result: the coefficient of the default premium is declining as the firm size rises.

4. Summary and Conclusion

This paper presents new tests of the proposition that asset expected returns are increasing in illiquidity. It is known from earlier studies that illiquidity explains differences in expected returns *across* stocks, a result that is confirmed here. The new tests in this paper propose that *over time*, market expected illiquidity affects the ex ante stock excess return. This implies that the stock excess return $RM - Rf$, usually referred to as "risk premium", also provides compensation for the lower liquidity of stocks relative to that of Treasury securities. And, expected stock excess returns are not constant but rather vary over time as a function of changes in market illiquidity.

The measure of illiquidity employed in this study is *ILLIQ*, the ratio of a stock absolute daily return to its daily dollar volume, averaged over some period. This measure is interpreted as the daily stock price reaction to a dollar of trading volume. While finer and better measures of illiquidity are available from market microstructure data on transactions and quotes,[23] *ILLIQ* can be easily obtained from databases that contain daily data on stock return and volume. This makes *ILLIQ* available for most stock markets and enables to construct a time series of illiquidity over a long period of time, which is necessary for the study of the effects of illiquidity over time.

In the cross-section estimations, *ILLIQ* has a positive effect, consistent with earlier studies. This is in addition to the usual negative effect of size (stock capitalization), which is another proxy for liquidity.

[23] Other measures of illiquidity are the bid–ask spread (Amihud and Mendelson, 1986, the effective bid–ask spread (Chalmers and Kadlec, 1998), transaction price impact (Brennan and Subrahmanyam, 1996) or the probability of information-based trading (Easley et al., 1999) – all shown to have a positive effect on the cross-section of stock expected return.

The new tests of the effects of illiquidity over time show that expected market illiquidity has a positive and significant effect on ex ante stock excess return, and *un*expected illiquidity has a negative and significant effect on contemporaneous stock return. Market illiquidity is the average *ILLIQ* across stocks in each period, and expected illiquidity is obtained from an autoregressive model. The negative effect of unexpected illiquidity is because higher realized illiquidity raises expected illiquidity, which in turn leads to higher stock expected return. Then, stock prices should decline to make the expected return rise (assuming that corporate cash flows are unaffected by market liquidity). The effects of illiquidity on stock excess return remain significant after including in the model two variables that are known to affect expected stock returns: the default yield premium on low-rated corporate bonds and the term yield premium on long-term Treasury bonds.

The effects over time of illiquidity on stock excess return differ across stocks by their liquidity or size: the effects of both expected and unexpected illiquidity are stronger on the returns of small stock portfolios. This suggests that the variations over time in the "small firm effect" – the excess return on small firms' stock – is partially due to changes in market illiquidity. This is because in times of dire liquidity, there is a "flight to liquidity" that makes large stocks relatively more attractive. The greater sensitivity of small stocks to illiquidity means that these stocks are subject to greater illiquidity risk which, if priced, should result in higher illiquidity risk premium.

The results suggest that the stock excess return, usually referred to as "risk premium", is in part a premium for stock illiquidity. This contributes to the explanation of the puzzle that the equity premium is too high. The results mean that stock excess returns reflect not only the higher risk but also the lower liquidity of stock compared to Treasury securities.

References

Amihud, Y., Mendelson, H., 1980. Dealership market: market making with inventory. Journal of Financial Economics 8, 311–53.

Amihud, Y., Mendelson, H., 1986. Asset pricing and the bid–ask spread. Journal of Financial Economics 17, 223–49.

Amihud, Y., Mendelson, H., 1989. The effects of beta, bid–ask spread, residual risk and size on stock returns. Journal of Finance 44, 479–86.

Amihud, Y., Mendelson, H., Wood, R., 1990. Liquidity and the 1987 stock market crash. Journal of Portfolio Management 16, 65–9.

Amihud, Y., Mendelson, H., 1991a. Liquidity, maturity and the yields on U.S. government securities. Journal of Finance 46, 1411–26.

Amihud, Y., Mendelson, H., 1991b. Liquidity, asset prices and financial policy. Financial Analysts Journal 47, 56–66.

Amihud, Y., Mendelson, H., Lauterbach, B., 1997. Market microstructure and securities values: evidence from the Tel Aviv exchange. Journal of Financial Economics 45, 365–90.

Atkins, A.B., Dyl, E.A., 1997. Transactions costs and holding periods for common stocks. Journal of Finance 52, 309–25.

Banz, R.W., 1981. The relationship between return and market value of common stocks. Journal of Financial Economics 9, 3–18.

Barry, C.B., Brown, S.J., 1984. Differential information and the small firm effect. Journal of Financial Information 13, 283–94.

Berk, J., 1995. A critique of size-related anomalies. Review of Financial Studies 8, 275–86.

Berkman, H., Eleswarapu, V.R., 1998. Short-term traders and liquidity: a test using Bombay stock exchange data. Journal of Financial Economics 47, 339–55.

Boudoukh, J., Richardson, M., Smith, T., 1993. Is the ex ante risk premium always positive? Journal of Financial Economics 34, 387–408.

Brennan, M.J., Subrahmanyam, A., 1996. Market microstructure and asset pricing: on the compensation for illiquidity in stock returns. Journal of Financial Economics 41, 441–64.

Brennan, M.J., Cordia, T., Subrahmanyam, A., 1998. Alternative factor specifications, security characteristics, and the cross-section of expected stock returns. Journal of Financial Economics 49, 345–73.

Brown, P., Kleidon, A.W., Marsh, T.A., 1983. New evidence on the nature of size-related anomalies in stock prices. Journal of Financial Econmics 12, 33–56.

Chakravarti, S., Sarkar, A., 1999. Liquidity in U.S. fixed income markets: a comparison of the bid–ask spread in corporate, government and municipal bond markets. Federal Reserve Bank of New York, Staff Report Number 73.

Chalmers, J.M.R., Kadlec, G.B., 1998. An empirical examination of the amortized spread. Journal of Financial Economics 48, 159–88.

Chordia, T., Subrahmanyam, A., Anshuman, V.R., 2001. Trading activity and expected stock returns. Journal of Financial Economics 59, 3–32.

Constantinides, G.M., Scholes, M.S., 1980. Optimal liquidation of assets in the presence of personal taxes: implications for asset pricing. Journal of Finance 35, 439–43.

Constantinides, G.M., 1986. Capital market equilibrium with transaction costs. Journal of Political Economy 94, 842–62.

Coopu, S.K., Goth, J.C., Avera, W.E., 1985. Liquidity, exchange listing and common stock performance. Journal of Economics and Business 37, 19–33.

Copeland, T.C., Galai, D., 1983. Information effect on the bid–ask spread. Journal of Finance 38, 1457–69.

Datar, V.T., Naik, N.Y., Radcliffe, R., 1998. Liquidity and stock returns: an alternative test. Journal of Financial Markets 1, 205–19.

Easley, D., O'Hara, M., 1987. Price, trade size and information in securities markets. Journal of Financial Economics 19, 69–90.

Easley, D., Hvidkjaer, S., O'Hara, M., 1999. Is information risk a determinant of asset returns? Working Paper, Cornell University.

Eleswarapu, V.R., Reinganum, M., 1993. The seasonal behavior of liquidity premium in asset pricing. Journal of Financial Economics 34, 373–86.

Eleswarapu, V.R., 1997. Cost of transacting and expected returns in the NASDAQ market. Journal of Finance 52, 2113–27.

Fama, E.F., MacBeth, J.D., 1973. Risk, return and equilibrium: empirical tests. Journal of Political Economy 81, 607–36.

Fama, E.F., French, K.R., 1989. Business conditions and expected returns on stocks and bonds. Journal of Financial Economics 25, 23–49.

Fama, E.F., 1990. Stock returns, expected returns, and real activity. Journal of Finance 45, 1089–108.

Fama, E.F., French, K.R., 1992. The cross section of expected stock returns. Journal of Finance 47, 427–65.

French, K.R., Schwert, G.W., Stambaugh, R.F., 1987. Expected stock returns and volatility. Journal of Financial Economics 19, 3–29.

Glosten, L.R., Milgrom, P.R., 1985. Bid, ask and transaction prices in a specialist market with heterogeneously informed traders. Journal of Financial Economics 14, 71–100.

Glosten, L., Harris, L., 1988. Estimating the components of the bid–ask spread. Journal of Financial Economics 21, 123–42.

Harris, M., Raviv, A., 1993. Differences of opinion make a horse race. Review of Financial Studies 6, 473–506.

Harris, L.E., 1994. Minimum price variation, discrete bid–ask spreads, and quotation sizes. Review of Financial Studies 7, 149–78.

Hasbrouck, J., 1991. Measuring the information content of stock trades. Journal of Finance 46, 179–207.

Haugen, R.A., Baker, N.L., 1996. Commonality in the determinants of expected stock returns. Journal of Financial Economics 41, 401–39.

Hu, S.-Y., 1997a. Trading turnover and expected stock returns: the trading frequency hypothesis and evidence from the Tokyo Stock Exchange. Working Paper, National Taiwan University.

Kamara, A., 1994. Liquidity, taxes, and short-term treasury yields. Journal of Financial and Quantitative Analysis 29, 403–16.

Keim, D.B., 1983. Size related anomalies and stock return seasonality. Journal of Financial Economics 12, 13–32.

Keim, D.B., Stambaugh, R.F., 1986. Predicting returns in the stock and bond market. Journal of Financial Economics 17, 357–96.

Keim, D.B., Madhavan, A., 1996. The upstairs market for large-block transactions: analysis and measurement of price effects. Review of Financial Studies 9, 1–36.

Kendall, M.G., 1954. Note on bias in the estimation of autocorrelation. Biometrica 41, 403–4.

Khan, W.A., Baker, H.K., 1993. Unlisted trading privileges, liquidity and stock returns. Journal of Financial Research 16, 221–36.

Kraus, A., Stoll, H.R., 1972. Price impacts of block trading on the New York Stock Exchange. Journal of Finance 27, 569–88.

Kyle, A., 1985. Continuous auctions and insider trading. Econometrica 53, 1315–35.

Levy, H., 1978. Equilibrium in an imperfect market: constraint on the number of securities in the portfolio. American Economic Review 68, 643–58.

Loughran, T., 1997. Book-to-market across firm size, exchange and seasonality: is there an effect? Journal of Financial and Quantitative Analysis 32, 249–68.

Merton, R.C., 1987. A simple model of capital market equilibrium with incomplete information. Journal of Finance 42, 483–511.

Newey, W.K., West, K.D., 1987. A simple, positive semi definite, heteroskedasticity and autocorrelation consistent covariance matrix. Econometrica 55, 703–6.

Pastor, L., Stambaugh, R.F., 2001. Liquidity risk and expected stock returns. Working paper, Wharton School, University of Pennsylvania, July.

Redding, L.S., 1997. Firm size and dividend payouts. Journal of Financial Intermediation 6, 224–48.

Reinganum, M.R., 1981. Misspecification of capital asset pricing: empirical anomalies based on earnings yields and market values. Journal of Financial Economics 9, 19–46.

Reinganum, M.R., 1990. Market microstructure and asset pricing. Journal of Financial Economics 28, 127–47.

Rouwenhorst, K.G., 1998. Local return factors and turnover in emerging stock markets. Working paper, Yale University.

Sawa, T., 1978. The exact moments of the least squares estimator for the autocorregressive model. Journal of Econometrics 8, 159–72.

Scholes, M., Williams, J., 1977. Estimating betas from non-synchronous data. Journal of Financial Economics 5, 309–27.

Shumway, T., 1997. The delisting bias in CRSP data. Journal of Finance 52, 327–40.

Silber, W.L., 1975. Thinness in capital markets: the case of the Tel Aviv Stock Exchange. Journal of Financial and Quantitative Analysis 10, 129–42.

Stambaugh, R.F., 1999. Predictive regressions. Journal of Financial Economics 54, 375–421.

Stigum, M., 1983. The Money Market. Dow Jones-Irwin, Homewood, IL.

Stoll, H.R., 1978. The pricing of security dealers services: an empirical study of NASDAQ stocks. Journal of Finance 33, 1153–72.

Stoll, H.R., Whaley, R.H., 1983. Transaction costs and the small firm effect. Journal of Financial Economics 12, 57–79.

Tinic, S.M., West, R.R., 1986. Risk, return and equilibrium: a revisit. Journal of Political Economy 94, 126–47.

CHAPTER 5

Asset Pricing with Liquidity Risk

Summary and Implications

Market-wide liquidity shocks are a source of systematic risk in securities markets, which affect investors' wealth and ability to trade. Risk-averse investors price this risk, requiring higher expected returns on assets with higher exposure to liquidity-related risk. This is the proposition of Acharya and Pedersen, who present a liquidity-adjusted Capital Asset Pricing Model (CAPM) that accounts for the risk of systematic shocks to liquidity. For example, in the Global Financial Crisis of 2008–2009, investors experienced severe reductions in liquidity and feared that liquidity would dry up even more; this is the liquidity risk that Acharya and Pedersen model. According to their model, liquidity risk reduces prices and increases the required return, thus contributing to the large drop in prices during the global financial crisis, and it can help explain why prices rebounded so strongly when, starting in March 2009, the liquidity crisis eased off.

In the model, diversified investors price systematic risk while they diversify away the idiosyncratic (i.e., unsystematic) risk. Investors care about their *net* return, which equals gross returns generated by the assets minus the cost of trading the assets. Thus, the risk of the net return is affected by the risk of both the gross returns and the trading costs. Indeed, trading costs vary significantly over time as seen in Figures 5.1 and PII.1. An asset's gross returns and transaction costs are exposed to two market-wide risk factors: gross market returns and market-wide shocks to transaction costs (or illiquidity costs). The sensitivity, or the *beta*, of the asset's net returns to these two market-wide risk factors determines the systematic risk to which the investor is exposed, and for which the investor demands a risk premium as compensation.

The total systematic risk the investor bears is therefore the sum of four (2 × 2) *betas* to the two market factors. First is the market return beta, that is, the sensitivity of the asset's gross return to the market gross return is measured by the familiar market beta coefficient, β^1. In addition, there are three *beta* coefficients that capture liquidity-related risks. The first, β^2, is the sensitivity of the asset's own illiquidity cost to the market-wide illiquidity cost. This *beta* is usually positive due to *commonality in liquidity*.[1] Investors require higher return for assets with higher β^2 as compensation for holding a security that becomes illiquid when the market in general becomes illiquid. For example, while the recent crisis induced a rise in market-wide trading costs, as depicted in Figure 5.1, the trading costs of small-cap stocks, which are less liquid, rose by more than the trading costs on the more liquid large-cap stocks. This means that the β^2 values of small-cap stocks are larger than those of large-cap stocks. In other words, less liquid stocks have not only a higher level of illiquidity, but also higher liquidity *risk*.

The second liquidity beta, β^3, measures the asset return's exposure to market-wide shocks in trading costs. This beta is usually negative because, as discussed earlier, a rise in market illiquidity makes investors require higher expected returns, which causes asset prices to fall and returns are then negative. Assets with more negative β^3 have a higher required return (or risk premium) because these assets are riskier, declining more sharply when market illiquidity worsens.

The third liquidity beta, β^4, reflects the sensitivity of an asset's illiquidity costs to market-wide returns. Usually, illiquidity costs rise when the market falls, thus reducing the investor's return net of trading costs. This is evident from Figure 8.1. At the height of the crisis from September 2008 to March 2009 when stock indices were at the bottom, trading costs peaked, thus hurting investors, who had to pay more for liquidating their positions at that time. Therefore, risk-averse investors prefer assets whose liquidity costs do not rise when market returns fall. Hence, the more negative is β^4, the greater the expected return required by investors. As shown in Figure 8.1, the rise in trading costs of small-cap stocks was greater than that of large-cap stocks when the S&P 500 index fell to its lowest level, which means that the less liquid small-cap stocks have a more negative β^4 and thus should generate higher expected returns.

In sum, Acharya and Pedersen show that the return required by investors (in excess of the risk-free rate) is an increasing function of the asset's expected transaction costs and its total market and liquidity risk, measured by the sum $\beta^1 + \beta^2 - \beta^3 - \beta^4$ (see Eq. (12) of their article in this book). The authors test this relation on NYSE and AMEX stock market data for 1964 through 1999 and find that the average return is indeed higher on stocks whose sum

---

[1] See Chordia, Roll, and Subrahmanyam (2000).

of these four betas is higher. Their analysis employs a modified *ILLIQ* as a measure of trading costs for 25 stock portfolios sorted on their illiquidity or standard deviation. After estimating the four β coefficients for each portfolio, the return–beta relation is estimated by a regression across stock portfolios of the portfolio average return on its liquidity-related systematic risk.

The results show that systematic liquidity risk has a significant positive effect on average stock returns. To illustrate, the differences in annualized expected returns between portfolio 1 and portfolio 25 (the two extreme liquidity-based portfolios) that can be attributed to differences in β^2, β^3, and β^4 are, respectively, 0.08%, 0.16%, and 0.82%. Therefore, the total effect of liquidity risk is 1.1% per year. The stronger effect of β^4 suggests that investors are most averse to the rise in the stock illiquidity (or transaction costs) when market prices decline. This brings us to the financial crisis of 2008–2009, when a sharp drop in market prices was associated with a sharp deterioration in the liquidity of some assets, such as less liquid stocks, low-grade corporate bonds, and convertible bonds.

The estimated effect of liquidity risk on required returns is illustrated in Figure PII.2. The estimated effect of liquidity risk reaches a return premium in excess of 1% (in addition to the effect of liquidity level). This estimate imposes the restriction that market risk and liquidity risk have the same risk premium. If the two risk premia are estimated separately, then the effect of liquidity risk is even larger, reaching more than 3% (Table 7.4, Panel A, line 4). This means that investors demand a very significant compensation for holding securities that are illiquid on average and especially those with liquidity risk.

The proposition that assets should earn a premium for the exposure of their returns to market-wide liquidity shocks is also tested by Pastor and Stambaugh (2003). These authors measure market illiquidity by the extent of the daily stock price reversal on the day after a given trading volume was associated with a price change. For example, a stock is considered relatively illiquid if a given trading volume associated with a price decline on one day is followed by a large upward bounce in price the next day. The greater the price reversal for a given volume, the more illiquid the stock. The extent of the reversal is estimated by a coefficient γ obtained from regressing the stock's daily stock return on the previous day's trading volume that has the same sign as that day's return. The market-wide measure of liquidity for a given month is the average across stocks of the price reversal coefficients in that month (modified in some ways). The market-wide aggregate liquidity measure fluctuates over time, and the unexpected changes in it are the liquidity shocks. The estimated sensitivity of each stock's return to these

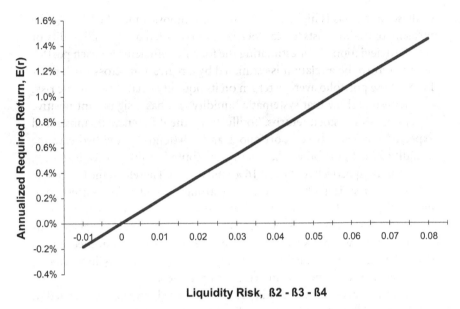

Figure PII.2 **Liquidity Risk and Required Returns.** The figure illustrates the return compensation for liquidity risk in Acharya and Pedersen's liquidity-adjusted CAPM. The model is estimated for U.S. stocks over the 1964–1999 period with all the model-implied restrictions imposed (Table 7.4, Panel A, line 1).

liquidity shocks (controlling for some benchmark return indexes) is the stock's liquidity beta, β^L. Higher β^L means greater exposure of stock return to systematic liquidity shocks. Consequently, a stock's expected return should be an increasing function of its β^L. Therefore, Pastor and Stambaugh focus on the pricing of the liquidity beta that Acharya and Pedersen denote by β^3. Given that the three liquidity betas in Acharya and Pedersen are closely related, this β^3 estimate can be viewed as proxying for the total effect of all three liquidity betas, as well as the effect of the level of liquidity.

Pastor and Stambaugh sort stocks by their β^L into ten portfolios. The authors obtain that the highest-β^L portfolio has a CAPM-based *alpha* (excess return after adjusting for risk factors) that is higher by an annual 6.4% than the *alpha* of the portfolio with the lowest β^L. Using *alpha* from the Fama–French (1993) benchmark portfolios, the difference between the portfolios' *alphas* is an annual 9.23%. This shows that investors earn significantly higher return on stocks with greater systematic liquidity risk.

Liquidity risk is also a significant determinant of the pricing of corporate bonds. Lin, Wang, and Wu (2011) estimate the liquidity *beta* (β^3 in Acharya and Pedersen) – the sensitivity of monthly corporate bond returns to liquidity shocks – using monthly unexpected changes in the liquidity measures of Amihud (2002) and of Pastor and Stambaugh (2003). The liquidity *beta* is estimated after controlling for using standard return factors of stocks and bonds that affect bond returns. Then, Lin et al. (2011) examine whether the liquidity *beta* is priced by estimating its effect across bonds, controlling for the *beta* coefficients of the other factors. They obtain that liquidity risk has a positive and significant effect on average excess bond returns. This positive return–liquidity *beta* relation holds after controlling for bond characteristics, such as rating, coupon, issue size, and age. They find that one standard deviation increase in beta above its mean across bonds raises the annual return on the bond by nearly 1%, which is quite considerable.

As an application of the theory of liquidity-adjusted CAPM, consider the hedge fund Long Term Capital Management (LTCM). LTCM constructed arbitrage positions by going long (i.e., buying) and short (i.e., selling) securities with similar fundamentals but different prices, buying the lower-price security and selling the one with the higher price. For instance, LTCM went long convertible bonds and short a replicating strategy of the underlying stock and risk-free bond. Similarly, LTCM went long off-the-run Treasuries and shorted corresponding newly issued on-the-run bonds. Therefore, by going both long and short, and by diversifying across a number of types of securities, LTCM eliminated the market risk (β^i) of its portfolio. Nevertheless, it suffered losses starting in the middle of 1998, eventually collapsing after sustaining severe losses in September of 1998. What went wrong?

One simple explanation is that while LTCM had hedged its market risk, it had significant exposure to *liquidity risk*. Since securities with liquidity risk have lower prices (consistent with the liquidity-adjusted CAPM), the securities that LTCM was long tended to have more liquidity risk than the securities that LTCM was short. Said differently, the "cheap" securities may have been cheap for a reason: they were exposed to liquidity risk. Convertible bonds were less liquid than the respective stocks and the bonds that were used to hedge them, and the off-the-run bonds were less liquid than on-the-run bonds. Therefore, while the values of these positions fluctuated somewhat independently during times of small liquidity shocks, almost all LTCM's positions lost value in September 1998, when market liquidity dropped significantly and the liquidity premium rose. Viewed in this light, the high return that LTCM earned in the years before 1998 was in part a compensation for taking liquidity risk, a risk that materialized dramatically in September 1998. When market liquidity deteriorated, the prices of its illiquid securities, in which it invested long, declined relative to the prices of the more liquid securities, which it shorted (i.e., LTCM had exposure to β^3). Furthermore, the transaction costs of trading out of these positions sharply increased when overall trading costs rose and the market fell, meaning that LTCM also had liquidity risk exposures to β^2 and β^4.

The experience of LTCM illustrates how the liquidity risk premium presents an opportunity for investors with long holding periods and good trading technology. These premia, however, are no free lunch. Investors pursuing such strategies should adopt risk management processes that account for liquidity risk, acknowledging how it affects returns and how rising transaction costs can limit maneuverability.

Evidence on the effect of liquidity risk on hedge fund performance is presented by Sadka (2011). He finds that hedge funds with greater exposure to liquidity shocks – that is, having higher liquidity *beta* – earn significantly higher average returns. Funds are grouped into ten deciles by their exposure to liquidity shocks, measured by liquidity beta, similar to Acharya and Pedersen's β^3. For the period 1994–2009, Sadka finds that the portfolio of hedge funds with the highest liquidity beta outperformed the hedge funds portfolio with the lowest liquidity beta by about 6% annually. This excess return is obtained after controlling for common return risk factors that affect hedge fund performance. Consistent with the example of LTCM, while high liquidity-beta funds did better on average, they underperformed during financial crises (September–November 1998, August–October 2007, and September–November 2008). This is evidence of the role of liquidity in financial crises, a topic discussed in detail in Part III.

In conclusion, Acharya and Pedersen's liquidity-adjusted CAPM proposes that investors price securities so they are compensated for liquidity risk. Empirically, the liquidity-adjusted CAPM fits the data significantly better than the standard CAPM as liquidity risk is found to be priced for stocks, bonds, and hedge funds, among other assets.

Asset Pricing with Liquidity Risk*

Viral V. Acharya and Lasse Heje Pedersen

Journal of Financial Economics 77, 2005

1. Introduction

Liquidity is risky and has commonalty: it varies over time both for individual stocks and for the market as a whole (Chordia et al., 2000; Hasbrouck and Seppi, 2001; Huberman and Halka, 1999). Liquidity risk is often noted in the financial press. For instance:

The possibility that liquidity might disappear from a market, and so not be available when it is needed, is a big source of risk to an investor. – The Economist, September 23, 1999

. . . there is also broad belief among users of financial liquidity – traders, investors and central bankers – that the principal challenge is not the average level of financial liquidity. . . but its variability and uncertainty. . . . – Persaud (2003)

This paper presents a simple theoretical model that helps explain how asset prices are affected by liquidity risk and commonality in liquidity. The model provides a unified theoretical framework that can explain the empirical findings that return sensitivity to market liquidity is priced (Pastor and Stambaugh, 2003), that average liquidity is priced (Amihud and Mendelson, 1986), and that liquidity comoves with returns and predicts future returns (Amihud, 2002; Chordia et al., 2001a; Jones, 2001; Bekaert et al., 2003).

* We are grateful for conversations with Andrew Ang, Joseph Chen, Sergei Davydenko, Francisco Gomes, Joel Hasbrouck, Andrew Jackson, Tim Johnson, Martin Lettau, Anthony Lynch, Stefan Nagel, Lubos Pastor, Tano Santos, Dimitri Vayanos, Luis Viceira, Jeff Wurgler, and seminar participants at London Business School, London School of Economics, New York University, the National Bureau of Economic Research (NBER) Summer Institute 2002, the Five Star Conference 2002, the Western Finance Association Meetings 2003, and the Texas Finance Festival 2004. We are especially indebted to Yakov Amihud and to an anonymous referee for help and many valuable suggestions.

In our model, risk-averse agents in an overlapping generations economy trade securities whose liquidity varies randomly over time. We solve the model explicitly and derive a liquidity-adjusted capital asset pricing model (CAPM). Our model of liquidity risk complements the existing theoretical literature on asset pricing with constant trading frictions (see, for instance, Amihud and Mendelson, 1986; Constantinides, 1986; Vayanos, 1998; Vayanos and Vila, 1999; Duffie et al., 2000, 2003; Huang, 2003; Gârleanu and Pedersen, 2004). In the liquidity-adjusted CAPM, the expected return of a security is increasing in its expected illiquidity and its "net beta," which is proportional to the covariance of its return, r^i, net of its exogenous[1] illiquidity costs, c^i, with the market portfolio's net return, $r^M - c^M$. The net beta can be decomposed into the standard market beta and three betas representing different forms of liquidity risk. These liquidity risks are associated with: (i) commonality in liquidity with the market liquidity, $\text{cov}(c^i, c^M)$; (ii) return sensitivity to market liquidity, $\text{cov}(r^i, c^M)$; and, (iii) liquidity sensitivity to market returns, $\text{cov}(c^i, r^M)$.

We explore the cross-sectional predictions of the model using NYSE and AMEX stocks over the period 1963 to 1999. We use the illiquidity measure of Amihud (2002) to proxy for c^i. We find that the liquidity-adjusted CAPM fares better than the standard CAPM in terms of R^2 for cross-sectional returns and p-values in specification tests, even though both models employ exactly one degree of freedom. The model has a good fit for portfolios sorted on liquidity, liquidity variation, and size, but the model cannot explain the cross-sectional returns associated with the book-to-market effect.

An interesting result that emerges from our empirical exercises based on Amihud's illiquidity measure is that illiquid securities also have high liquidity risk, consistent with "flight to liquidity" in times of down markets or generally illiquid markets. In particular, a security that has high average illiquidity, c^i, also tends to have high commonality in liquidity with the market liquidity, high return sensitivity to market liquidity, and high liquidity sensitivity to market returns.

While this collinearity is itself interesting, it also complicates the task of distinguishing statistically the relative return impacts of liquidity, liquidity risk, and market risk. There is, however, some evidence that the total effect

---

[1] While research on endogenous time-variation in illiquidity is sparse, Eisfeldt (2004) presents a model in which real-sector liquidity fluctuates with productivity, Brunnermeier and Pedersen (2004b) show how predatory trading can lead to illiquidity when liquidity is most needed, and Brunnermeier and Pedersen (2004a) show how market liquidity varies with dealers' "funding liquidity."

of the three liquidity risks matters over and above market risk and the level of liquidity.

It is interesting to consider the total and relative economic significance of liquidity level and each of the three liquidity risks by evaluating their contribution to cross-sectional return differences. It is difficult, however, to accurately distinguish the relative economic effects because of the inherent collinearity in the data. One of the benefits of having an economic model is that it provides a restrictive structure under which the identification problem is alleviated. Under the model's restrictions, liquidity risk contributes on average about 1.1% annually to the difference in risk premium between stocks with high expected illiquidity and low expected illiquidity. We decompose the effect of liquidity risk into the contribution from each of the three kinds of risk, recognizing that these estimates are subject to error and rely on the validity of the model:

- First, we estimate that the return premium due to commonality in liquidity, $\text{cov}(c^i, c^M)$, is 0.08%. Hence, while the model shows that investors require a return premium for a security that is illiquid when the market as a whole is illiquid, this effect appears to be small. The commonality in liquidity has been documented by Chordia et al. (2000), Huberman and Halka (1999), and Hasbrouck and Seppi (2001), but these papers do not study the implications for required returns.
- Second, we estimate that the return premium due to $\text{cov}(r^i, c^M)$ is 0.16%. This model-implied premium stems from the preference of investors for securities with high returns when the market is illiquid. Pastor and Stambaugh (2003) find empirical support for this effect using monthly data over 34 years with a measure of liquidity that they construct based on the return reversals induced by order flow.
- Third, we estimate that the return premium due to $\text{cov}(c^i, r^M)$ is 0.82%. Intuitively, investors are willing to pay a premium for a security that is liquid when the market return is low. We note that $\text{cov}(c^i, r^M)$ appears to be the most important source of liquidity risk although it has not previously been considered in the academic literature. However, it is reflected in industry practices such as legal disclaimers for certain asset management firms; e.g.,

Risks of investing in smaller companies include . . . the potential difficulty of selling these stocks during market downturns (illiquidity). – Legal Disclaimer, Investec Asset Management, 2004.[2]

[2] Source: http://wvvw2.investecfunds.com/US/LegalDisclaimer/lndex.cfm.

The return premium due to the level of liquidity is calibrated based on the average turnover to be 3.5%, thus the combined effect of the differences in liquidity risks and differences in the level of liquidity is estimated to be 4.6% per year. These estimates of the relative importance of liquidity level and the liquidity risks depend on the model-implied restrictions of a single risk premium and a level effect consistent with the turnover. If we depart from the model restrictions and estimate each liquidity risk premium as a free parameter then the economic effect of liquidity risk appears to be larger, but the unrestricted premia are estimated with little precision. Pastor and Stambaugh (2003) find a large (7.5%) effect of liquidity risk ($\text{cov}(r^i, c^M)$) using an unrestricted liquidity risk premium and without controlling for the level of liquidity.

Finally, the model also shows that since liquidity is persistent,[3] liquidity predicts future returns and liquidity co-moves with contemporaneous returns. This is because a positive shock to illiquidity predicts high future illiquidity, which raises the required return and lowers contemporaneous prices. This may help explain the empirical findings of Amihud et al. (1990), Amihud (2002), Chordia et al. (2001a), Jones (2001), and Pastor and Stambaugh (2003) in the U.S. stock market, and of Bekaert et al. (2003) in emerging markets.

In summary, we offer a simple theoretical framework that illustrates several channels through which liquidity risk can affect asset prices. The model is a useful first step in understanding how a number of recent empirical findings fit together. Finally, our empirical analysis suggests that the effects of liquidity level and liquidity risk are separate, although the analysis is made difficult by collinearity, and that one channel for liquidity risk that has not been treated in the prior literature, namely $\text{cov}(c^i, r^M)$, may be of empirical importance.

The paper is organized as follows. Section 2 describes the economy. Section 3 derives the liquidity-adjusted capital asset pricing model and outlines how liquidity predicts and co-moves with returns. Section 4 contains an empirical analysis. Section 5 concludes. Proofs are in the Appendix.

2. Assumptions

The model assumes a simple overlapping generations economy in which a new generation of agents is born at any time $t \in \{\ldots, -2, -1, 0, 1, 2, \ldots\}$

---

[3] Amihud (2002), Chordia et al. (2000, 2001a,b), Hasbrouck and Seppi (2001), Huberman and Halka (1999), Jones (2001), and Pastor and Stambaugh (2003).

(Samuelson, 1958). Generation t consists of N agents, indexed by n, who live for two periods, t and $t + 1$. Agent n of generation t has an endowment at time t and no other sources of income, trades in periods t and $t + 1$, and derives utility from consumption at time $t + 1$. He has constant absolute risk aversion A^n so that his preferences are represented by the expected utility function $-E_t \exp(-A^n x_{t+1})$, where x_{t+1} is his consumption at time $t + 1$.

There are I securities indexed by $i = 1, \ldots, I$ with a total of S^i shares of security i. At time t, security i pays a dividend of D_t^i, has an ex-dividend share price of P_t^i, and has an illiquidity cost of C_t^i, where D_t^i and C_t^i are random variables. All random variables are defined on a probability space $(\Omega, \mathscr{F}, \mathscr{P})$, and all random variables indexed by t are measurable with respect to the filtration $\{\mathscr{F}_t\}$, representing the information commonly available to investors. The illiquidity cost, C_t^i, is modeled simply as the per-share cost of selling security i. Hence, agents can buy at P_t^i but must sell at $P_t^i - C_t^i$. Short-selling is not allowed.

Uncertainty about the illiquidity cost is what generates the liquidity risk in this model. Specifically, we assume that D_t^i and C_t^i are autoregressive processes of order one, that is:

$$D_t = \bar{D} + \rho^D (D_{t-1} - \bar{D}) + \varepsilon_t \tag{1}$$

$$C_t = \bar{C} + \rho^C \left(C_{t-1} - \bar{C}\right) + \eta_t, \tag{2}$$

where[4] $\bar{D}, \bar{C} \in \mathbb{R}_+^I$ are positive real vectors, $\rho^D, \rho^C \in [0, 1]$, and (ε_t, η_t) is an independent identically distributed normal process with mean $E(\varepsilon_t) = E(\eta_t) = 0$ and variance-covariance matrices $\text{var}(\varepsilon_t) = \Sigma^D$, $\text{var}(\eta_t) = \Sigma^C$, and $E(\varepsilon_t \eta_t^\tau) = \Sigma^{CD}$.

We assume that agents can borrow and lend at a risk-free real return of $r^f > 1$, which is exogenous. This can be interpreted as an inelastic bond market, or a generally available production technology that turns a unit of consumption at time t into r^f units of consumption at time $t + 1$.

The assumptions with respect to agents, preferences, and dividends are strong. These assumptions are made for tractability, and, as we shall see, they imply natural closed-form results for prices and expected returns. The main result (Proposition 1) applies more generally, however. It holds for an arbitrary increasing and concave utility function defined on $(-\infty, \infty)$ as long as conditional expected net returns are normal,[5] and also for an

---

[4] For notational convenience, we assume that all securities have the same autocorrelation of dividends and liquidity (ρ^D and ρ^C) although our results apply more generally.

[5] The normal returns assumption is an assumption about endogenous variables that is used in standard CAPM analysis (for instance, Huang and Litzenberger, 1988). This assumption is satisfied in the equilibrium of the model of this paper.

arbitrary return distribution and quadratic utility. Furthermore, it can be viewed as a result of near-rational behavior, for instance, by using a Taylor expansion of the utility function (see, for example, Huang and Litzenberger, 1988; Markowitz, 2000; Cochrane, 2001). Our assumptions also allow us to study return predictability caused by illiquidity (Proposition 2) and the co-movements of returns and illiquidity (Proposition 3), producing insights that also seem robust to the specification.

Perhaps the strongest assumption is that investors need to sell all their securities after one period (when they die). In a more general setting with endogenous holding periods, deriving a general equilibrium with time-varying liquidity is an onerous task. While our model is mostly suggestive, it is helpful since it provides guidelines concerning the first-order effect of liquidity risk, showing which risks are priced. The assumption of overlapping generations can capture investors' life-cycle motives for trade (as in Vayanos, 1998; Constantinides et al., 2002), or can be viewed as a way of capturing short investment horizons (as in De Long et al., 1990) and the large turnover observed empirically in many markets.

It should also be noted that a narrow interpretation of the illiquidity cost, C_t^i, is that it represents transactions costs such as broker fees and bid–ask spread, in line with the literature on exogenous transactions costs. More broadly, however, the illiquidity cost could represent other real costs, for instance, those arising from delay and search associated with trade execution as in Duffle et al. (2000, 2002, 2003). The novelty in our model arises from the fact that we allow this cost to be time-varying.

3. Liquidity-Adjusted Capital Asset Pricing Model

This section derives a liquidity-adjusted version of the capital asset pricing model (CAPM) and studies its asset pricing implications.

We are interested in how an asset's expected (gross) return,

$$r_t^i = \frac{D_t^i + P_t^i}{P_{j-1}^i}, \tag{3}$$

depends on its relative illiquidity cost,

$$c_t^i = \frac{C_t^i}{P_{t-1}^i}, \tag{4}$$

on the market return,

$$r_t^M = \frac{\sum_i S^i \left(D_t^i + P_t^i \right)}{\sum_i S^i P_{t-1}^i}, \tag{5}$$

and on the relative market illiquidity,

$$c_t^M = \frac{\sum_i S^i C_t^i}{\sum_i S^i P_{t-1}^i}.$$ (6)

In a competitive equilibrium of the model (henceforth referred to simply as equilibrium), agents choose consumption and portfolios so as to maximize their expected utility taking prices as given, and prices are determined such that markets clear.

To determine equilibrium prices, consider first an economy with the same agents in which asset i has a dividend of $D_t^i - C_t^i$ and no illiquidity cost. In this imagined economy, standard results imply that the CAPM holds (Markowitz, 1952; Sharpe, 1964; Lintner, 1965; Mossin, 1966). We claim that the equilibrium prices in the original economy with frictions are the same as those of the imagined economy. This follows from two facts: (i) the net return on a long position is the same in both economies; and, (ii) all investors in the imagined economy hold a long position in the market portfolio, and a (long or short) position in the risk-free asset. Hence, an investor's equilibrium return in the frictionless economy is feasible in the original economy, and is also optimal, given the more limited investment opportunities due to the short-selling constraints. (This argument applies more generally since positive transactions costs imply that a short position has a worse payoff than minus the payoff of a long position. We impose the short-sale constraint because C can be negative in a setting with normal distributions.)

These arguments show that the CAPM in the imagined frictionless economy translates into a CAPM in net returns for the original economy with illiquidity costs. Rewriting the one-beta CAPM in net returns in terms of gross returns, we get a liquidity-adjusted CAPM for gross returns. This is the main testable[6] implication of this paper:

Proposition 1. *In the unique linear equilibrium, the conditional expected net return of security i is*

$$E_t\left(r_{t+1}^i - c_{t+1}^i\right) = r^f + \lambda_t \frac{\mathrm{cov}_t\left(r_{t+1}^i - c_{t+1}^i, r_{t+1}^M - c_{t+1}^M\right)}{\mathrm{var}_t\left(r_{t+1}^M - c_{t+1}^M\right)},$$ (7)

---

[6] Difficulties in testing this model arise from the fact that it makes predictions concerning conditional moments as is standard in asset pricing. See Hansen and Richard (1987), Cochrane (2001), and references therein. An unconditional version of (8) applies under stronger assumptions as discussed in Section 3.3.

where $\lambda_t = E_t(r_{t+1}^M - c_{t+1}^M - r^f)$ is the risk premium. Equivalently, the conditional expected gross return is

$$
E_t\left(r_{t+1}^i\right) = r^f + E_t\left(c_{t+1}^i\right) + \lambda_t \frac{\text{cov}_t\left(r_{t+1}^i, r_{t+1}^M\right)}{\text{var}_t\left(r_{t+1}^M - c_{t+1}^M\right)} + \lambda_t \frac{\text{cov}_t\left(c_{t+1}^i, c_{t+1}^M\right)}{\text{var}_t\left(r_{t+1}^M - c_{t+1}^M\right)}
$$
$$
- \lambda_t \frac{\text{cov}_t\left(r_{t+1}^i, c_{t+1}^M\right)}{\text{var}_t\left(r_{t+1}^M - c_{t+1}^M\right)} - \lambda_t \frac{\text{cov}_t\left(c_{t+1}^i, r_{t+1}^M\right)}{\text{var}_t\left(r_{t+1}^M - c_{t+1}^M\right)}. \tag{8}
$$

Eq. (8) is simple and natural. It states that the required excess return is the expected relative illiquidity cost, $E_t(c_{t+1}^i)$, as found theoretically and empirically[7] by Amihud and Mendelson (1986)), plus four betas (or covariances) times the risk premium. These four betas depend on the asset's payoff and liquidity risks. As in the standard CAPM, the required return on an asset increases linearly with the market beta, that is, covariance between the asset's return and the market return. This model yields three additional effects which could be regarded as three forms of liquidity risks.

3.1. Three Liquidity Risks

1. $\text{cov}_t(c_{t+1}^i, c_{t+1}^M)$: The first effect is that the return increases with the covariance between the asset's illiquidity and the market illiquidity. This is because investors want to be compensated for holding a security that becomes illiquid when the market in general becomes illiquid. The potential empirical significance of this pricing implication follows from the presence of a time-varying common factor in liquidity, which is documented by Chordia et al. (2000), Hasbrouck and Seppi (2001), and Huberman and Halka (1999). These papers find that most stocks' illiquidities are positively related to market illiquidity, so the required return should be raised by the commonality-in-liquidity effect. The effect of commonality in liquidity on asset prices is not studied, however, by these authors; we study this effect empirically in Section 4.

---

[7] Empirically, Amihud and Mendelson (1986, 1989) find the required rate of return on NYSE stocks to increase with the relative bid-ask spread. This result is questioned for NYSE stocks by Eleswarapu and Reinganum (1993), but supported for NYSE stocks (especially for amortized spreads) by Chalmers and Kadlec (1998), and for Nasdaq stocks by Eleswarapu (1997). Gârleanu and Pedersen (2004) show theoretically that adverse-selection costs are priced only to the extent that they render allocations inefficient. The ability of a market to allocate assets efficiently may be related to market depth, and, consistent with this view, the required rate of return has been found to decrease with measures of depth (Brennan and Subrahmanyam, 1996; Amihud, 2002). Easley et at. (2002) find returns to increase with a measure of the probability of informed trading.

In this model, the risk premium associated with commonality in liquidity is caused by the wealth effects of illiquidity. Also, this risk premium would potentially apply in an economy in which investors can choose which securities to sell. In such a model, an investor who holds a security that becomes illiquid (i.e., has a high cost c_t^i) can choose to not trade this security and instead trade other (similar) securities. It is more likely that an investor can trade other (similar) securities, at low cost, if the liquidity of this asset does not co-move with the market liquidity. Hence, investors would require a return premium for assets with positive covariance between individual and market illiquidity.

2. $\text{cov}_t(r_{t+1}^i, c_{t+1}^M)$: The second effect on expected returns is due to covariation between a security's return and the market liquidity. We see that $\text{cov}_t(r_{t+1}^i, c_{t+1}^M)$ affects required returns negatively because investors are willing to accept a lower return on an asset with a high return in times of market illiquidity. Related effects also arise in the theoretical models of Holmstrom and Tirole (2000), who examine implications of corporate demand for liquidity, and Lustig (2001), who studies the equilibrium implications of solvency constraints. Empirical support for this effect is provided by Pastor and Stambaugh (2003), who find that "the average return on stocks with high sensitivities to [market] liquidity exceeds that for stocks with low sensitivities by 7.5% annually, adjusted for exposures to the market return as well as size, value, and momentum factors." Sadka (2002) and Wang (2002) also present consistent evidence for this effect using alternative measures of liquidity.

3. $\text{cov}_t(c_{t+1}^i, r_{t+1}^M)$: The third effect on required returns is due to covariation between a security's illiquidity and the market return. This effect stems from the willingness of investors to accept a lower expected return on a security that is liquid in a down market. When the market declines, investors are poor and the ability to sell easily is especially valuable. Hence, an investor is willing to accept a discounted return on stocks with low illiquidity costs in states of poor market return. We find consistent evidence for this liquidity risk in the stock market in Section 4, and the effect seems economically important. Also, anecdotal evidence[8] suggests that private equity is illiquid during down markets, which, together with our model, may help explain the high average return documented by Ljungqvist and Richardson (2003).

---

[8] For example, the Institute for Fiduciary Education (2002) characterizes private equity as an "illiquid asset class" and points out that "In down equity markets, exits are more difficult and little cash is returned." Source: http://www.ifecorp.com/Papers-PDFs/Wenderl 102.PDF.

Outside our model, intuition suggests that a low market return causes wealth problems for some investors, who then need to sell. If a selling investor holds securities that are illiquid at this time, then his problems are magnified. Consistent with this intuition, Lynch and Tan (2003) find that the liquidity premium is large if the transaction costs covary negatively with wealth shocks, among other conditions. This is consistent with our effect of $\mathrm{cov}_t(c^i_{t+1}, r^M_{t+1})$ to the extent that r^M proxies for wealth shocks. Lynch and Tan (2003) complement our paper by showing through calibration that, even if an investor chooses his holding period endogenously, the liquidity premium can be large (3.55% in one calibration). They follow Constantinides (1986) in using a partial-equilibrium framework and defining the liquidity premium as the decrease in expected return that makes an investor indifferent between having access to the asset without transaction costs and the asset with transaction costs.

The three covariances thus provide a characterization of the liquidity risk of a security. We note that all these covariances can be accounted for by simply using the conditional CAPM in net returns as in (7). It is useful, however, to use gross returns and illiquidity as the basic inputs for several reasons: First, computing the net return is not straightforward since it depends on the investor's holding period, and the holding period may be different from the econometrician's sampling period. We explain in Section 4 how we overcome this problem. Second, the empirical liquidity literature is based on measures of gross return and illiquidity costs, and the model provides a theoretical foundation for the empirical relations between these security characteristics. Third, a pricing relation for gross returns and illiquidity, which is similar in spirit to (8), may hold in richer models in which net returns are not sufficient state variables. As argued above, additional liquidity effects outside the model suggest risk premia of the same sign for the covariance terms in (8). These additional liquidity effects also suggest that the size of the risk premia need not be identical across the covariance terms. To accommodate the possibility of a richer liquidity framework, we also consider a generalization of (8) in our empirical work in Section 4.

3.2. Implications of Persistence of Liquidity

This section shows that persistence of liquidity implies that liquidity predicts future returns and co-moves with contemporaneous returns.

Empirically, liquidity is time-varying and persistent, that is, $\rho^C > 0$ (Amihud, 2002; Chordia et al., 2000, 2001a,b; Hasbrouck and Seppi, 2001;

Huberman and Halka, 1999; Jones, 2001; Pastor and Stambaugh, 2003). This model shows that persistent liquidity implies that returns are predictable. Intuitively, high illiquidity today predicts high expected illiquidity next period, implying a high required return. The following proposition makes this intuition precise for a portfolio $q \in \mathbb{R}^I$. We use the obvious notation for portfolio dividend $D_t^q = q^T D_t$, return $r_t^q = \frac{\sum_i q^i (D_t^i + P_t^i)}{\sum_i q^i P_{t-1}^i}$, and so on.

Proposition 2. *Suppose that $\rho^C > 0$, and that $q \in \mathbb{R}^I$ is a portfolio with $E_t(P_{t+1}^q + D_{t+1}^q) > \rho^C P_t^q$. Then, the conditional expected return increases with illiquidity,*

$$\frac{\partial}{\partial C_t^q} E_t \left(r_{t+1}^q - r^f \right) > 0. \tag{9}$$

Proposition 2 relies on a mild technical condition, which is satisfied, for instance, for any portfolio with positive price and with $E_t(P_{t+1}^q + D_{t+1}^q)/P_t^q \geq 1$. The proposition states that the conditional expected return depends positively on the current illiquidity cost, that is, the current liquidity predicts the return.

Jones (2001) finds empirically that the expected annual stock market return increases with the previous year's bid–ask spread and decreases with the previous year's turnover. Amihud (2002) finds that illiquidity predicts excess return both for the market and for size-based portfolios, and Bekaert et al. (2003) find that illiquidity predicts returns in emerging markets.

Predictability of liquidity further implies a negative conditional covariance between contemporaneous returns and illiquidity. Naturally, when illiquidity is high, the required return is high also, which depresses the current price, leading to a low return. This intuition applies as long as liquidity is persistent ($\rho^C > 0$) and innovations in dividends and illiquidity are not too correlated ($q^T \Sigma^{CD} q$ low for a portfolio q), as is formalized in the following proposition.

Proposition 3. *Suppose $q \in \mathbb{R}^I$ is a portfolio such that $\rho^C (r^f q^T \Sigma^{CD} q + (r^f - \rho^D) q^T \Sigma^C q) > (r^f)^2 q^T \Sigma^{CD} q$. Then, returns are low when illiquidity increases,*

$$\text{cov}_t \left(c_{t+1}^q, r_{t+1}^q \right) < 0. \tag{10}$$

Consistent with this result, Chordia et al. (2001a), Jones (2001), and Pastor and Stambaugh (2003) find a negative relation between the market return and measures of market illiquidity, Amihud (2002) finds a negative relation between the return on size portfolios and their corresponding unexpected illiquidity, and Bekaert et al. (2003) find a negative relationship between illiquidity and returns for emerging markets.

3.3. An Unconditional Liquidity-Adjusted CAPM

To estimate the liquidity-adjusted CAPM, we derive an unconditional version. An unconditional result obtains, for instance, under the assumption of independence over time of dividends and illiquidity costs. Empirically, however, illiquidity is persistent. Therefore, we rely instead on an assumption of constant conditional covariances of innovations in illiquidity and returns.[9] This assumption yields the unconditional result that

$$E\left(r_t^i - r_t^f\right) = E\left(c_t^i\right) + \lambda\beta^{1i} + \lambda\beta^{2i} - \lambda\beta^{3i} - \lambda\beta^{4i}, \tag{12}$$

where

$$\beta^{1i} = \frac{\mathrm{cov}\left(r_t^i, r_t^M - E_{t-1}\left(r_t^M\right)\right)}{\mathrm{var}\left(r_t^M - E_{t-1}\left(r_t^M\right) - \left[c_t^M - E_{t-1}\left(c_t^M\right)\right]\right)}, \tag{13}$$

$$\beta^{2i} = \frac{\mathrm{cov}\left(c_t^i - E_{t-1}\left(c_t^i\right), c_t^M - E_{t-1}\left(c_t^M\right)\right)}{\mathrm{var}\left(r_t^M - E_{t-1}\left(r_t^M\right) - \left[c_t^M - E_{t-1}\left(c_t^M\right)\right]\right)}, \tag{14}$$

$$\beta^{3i} = \frac{\mathrm{cov}\left(r_t^i, c_t^M - E_{t-1}\left(c_t^M\right)\right)}{\mathrm{var}\left(r_t^M - E_{t-1}\left(r_t^M\right) - \left[c_t^M - E_{t-1}\left(c_t^M\right)\right]\right)}, \tag{15}$$

$$\beta^{4i} = \frac{\mathrm{cov}\left(c_t^i - E_{t-1}\left(c_t^i\right), r_t^M - E_{t-1}\left(r_t^M\right)\right)}{\mathrm{var}\left(r_t^M - E_{t-1}\left(r_t^M\right) - \left[c_t^M - E_{t-1}\left(c_t^M\right)\right]\right)}, \tag{16}$$

and $\lambda = E(\lambda_t) = E(r_t^M - c_t^M - r^f)$. Next, we describe the empirical tests of this unconditional relation.

4. Empirical Results

In this section, we estimate and test the liquidity-adjusted CAPM as specified in Equation (12). We do this in five steps:

[9] Alternatively, the same unconditional model can be derived by assuming a constant risk premium λ and using the fact that for any random variables X and Y, it holds that

$$E(\mathrm{cov}_t(X, Y)) = \mathrm{cov}(X - E_t(X), Y) = \mathrm{cov}(X - E_t(X), Y - E_t(Y)). \tag{11}$$

We note that the possible time-variation of risk premium is driven by constant absolute risk aversion in our model, but with constant relative risk aversion, the risk premium is approximately constant. See Friend and Blume (1975).

(i) We estimate, in each month t of our sample, a measure of illiquidity, c_t^i, for each individual security i. (Section 4.1).

(ii) We form a "market portfolio" and sets of 25 test portfolios sorted on the basis of illiquidity, illiquidity variation, size, and book-to-market by size, respectively. We compute the return and illiquidity for each portfolio in each month (Section 4.2).

(iii) For the market portfolio as well as the test portfolios, we estimate the innovations in illiquidity, $c_t^p - E_{t-1}\left(c_t^p\right)$ (Section 4.3).

(iv) Using these illiquidity innovations and returns, we estimate and analyze the liquidity betas (Section 4.4).

(v) Finally, we consider the empirical fit of the (unconditional) liquidity-adjusted CAPM by running cross-sectional regressions. To check the robustness of our results, we do the analysis with a number of different specifications (Section 4.5).

4.1. The Illiquidity Measure

Liquidity is (unfortunately) not an observable variable. There exist, however, many proxies for liquidity. Some proxies, such as the bid–ask spread, are based on market microstructure data, which is not available for a time series as long as is usually desirable for studying the effect on expected returns. Further, the bid–ask spread measures well the cost of selling a small number of shares, but it does not necessarily measure well the cost of selling many shares. We follow Amihud (2002) in estimating illiquidity using only daily data from the Center for Research in Security Prices (CRSP). In particular, Amihud (2002) defines the illiquidity of stock i in month t as

$$ILLIQ_t^i = \frac{1}{Days_t^i} \sum_{d=1}^{Days_t^i} \frac{\left|R_{td}^i\right|}{V_{td}^i}, \tag{17}$$

where R_{td}^i and V_{td}^i are, respectively, the return and dollar volume (in millions) on day d in month t, and $Days_t^i$ is the number of valid observation days in month t for stock i.

The intuition behind this illiquidity measure is as follows. A stock is illiquid – that is, has a high value of $ILLIQ_t^i$ – if the stock's price moves a lot in response to little volume. In our model, illiquidity is the cost of selling and, as discussed in Section 2, real markets have several different selling costs including broker fees, bid-ask spreads, market impact, and search costs. Our empirical strategy is based on an assumption that $ILLIQ$ is a valid instrument for the costs of selling, broadly interpreted. Consistent with this view, Amihud (2002) shows empirically that *ILLIQ* is positively related to measures of price impact and fixed trading costs over the time period in which he has the microstructure data. Similarly, Hasbrouck (2002) computes a measure of Kyle's lambda using microstructure data for NYSE, AMEX, and NASDAQ stocks, and finds that its Spearman (Pearson) correlation with *ILLIQ* in the cross-section of stocks is 0.737 (0.473). Hasbrouck (2002) concludes that "[a]mong the proxies considered here, the illiquidity measure [*ILLIQ*] appears to be the best." Furthermore, *ILLIQ* is closely related to the Amivest measure of illiquidity, which has often been used in the empirical microstructure literature.

There are two problems with using *ILLIQ*. First, it is measured in "percent per dollar," whereas the model is specified in terms of "dollar cost per dollar invested." This is a problem because it means that *ILLIQ* is not stationary (e.g., inflation is ignored). Second, while *ILLIQ* is an instrument for the cost of selling, it does not directly measure the cost of a trade. To solve these problems, we define a normalized measure of illiquidity, c_t^i, by

$$c_t^i = \min\left(0.25 + 0.30 ILLIQ_t^i P_{t-1}^M, 30.00\right),\qquad(18)$$

where P_{t-1}^M is the ratio of the capitalizations of the market portfolio at the end of month $t-1$ and of the market portfolio at the end of July 1962. The P_{t-1}^M adjustment solves the first problem mentioned above, and it makes this measure of illiquidity relatively stationary. The coefficients 0.25 and 0.30 are chosen such that the cross-sectional distribution of normalized illiquidity (c_t^i) for size-decile portfolios has approximately the same level and variance as does the effective half spread – i.e., the difference between the transaction price and the midpoint of the prevailing bid–ask quote – reported by Chalmers and Kadlec (1998), Table 5.1. This normalized illiquidity is capped at a maximum value of 30% in order to ensure that our results are not driven by the extreme observations $ILLIQ_t^i$. Furthermore, a per-trade cost greater than 30% seems unreasonable and is an artifact of the effect of low volume days on $ILLIQ_t^i$.

Chalmers and Kadlec (1998) report that the mean effective spread for size-decile portfolios of NYSE and AMEX stocks over the period 1983–1992 ranges from 0.29% to 3.41% with an average of 1.11%. The normalized illiquidity, c_t^i, for identically formed portfolios has an average of 1.24%, a standard deviation of 0.37%, and matches the range as well as the cross-sectional variation reported by Chalmers and Kadlec (1998). This means that we can interpret the illiquidity measure c_t^i as directly related to (a lower bound of) the per-trade cost.

Table 5.1. *Properties of illiquidity portfolios*

This table reports the properties of the odd-numbered portfolios of twenty-five value-weighted illiquidity portfolios formed each year during 1964–1999. The market beta (β^{1p}) and the liquidity betas(β^{2p}, β^{3p}, and β^{4p}) are computed using all monthly return and illiquidity observations for each portfolio and for an equal-weighted market portfolio; t-statistics are reported in parentheses. The standard deviation of a portfolio's illiquidity innovations is reported under the column of $\sigma(\Delta c^p)$. The average illiquidity, $E(c^p)$, the average excess return, $E(r^{e,p})$, the turnover (trn), the market capitalization (size), and book-to-market (BM) are computed for each portfolio as time-series averages of the respective monthly characteristics. Finally, $\sigma(r^p)$ is the average of the standard deviation of daily returns for the portfolio's constituent stocks computed each month.

	β^{1p} ($\cdot$100)	β^{2p} ($\cdot$100)	β^{3p} ($\cdot$100)	β^{4p} ($\cdot$100)	$E(c^p)$ (%)	$\sigma(\Delta c^p)$ (%)	$E(r^{e,p})$ (%)	$\sigma(r^p)$ (%)	trn (%)	Size (bl$)	BM
1	55.10 (14.54)	0.00 (0.08)	− 0.80 (− 5.90)	− 0.00 (− 0.10)	0.25	0.00	0.48	1.43	3.25	12.50	0.53
3	67.70 (16.32)	0.00 (0.58)	− 1.05 (− 7.14)	− 0.03 (− 0.62)	0.26	0.00	0.39	1.64	4.19	2.26	0.72
5	74.67 (20.44)	0.00 (1.27)	− 1.24 (− 7.43)	− 0.07 (− 1.36)	0.27	0.01	0.60	1.74	4.17	1.20	0.71
7	76.25 (20.63)	0.00 (2.18)	− 1.27 (− 7.49)	− 0.10 (− 2.03)	0.29	0.01	0.57	1.83	4.14	0.74	0.73
9	81.93 (33.25)	0.01 (3.79)	− 1.37 (− 8.00)	− 0.18 (− 3.74)	0.32	0.02	0.71	1.86	3.82	0.48	0.73
11	84.59 (34.21)	0.01 (5.07)	− 1.41 (− 7.94)	− 0.33 (− 5.85)	0.36	0.04	0.73	1.94	3.87	0.33	0.76
13	85.29 (34.15)	0.01 (6.84)	− 1.47 (− 8.01)	− 0.40 (− 7.46)	0.43	0.05	0.77	1.99	3.47	0.24	0.77
15	88.99 (42.88)	0.02 (6.87)	− 1.61 (− 8.35)	− 0.70 (− 8.45)	0.53	0.08	0.85	2.04	3.20	0.17	0.83
17	87.89 (27.54)	0.04 (8.16)	− 1.59 (− 8.18)	− 0.98 (− 9.30)	0.71	0.13	0.80	2.11	2.96	0.13	0.88
19	87.50 (40.74)	0.05 (7.63)	− 1.58 (− 8.75)	− 1.53 (− 8.77)	1.01	0.21	0.83	2.13	2.68	0.09	0.92
21	92.73 (37.85)	0.09 (7.33)	− 1.69 (− 8.34)	− 2.10 (− 6.11)	1.61	0.34	1.13	2.28	2.97	0.06	0.99
23	94.76 (39.71)	0.19 (6.85)	− 1.71 (− 8.68)	− 3.35 (− 5.91)	3.02	0.62	1.12	2.57	2.75	0.04	1.09
25	84.54 (20.86)	0.42 (6.40)	− 1.69 (− 8.23)	− 4.52 (− 3.35)	8.83	1.46	1.10	2.87	2.60	0.02	1.15

Admittedly, this is a noisy measure of illiquidity. This makes it harder for us to find an empirical connection between return and illiquidity, and it can enhance omitted-variable problems. The noise is reduced by considering portfolios rather than individual stocks.

4.2. Portfolios

We employ daily return and volume data from CRSP from July 1, 1962, until December 31, 1999, for all common shares listed on NYSE and AMEX. To keep our liquidity measure consistent across stocks, we do not include Nasdaq since the volume data includes interdealer trades (and only starts in 1982). Also, we use book-to-market data based on the COMPUSTAT measure of book value.[10]

We form a market portfolio for each month t during this sample period based on stocks with beginning-of-month price between $5 and $1000, and with at least 15 days of return and volume data in that month.

We form twenty-five illiquidity portfolios for each year y during the period 1964 to 1999 by sorting stocks with price, at the beginning of the year, between $5 and $1000, and return and volume data in year $y - 1$ for at least 100 days.[11] We compute the annual illiquidity for each eligible stock as the average over the entire year $y - 1$ of daily illiquidities, analogously to the monthly illiquidity calculation in (17). The eligible stocks are then sorted into twenty-five portfolios, $p \in \{1, 2, \ldots, 25\}$, based on their year $y - 1$ illiquidities.

Similarly, we form twenty-five illiquidity-variation portfolios (denoted "σ(illiquidity) portfolios") by ranking the eligible stocks each year based on the standard deviation of daily illiquidity measures in the previous year, and twenty-five size portfolios by ranking stocks based on their market capitalization at the beginning of the year.

Finally, we form portfolios sorted first into five book-to-market quintiles and then into five size quintiles within the book-to-market groups. This sample is restricted to stocks with book-to-market data in year $y - 1$. When considering the portfolio properties, we use the year-y book-to-market, averaging across stocks with available book-to-market data in that year.

---

[10] We are grateful to Joe Chen for providing us with data on book-to-market ratios. The book-to-market ratios are computed as described in Ang and Chen (2002): [For a given month] the book-to-market ratio is calculated using the most recently available fiscal year-end balance sheet data on COMPUSTAT. Following Fama and French (1993), we define "book value" as the value of common stockholders' equity, plus deferred taxes and investment tax credit, minus the book value of preferred stock. The book value is then divided by the market value on the day of the firm's fiscal year-end.

[11] Amihud (2002) and Pastor and Stambaugh (2003) employ similar requirements for the inclusion of stocks in their samples. These requirements help reduce the measurement error in the monthly illiquidity series.

For each portfolio p (including the market portfolio), we compute its return in month t as

$$r_t^p = \sum_{i \text{ in } p} w_t^{ip} r_t^i, \tag{19}$$

where the sum is taken over the stocks included in portfolio p in month t, and where w_t^{ip} are either equal weights or value-based weights, depending on the specification.[12]

Similarly, we compute the normalized illiquidity of a portfolio, p, as

$$c_t^p = \sum_{i \text{ in } p} w_t^{ip} c_t^i, \tag{20}$$

where, as above, w_t^{ip} are either equal weights or value-based weights, depending on the specification.

The model's results are phrased in terms of value-weighted returns and value-weighted illiquidity for the market portfolio. Several studies, however, focus on equal-weighted return and illiquidity measures, for instance Amihud (2002) and Chordia et al. (2000). Computing the market return and illiquidity as equal-weighted averages is a way of compensating for the over-representation in our sample of large liquid securities, as compared to the "true" market portfolio in the economy. In particular, our sample does not include illiquid assets such as corporate bonds, private equity, real estate, and many small stocks, and these assets constitute a significant fraction of aggregate wealth. In particular, Heaton and Lucas (2000) report that stocks constitute only 13.6% of national wealth, while noncorporate (i.e. private) equity is 13.8%, other financial wealth is 28.2%, owner-occupied real estate is 33.3%, and consumer durables is 11.1%. Therefore, we focus in our empirical work on an equal-weighted market portfolio, although we also estimate the model with a value-weighted market portfolio for robustness. Also, we use both equal- and value-weighted averages for the test portfolios.

[12] The returns, r_t^i, are adjusted for stock delisting to avoid survivorship bias, following Shumway (1997). In particular, the last return used is either the last return available on CRSP, or the delisting return, if available. While a last return for the stock of -100% is naturally included in the study, a return of -30% is assigned if the deletion reason is coded in CRSP as 500 (reason unavailable), 520 (went to OTC), 551–573 and 580 (various reasons), 574 (bankruptcy), and 584 (does not meet exchange financial guidelines). Shumway (1997) obtains that -30% is the average delisting return, examining the OTC returns of delisted stocks.

4.3. Innovations in Illiquidity

Illiquidity is persistent. The autocorrelation of the market illiquidity, for instance, is 0.87 at a monthly frequency. Therefore, we focus on the innovations, $c_t^p - E_{t-1}(c_t^p)$, in illiquidity of a portfolio when computing its liquidity betas as explained in Section 3.3.

To compute these innovations, we first define the un-normalized illiquidity, truncated for outliers, of a portfolio p as

$$\overline{ILLIQ}_t^p := \sum_{i\,in\,p} w_t^{ip} \min\left(ILLIQ_t^i, \frac{30.00 - 0.25}{0.30 P_{t-1}^M} \right), \qquad (21)$$

where w_t^{ip} is the portfolio weight. As explained in Section 4.1, we normalize illiquidity to make it stationary and to put it on a scale corresponding to the cost of a single trade.

To predict market illiquidity, we run the following regression:

$$(0.25 + 0.30\overline{ILLIQ}_t^M P_{t-1}^M) = a_0 + a_1(0.25 + 0.30\overline{ILLIQ}_{t-1}^M P_{t-1}^M)$$
$$+ a_2(0.25 + 0.30\overline{ILLIQ}_{t-2}^M P_{t-1}^M)$$
$$+ u_t. \qquad (22)$$

Note that the three terms inside parentheses in this specification correspond closely to c_t^M, c_{t-1}^M, and c_{t-2}^M, respectively, as given by (18) and (20), with the difference that the same date is used for the market index (P_{t-1}^M) in all three terms. This is to ensure that we are measuring innovations only in illiquidity, not changes in P^M. Our results are robust to the specification of liquidity innovations and, in particular, employing other stock-market variables available at time $t - 1$ does not improve significantly the explanatory power of the regression. Pastor and Stambaugh (2003) employ a specification to compute market liquidity innovations that is similar in spirit to the AR(2) specification in (22).

The residual, u, of the regression in (22) is interpreted as the market illiquidity innovation, $c_t^M - E_{t-1}(c_t^M)$ that is,

$$c_t^M - E_{t-1}\left(c_t^M\right) := u_t, \qquad (23)$$

and innovations in portfolio illiquidity are computed in the same way using the same AR coefficients.

For the market illiquidity series, the AR(2) specification has a R^2 of 78%. The resulting innovations in market illiquidity, $c_t^M - E_{t-1}(c_t^M)$, have a standard deviation of 0.17%. Figure 5.1 plots the time series of these innovations, scaled to have unit standard deviation. The autocorrelation

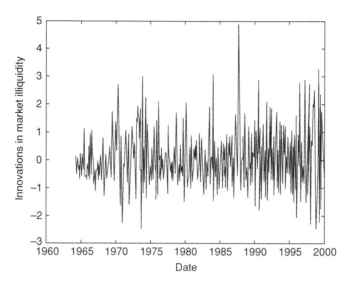

Figure 5.1. Standardized innovations in market illiquidity from 1964–1999.

of these illiquidity innovations is low (−0.03) and, visually, they appear stationary. Employing an AR(1) specification produces a significantly greater correlation of innovations (−0.29), whereas employing an AR(3) specification produces little improvement in the explanatory power.

The measured innovations in market illiquidity are high during periods that anecdotally were characterized by liquidity crisis, for instance, in 5/1970 (Penn Central commercial paper crisis), 11/1973 (oil crisis), 10/1987 (stock market crash), 8/1990 (Iraqi invasion of Kuwait), 4,12/1997 (Asian crisis), and 6–10/1998 (Russian default and Long Term Capital Management crisis). The correlation between this measure of innovations in market illiquidity and the measure of innovations in liquidity used by Pastor and Stambaugh (2003) is −0.33.[13] (The negative sign is due to the fact that Pastor and Stambaugh (2003) measure liquidity, whereas we follow Amihud (2002) in considering *il*liquidity.)

4.4. Liquidity Risk

In this section, we present the descriptive statistics of liquidity risk, measured by the betas β^{2p}, β^{3p}, and β^{4p}. We focus on the value-weighted illiquidity portfolios whose properties are reported in Table 5.1. Similar conclusions

[13] We thank Pastor and Stambaugh for providing their data on innovations in market liquidity.

are drawn from examining the properties of equal-weighted illiquidity port-folios or size portfolios (not reported). The four betas, β^{1p}, β^{2p}, β^{3p}, and β^{4p}, for each portfolio are computed as per Eqs. (13)–(16) using the entire monthly time-series 1964 to 1999, where the illiquidity innovations are computed as described in Section 4.3 and the innovations in market port-folio returns are computed using an AR(2) that also employs available market characteristics at the beginning of the month (return, volatility, average illiquidity, log of average dollar volume, log of average turnover, all measured over the past six months, and log of one-month lagged market capitalization).

Table 5.1 shows that the sort on past illiquidity successfully produces portfolios with monotonically increasing average illiquidity from portfolio 1 through portfolio 25. Not surprisingly, we see that illiquid stocks – that is, stocks with high average illiquidity $E(c^p)$ – tend to have a high volatility of stock returns, a low turnover, and a small market capitalization. Further-more, we find that illiquid stocks also have high liquidity *risk* – they have large values of β^{2p} and large negative values of β^{3p} and β^{4p}. In other words, a stock, which is illiquid in absolute terms *(c^p)*, also tends to have a lot of commonality in liquidity with the market (cov(c^p, c^M)), a lot of return sensitivity to market liquidity (cov(r^p, c^M)), and a lot of liquidity sensitivity to market returns (cov(c^p, r^M)). This result is interesting on its own since it is consistent with the notion of flight to liquidity. We note that all of the betas are estimated with a small error (i.e., a small asymptotic variance). Indeed, almost all of the betas are statistically significant at conventional levels.

A liquidity beta is proportional to the product of the correlation between its respective arguments and their standard deviations. As noted before, more illiquid stocks have greater volatility of returns. Furthermore, since illiquidity is bounded below by zero, it is natural that more illiquid stocks also have more volatile illiquidity innovations. This is verified in Table 5.1 which shows that the standard deviation of portfolio illiquidity innova-tions, $\sigma(\Delta c^p)$, increases monotonically in portfolio illiquidity. However, the higher variability of returns and illiquidity innovations are not the sole drivers of the positive relation between illiquidity and liquidity risk. The correlation coefficients between c^p and $c^M(r^p$ and $c^M)$ are also increasing (decreasing) in portfolio illiquidity. The correlation coefficients between c^p and r^M are decreasing in illiquidity between portfolios 1–15 and are gradually increasing thereafter. Nevertheless, the variability of c^p ensures that the covariances between c^p and r^M are decreasing in illiquidity. (These correlations are not reported in the table for sake of brevity.)

Table 5.2. *Beta correlations for illiquidity portfolios*

This table reports the correlations of β^{1p}, β^{2p}, β^{3p}, and β^{4p}, for the twenty-five value-weighted illiquidity portfolios formed for each year during 1964–1999.

	β^{1p}	β^{2p}	β^{3p}	β^{4p}
β^{1p}	1.000	0.441	-0.972	-0.628
β^{2p}		1.000	-0.573	-0.941
β^{3p}			1.000	0.726
β^{4p}				1.000

The collinearity of measures of liquidity risk is confirmed by considering the correlation among the betas, reported in Table 5.2. The collinearity problem is not just a property of the liquidity-sorted portfolios; it also exists at an individual stock level as is seen in Table 5.3. The collinearity at the stock level is smaller, which could be due in part to larger estimation errors. While this collinearity is theoretically intriguing, it makes it hard to empirically distinguish the separate effects of illiquidity and the individual liquidity betas.

4.5. How Liquidity Risk Affects Returns

In this section, we study how liquidity risk affects expected returns. We do this by running cross-sectional regressions on our test portfolios using a GMM framework that takes into account the pre-estimation of the betas

Table 5.3. *Beta correlations for individual stocks*

This table reports the correlations of β^{1i}, β^{2i}, β^{3i}, and β^{4i} for the common shares listed on NYSE and AMEX during the period 1964–1999. The correlations are computed annually for all eligible stocks in a year and then averaged over the sample period. The four betas are computed for each stock using all monthly return and illiquidity observations for the stock and the market portfolio.

	β^{1i}	β^{2i}	β^{3i}	β^{4i} ,
β^{1i}	1.000	0.020	-0.685	-0.164
β^{2i}		1.000	-0.072	-0.270
β^{3i}			1.000	0.192
β^{4i}				1.000

(as in Cochrane, 2001). Standard errors are computed using the Newey and West (1987) method with two lags. Our point estimates are the same as those derived using OLS (either in a pooled regression or using the Fama and MacBeth (1973) method), and our standard errors correspond to those of Shanken (1992) except that the GMM method also takes serial correlation into account.

Illiquidity and σ (illiquidity) portfolios. The potential effect of liquidity and liquidity risk is, of course, detected by considering portfolios that differ in their liquidity attributes. Hence, we consider first the liquidity-adjusted CAPM (12) for portfolios sorted by illiquidity and the illiquidity variation.

To impose the model-implied constraint that the risk premia of the different betas is the same, we define the "net beta" as

$$\beta^{\text{net},p} := \beta^{1p} + \beta^{2p} - \beta^{3p} - \beta^{4p}. \tag{24}$$

With this definition, the liquidity-adjusted CAPM becomes

$$E\left(r_t^p - r_t^f\right) = \alpha + \kappa E\left(c_t^p\right) + \lambda \beta^{\text{net},p}, \tag{25}$$

where we allow a nonzero intercept, α, in the estimation, although the model implies that the intercept is zero. Also, in our model $\kappa = 1$. This is because investors incur the illiquidity cost exactly once each model period. Our monthly estimation period is, however, different from a typical investor's holding period – the period implicitly considered in the model. When the estimation period is κ times the holding period, then the estimated $E(r_t^p - r_t^f)$ is approximately κ times the expected holding period return, and the estimated $\beta^{\text{net},p}$ is assumed to be approximately κ times the holding-period net beta. This is because a κ-period return (or illiquidity innovation) is approximately a sum of κ one-period returns (or illiquidity innovations), and because returns and illiquidity innovations have low correlation across time. The illiquidity, $E(c^p)$, however, does not scale with time period because it is an average of daily illiquidities (not a sum of such terms). Therefore, the $E(c^p)$ term is scaled by κ in (25) to adjust for the difference between estimation periods and holding periods.

The average holding period is proxied empirically by the period over which all shares are turned over once. Hence, we calibrate κ as the average monthly turnover across all stocks in the sample. In the sample of liquidity portfolios, κ is calibrated to 0.034, which corresponds to a holding period of $1/0.034 \cong 29$ months. The expected illiquidity, $E(c_t^p)$, is computed as the portfolio's average illiquidity. To run the regression (25) with a fixed

κ, we treat the net return, $E(r_t^p - r_t^f) - \kappa E(c_t^p)$, as the dependent variable. However, all R^2 are based on the same dependent variable, namely, $E(r_t^p - r_t^f)$. Note that the structure of the liquidity-adjusted CAPM and the calibration of κ make the estimation different from the typical cross-sectional regression study in which the asset-pricing relationship is backed out from the return series and data on security characteristics such as beta, size, book-to-market, etc.

The liquidity-adjusted CAPM (25) has only one risk premium, λ, that needs to be estimated as in the standard CAPM. Here, the risk factor is the net beta instead of the standard market beta. Hence, the empirical improvement in fit relative to the standard CAPM is not achieved by adding factors (or otherwise adding degrees of freedom), but simply by making a liquidity adjustment.

The estimated results for Eq. (25) are reported in line 1 of Table 5.4, with illiquidity portfolios in Panel A and σ (illiquidity) portfolios in Panel B. With either portfolio, the risk premium λ is positive and significant at a 1% level and α is insignificant, both results lending support to our model. The R^2 of the liquidity-adjusted CAPM is high relative to the standard CAPM, reported in line 3. In line 2, we estimate the liquidity-adjusted CAPM with κ as a free parameter, which results in only modest changes in κ and X.

While the improvement in fit of the liquidity-adjusted CAPM over the CAPM is encouraging, it does not constitute a test of the effect of liquidity risk. To isolate the effect of liquidity risk (β^2, β^3, and β^4) over liquidity level ($E(c)$) and market risk (β^1), we consider the relation

$$E\left(r_t^p - r_t^f\right) = \alpha + \kappa E\left(c_t^p\right) + \lambda^1 \beta^{1p} + \lambda \beta^{\text{net},p}. \tag{26}$$

In line 4, this relation is estimated with κ at its calibrated value. We see that β^{net} is insignificant for illiquidity portfolios, but significant for σ (illiquidity) portfolios. In line 5, the relation is estimated with κ as a free parameter. In this regression, the support for the model is stronger in that β^{net} is significant with either portfolio. We note that κ is estimated to be negative in Panel A, although it is statistically insignificant. Since the model implies that κ should be positive, we estimate in line 6 with the restriction that $\kappa = 0$. With this specification, β^{net} remains significant in both panels. In conclusion, there is some evidence that liquidity risk matters over and above market risk and liquidity level. The collinearity problems imply, however, that this evidence is weak.

We note that a negative coefficient on β^1 does not imply a negative risk premium on market risk since β^1 is also contained in β^{net}. Rather, a negative

Table 5.4. *Illiquidity and σ (illiquidity) portfolios*

This table reports the estimated coefficients from cross-sectional regressions of the liquidity-adjusted CAPM for twenty-five value-weighted portfolios using monthly data during 1964–1999 with an equal-weighted market portfolio. We consider special cases of the relation

$$E(r^p_t - r^f_t) = \alpha + \kappa E\left(c^p_t\right) + \lambda^1\beta^{1p} + \lambda^2\beta^{2p} + \lambda^3\beta^{3p} + \lambda^4\beta^{4p} + \lambda\beta^{net,p},$$

where $\beta^{net,p} = \beta^{1p} + \beta^{2p} - \beta^{3p} - \beta^{4p}$. In some specifications, κ is set to be the average monthly turnover. The t-statistic, reported in the parentheses, is estimated using a GMM framework that takes into account the pre-estimation of the betas. The R^2 is obtained in a single cross-sectional regression, and the adjusted R^2 is reported in parentheses.

	Constant	$E(c^p)$	β^{1p}	β^{2p}	β^{3p}	β^{4p}	$\beta^{net,p}$	R^2
Panel A: illiquidity portfolios								
1	− 0.556	0.034					1.512	0.732
	(− 1.450)	(–)					(2.806)	(0.732)
2	− 0.512	0.042					1.449	0.825
	(− 1.482)	(2.210)					(2.532)	(0.809)
3	− 0.788		1.891					0.653
	(− 1.910)		(3.198)					(0.638)
4	− 0.333	0.034	− 3.181				4.334	0.843
	(− 0.913)	(–)	(− 0.998)				(1.102)	(0.836)
5	0.005	− 0.032	− 13.223				13.767	0.878
	(0.013)	(− 0.806)	(− 1.969)				(2.080)	(0.861)
6	− 0.160		− 8.322				9.164	0.870
	(− 0.447)		(− 2.681)				(3.016)	(0.858)
7	− 0.089	0.034	0.992	− 153.369	7.112	− 17.583		0.881
	(− 0.219)	(–)	(0.743)	(− 1.287)	(0.402)	(− 1.753)		(0.865)
8	− 0.089	0.033	0.992	− 151.152	7.087	− 17.542		0.881
	(− 0.157)	(0.166)	(0.468)	(− 0.280)	(0.086)	(− 1.130)		(0.850)
Panel B: σ (illiquidity) portfolios								
1	− 0.528	0.035					1.471	0.865
	(− 1.419)	(–)					(2.817)	(0.865)
2	− 0.363	0.062					1.243	0.886
	(− 1.070)	(2.433)					(2.240)	(0.875)
3	− 0.827		1.923					0.726
	(− 2.027)		(3.322)					(0.714)
4	− 0.014	0.035	− 7.113				7.772	0.917
	(− 0.037)	(–)	(− 1.939)				(2.615)	(0.914)
5	0.094	0.007	− 11.013				11.467	0.924
	(0.235)	(0.158)	(− 2.080)				(2.480)	(0.914)
6	0.119		− 11.914				12.320	0.924
	(0.305)		(− 2.413)				(2.608)	(0.917)
7	0.464	0.035	− 1.105	− 83.690	− 74.538	− 14.560		0.940
	(0.913)	(–)	(− 0.728)	(− 0.663)	(− 1.175)	(− 1.662)		(0.931)
8	0.459	0.148	− 1.125	− 390.588	− 73.552	− 21.688		0.942
	(0.565)	(0.140)	(− 0.485)	(− 0.140)	(− 1.943)	(− 0.335)		(0.927)

coefficient suggests that liquidity risk may have a higher risk premium than market risk. For instance, line 4 of Table 5.4A means that

$$E\left(r_t^p - r_t^f\right) = -0.333 + 0.034E\left(c_t^p\right) - 3.181\beta^{1p} + 4.334\beta^{\text{net},p}$$
$$= -0.333 + 0.034E\left(c_t^p\right) + 1.153\beta^{1p}$$
$$+4.334(\beta^{2p} - \beta^{3p} - \beta^{4p}). \tag{27}$$

Finally, in line 7, we allow all of the betas to have different risk premia λ^i, and in line 8, we further let κ be a free parameter. That is, lines 7–8 estimate the generalized relation

$$E\left(r_t^p - r_t^f\right) = \alpha + \kappa E\left(c_t^p\right) + \lambda^1\beta^{1p} + \lambda^2\beta^{2p} + \lambda^3\beta^{3p} + \lambda^4\beta^{4p} \tag{28}$$

without the model restrictions that $\lambda^1 = \lambda^2 = -\lambda^3 = -\lambda^4$. We see that the multi-collinearity problems are severe, and, hence, statistical identification of the separate effects of the different liquidity risks is difficult. Of course, we must also entertain the possibility that not all of these risk factors are empirically relevant.

The empirical fit of the standard CAPM is illustrated in the top left panel of Figure 5.2 for illiquidity portfolios and of Figure 5.3 for σ (illiquidity) portfolios. The top right and bottom panels show, respectively, the fit of the constrained and unconstrained liquidity-adjusted CAPM, that is, lines 1 and 8, respectively, from Table 5.4. We see that the liquidity adjustment improves the fit especially for the illiquid portfolios, consistent with what our intuition would suggest. We note that the number of free parameters is the same in the top right and top left panels, so the improvement in fit is not a consequence of more degrees of freedom.

Economic significance of results. It is interesting to consider the economic significance of liquidity risk. To get a perspective on the magnitude of the effect, we compute the annual return premium required to hold illiquid rather than liquid securities. This is computed as the product of the risk premium and the difference in liquidity risk across liquidity portfolios. If we use the unrestricted model in line 8 of Table 5.4A, then our estimates are very noisy because of the multicollinearity problem. Instead, the benefit of having an economic model is that we can impose its structure and can get relatively tight estimates. Hence, we use the calibrated value of κ and the common risk premium, $\lambda = 1.512$, from line 1. Of course, when interpreting the results, one must bear in mind that they rely on the validity of the model.

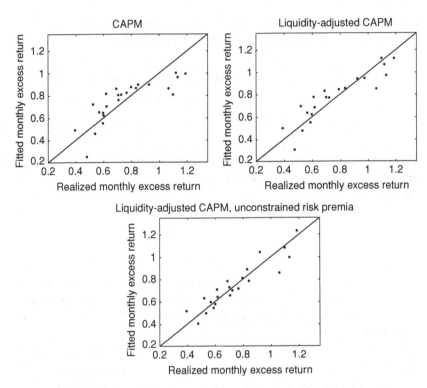

Figure 5.2. *Illiquidity portfolios:* the top left panel shows the fitted CAPM returns vs. realized returns using monthly data 1964–1999 for value-weighted illiquidity portfolios. The top right panel shows the same for the liquidity-adjusted CAPM, and the lower panel shows the relation for the liquidity-adjusted CAPM with unconstrained risk premia.

The difference in annualized expected returns between portfolio 1 and 25 that can be attributed to a difference in β^2, the commonality between the portfolio illiquidity and market illiquidity, is

$$\lambda(\beta^{2,P_{25}} - \beta^{2,P_1})12 = 0.08\%. \tag{29}$$

Similarly, the annualized return difference stemming from the difference in β^3, the sensitivity of the portfolio return to market illiquidity, is

$$-\lambda(\beta^{3,P_{25}} - \beta^{3,P_1})12 = 0.16\%, \tag{30}$$

and the effect of β^4, the sensitivity of the portfolio illiquidity to market return, is

$$-\lambda(\beta^{4,P_{25}} - \beta^{4,P_1})12 = 0.82\%. \tag{31}$$

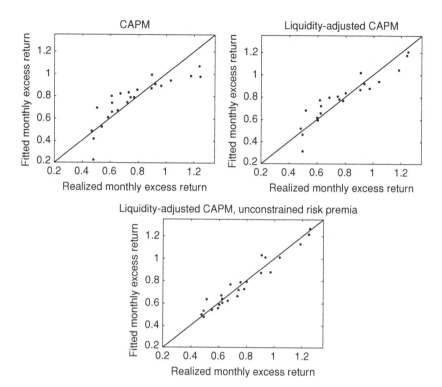

Figure 5.3. σ (*illiquidity*) *portfolios*: the top left panel shows the fitted CAPM returns vs. realized returns using monthly data 1964–1999 for value weighted σ (illiquidity) portfolios. The top right panel shows the same for the liquidity-adjusted CAPM, and the lower panel shows the relation for the liquidity-adjusted CAPM with unconstrained risk premia.

The total effect of liquidity risk is therefore 1.1% per year. Using the standard error of the estimates of λ and the betas, the 95% confidence interval for the total effect of $\beta^2 - \beta^3 - \beta^4$ is [0.24%, 1.88%]. Hence, under the model restrictions and using the calibrated κ, the effect of liquidity risk is significantly different from zero.

Interestingly, of the three liquidity risks the effect of β^4, the covariation of a security's illiquidity to market returns, appears to have the largest economic impact on expected returns. (Also, it has the highest t-statistics in the unrestricted regression of lines 7–8 in Table 5.4). This liquidity risk has not been studied before either theoretically or empirically.

The difference in annualized expected returns between portfolios 1 and 25 that can be attributed to a difference in the expected illiquidity, $E(c)$, is 3.5%, using the calibrated coefficient. The overall effect of expected illiquidity and liquidity risk is thus 4.6% per year.

While the magnitude of liquidity risk is economically significant, it is lower than the magnitude estimated by Pastor and Stambaugh (2003). This could be due to the fact that they employ a different measure of liquidity, or due to the fact that they sort portfolios based on liquidity risk (in their case, β^3) whereas we sort based on the level of illiquidity. Also, this could be because they do not control for the level of illiquidity which has been shown to command a significant premium in a number of studies including Amihud and Mendelson (1986), Brennan and Subrahmanyam (1996), Brennan et al. (1998), Datar et al. (1998), Swan (2002), and Dimson and Hanke (2002). Finally, the difference could also arise because we restrict the risk premia on different liquidity betas to be the same. For instance, the magnitude of the risk premium related to β^4 is estimated to be higher in lines 7–8 of Table 5.4A. This higher risk premium results in a per-year effect of about 9% from β^4 alone.[14]

The collinearity between liquidity and liquidity risk implies that the most robust number is their overall effect. Further, our results suggest that studies that focus on the separate effect of liquidity (or liquidity risk) can possibly be reinterpreted as providing an estimate of the overall effect of liquidity and liquidity risk.

Robustness, size, and book-to-market. To check the robustness of our results, we consider different specifications and portfolios. First, we consider whether our results are robust to the choice of value weighting versus equal weighting. Table 5.5A reports the results with equal-weighted illiquidity portfolios and equal-weighted market, and Table 5.5B with value-weighted illiquidity portfolios and value-weighted market. The results and their significance are similar to those of Table 5.4A. First, β^{net} is borderline significant at a 5% level in line 1 of Table 5.5A, but insignificant at this level in Table 5.5B. In both tables, the liquidity-adjusted CAPM has a higher R-square than the standard CAPM. In particular, with value-weighted portfolios in Table 5.5B, the standard CAPM has an R-square of 0.0%, whereas the liquidity-adjusted CAPM has an R-square of 48.6%. There is further evidence that liquidity risk matters over and above liquidity level and market risk. In particular, β^{net} is significant in line 5 of Table 5.5A, and in all of

---

[14] In another recent paper, Chordia et al. (2001b) find that expected returns in the cross-section are higher for stocks with low variability or liquidity, measured using variables such as trading volume and turnover. They examine the firm-specific variability of liquidity. By contrast, our model and tests suggest that it is the co-movement of firm-specific liquidity with market return and market liquidity that affects expected returns.

Table 5.5. *Illiquidity portfolios: robustness of weighting method*

This table reports the estimated coefficients from cross-sectional regressions of the liquidity-adjusted CAPM for twenty-five illiquidity portfolios using monthly data during 1964–1999. We consider special cases of the relation

$$E\left(r_t^p - r_t^f\right) = \alpha + \kappa E(c_t^p) + \lambda^1 \beta^{1p} + \lambda^2 \beta^{2p} + \lambda^3 \beta^{3p} + \lambda^4 \beta^{4p} + \lambda \beta^{\mathrm{net},p},$$

where $\beta^{\mathrm{net},p} = \beta^{1p} + \beta^{2p} - \beta^{3p} - \beta^{4p}$. In some specifications, κ is set to be the average monthly turnover. The t-statistic, reported in the parentheses, is estimated using a GMM framework that takes into account the pre-estimation of the betas. The R^2 is obtained in a single cross-sectional regression, and the adjusted R^2 is reported in parentheses.

	Constant	$E(c^p)$	β^{1p}	β^{2p}	β^{3p}	β^{4p}	$\beta^{\mathrm{net},p}$	R^2
Panel A: equal-weighted portfolios, equal-weighted market								
1	− 0.391	0.046					1.115	0.825
	(− 0.889)	(–)					(1.997)	(0.825)
2	− 0.299	0.062					0.996	0.846
	(− 0.737)	(3.878)					(4.848)	(0.832)
3	− 0.530		1.374					0.350
	(− 1.082)		(2.085)					(0.322)
4	− 0.088	0.046	− 2.699				3.395	0.879
	(− 0.249)	(–)	(− 1.441)				(1.782)	(0.873)
5	0.105	0.008	− 6.392				6.800	0.901
	(0.296)	(0.318)	(− 2.238)				(2.427)	(0.886)
6	0.143		− 7.115				7.467	0.900
	(0.397)		(− 3.623)				(3.871)	(0.891)
7	− 0.132	0.046	1.568	− 141.416	47.823	− 12.784		0.911
	(− 0.633)	(–)	(1.295)	(− 1.032)	(0.469)	(− 1.553)		(0.898)
8	− 0.053	0.117	1.207	− 346.547	33.043	− 17.356		0.913
	(− 0.060)	(0.837)	(0.343)	(− 0.796)	(0.186)	(− 0.981)		(0.890)
Panel B: value-weighted portfolios, value-weighted market								
1	1.938	0.034					2.495	0.486
	(− 1.203)	(–)					(1.627)	(0.486)
2	− 2.059	0.081					2.556	0.642
	(− 1.755)	(2.755)					(2.107)	(0.609)
3	0.700		0.062					0.000
	(0.272)		(0.025)					(− 0.043)
4	− 1.536	0.034	− 6.070				8.099	0.754
	(− 2.033)	(–)	(− 1.540)				(2.040)	(0.743)
5	− 0.583	− 0.076	− 16.226				17.333	0.841
	(− 0.718)	(− 0.902)	(− 2.978)				(3.543)	(0.819)
6	− 1.241		− 9.210				10.954	0.800
	(− 1.271)		(− 2.733)				(3.183)	(0.781)
7	− 0.301	0.034	0.363	− 4494.924	− 370.840	− 26.044		0.850
	(− 0.285)	(–)	(0.268)	(− 1.060)	(− 0.806)	(− 1.366)		(0.828)
8	0.039	− 0.056	0.015	− 116.450	− 405.451	− 13.135		0.865
	(0.031)	(− 0.140)	(0.007)	(− 0.010)	(− 0.413)	(− 0.270)		(0.829)

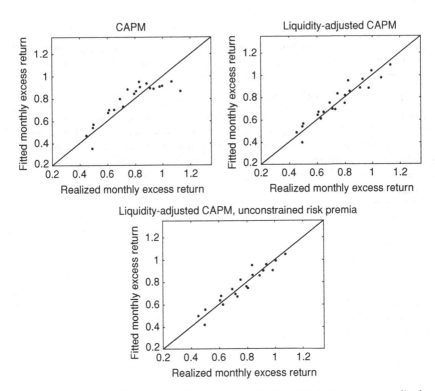

Figure 5.4. *Size portfolios*: the top left panel shows the fitted CAPM returns vs. realized returns using monthly data 1964–1999 for value-weighted size portfolios. The top right panel shows the same for the liquidity-adjusted CAPM, and the lower panel shows the relation for the liquidity-adjusted CAPM with unconstrained risk premia.

lines 4–6 in Table 5.5B. (Also, β^{net} is significant in line 6 of Table 5.5A, but this line is not relevant since the coefficient on $E(c^p)$ has the correct sign in line 5.)

As a further robustness check, we re-estimate our model with size-based portfolios and portfolios sorted first into five book-to-market quintiles and then into five size quintiles within the book-to-market groups.

Small-sized stocks are illiquid (in absolute terms as measured by $E(c)$) and also have high liquidity risk (as measured by the three betas β^{2p}, β^{3p}, and β^{4p}). Table 5.6A shows that the cross-sectional regressions have coefficients that are similar to our earlier results, but the statistical significance is reduced. The coefficient of β^{net} is estimated to be positive and the liquidity-adjusted CAPM still has a higher R^2 than the standard CAPM. Figure 5.4 shows graphically the fit for size portfolios of the standard CAPM, and the liquidity-adjusted CAPM, with constrained and unconstrained risk premia.

Table 5.6. *Size and B/M-by-size portfolios*

This table reports the estimated coefficients from cross-sectional regressions of the liquidity-adjusted CAPM for twenty-five value-weighted size and B/M-by-size portfolios using monthly data during 1964–1999 with an equal-weighted market portfolio. We consider special cases of the relation

$$E\left(r_t^p - r_t^f\right) = \alpha + \kappa E(c_t^p) + \lambda^1 \beta^{1p} + \lambda^2 \beta^{2p} + \lambda^3 \beta^{3p} + \lambda^4 \beta^{4p} + \lambda \beta^{\text{net},p},$$

where $\beta^{\text{net},p} = \beta^{1p} + \beta^{2p} - \beta^{3p} - \beta^{4p}$. In some specifications, κ is set to be the average monthly turnover. The t-statistic, reported in the parentheses, is estimated using a GMM framework that takes into account the pre-estimation of the betas. The R^2 is obtained in a single cross-sectional regression, and the adjusted R^2 is reported in parentheses.

	Constant	$E(c^p)$	β^{1p}	β^{2p}	β^{3p}	β^{4p}	$\beta^{\text{net},p}$	R^2
Panel A: size portfolios								
1	− 0.087	0.047					0.865	0.910
	(− 0.274)	(–)					(1.864)	(0.910)
2	− 0.059	0.056					0.823	0.912
	(− 0.201)	(2.139)					(1.768)	(0.904)
3	− 0.265		1.144					0.757
	(− 0.789)		(2.270)					(0.747)
4	− 0.043	0.047	− 0.770				1.562	0.912
	(− 0.151)	(–)	(− 0.323)				(0.685)	(0.908)
5	− 0.055	0.054	− 0.168				0.984	0.912
	(− 0.186)	(1.180)	(− 0.050)				(0.266)	(0.900)
6	0.032		− 4.633				5.278	0.902
	(0.112)		(− 1.899)				(2.104)	(0.893)
7	− 0.073	0.047	0.887	27.387	1.741	0.038		0.913
	(− 0.122)	(–)	(0.304)	(0.342)	(0.009)	(0.006)		(0.901)
8	0.224	− 0.408	− 0.079	742.841	− 42.800	7.933		0.929
	(0.552)	(− 1.206)	(− 0.047)	(1.157)	(− 0.845)	(0.691)		(0.911)
Panel B: B/M-by-size properties								
1	0.200	0.045					0.582	0.406
	(0.680)	(–)					(1.197)	(0.406)
2	0.453	0.167					0.182	0.541
	(1.657)	(3.452)					(0.377)	(0.499)
3	0.109		0.748					0.262
	(0.348)		(1.406)					(0.229)
4	0.529	0.045	− 8.289				8.275	0.502
	(1.665)	(–)	(− 2.013)				(2.198)	(0.481)
5	0.187	0.387	18.229				− 17.458	0.571
	(0.626)	(3.061)	(2.344)				(− 2.265)	(0.510)
6	0.574		− 11.787				11.671	0.483
	(1.959)		(− 3.102)				(2.902)	(0.436)
7	− 0.425	0.045	4.606	203.397	198.027	− 3.330		0.788
	(− 0.254)	(–)	(0.483)	(0.200)	(0.526)	(− 0.049)		(0.758)
8	− 0.395	− 0.031	4.545	397.770	195.128	0.380		0.789
	(− 0.638)	(− 0.028)	(1.722)	(0.115)	(1.612)	(0.004)		(0.733)

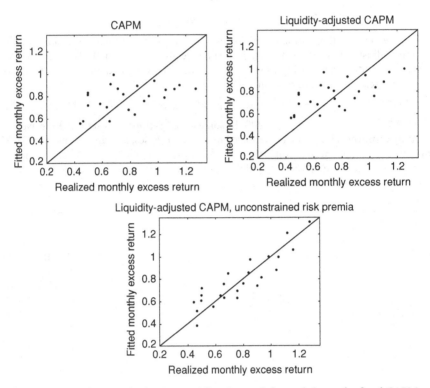

Figure 5.5. *Book-to-market by size portfolios*: the top left panel shows the fitted CAPM returns vs. realized returns using monthly data 1964–1999 for value-weighted BM-size portfolios. The top right panel shows the same for the liquidity-adjusted CAPM, and the lower panel shows the relation for the liquidity-adjusted CAPM with unconstrained risk premia.

We see that the liquidity adjustment improves the fit, particularly for the smaller size portfolios.

Table 5.6B and Figure 5.5 show the model's fit of the B/M-by-size portfolios. We recover the well-known result (see Fama and French, 1992, 1993) that CAPM does relatively poorly for B/M-by-size portfolios (adjusted $R^2 = 22.9\%$) since market beta is relatively "flat" across these portfolios. The liquidity-adjusted CAPM in line 1 provides a moderate improvement in the fit (adjusted $R^2 = 40.6\%$) whereas the model with unconstrained risk premia produces a significant improvement in the fit (adjusted $R^2 = 73.3\%$). It should be noted, however, that the unconstrained specification may be "over fitted" in the sense that some of the risk premia estimated have an incorrect sign and they are all insignificant. The negative coefficient on β^{net} in line 5 suggests that the model is misspecified for these portfolios.

To further consider the model's ability to explain the size and book-to-market effects, we run our regressions while controlling for size and book-to-market (Table 5.7). We do this both for illiquidity portfolios (Panel A) and for B/M-by-size portfolios (Panel B). The results with illiquidity portfolios are similar to the earlier results, although the standard errors increase because of the additional variables. The coefficient on β^{net} is significant in the liquidity-adjusted CAPM of line 1. The coefficient on size is always insignificant and the coefficient on book-to-market is insignificant in all specifications except line 2. (Including volatility does not change the results, and volatility is not significant. These results are not reported.) With B/M-by-size portfolios (Table 5.7B), the model performs poorly. Indeed, the coefficient on β^{net} is negative, although insignificant, and the coefficient on B/M is significant in most specifications. To summarize, the results with illiquidity portfolios suggest that liquidity risk matters while controlling for book to market, while the results with B/M-by-size portfolios suggest that liquidity risk does not explain the book-to-market effect. (Pastor and Stambaugh, 2003 reach a similar conclusion.) Hence, our simple model fails to explain the entire investment universe.

Specification tests. We perform several specification tests of the liquidity-adjusted CAPM. First, we note that we fail to reject at conventional levels the model-implied restriction that $\alpha = 0$ in the liquidity-adjusted CAPM (lines 1–2 and 4–8 of Table 5.4), whereas this restriction is rejected for the standard CAPM (at a 10% level in line 3 Table 5.4A, and at a 5% level in Table 5.4B). Second, in context of the model with unrestricted risk premia in line 8 of Table 5.4, a Wald test fails to reject the five model-implied restrictions $\lambda^1 = \lambda^2 = -\lambda^3 = -\lambda^4, \alpha = 0$, and $\kappa = k$, where k is the calibrated value. The p-value is 47% in Table 5.4A and 28% in Table 5.4B. The CAPM restrictions $\lambda^2 = \lambda^3 = \lambda^4 = 0$, $\alpha = 0$, and $\kappa = 0$ have p-values of 15% and 8.7%, respectively. The CAPM is rejected in lines 5 and 6 since β^{net} is significant.

Another testable restriction implied by the model is that the risk premium equals the expected net return on the market in excess of the risk-free rate. The point estimate of the risk premium, λ, is larger than the sample average of the excess return of the market net of transaction costs, $E(r_t^M - r_t^f - \kappa c_t^M)$, and the p-value is 6.6% in regression 1 of Table 5.4A and 7.3% in Table 5.4B. In comparison, the test that the standard CAPM risk premium equals the $E(r_t^M - r_t^f)$ has p-values of 1.2% and 0.8%, respectively.

Lastly, we test that the linear model has zero average pricing error for all of the portfolios, a stringent test since it requires that the model is pricing all

Table 5.7. *Controlling for size and book-to-market*

This table reports the estimated coefficients from cross-sectional regressions of the liquidity-adjusted CAPM for twenty-five value-weighted size and B/M-by-size portfolios using monthly data during 1964–1999 with an equal-weighted market portfolio. We consider special cases of the relation

$$E\left(r_t^p - r_t^f\right) = \alpha + \kappa E(c_t^p) + \lambda^1 \beta^{1p} + \lambda^2 \beta^{2p} + \lambda^3 \beta^{3p} + \lambda^4 \beta^{4p} + \lambda \beta^{\mathrm{net},p} \\ + \lambda^5 \ln(\mathrm{size}^p) + \lambda^6 BM^p,$$

where $\beta^{\mathrm{net},p} = \beta^{1p} + \beta^{2p} - \beta^{3p} - \beta^{4p}$, $\ln(\mathrm{size}^p)$ is the time-series average of the natural log of the ratio of the portfolio's market capitalization at the beginning of the month to the total market capitalization, and BM^p is the time-series average of the average monthly book-to-market of the stocks constituting the portfolio. In some specifications, κ is set to be the average monthly turnover. The t-statistic, reported in the parentheses, is estimated using a GMM framework that takes into account the pre-estimation of betas. The R^2 is obtained in a single cross-sectional regression, and the adjusted R^2 is reported in parentheses.

	Constant	$E(c^p)$	β^{1p}	β^{2p}	β^{3p}	β^{4p}	$\beta^{\mathrm{net},p}$	$\ln(\mathrm{size}^p)$	B/M	R^2
Panel A: liquidity portfolios										
1	−1.358	0.034					2.158	0.142	1.076	0.865
	(1.843)	(–)					(2.114)	(1.247)	(1.871)	(0.852)
2	−1.286	0.028					1.970	0.129	1.120	0.865
	(−1.501)	(1.129)					(1.869)	(0.950)	(2.215)	(0.838)
3	−0.818		0.798					0.043	1.350	0.850
	(−0.837)		(0.651)					(0.302)	(1.724)	(0.829)
4	−1.273	0.034	−3.740				6.145	0.155	0.679	0.869
	(−1.459)	(–)	(−0.576)				(0.891)	(1.054)	(0.814)	(0.850)
5	−0.441	−0.018	−12.278				13.565	0.068	0.159	0.882
	(−0.613)	(−0.227)	(−1.292)				(1.453)	(0.871)	(0.229)	(0.850)
6	−0.730		−9.313				10.988	0.098	0.339	0.880
	(−0.939)		(−1.884)				(2.106)	(0.788)	(0.598)	(0.856)
7	−0.491	0.034	1.253	−124.221	−18.359	−16.421		0.078	0.205	0.884
	(−0.369)	(–)	(0.714)	(−0.818)	(−0.180)	(−1.230)		(0.313)	(0.208)	(0.853)
8	−0.557	0.059	1.300	−183.466	−19.865	−17.238		0.087	0.253	0.884
	(−0.912)	(0.298)	(2.043)	(−0.325)	(−0.208)	(−0.922)		(0.773)	(0.376)	(0.836)
Panel B: B/M-by-size portfolios										
1	0.310	0.045					−0.199	−0.084	0.251	0.924
	(1.040)	(–)					(−0.345)	(−1.415)	(2.892)	(0.917)
2	0.317	0.035					−0.236	−0.091	0.250	0.925
	(1.206)	(0.684)					(−0.311)	(−1.176)	(2.905)	(0.910)
3	0.365		−0.403					−0.119	0.246	0.920
	(1.177)		(−0.516)					(−2.155)	(2.749)	(0.909)
4	0.311	0.045	0.484				−0.696	−0.089	0.249	0.924
	(1.170)	(–)	(0.155)				(−0.262)	(−1.598)	(2.960)	(0.913)
5	0.340	−0.003	−3.145				2.850	−0.087	0.259	0.925
	(1.083)	(−0.039)	(−0.894)				(0.846)	(−1.224)	(3.108)	(0.906)
6	0.338		−2.930				2.639	−0.087	0.259	0.925
	(1.003)		(−1.366)				(0.613)	(−1.065)	(3.314)	(0.910)
7	0.237	0.045	0.490	−286.927	38.480	−14.711		−0.095	0.226	0.932
	(1.483)	(–)	(0.284)	(−1.063)	(0.615)	(−1.069)		(−1.613)	(2.868)	(0.915)
8	0.171	0.284	0.529	−916.982	42.353	−26.730		−0.100	0.233	0.937
	(0.249)	(0.308)	(0.232)	(−0.344)	(0.181)	(−0.391)		(−0.735)	(0.746)	(0.911)

portfolios correctly. With illiquidity portfolios, the p-values for the liquidity-adjusted CAPM in regressions 1, 5, and 8 are, respectively, 8.5%, 9.9%, and 6.8% using a GMM test (as in Cochrane, 2001, p. 241), which is similar to the cross-sectional regression test of Shanken (1985). In comparison, the standard CAPM has p-value of 0.5%. With σ (illiquidity) portfolios the GMM p-values for the liquidity-adjusted CAPM are, respectively, 16%, 42%, and 65%, and the p-value for the standard CAPM is 6.6%. The specification tests for size portfolios are similar. This confirms the visual evidence from Figures 5.2–5.4 that the liquidity-adjusted CAPM has a better fit than the standard CAPM for these portfolios.

With B/M-by-size portfolios, the Wald test of the liquidity-adjusted CAPM has a p-value of 47% and the test of zero pricing errors for regressions 1, 5, and 8 are, respectively, 15.7%, 38%, and 85%. The standard CAPM has a p-value of 23% for the Wald test and 3.2% for the test of zero pricing errors. The failure to reject the liquidity-adjusted CAPM using B/M-by-size portfolios may be due to low power since, as discussed above, the model fit is not good for these portfolios.

5. Conclusion

This paper derives a simple model of liquidity risk. The model shows that the CAPM applies for returns net of illiquidity costs. This implies that investors should worry about a security's performance and tradability both in market downturns and when liquidity "dries up." Said differently, the required return of a security i is increasing in the covariance between its illiquidity and the market illiquidity, $\mathrm{cov}_t(c^i_{t+1}, c^M_{t+1})$, decreasing in the covariance between the security's return and the market illiquidity, $\mathrm{cov}_t(r^i_{t+1}, c^M_{t+1})$, and decreasing in the covariance between its illiquidity and market returns, $\mathrm{cov}_t(c^i_{t+1}, r^M_{t+1})$. The model further shows that positive shocks to illiquidity, if persistent, are associated with a low contemporaneous returns and high predicted future returns.

Hence, the model gives an integrated view of the existing empirical evidence related to liquidity and liquidity risk, and it generates new testable predictions. We find that the liquidity-adjusted CAPM explains the data better than the standard CAPM, while still exploiting the same degrees of freedom. Further, we find weak evidence that liquidity risk is important over and above the effects of market risk and the level of liquidity. The model has a reasonably good fit for portfolios sorted by liquidity, liquidity variation, and size, but it fails to explain the book-to-market effect.

The model provides a framework in which we can study the economic significance of liquidity risk. We find that liquidity risk explains about 1.1% of cross-sectional returns when the effect of average liquidity is calibrated to the typical holding period in the data and the model restriction of a single risk premium is imposed. About 80% of this effect is due to the liquidity sensitivity to the market return, $\text{cov}_t(c^i_{t+1}, r^M_{t+1})$, an effect not previously studied in the literature. Freeing up risk premia leads to larger estimates of the liquidity risk premium, but these results are estimated imprecisely because of collinearity between liquidity and liquidity risk.

While the model gives clear predictions that seem to have some bearing in the data, it is obviously simplistic. The model and the empirical results are suggestive of further theoretical and empirical work. In particular, it would be of interest to explain the time-variation in liquidity, and our finding of "flight to liquidity" namely that stocks that are illiquid in absolute terms also are more liquidity risky in the sense of having high values of all three liquidity betas. Another interesting topic is the determination of liquidity premia in a general equilibrium with liquidity risk and endogenous holdings periods. We note that if investors live several periods, but their probability of living more than one period approaches zero, then our equilibrium economy is approached, assuming continuity. Hence, our effects would also be present in the more general economy, although endogenous holding periods may imply a smaller effect of liquidity risk (as in Constantinides, 1986). The effect of liquidity risk is strengthened, however, if investors have important reasons to trade frequently. Such reasons include return predictability and wealth shocks (as considered in the context of liquidity by Lynch and Tan, 2003), differences of opinions (e.g., Harris and Raviv, 1993), asymmetric information (e.g., He and Wang, 1995), institutional effects (e.g., Allen, 2001), taxes (e.g., Constantinides, 1983), etc. It would be interesting to determine the equilibrium impact of liquidity risk in light of such trading motives.

APPENDIX

Proof of Proposition 1

We first solve the investment problem of any investor n at time t. We assume, and later confirm, that the price at time $t + 1$ is normally distributed conditional on time-t information. Hence, the investor's problem is to choose optimally the number of shares, $y^n = (y^{n,1}, \ldots, y^{n,I})$, to purchase according to

$$\max_{y^n \in \mathbb{R}_+^I} \left(E_t\left(W_{t+1}^n\right) - \frac{1}{2}A^n \mathrm{var}_t\left(W_{t+1}^n\right) \right), \tag{1}$$

where

$$W_{t+1}^n = (P_{t+1} + D_{t+1} - C_{t+1})^{\mathrm{T}} y^n + r^f \left(e_t^n - P_t^{\mathrm{T}} y^n\right) \tag{2}$$

and e_t^n is this agent's endowment. If we disregard the no-short-sale constraint, the solution is

$$y^n = \frac{1}{A^n}(\mathrm{var}_t(P_{t+1} + D_{t+1} - C_{t+1}))^{-1}(E_t(P_{t+1} + D_{t+1} - C_{t+1}) - r^f P_t). \tag{3}$$

We shortly verify that, in equilibrium, this solution does not entail short-selling. In equilibrium, $\sum_n y^n = S$, where $S = (S^1, \ldots, S^I)$ is the total supply of shares. This implies the equilibrium condition that

$$P_t = \frac{1}{r^f}[E_t(P_{t+1} + D_{t+1} - C_{t+1}) - A\,\mathrm{var}_t(P_{t+1} + D_{t+1} - C_{t+1})S], \tag{4}$$

where $A = \left(\sum_n 1/A^n\right)^{-1}$. The unique stationary linear equilibrium is

$$P_t = \Upsilon + \frac{\rho^D}{r^f - \rho^D}D_t - \frac{\rho^C}{r^f - \rho^C}C_t, \tag{5}$$

where

$$\Upsilon = \frac{1}{r^f - 1} \left(\frac{r^f(1 - \rho^D)}{r^f - \rho^D}\bar{D} - \frac{r^f(1 - \rho^C)}{r^f - \rho^C}\bar{C} \right.$$
$$\left. - A\,\mathrm{var}\left[\frac{r^f}{r^f - \rho^D}\varepsilon_t - \frac{r^f}{r^f - \rho^C}\eta_t\right]S \right). \tag{6}$$

With this price, conditional expected net returns are normally distributed, and any investor n holds a fraction $A/A^n > 0$ of the market portfolio $S > 0$ so he is not short-selling any securities. Therefore, our assumptions are satisfied in equilibrium.

Finally, since investors have mean-variance preferences, the conditional CAPM holds for net returns. See, for instance, Huang and Litzenberger (1988). Rewriting in terms of net returns yields the result stated in the proposition. $\qquad\square$

Proof of Proposition 2

The conditional expected return on a portfolio q is computed using (5):

$$
E_t\left(r_{t+1}^q\right) = E_t\left(\frac{P_{t+1}^q + D_{t+1}^q}{P_t^q}\right)
$$

$$
= \frac{E_t\left(\Upsilon^q + \frac{r^f}{r^f - \rho^D}D_{t+1}^q - \frac{\rho^C}{r^f - \rho^C}C_{t+1}^q\right)}{\Upsilon^q + \frac{\rho^D}{r^f - \rho^D}D_t^q - \frac{\rho^C}{r^f - \rho^C}C_t^q}, \tag{7}
$$

so, we have

$$
\frac{\partial}{\partial C_t^q}E_t\left(r_{t+1}^q - r^f\right)
$$

$$
\frac{1}{\left(P_t^q\right)^2}\left(-\frac{(\rho^C)^2}{r^f - \rho^C}P_t^q + \frac{\rho^C}{r^f - \rho^C}E_t\left(P_{t+1}^q + D_{t+1}^q\right)\right). \tag{8}
$$

This partial derivative is greater than zero under the conditions given in the proposition. □

Proof of Proposition 3

The conditional covariance between illiquidity and return for a portfolio q is

$$
\text{cov}_t\left(c_{t+1}^q, r_{t+1}^q\right) = \frac{1}{\left(P_t^q\right)^2}\text{cov}_t\left(C_{t+1}^q, P_{t+1}^q + D_{t+1}^q\right)
$$

$$
= \frac{1}{\left(P_t^q\right)^2}\text{cov}_t\left(C_{t+1}^q, \frac{r^f}{r^f - \rho^D}D_{t+1}^q - \frac{\rho^C}{r^f - \rho^C}C_{t+1}^q\right)
$$

$$
= \frac{1}{\left(P_t^q\right)^2}\left(\frac{r^f}{r^f - \rho^D}q^{\mathrm{T}}\Sigma^{CD}q - \frac{\rho^C}{r^f - \rho^C}q^{\mathrm{T}}\Sigma^C q\right), \tag{9}
$$

which yields the proposition. □

References

Allen, F., 2001. Do financial institutions matter? Journal of Finance 56, 1165–1175.

Amihud, Y., 2002. Illiquidity and stock returns: cross-section and time-series effects. Journal of Financial Markets 5, 31–56.

Amihud, Y., Mendelson, H., 1986. Asset pricing and the bid-ask spread. Journal of Financial Economics 17, 223–49.

Amihud, Y., Mendelson, H., 1989. The effect of beta, bid-ask spread, residual risk and size on stock returns. Journal of Finance 44, 479–86.

Amihud, Y., Mendelson, H., Wood, R., 1990. Liquidity and the 1987 stock market crash. Journal of Portfolio Management, 65–9.

Ang, A., Chen, J., 2002. Asymmetric correlations of equity portfolios. Journal of Financial Economics 63, 443–94.

Bekaert, G., Harvey, C.R., Lundblad, C., 2003. Liquidity and Expected Returns: Lessons from Emerging Markets. Columbia University.

Brennan, M.J., Subrahmanyam, A., 1996. Market microstructure and asset pricing: on the compensation for illiquidity in stock returns. Journal of Financial Economics 41, 441–64.

Brennan, M.J., Chordia, T., Subrahmanyam, A., 1998. Alternative factor specifications, security characteristics, and the cross-section of expected returns. Journal of Financial Economics 49, 345–73.

Brunnermeier, M., Pedersen, L.H., 2004a. Market liquidity and funding liquidity, Unpublished working paper, Princeton University.

Brunnermeier, M., Pedersen, L.H., 2004b. Predatory trading. Journal of Finance, forthcoming.

Chalmers, J.M., Kadlec, G.B., 1998. An empirical examination of the amortized spread. Journal of Financial Economics 48, 159–88.

Chordia, T., Roll, R., Subrahmanyam, A., 2000. Commonality in liquidity. Journal of Financial Economics 56, 3–28.

Chordia, T., Roll, R., Subrahmanyam, A., 2001a. Market liquidity and trading activity. Journal of Finance 56, 501–30.

Chordia, T., Subrahmanyam, A., Anshuman, V.R., 2001b. Trading activity and expected stock returns. Journal of Financial Economics 59, 3–32.

Cochrane, J.H., 2001. Asset Pricing. Princeton University Press, Princeton, NJ.

Constantinides, G.M., 1983. Capital market equilibrium with personal tax. Econometrica 51, 611–36.

Constantinides, G.M., 1986. Capital market equilibrium with transaction costs. Journal of Political Economy 94, 842–62.

Constantinides, G.M., Donaldson, J.B., Mehra, R., 2002. Junior can't borrow: a new perspective on the equity premium puzzle. Quarterly Journal of Economics 117, 269–96.

Datar, V.T., Naik, N.Y., Radcliffe, R., 1998. Liquidity and stock returns: an alternative test. Journal of Financial Markets 1, 203–19.

DeLong, J.B., Shleifer, A., Summers, L.H., Waldmann, R.J., 1990. Noise trader risk in financial markets. Journal of Political Economy 98, 703–38.

Dimson, E., Hanke, B., 2002. The expected illiquidity premium. Unpublished working paper, London Business School.

Duffie, D., Gârleanu, N., Pedersen, L.H., 2000. Over-the-counter markets. Econometrica, forthcoming.

Duffie, D., Gârleanu, N., Pedersen, L.H., 2002. Securities lending, shorting, and pricing. Journal of Financial Economics 66 (2,3), 307–39.

Duffie, D., Gârleanu, N., Pedersen, L.H., 2003. Valuation in over-the-counter markets. Unpublished working paper, Graduate School of Business, Stanford University.

Easley, D., Hvidkjær, S., O'Hara, M., 2002. Is information risk a determinant of asset returns? Journal of Finance 57, 2185–221.

Eisfeldt, A.L., 2004. Endogenous liquidity in asset markets. Journal of Finance 59, 1–30.

Eleswarapu, V.R., 1997. Cost of transacting and expected returns in the Nasdaq market. Journal of Finance 52, 2113–27.

Eleswarapu, V.R., Reinganum, M.R., 1993. The seasonal behavior of liquidity premium in asset pricing. Journal of Financial Economics 34, 373–86.

Fama, E.F., French, K.R., 1992. The cross-section of expected stock returns. Journal of Finance 47, 427–65.

Fama, E.F., French, K.R., 1993. Common risk factors in the returns on stocks and bonds. Journal of Financial Economics 33, 3–56.

Fama, E.F., MacBeth, J.D., 1973. Risk, return, and equilibrium: Empirical tests. Journal of Political Economy 81, 607–36.

Friend, I., Blume, M., 1975. The demand for risky assets. American Economic Review 65, 900–22.

Gârleanu, N., Pedersen, L.H., 2004. Adverse selection and the required return. Review of Financial Studies 17(3), 643–65.

Hansen, L.P., Richard, S.F., 1987. The role of conditioning information in deducing testable restrictions implied by dynamic asset pricing models. Econometrica 55, 587–614.

Harris, M., Raviv, A., 1993. Differences of opinion make a horse race. Review of Financial Studies 6, 473–506.

Hasbrouck, J., 2002. Inferring trading costs from daily data: US equities from 1962 to 2001. Unpublished working paper, New York University.

Hasbrouck, J., Seppi, D.J., 2001. Common factors in prices, order flows and liquidity. Journal of Financial Economics 59, 383–411.

He, H., Wang, J., 1995. Differential information and dynamic behavior of stock trading volume. The Review of Financial Studies 8, 919–72.

Heaton, J., Lucas, D., 2000. Portfolio choice and asset prices: the importance of entrepreneurial risk. Journal of Finance 55, 1163–98.

Holmstrom, B., Tirole, J., 2000. LAPM: a liquidity-based asset pricing model. Journal of Finance 56, 1837–67.

Huang, M., 2003. Liquidity shocks and equilibrium liquidity premia. Journal of Economic Theory 109, 104–29.

Huang, C, Litzenberger, R.H., 1988. Foundations for Financial Economics. Prentice-Hall, Englewood Cliffs, NJ.

Huberman, C, Halka, D., 1999. Systematic Liquidity. Columbia Business School.

Jones, C.M., 2001. A century of stock market liquidity and trading costs. Graduate School of Business, Columbia University.

Lintner, J., 1965. The valuation of risk assets and the selection of risky investments in stock portfolios and capital budgets. Review of Economics and Statistics 47, 13–37.

Ljungqvist, A., Richardson, M., 2003. The cash flow, return and risk characteristics of private equity. New York University.

Lustig, H., 2001. The market price of aggregate risk and the wealth distribution. Unpublished working paper, Stanford University.

Lynch, A.W., Tan, S., 2003. Explaining the magnitude of liquidity premia: the roles of return predictability, wealth shocks and state-dependent transaction costs. Unpublished working paper, New York University.

Markowitz, H., 1952. Portfolio selection. Journal of Finance 7, 77–91.

Markowitz, H., 2000. Mean-Variance Analysis in Portfolio Choice and Capital Markets. Frank J. Fabozzi Associates, New Hope, Pennsylvania.

Mossin, J., 1966. Equilibrium in a capital asset market. Econometrica 35, 768–83.

Newey, W., West, K., 1987. A simple, positive semi-definite, heteroskedasticity and autocorrelation consistent covariance matrix. Econometrica 55, 703–8.

Pastor, L., Stambaugh, R.F., 2003. Liquidity risk and expected stock returns. Journal of Political Economy 111, 642–85.

Persaud, A.D., 2003. Introduction. In: Persaud, A.D. (Ed.), Liquidity Black Holes. Risk.

Sadka, R., 2002. Momentum, liquidity risk, and limits to arbitrage. Unpublished working paper, Northwestern University.

Samuelson, P.A., 1958. An exact consumption-loan model of interest with or without the social contrivance of money. Journal of Political Economy 66, 467–82.

Shanken, J., 1985. Multivariate tests of the zero-beta CAPM. Journal of Financial Economics 14, 327–48.

Shanken, J., 1992. On the estimation of beta pricing models. Review of Financial Studies 5, 1–34.

Sharpe, W., 1964. Capital asset prices: a theory of capital market equilibrium under conditions of risk. Journal of Finance 19, 425–42.

Shumway, T., 1997. The delisting bias in CRSP data. Journal of Finance 52, 327–40.

Swan, P.L., 2002. Does "illiquidity" rather than "risk aversion" explain the equity premium puzzle? The value of endogenous market trading. Unpublished working paper, University of New South Wales.

Vayanos, D., 1998. Transaction costs and asset prices: a dynamic equilibrium model. Review of Financial Studies 11, 1–58.

Vayanos, D., Vila, J.-L., 1999. Equilibrium interest rate and liquidity premium with transaction costs. Economic Theory 13, 509–39.

Wang, A.W., 2002. Institutional equity flows, liquidity risk and asset pricing, Unpublished working paper, University of California, Los Angeles.

PART III

LIQUIDITY CRISES

Introduction and Overview

This chapter studies liquidity crises. A liquidity crisis is a situation where market liquidity drops dramatically as dealers widen bid–ask spreads, take the phone off the hook, or close down operations as their trading houses run out of cash and take their money off the table, security prices drop sharply, and volatility increases.

Brunnermeier and Pedersen (2009; Chapter 6 in this book) provide a theory explaining the origins and underlying dynamics that drive a liquidity crisis. It distinguishes between two kinds of liquidity: market liquidity and funding liquidity.

Market liquidity – the subject of much of this book – is the ease of trading a security. A security is liquid if the cost of trading it is low; for instance, it has a low bid–ask spread and a small market impact. *Funding liquidity* is a property of both securities and the agents that trade. A security has good funding liquidity if it is easy to borrow using the security as collateral. For instance, if a trader buys a security for $100, he may be able to borrow $80 with the security as collateral. The 20% of its value that must be financed with the trader's own capital is called a margin requirement (or "haircut"). A 20% margin requirement means that a trader can leverage this security 5-to-1 while a higher margin requirement would mean that less leverage is available. A trader (e.g., a market maker, dealer, or hedge fund) has good funding liquidity if it has ample capital and access to financing with low margin requirements so it can take desirable positions with few constraints.

A key insight in Brunnermeier and Pedersen is that the two kinds of liquidity interact and that this interaction creates *liquidity spirals*: First, when traders have good funding liquidity, they can trade a lot, which improves market liquidity. Indeed, when market makers, dealers, and other liquidity-providing traders have ample access to funding, they can better accommodate customers' demands to buy or sell securities and, therefore, customers experience lower transaction costs. For instance, when a market maker working for a large bank is allocated plenty of funding and allowed to take large positions, he can aggressively try to absorb many large customers orders. In contrast, when constrained, the market maker must limit the size of the positions that he takes on and will increase the price of his liquidity services, which translates into higher transaction costs for customers.

Interestingly, just as funding affects market liquidity, market liquidity also affects funding: Favorable market liquidity and lower volatility make it easier to finance traders' positions, lowering their margin requirement. Thus, market liquidity improves funding liquidity and vice versa: a positive feedback loop that creates the potential for a credit boom in good times.

This two-way interaction works in reverse during a downturn, and potentially more violently, since institutions are forced to make fire sales and even default when they cannot meet their margin requirements. The start of a downward liquidity spiral is a shock to traders' funding liquidity coming, for instance, from news about subprime mortgages, as in the Global Financial Crisis of 2007–2009. This makes dealers reduce their trading and the extent to which they accommodate order imbalances, which reduces market liquidity, increases liquidity risk, and leads to price drops of securities with higher liquidity risk. Financiers who observe dropping prices, illiquid and volatile markets, and further liquidity risk on the horizon naturally cut back their funding and increase margin requirements, thus fueling the liquidity spiral: worsening market liquidity leads to worsening funding liquidity, and so on, back and forth, until a new equilibrium is reached.

Brunnermeier and Pedersen show that such liquidity spirals induce fragility in the financial system, because a shock to one market can have a disproportionate effect as the spiral spreads throughout the financial system, affecting other markets. Therefore, this theory can explain why there is a link between the market liquidity of different securities ("commonality of liquidity"): the market liquidity of all securities depend on the funding liquidity of the banks and traders. This connection between market and funding liquidity also explains why market liquidity is worse in down markets on average: because funding liquidity is worse during bad times. Finally, it helps explain the phenomena of flight to quality and of asset prices that trade at fire-sale prices during a funding crisis and later rebound.

The Global Financial Crisis of 2007–2009 is a case in point: A shock to the valuation of subprime mortgages led to losses in the financial sector and liquidations in various markets as leveraged traders were compelled to raise cash to satisfy their margin requirements, and these sell-offs led to further

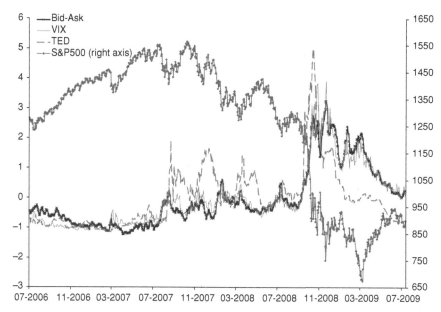

Figure PIII.1. Market and funding liquidity risks during the Global Financial Crisis. The chart shows the average bid–ask spread for large-cap U.S. stocks (a measure of market illiquidity), the equity volatility index VIX, and the TED spread, which is the difference between the LIBOR and Treasury Bill interest rates (a measure of funding illiquidity) from July 2006 to July 2009. These liquidity series have been scaled to have a zero mean and a unit standard deviation and are shown on the left axis. The stock market index S&P 500 is shown on the right axis. See, "when everyone runs for the exit," Pedersen (2010).

losses. With traditional providers of liquidity facing funding constraints, market liquidity dried up. The simultaneous spiraling of market liquidity (measured by the bid–ask spread), funding liquidity (proxied by the TED spread, that is, the spread between Treasury Bill rate and the EuroDollar LIBOR rate), and volatility (measured by the VIX index of option-implied volatility) are clearly depicted in Figure PIII.1, which shows what happens "when everyone runs for the exit" (Pedersen 2010). As market and funding liquidity dried up (seen in the figure as rising bid–ask spread, TED, and VIX), the stock market collapsed (seen as a sharp decline in the S&P 500 stock market index).

The fact that funding liquidity is a driver of market liquidity means that a liquidity crisis spreads across markets. This is because many institutions provide liquidity across different markets. When a liquidity spiral in one market erodes the funding of key dealers, then liquidity also dries up in other markets in which these dealers are active. In this way, the Global Financial

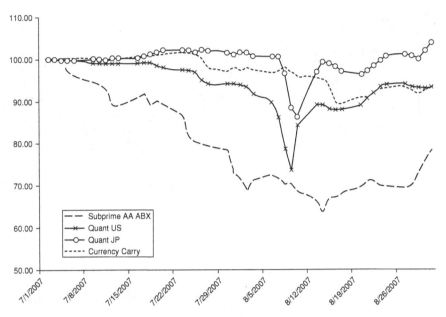

Figure PIII.2. Spillover at the beginning of the Global Financial Crisis (July–August 2007). This figure shows how the crisis started with a decline in the price of subprime credit. In July 2007, quantitative long–short stock selection strategies based on value and momentum in the United States (Quant US) began to experience losses, and this subsequently spilled over to similar strategies in Japan (Quant JP). The currency carry trade experienced an unwinding in the end of August. The price series and cumulative returns have been normalized to be 100 at the beginning of July. Source: Pedersen (2010).

Crisis spread from the subprime market to other mortgage markets, then more broadly to credit markets, before spreading to quantitative equity strategies and currency markets as seen in Figure PIII.2. As the money markets faltered and LIBOR spreads widened, the Global Financial Crisis spread even more broadly to equity markets, to corporate bond markets, and convertible bond markets. Finally, the crisis spread to emerging markets, commodities markets, and beyond.

In summary, Brunnermeier and Pedersen show that funding liquidity is a driver of market liquidity, which helps explain the variation of market liquidity over time and across securities, as well as the liquidity dynamics during crises. Funding liquidity thus affects required returns because market liquidity does.

Funding liquidity and asset prices. Funding liquidity also directly affects required returns, as argued by Garleanu and Pedersen (2011), Ashcraft, Garleanu, and Pedersen (2010), and Frazzini and Pedersen (2010). These authors show how asset prices depend on funding conditions and margin requirements, giving rise to a margin-CAPM formula. In particular, since investors have limited funding and face leverage constraints, they prefer to hold assets with lower margin requirements, that is, assets that use less capital. Indeed, securities differ in their margin requirements because of differences in risk, market liquidity, or institutional and contractual issues. Since an asset "ties up" more of an investor's scarce capital if it has a higher margin requirement, a security's required return $E(R_j)$ increases in its margin requirements, m_j:

$$E(R_j) = CAPM\ return + market\ liquidity\ risk\ compensation + \psi\, m_j,$$

Here, ψ is the tightness of the overall funding liquidity, which varies over time, being high during liquidity crises. Garleanu and Pedersen (2011) show that the law of one price breaks down during liquidity crises because securities with high margin requirements drop in price relative to lower-margin securities with identical cash flows. For instance, in 2008, credit default swaps (CDS) traded at lower credit spreads than comparable corporate bonds, consistent with the fact that the CDS had lower margin requirements. Ashcraft, Garleanu, and Pedersen (2010) show how the Federal Reserve's lending facilities alleviated liquidity-funding problems and find strong evidence that this lowered required returns and raised asset prices. In particular, as the Federal Reserve lowered the margin requirement m_j for certain bonds, these bond yields dropped, helping to restart credit markets such as the student loan market. In addition to the direct effect of lowering the margin requirement for these bonds, these central bank lending facilities had the added benefit of easing funding problems more broadly such that the tightness of the overall funding liquidity ψ came down, lowering required returns in general.

Funding liquidity affects asset prices even when their margin requirements are the same. While securities with the same margin have the same funding-induced increase in required return, ψm, the effect *per unit of risk* is larger for safer assets. Said differently, this funding effect will raise the Sharpe ratio of safe assets more than it raises the Sharpe ratio of risky assets. Therefore, the margin-CAPM implies that risk-adjusted returns depend on how difficult a security is to fund per unit of risk. Consequently, it can be tested by examining securities with similar risk and different margin requirements, as in Garleanu and Pedersen (2011) and Ashcraft, Garleanu, and Pedersen (2010), or securities with similar margin requirement but different risk. This latter approach is taken by Frazzini and Pedersen (2010, 2011) and

Asness, Frazzini, and Pedersen (2012). Consistent with the margin-CAPM, these authors show that low-beta assets earn higher risk-adjusted returns than high-risk assets because low-risk assets are more difficult to fund per unit of risk. That is, a betting-against-beta (BAB) portfolio that goes long a leveraged basket of low-risk assets and short sells a basket of high-risk assets earns significant positive return on average. This pattern holds in stock markets, bond markets, credit markets, and option markets. However, such BAB portfolios tend to lose money during liquidity crises, consistent with the idea that liquidity crises are associated with de-leveraging due to liquidity spirals.

The recent liquidity crisis is by no means the first of its kind, and, in fact, the theory of market liquidity and funding liquidity spirals was derived before the onset of the crisis. Just two years prior, a liquidity crisis occurred in the convertible bond market, as described by Mitchell, Pedersen, and Pulvino (2007; Chapter 8 in this book). Mitchell, Pedersen, and Pulvino use the term *slow moving capital* to capture the idea that arbitrageurs face funding constraints and raising new capital takes times, especially during market downturns. Convertible bonds are very illiquid and therefore have high average returns to compensate investors for the illiquidity and liquidity risk. They are issued by firms with an immediate need for capital and often sold to convertible bond hedge funds. The hedge funds buy convertible bonds and eliminate most of the risk by hedging – dynamically shorting stocks in the right proportion – thus earning the convertible bond's liquidity premium, on average. Convertible bonds are very suitable for the study of liquidity effects, because their "theoretical value" can be computed using the more liquid stocks of which the bonds are derivatives. This means that it is possible to estimate the convertible bonds' liquidity-driven value discount ("cheapness") over time.

The convertible bonds' illiquidity makes them susceptible to liquidity crises. When convertible bond hedge funds had large capital redemptions in 2005, a liquidity crisis ensued. The hedge funds were forced to sell, which led to a drop in convertible bond liquidity and prices, leading to losses for the hedge funds, further outflows, worsening funding conditions, a greater need to sell, and so on, a liquidity spiral at work.

While multi-strategy hedge funds that were not capital constrained increased their positions, a large fraction of these funds actually acted as net *sellers*, consistent with the view that information barriers within a firm (not just relative to outside investors) can lead to capital constraints for trading desks with mark-to-market losses.

The convertible bond market also experienced a liquidity crisis during the broader liquidity event of 1998 surrounding the collapse of the hedge fund Long Term Capital Management (LTCM), the Russian default, and other events. LTCM faced losses in various markets and, as a result, had to liquidate their convertible bonds. As in 2005, liquidity dried up, and prices spiraled down, rebounding months later as liquidity came back.

Liquidity spirals can break out even in markets that are commonly the world's most liquid markets. For instance, in early August 2007, unwinding an equity portfolio by certain quantitative funds caused a liquidity spiral in exchange-traded large-cap stocks, which are normally highly liquid. A sell-off by quantitative equity traders in investment banks and hedge funds who lost substantial capital and had to downscale their positions pushed prices against other quantitative traders with similar positions and reduced market liquidity. As a result, the funding problems spread across the market, leading to further price disruptions and illiquidity. Panel A of Figure PIII.3 illustrates that drop-and-rebound in prices that followed as a consequence of the liquidity spiral. Panel B shows the theoretically predicted price path when everyone runs for the exit in a liquidity crisis based on the model of Brunnermeier and Pedersen (2005).

Further evidence on liquidity crisis is provided by Amihud, Mendelson, and Wood (1990; Chapter 7 in this book). This paper shows how a drop in market liquidity leads to a fall in asset prices during a crisis. It suggests that the stock market crash of October 19, 1987 can be partly explained by a decline in investors' perceptions of the market's liquidity. At the time, a popular investment strategy was "portfolio insurance," by which stockholdings are reduced when prices fall, to protect the portfolio from further losses, and increased as prices rise. In an infinitely liquid market, such a strategy would have no impact on prices, even when exercised by many investors. However, in the days prior to the crash, there were massive stock sales with associated price declines, which may have caused investors to realize that market liquidity was not as good as they had thought, especially when they needed the liquidity. Given the increased market illiquidity and liquidity risk, the liquidity-based asset pricing theory presented in this book predicts a decline in stock prices, especially for stocks with greater drop in liquidity.

Amihud, Mendelson, and Wood consider the connection between the risk-adjusted return of NYSE stocks and the change in their liquidity during October 19, 1987. They measure market liquidity by the average daily bid–ask spread or by depth (the number of shares that could be traded at the quoted bid and ask prices). The finding is that stocks whose illiquidity

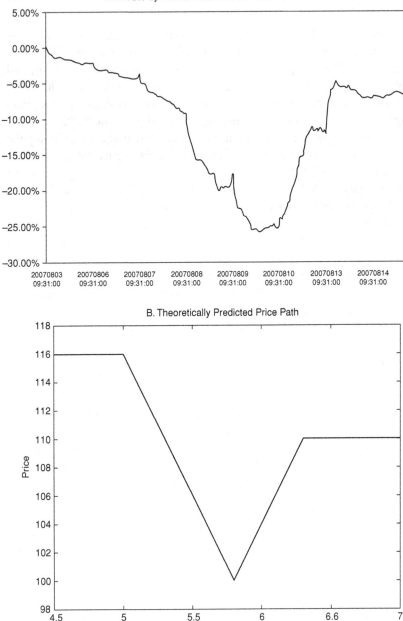

Figure PIII.3. Everyone Runs for the Exit: Quant Equity vs. Theory. Panel A shows the cumulative return to a long-short market-neutral value and momentum strategy for U.S. large-cap stocks, scaled to 6% annualized volatility during August 3–14, 2007 (Pedersen 2010). Panel B illustrates the Brunnermeier and Pedersen (2005) model's predicted price path when everyone runs for the exit.

declined more on that day also suffered greater decline in price. Furthermore, stocks whose liquidity recovered more by the end of the month of October 1987 also enjoyed a greater recovery in price. This evidence suggests a tight link between market liquidity and asset prices and illustrates how both drop and recover during a crisis.

The liquidity problems in the 1987 crash especially affected merger targets, as documented by Mitchell, Pedersen, and Pulvino. When a merger is announced, the acquirer usually offers to buy the target stock at a premium of 20–30% of its current stock price. The target stock price immediately rises to reflect most of this premium, but the stock tends to trade at a small discount below the offer price. This discount reflects the risk that the deal will fail, but also a liquidity effect, driven by selling pressure from the many mutual funds that held the target stock before the announcement and who want to avoid any risk of deal failure. This selling of the target stock gives rise to a liquidity and insurance premium that is earned by merger arbitrage hedge funds and proprietary traders who hold a portfolio of targets. In 1987, the merger arbitrageurs had large losses due to proposed anti-takeover legislation and to the stock market crash, and they started selling merger targets instead of buying them. Targets became less liquid and, importantly, the spread between offer prices and target stock prices widened substantially. Hence, this is another example of a crisis in which illiquid securities become even more illiquid as liquidity providers become funding constrained, leading to price drops and losses in the short term and high returns for investors who are able to hold on to the positions.

The "flash crash" of 2010 is a recent example of a liquidity event (see CFTC-SEC 2010). On May 6, 2010, market uncertainty about macroeconomic risks in Europe led to selling pressure, high turnover, and high volatility. Liquidity providers approached their funding and risk limits when the order imbalances escalated due in part to a large sell order of more than $4B that hit the market at 2:32 PM and was executed over the 20 minutes that followed. Adding further strain to the system were data latency issues across exchanges that led traders to question the integrity of market data. The result was that some traders, including systematic high-frequency traders, reduced or temporarily stopped providing liquidity to the market.[1] As seen in Figure PIII.4, the resulting price pattern for the S&P 500 resembles that of Figure PIII.3. The liquidity event spread from the S&P 500 to

---

[1] Kirilenko et al. (2011) document that high-frequency traders exacerbated the price movements by their aggressive trading, causing liquidity problem at the peak of the crisis: "HFTs aggressively sold on the way down and aggressively bought on the way up."

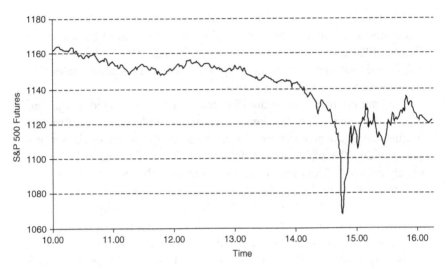

Figure PIII.4. The Flash Crash of 2010. This figure shows the price of the S&P 500 index futures on May 6, 2010.

ETFs and to individual stocks because of the interrelations across markets and the fact that the same traders often provide liquidity to many of these markets.

In conclusion, the liquidity crises of 1987, 1998, 2005, 2007, 2008, and 2010 vividly illustrate how real-world liquidity risk leads to a drop and rebound of illiquid securities as capital becomes tight and comes back over time, slower in more illiquid markets. Duffie (2010) and Reinhart and Rogoff (2009) describe a large number of other historical liquidity events and crises with similar characteristics. Duffie, Garleanu, and Pedersen (2005, 2007) model illiquidity in over-the-counter (OTC) search markets and show how liquidity shocks produce drop-and-rebound price patterns. They find that the price jump is larger and the recovery is slower in less liquid markets, consistent with quick resolution of the 2010 flash crash in the liquid futures markets and the slow resolution of the convertible bond crises documented by Mitchell, Pulvino, and Pedersen.

Notably, these liquidity-driven changes in required returns have important consequences for the real economy, as modeled by Ashcraft, Garleanu, and Pedersen (2010). For instance, when real estate assets became very liquid up until 2006 (low transaction costs and low "margin requirement" in the sense of high possible loan-to-value ratios), real estate prices rose dramatically, which led to an increase in construction. When the crisis hit, both market liquidity and funding liquidity dried up (houses became

difficult to sell and difficult to borrow against) and prices and construction dropped substantially. More generally, liquidity-driven changes in
the required returns over time and across sectors of the economy affect
firms' and households' ability to raise capital, real investment, and real
output.

CHAPTER 6

Market Liquidity and Funding Liquidity

Summary and Implications

This article derives a theory of the origins of liquidity crises. The basic idea, which was put forth before the recent global financial crisis, is that liquidity spirals amplify a shock to the system, leading to a breakdown of market liquidity, a sharp drop in prices, and large losses by key banks and traders. Liquidity spirals evolve as follows: Banks and financial intermediaries have an initial shock to their funding, for instance, a loss on some of their security positions. This makes them reduce their trading and take smaller positions, which reduces market liquidity as order imbalances become more difficult and costly to absorb for market makers. The reduced market liquidity and associated increased volatility make it riskier to finance security positions and lead to increased margin requirements, which are set endogenously in the model (and, of course, in the real world). This is because margin requirements are set to make the lender relatively immune against a scenario in which the borrower defaults and, at the same time, the asset price drops. Since larger volatility increases the risk of a large price drop and higher illiquidity makes it costly to sell the collateral in case of default, both of these effects push lenders to increase their margin of safely, that is, the margin requirement. When margin requirements rise, intermediaries face exacerbated funding problems and are forced to de-leverage and divest their positions.

In summary, funding problems lead to market illiquidity, and market illiquidity worsens funding problems, creating an adverse feedback loop that makes the markets spiral into crisis. During the recent liquidity crisis, global central banks recognized the liquidity spirals that deteriorate market and funding liquidity. In a speech on liquidity provision on May 13, 2008, the Chairman of the Federal Reserve Board Ben Bernanke said:

"Another crucial lesson from recent events is that financial institutions must understand their liquidity needs at an enterprise-wide level and be prepared for the possibility that market liquidity may erode quickly and unexpectedly."

In recognition of the importance of alleviating liquidity-spiral problems for financial stability, Chairman Bernanke also said:

"Consistent with its role as the nation's central bank, the Federal Reserve has responded not only with an easing of monetary policy but also with a number of steps aimed at reducing funding pressures for depository institutions and primary securities dealers and at improving overall market liquidity and market functioning."

This paper shows that these liquidity spirals can help explain why liquidity suddenly dries up when margin requirements are hit and liquidity spirals play out, as well as the commonality of liquidity across securities that arise, because many securities are affected by the same funding liquidity of the financial sector. It also predicts that crises are associated with "flight to quality," whereby more illiquid high-margin securities are most affected.

This article thus lays out a theory where the financial sector's capital and access to debt financing are key underlying state variables that drive market liquidity risk and risk premiums. It also addresses crash risk and negatively skewed returns of intermediaries, or, said differently, why some speculators realize "hundred-year flood losses" every couple of years. This is because of the endogenous spiral effect, where the losses of leveraged investors are amplified by their forced liquidation, while gains are not amplified similarly. Finally, the paper shows why collateralized lending can be fragile and subject to "collateral runs" due to liquidity spirals.

In a speech on April 13, 2012, Ben Bernanke, the Chairman of the Federal Reserve Bank, discussed the Global Financial Crisis, making reference to the Brunnermeier and Pedersen (2009) model. Bernanke explained how a liquidity spiral played out:

"panic-like phenomena arose in multiple contexts and in multiple ways during the crisis. The repo market, a major source of short-term credit for many financial institutions, notably including the independent investment banks, was an important example. In repo agreements, loans are collateralized by financial assets, and the maximum amount of the loan is the current assessed value of the collateral less a safety margin, or haircut. The secured nature of repo agreements gave firms and regulators confidence that runs were unlikely. But this confidence was misplaced.

Once the crisis began, repo lenders became increasingly concerned about the possibility that they would be forced to receive collateral instead of cash, collateral that would then have to be disposed of in falling and illiquid markets. In some contexts, lenders responded by imposing increasingly higher haircuts, cutting the effective amount of funding available to borrowers. In other contexts, lenders simply pulled away, as in a deposit run; in these cases, some borrowers lost access to repo entirely, and some securities became unfundable in the repo market. In either case, absent sufficient funding, borrowers were frequently left with no option but to sell assets into illiquid markets. These forced sales drove down asset prices, increased volatility, and weakened the financial positions of all holders of similar assets. Volatile asset prices and weaker borrower balance sheets in turn heightened the risks borne by repo lenders, further boosting the incentives to demand higher haircuts or withdraw funding entirely. This unstable dynamic was operating in full force around the time of the near failure of Bear Stearns in March 2008, and again during the worsening of the crisis in mid-September of that year."

In addition to explaining these stylized facts, the model has been tested in a number of markets. Comerton-Forde et al. (2010) provide compelling evidence by showing directly that market-makers' balance sheet and income-statement variables explain time variation in market liquidity. This shows that the funding of liquidity suppliers matter. Consistent with the idea that funding liquidity is more important when market makers are near their capital constraints, Comerton-Forde et al. (2010) find that the effect of market makers' financial situations is the strongest when market makers' "inventories are big or their trading results have been particularly poor. These sensitivities are smaller after specialist firm mergers, consistent with deep pockets easing."

Further evidence is provided by Aragon and Strahan (2010) who study how the funding liquidity of hedge funds affects the market liquidity of the stocks that they hold. The authors use the failure of Lehman as an exogenous instrument, considering the differential effect for stocks largely held by hedge funds using Lehman as prime broker versus stocks that were held by otherwise similar hedge funds. They find that "stocks held by these Lehman-connected funds experienced greater declines in market liquidity following the bankruptcy than other stocks." This suggests that market liquidity is affected by traders' funding liquidity.

Finally, Dick-Nielsen, Feldhutter, and Lando (2011) provide consistent evidence from corporate bond markets. They find that a corporate bond's market liquidity drops when its lead underwriter – typically, one of the main liquidity providers – is facing funding problems.

Market Liquidity and Funding Liquidity*
Markus K. Brunnermeier and
Lasse Heje Pedersen
The Review of Financial Studies, 2009

Trading requires capital. When a trader (e.g., a dealer, hedge fund, or investment bank) buys a security, he can use the security as collateral and borrow against it, but he cannot borrow the entire price. The difference between the security's price and collateral value, denoted as the margin or haircut, must be financed with the trader's own capital. Similarly, short-selling requires capital in the form of a margin; it does not free up capital. Therefore, the total margin on all positions cannot exceed a trader's capital at any time.

Our model shows that the funding of traders affects – and is affected by – market liquidity in a profound way. When funding liquidity is tight, traders become reluctant to take on positions, especially "capital intensive" positions in high-margin securities. This lowers market liquidity, leading

* We are grateful for helpful comments from Tobias Adrian, Franklin Allen, Yakov Amihud, David Blair, Bernard Dumas, Denis Gromb, Charles Johns, Christian Julliard, John Kambhu, Markus Konz, Stefan Nagel, Michael Brennan, Martin Oehmke, Ketan Patel, Guillaume Plantin, Felipe Schwartzman, Hyun Shin, Matt Spiegel (the editor), Jeremy Stein, Dimitri Vayanos, Jiang Wang, Pierre-Olivier Weill, and from an anonymous referee and Filippos Papakonstantinou and Felipe Schwartzman for outstanding research assistantship. We also thank seminar participants at the New York Federal Reserve Bank, the New York Stock Exchange, Citigroup, Bank for International Settlement, University of Zürich, INSEAD, Northwestern University, Stockholm Institute for Financial Research, Goldman Sachs, IMF, the World Bank, UCLA, LSE, Warwick University, Bank of England, University of Chicago, Texas A&M, University of Notre Dame, HEC, University of Maryland, University of Michigan, Virginia Tech, Ohio State University, University of Mannheim, ECB-Bundesbank, MIT, and conference participants at the American Economic Association Meeting, FMRC conference in honor of Hans Stoll at Vanderbilt, NBER Market Microstructure Meetings, NBER Asset Pricing Meetings, NBER Risks of Financial Institutions conference, the Five Star conference, and American Finance Association Meeting. Brunnermeier acknowledges financial support from the Alfred P. Sloan Foundation. Send correspondence to Markus K. Brunnermeier, Princeton University, NBER and CEPR, Department of Economics, Bendheim Center for Finance, Princeton University, 26 Prospect Avenue, Princeton. NJ 08540-5296. E-mail: markus@princeton.edu.

to higher volatility. Further, under certain conditions, low future market liquidity increases the risk of financing a trade, thus increasing margins. Based on the links between funding and market liquidity, we provide a unified explanation for the main empirical features of market liquidity. In particular, our model implies that market liquidity (i) can suddenly dry up, (ii) has commonality across securities, (iii) is related to volatility, (iv) is subject to "flight to quality," and (v) co-moves with the market. The model has several new testable implications that link margins and dealer funding to market liquidity: We predict that (i) speculators' (mark-to-market) capital and volatility (as, e.g., measured by VIX) are state variables affecting market liquidity and risk premiums; (ii) a reduction in capital reduces market liquidity, especially if capital is already low (a nonlinear effect) and for high-margin securities; (iii) margins increase in illiquidity if the fundamental value is difficult to determine; and (iv) speculators' returns are negatively skewed (even if they trade securities without skewness in the fundamentals).

Our model is similar in spirit to Grossman and Miller (1988) with the added feature that speculators face the real-world funding constraint discussed above. In our model, different customers have offsetting demand shocks, but arrive sequentially to the market. This creates a temporary order imbalance. Speculators smooth price fluctuations, thus providing market liquidity. Speculators finance their trades through collateralized borrowing from financiers who set the margins to control their value-at-risk (VaR). Since financiers can reset margins in each period, speculators face funding liquidity risk due to the risk of higher margins or losses on existing positions. We derive the competitive equilibrium of the model and explore its liquidity implications. We define market liquidity as the difference between the transaction price and the fundamental value, and funding liquidity as speculators' scarcity (or shadow cost) of capital.

We first analyze the properties of margins, which determine the investors' capital requirement. We show that margins can increase in illiquidity when margin-setting financiers are unsure whether price changes are due to fundamental news or to liquidity shocks, and volatility is time varying. This happens when a liquidity shock leads to price volatility, which raises the financier's expectation about future volatility, and this leads to increased margins. Figure 6.1 shows that margins did increase empirically for S&P 500 futures during the liquidity crises of 1987, 1990, 1998, and 2007. More generally, the October 2007 IMF Global Stability Report documents a significant widening of the margins across most asset classes during the summer of 2007. We denote margins as "destabilizing" if they can increase in illiquidity, and note that anecdotal evidence from prime brokers suggests that

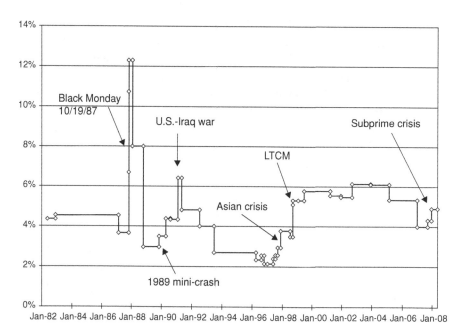

Figure 6.1. Margins for S&P 500 futures. The figure shows margin requirements on S&P 500 futures for members of the Chicago Mercantile Exchange as a fraction of the value of the underlying S&P 500 index multiplied by the size of the contract. (Initial or maintenance margins are the same for members.) Each dot represents a change in the dollar margin.

margins often behave in this way. Destabilizing margins force speculators to de-lever their positions in times of crisis, leading to pro-cyclical market liquidity provision.[1]

In contrast, margins can theoretically decrease with illiquidity and thus can be "stabilizing." This happens when financiers know that prices diverge due to temporary market illiquidity and know that liquidity will be improved shortly as complementary customers arrive. This is because a current price divergence from fundamentals provides a "cushion" against future adverse price moves, making the speculators' position less risky in this case.

Turning to the implications for market liquidity, we first show that, as long as speculators' capital is so abundant that there is no risk of hitting the funding constraint, market liquidity is naturally at its highest level and is insensitive to marginal changes in capital and margins. However, when speculators hit their capital constraints – or risk hitting their capital

---

[1] The pro-cyclical nature of banks' regulatory capital requirements and funding liquidity is another application of our model, which we describe in Appendix A.2.

constraints over the life of a trade – then they reduce their positions and market liquidity declines. At that point, prices are more driven by funding liquidity considerations rather than by movements in fundamentals, as was apparent during the quant hedge fund crisis in August 2007, for instance.

When margins are destabilizing or speculators have large existing positions, there can be multiple equilibria and liquidity can be *fragile*. In one equilibrium, markets are liquid, leading to favorable margin requirements for speculators, which in turn helps speculators make markets liquid. In another equilibrium, markets are illiquid, resulting in larger margin requirements (or speculator losses), thus restricting speculators from providing market liquidity. Importantly, any equilibrium selection has the property that small speculator losses can lead to a discontinuous drop of market liquidity. This "sudden dry-up" or fragility of market liquidity is due to the fact that with high levels of speculator capital, markets must be in a liquid equilibrium, and, if speculator capital is reduced enough, the market must eventually switch to a low-liquidity/high-margin equilibrium.[2] The events following the Russian default and LTCM collapse in 1998 are a vivid example of fragility of liquidity since a relatively small shock had a large impact. Compared to the total market capitalization of the U.S. stock and bond markets, the losses due to the Russian default were minuscule but, as Figure 6.1 shows, caused a shiver in world financial markets. Similarly, the subprime losses in 2007–2008 were in the order of several hundred billion dollars, corresponding to only about 5% of overall stock market capitalization. However, since they were primarily borne by levered financial institutions with significant maturity mismatch, spiral effects amplified the crisis so, for example, the overall stock market losses amounted to more than 8 trillion dollars as of this writing (see Brunnermeier 2009).

Further, when markets are illiquid, market liquidity is highly sensitive to further changes in funding conditions. This is due to two liquidity spirals, as illustrated in Figure 6.2. First, a *margin spiral* emerges if margins are increasing in market illiquidity. In this case, a funding shock to the speculators lowers market liquidity, leading to higher margins, which tightens speculators' funding constraint further, and so on. For instance, Figure 6.1 shows how margins gradually escalated within a few days after Black Monday in 1987. The subprime crisis that started in 2007 led to margin increases at the end of August and end of November 2007 for the S&P futures contract. For other assets, margins and haircuts widened significantly more (see, for

---

[2] Fragility can also be caused by asymmetric information on the amount of trading by portfolio insurance traders (Gennotte and Leland 1990), and by losses on existing positions (Chowdhry and Nanda 1998).

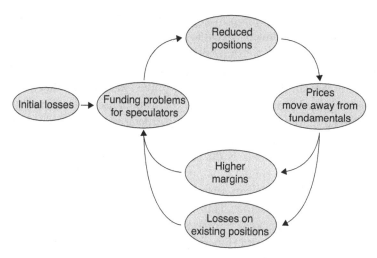

Figure 6.2. Liquidity spirals. The figure shows the loss spiral and the margin/haircut spiral.

example, IMF Global Stability Report, October 2007). The margin spiral forces traders to de-lever during downturns and recently, Adrian and Shin (2009) found consistent evidence for investment banks. Second, a *loss spiral* arises if speculators hold a large initial position that is negatively correlated with customers' demand shock. In this case, a funding shock increases market illiquidity, leading to speculator losses on their initial position, forcing speculators to sell more, causing a further price drop, and so on.[3] These liquidity spirals reinforce each other, implying a larger total effect than the sum of their separate effects. Paradoxically, liquidity spirals imply that a larger shock to the customers' demand for immediacy leads to a reduction in the provision of immediacy during such times of stress. Consistent with our predictions, Mitchell, Pedersen, and Pulvino (2007) find significant liquidity-driven divergence of prices from fundamentals in the convertible bond markets after capital shocks to the main liquidity providers, namely convertible arbitrage hedge funds. Also, Garleanu, Pedersen, and Poteshman

---

[3] The loss spiral is related to the multipliers that arise in Grossman (1988); Kiyotaki and Moore (1997); Shleifer and Vishny (1997); Chowdhry and Nanda (1998); Xiong (2001); Kyle and Xiong (2001); Gromb and Vayanos (2002); Morris and Shin (2004); Plantin, Sapra, and Shin (2005); and others. In Geanakoplos (2003) and in Fostel and Geanakoplos (2008), margins increase as risk increases. Our paper captures the margin spiral – i.e., the adverse feedback loop between margins and prices – and the interaction between the margin and loss spirals. Garleanu and Pedersen (2007) show how a risk management spiral can arise.

(2008) document that option market makers' unhedgeable risk is priced, especially in times following recent losses.

In the cross section, we show that the ratio of illiquidity to margin is the same across all assets for which speculators provide market liquidity. This is the case since speculators optimally invest in securities that have the greatest expected profit (i.e., illiquidity) per capital use (determined by the asset's dollar margin). This common ratio is determined in equilibrium by the speculators' funding liquidity (i.e., capital scarcity). Said differently, a security's market illiquidity is the product of its margin and the shadow cost of funding. Our model thus provides a natural explanation for the *commonality* of liquidity across assets since shocks to speculators' funding constraint affect all securities. This may help explain why market liquidity is correlated across stocks (Chordia, Roll, and Subrahmanyam 2000; Hasbrouck and Seppi 2001; and Huberman and Halka 2001), and across stocks and bonds (Chordia, Sarkar, and Subrahmanyam 2005). In support of the idea that commonality is driven at least in part by our funding-liquidity mechanism, Chordia, Roll, and Subrahmanyam (2005) find that "money flows...account for part of the commonality in stock and bond market liquidity." Moreover, their finding that "during crisis periods, monetary expansions are associated with increased liquidity" is consistent with our model's prediction that the effects are largest when traders are near their constraint. Acharya, Schaefer, and Zhang (2008) document a substantial increase in the co-movement among credit default swaps (CDS) during the GM/Ford rating downgrade in May 2005 when dealer funding was stretched. Coughenour and Saad (2004) provide further evidence of the funding-liquidity mechanism by showing that the co-movement in liquidity among stocks handled by the same NYSE specialist firm is higher than for other stocks, commonality is higher for specialists with less capital, and decreases after a merger of specialists.

Next, our model predicts that market liquidity declines as fundamental volatility increases, which is consistent with the empirical findings of Benston and Hagerman (1974) and Amihud and Mendelson (1989).[4] Further, the model can shed new light on "flight to quality," referring to episodes in which risky securities become especially illiquid. In our model, this happens when speculators' capital deteriorates, which induces them to mostly

---

[4] The link between volatility and liquidity is shared by the models of Stoll (1978); Grossman and Miller (1988); and others. What sets our theory apart is that this link is connected with margin constraints. This leads to testable differences since, according to our model, the link is stronger when speculators are poorly financed, and high-volatility securities are more affected by speculator wealth shocks – our explanation of flight to quality.

provide liquidity in securities that do not use much capital (low-volatility stocks with lower margins), implying that the liquidity differential between high-volatility and low-volatility securities increases. This capital effect means that illiquid securities are predicted to have more liquidity risk.[5] Recently, Comerton-Forde, Hendershott, Jones, Moulton, and Seasholes (2008) test these predictions using inventory positions of NYSE specialists as a proxy for funding liquidity. Their findings support our hypotheses that market liquidity of high-volatility stocks is more sensitive to inventory shocks and that this is more pronounced at times of low funding liquidity. Moreover, Pastor and Stambaugh (2003) and Acharya and Pedersen (2005) document empirical evidence consistent with flight to liquidity and the pricing of this liquidity risk.

Market-making firms are often net long in the market. For instance, Ibbotson (1999) reports that security brokers and speculators have median market betas in excess of one. Therefore, capital constraints are more likely to be hit during market downturns, and this, together with the mechanism outlined in our model, helps to explain why sudden liquidity dry-ups occur more often when markets decline. Further, capital constraints affect the liquidity of all securities, leading to co-movement as explained above. The fact that this effect is stronger in down markets could explain that co-movement in liquidity is higher during large negative market moves, as documented empirically by Hameed, Kang, and Viswanathan (2005).

Finally, the very risk that the funding constraint becomes binding limits speculators' provision of market liquidity. Our analysis shows that speculators' optimal (funding) risk management policy is to maintain a "safety buffer." This affects initial prices, which increase in the covariance of future prices with future shadow costs of capital (i.e., with future funding illiquidity).

Our paper is related to several literatures.[6] Traders rely both on (equity) investors and counterparties, and, while the limits to arbitrage literature

---

[5] In Vayanos (2004), liquidity premiums increase in volatile times. Fund managers become effectively more risk-averse because higher fundamental volatility increases the likelihood that their performance falls short of a threshold, leading to costly performance-based withdrawal of funds.

[6] Market liquidity is the focus of market microstructure (Stoll 1978; Ho and Stoll 1981, 1983; Kyle 1985; Glosten and Milgrom 1985; Grossman and Miller 1988), and is related to the limits of arbitrage (DeLong et al. 1990; Shleifer and Vishny 1997; Abreu and Brunnermeier 2002). Funding liquidity is examined in corporate finance (Shleifer and Vishny 1992; Holmström and Tirole 1998, 2001) and banking (Bryant 1980; Diamond and Dybvig 1983; Allen and Gale 1998, 2004, 2005, 2007). Funding and collateral constraints are also studied in macroeconomics (Aiyagari and Gertler 1999; Bemanke and Gertler 1989; Fisher 1933; Kiyotaki and Moore 1997; Lustig and Chien 2005), and general equilibrium with incomplete markets (Geanakoplos 1997, 2003). Finally, recent papers consider illiquidity

following Shleifer and Vishny (1997) focuses on the risk of investor redemp-tions, we focus on the risk that counterparty funding conditions may worsen. Other models with margin-constrained traders are Grossman and Vila (1992) and Liu and Longstaff (2004), which derive optimal strategies in a partial equilibrium with a single security; Chowdhry and Nanda (1998) focus on fragility due to dealer losses; and Gromb and Vayanos (2002) derive a general equilibrium with one security (traded in two segmented markets) and study welfare and liquidity provision. We study the endoge-nous variation of margin constraints, the resulting amplifying effects, and differences across high- and low-margin securities in our setting with mul-tiple securities. Stated simply, whereas the above-cited papers use a fixed or decreasing margin constraint, say, $5000 per contract, we study how market conditions lead to changes in the margin requirement itself, e.g., an increase from $5000 to $15,000 per futures contract as happened in October 1987, and the resulting feedback effects between margins and market conditions as speculators are forced to de-lever.

We proceed as follows. We describe the model (Section 1) and derive our four main new results: (i) margins increase with market illiquidity when financiers cannot distinguish fundamental shocks from liquidity shocks and fundamentals have time-varying volatility (Section 2); (ii) this makes margins destabilizing, leading to sudden liquidity dry-ups and margin spi-rals (Section 3); (iii) liquidity crises simultaneously affect many securities, mostly risky high-margin securities, resulting in commonality of liquidity and flight to quality (Section 4); and (iv) liquidity risk matters even before speculators hit their capital constraints (Section 5). Then, we outline how our model's new testable predictions may be helpful for a novel line of empirical work that links measures of speculators' funding conditions to measures of market liquidity (Section 6). Section 7 concludes. Finally, we describe the real-world funding constraints for the main liquidity providers, namely market makers, banks, and hedge funds (Appendix A), and provide proofs (Appendix B).

1. Model

The economy has J risky assets, traded at times $t = 0, 1, 2, 3$. At time $t = 3$, each security j pays off v^j, a random variable defined on a probability space $(\Omega, \mathcal{F}, \mathcal{P})$. There is no aggregate risk because the aggregate supply is zero and

with constrained traders (Attari, Mello, and Ruckes 2005; Bernardo and Welch 2004; Brunnermeier and Pedersen 2005; Eisfeldt 2004; Morris and Shin 2004; Weill 2007).

the risk-free interest rate is normalized to zero, so the fundamental value of each stock is its conditional expected value of the final payoff $v_t^j = E_t[v^j]$. Fundamental volatility has an autoregressive conditional heteroscedasticity (ARCH) structure. Specifically, v_t^j evolves according to

$$v_{t+1}^j = v_t^j + \Delta v_{t+1}^j = v_t^j + \sigma_{t+1}^j \varepsilon_{t+1}^j, \tag{1}$$

where all ε_t^j are i.i.d. across time and assets with a standard normal cumulative distribution function Φ with zero mean and unit variance, and the volatility σ_t^j has dynamics

$$\sigma_{t+1}^j = \underline{\sigma}^j + \theta^j |\Delta v_t^j|, \tag{2}$$

where $\underline{\sigma}^j, \theta^j \geq 0$. A positive θ^j implies that shocks to fundamentals increase future volatility.

There are three groups of market participants: "customers" and "speculators" trade assets while "financiers" finance speculators' positions. The group of customers consists of three risk-averse agents. At time 0, customer $k = 0, 1, 2$ has a cash holding of W_0^k bonds and zero shares, but finds out that he will experience an endowment shock of $\mathbf{z}^k = \{z^{1,k}, \ldots, z^{j,k}\}$ shares at time $t = 3$, where $\mathbf{z}$ are random variables such that the aggregate endowment shock is zero, $\sum_{k=0}^2 z^{j,k} = 0$.

With probability $(1 - a)$, all customers arrive at the market at time 0 and can trade securities in each time period 0, 1, 2. Since their aggregate shock is zero, they can share risks and have no need for intermediation.

The basic liquidity problem arises because customers arrive sequentially with probability a, which gives rise to order imbalance. Specifically, in this case customer 0 arrives at time 0, customer 1 arrives at time 1, and customer 2 arrives at time 2. Hence, at time 2 all customers are present, at time 1 only customers 0 and 1 can trade, and at time 0 only customer 0 is in the market.

Before a customer arrives in the marketplace, his demand is $\mathbf{y}_t^k = 0$, and after he arrives he chooses his security position each period to maximize his exponential utility function $U(W_3^k) = -\exp\{-\gamma W_3^k\}$ over final wealth. Wealth W_t^k, including the value of the anticipated endowment shock of $\mathbf{z}^k$ shares, evolves according to

$$W_{t+1}^k = W_t^k + (\mathbf{p}_{t+1} - \mathbf{p}_t)'(\mathbf{y}_t^k + \mathbf{z}^k). \tag{3}$$

The vector of total demand shock of customers who have arrived in the market at time t is denoted by $Z_t := \sum_{k=0}^t \mathbf{z}^k$.

The early customers' trading need is accommodated by speculators who provide liquidity/immediacy. Speculators are risk-neutral and maximize expected final wealth W_3. Speculators face the constraint that the total margin on their position x_t cannot exceed their capital W_t:

$$\sum_j \left(x_t^{j+} m_t^{j+} + x_t^{j-} m_t^{j-} \right) \leq W_t, \qquad (4)$$

where $x_t^{j+} \geq 0$ and $x_t^{j-} \geq 0$ are the positive and negative parts of $x_t^j = x_t^{j+} - x_t^{j-}$, respectively, and $m_t^{j+} \geq 0$ and $m_t^{j-} \geq 0$ are the dollar margin on long and short positions, respectively. The institutional features related to this key constraint for different types of speculators like hedge funds, banks, and market makers are discussed in detail in Appendix A.

Speculators start out with a cash position of W_0 and zero shares, and their wealth evolves according to

$$W_t = W_{t-1} + (\mathbf{p}_t - \mathbf{p}_{t-1})' \mathbf{x}_{t-1} + \eta_t, \qquad (5)$$

where η_t is an independent wealth shock arising from other activities (e.g., a speculator's investment banking arm). If a speculator loses all his capital, $W_t \leq 0$, he can no longer invest because of the margin constraint (4), i.e., he must choose $x_t = 0$. We let his utility in this case be $\varphi_t W_t$, where $\varphi_t \geq 0$. Limited liability corresponds to $\varphi_t = 0$, and a proportional bankruptcy cost (e.g., monetary, reputational, or opportunity costs) corresponds to $\varphi_t > 0$. We focus on the case in which $\varphi_2 = 1$, that is, negative consumption equal to the dollar loss in $t = 2$. We discuss φ_1 in Section 5. Our results would be qualitatively the same with other bankruptcy assumptions.

We could allow the speculators to raise new capital as long as this takes time. Indeed, the model would be the same if the speculators could raise capital only at time 2 (and in this case we need not assume that the customers' endowment shocks z^j aggregate to zero). Hence, in this sense, we can view our model as one of "slow moving capital," consistent with the empirical evidence of Mitchell, Pedersen, and Pulvino (2007).

Each financier sets the margins to limit his counterparty credit risk. Specifically, each financier ensures that the margin is large enough to cover the position's π-value-at-risk (where π is a non-negative number close to zero, e.g., 1%):

$$\pi = \Pr\left(-\Delta p_{t+1}^j > m_t^{j+} | \mathcal{F}_t \right), \qquad (6)$$

$$\pi = \Pr\left(\Delta p_{t+1}^j > m_t^{j-} | \mathcal{F}_t \right). \qquad (7)$$

Equation (6) means that the margin on a long position m^+ is set such that price drops that exceed the amount of the margin only happen with a small probability π. Similarly, Equation (7) means that price increases larger than the margin on a short position only happen with small probability. Clearly, the margin is larger for more volatile assets. The margin depends on financiers' information set $\mathcal{F}_t$. We consider two important benchmarks: "informed financiers," who know the fundamental value and the liquidity shocks $\mathbf{z}$, $\mathcal{F}_t = \sigma\{\mathbf{z}, v_0, \ldots, v_t, \mathbf{p}_0, \ldots, \mathbf{p}_t, \eta_1, \ldots, \eta_t\}$, and "uninformed financiers," who only observe prices, $\mathcal{F}_t = \sigma\{\mathbf{p}_0, \ldots, \mathbf{p}_t\}$. This margin specification is motivated by the real-world institutional features described in Appendix A. Theoretically, Stiglitz and Weiss (1981) show how credit rationing can be due to adverse selection and moral hazard in the lending market, and Geanakoplos (2003) considers endogenous contracts in a general-equilibrium framework of imperfect commitment.

We let Λ_t^j be the (signed) deviation of the price from fundamental value:

$$\Lambda_t^j = p_t^j - v_t^j, \tag{8}$$

and we define our measure of market illiquidity as the absolute amount of this deviation, $|\Lambda_t^j|$. We consider competitive equilibria of the economy:

Definition 1. An *equilibrium* is a price process $\mathbf{p}_t$ such that (i) $\mathbf{x}_t$ maximizes the speculators' expected final profit subject to the margin constraint (4); (ii) each $\mathbf{y}_t^k$ maximizes customer k's expected utility after their arrival at the marketplace and is zero beforehand; (iii) margins are set according to the VaR specification (6–7); and (iv) markets clear, $\mathbf{x}_t + \sum_{k=0}^{2} \mathbf{y}_t^k = 0$.

Equilibrium. We derive the optimal strategies for customers and speculators using dynamic programming, starting from time 2, and working backwards. A customer's value function is denoted Γ and a speculator's value function is denoted J. At time 2, customer k's problem is

$$\Gamma_2(W_2^k, p_2, v_2) = \max_{y_2^k} -E_2\left[e^{-\gamma W_3^k}\right] \tag{9}$$

$$= \max_{y_2^k} -e^{-\gamma(E_2[W_3^k])-\frac{\gamma}{2}Var_2[W_3^k])}, \tag{10}$$

which has the solution

$$y_2^{j,k} = \frac{v_2^j - p_2^j}{\gamma(\sigma_3^j)^2} - z^{j,k}. \tag{11}$$

Clearly, since all customers are present in the market at time 2, the unique equilibrium is $p_2 = v_2$. Indeed, when the prices are equal to fundamentals, the aggregate customer demand is zero, $\sum_k y_2^{j,k} = 0$, and speculators also has a zero demand. We get the customer's value function $\Gamma_2(W_2^k, p_2 = v_2, v_2) = -e^{-\gamma W_2^k}$, and the speculator's value function $J_2 (W_2, p_2 = v_2, v_2) = W_2$.

The equilibrium before time 2 depends on whether the customers arrive sequentially or simultaneously. If all customers arrive at time 0, then the simple arguments above show that $p_t = v_t$, at any time $t = 0, 1, 2$.

We are interested in the case with sequential arrival of the customers such that the speculators' liquidity provision is needed. At time 1, customers 0 and 1 are present in the market, but customer 2 has not arrived yet. As above, customer $k = 0, 1$ has a demand and value function of

$$y_1^{j,k} = \frac{v_1^j - p_1^j}{\gamma(\sigma_2^j)^2} - z^{j,k} \qquad (12)$$

$$\Gamma_1(W_1^k, p_1, v_1) = -\exp\left\{-\gamma\left[W_1^k + \sum_j \frac{(v_1^j - p_1^j)^2}{2\gamma(\sigma_2^j)^2}\right]\right\}. \qquad (13)$$

At time 0, customer $k = 0$ arrives in the market and maximizes $E_0[\Gamma_1(W_1^k, p_1, v_1)]$.

At time $t = 1$, if the market is perfectly liquid so that $p_1^j = v_1^j$ for all j, then the speculators are indifferent among all possible positions x_1. If some securities have $p_1 \neq v_1$, then the risk-neutral speculators invest all his capital such that his margin constraint binds. The speculators optimally trade only in securities with the highest expected profit per dollar used. The profit per dollar used is $(v_1^j - p_1^j)/m_1^{j+}$ on a long position and $-(v_1^j - p_1^j)/m_1^{j-}$ on a short position. A speculators' shadow cost of capital, denoted ϕ_1, is 1 plus the maximum profit per dollar used as long as he is not bankrupt:

$$\phi_1 = 1 + \max_j\left\{\max\left(\frac{v_1^j - p_1^j}{m_1^{j+}}, \frac{-(v_1^j - p_1^j)}{m_1^{j-}}\right)\right\}, \qquad (14)$$

where the margins for long and short positions are set by the financiers, as described in the next section. If the speculators are bankrupt, $W_1 < 0$, then $\phi_1 = \varphi_1$. Each speculator's value function is therefore

$$J_1 (W_1, p_1, v_1, p_0, v_0) = W_1\phi_1. \qquad (15)$$

At time $t = 0$, the speculator maximizes $E_0[W_1\phi_1]$ subject to his capital constraint (4).

The equilibrium prices at times 1 and 0 do not have simple expressions but we can characterize their properties, starting with a basic result from which much intuition derives:

Proposition 1 (market and funding liquidity). *In equilibrium, any asset j's market illiquidity* $|\Lambda_1^j|$ *is linked to its margin* m_1^j *and the common funding illiquidity as measured by the speculators' marginal value of an extra dollar* ϕ_1:

$$\left|\Lambda_1^j\right| = m_1^j\,(\phi_1 - 1), \tag{16}$$

where $m_1^j = m_1^{j+}$ *if the speculator is long and* $m_1^j = m_1^{j-}$ *otherwise. If the speculators have a zero position for asset j, the equation is replaced by* $\leq$.

We next go on to show the (de-)stabilizing properties of margins, and then we further characterize the equilibrium connection between market liquidity and speculators' funding situation, and the role played by liquidity risk at time 0.

2. Margin Setting and Liquidity (Time 1)

A key determinant of speculators' funding liquidity is their margin requirement for collateralized financing. Hence, it is important to determine the margin function, m_1, set by, respectively, informed and uninformed financiers. The margin at time 1 is set to cover a position's value-at-risk, knowing that prices equal the fundamental values in the next period 2, $p_2 = v_2$.

We consider first, informed financiers who know the fundamental values v_1 and, hence, price divergence from fundamentals Λ_1. Since $\Lambda_2 = 0$, they set margins on long positions at $t = 1$, according to

$$\begin{aligned}
\pi &= \Pr(-\Delta p_2^j > m_1^{j+}|\mathcal{F}_1) \\
&= \Pr(-\Delta v_2^j + \Lambda_1^j > m_1^{j+}|\mathcal{F}_1) \\
&= 1 - \Phi\left(\frac{m_1^{j+} - \Lambda_1^j}{\sigma_2^j}\right),
\end{aligned} \tag{17}$$

which implies that

$$\begin{aligned}
m_1^{j+} &= \Phi^{-1}(1 - \pi)\sigma_2^j + \Lambda_1^j \\
&= \bar{\sigma}^j + \bar{\theta}|\Delta v_1^j| + \Lambda_1^j,
\end{aligned} \tag{18}$$

where we define

$$\bar{\sigma}^j = \underline{\sigma}^j\,\Phi^{-1}\,(1 - \pi), \tag{19}$$

$$\bar{\theta}^j = \theta^j\,\Phi^{-1}\,(1 - \pi). \tag{20}$$

The margin on a short position can be derived similarly and we arrive at the following surprising result:

Proposition 2 (stabilizing margins and the cushioning effect). *When the financiers are informed about the fundamental value and knows that prices will equal fundamentals in the next period, $t = 2$, then the margins on long and short positions are, respectively,*

$$m_1^{j+} = \max\{\bar{\sigma}^j + \bar{\theta}^j |\Delta v_1^j| + \Lambda_1^j, 0\}, \tag{21}$$

$$m_1^{j-} = \max\{\bar{\sigma}^j + \bar{\theta}^j |\Delta v_1^j| - \Lambda_1^j, 0\}. \tag{22}$$

The more prices are below fundamentals $\Lambda_1^j < 0$, the lower is the margin on a long position m_1^{j+}, and the more prices are above fundamentals $\Lambda_1^j > 0$, the lower is the margin on a short position m_1^{j-}. Hence, in this case illiquidity reduces margins for speculators who buy low and sell high.

The margins are reduced by illiquidity because the speculators are expected to profit when prices return to fundamentals at time 2, and this profit "cushions" the speculators from losses due to fundamental volatility. Thus, we denote the margins set by informed financiers at $t = 1$ as *stabilizing margins*.

Stabilizing margins are an interesting benchmark, and they are hard to escape in a theoretical model. However, real-world liquidity crises are often associated with increases in margins, not decreases. To capture this, we turn to the case of a in which financiers are uninformed about the current fundamental so that he must set his margin based on the observed prices p_0 and p_1. This is in general a complicated problem since the financiers need to filter out the probability that customers arrive sequentially, and the values of z_0 and z_1. The expression becomes simple, however, if the financier's prior probability of an asynchronous arrival of endowment shocks is small so that he finds it likely that $p_t^j = v_t^j$, implying a common margin $m_1^j = m_1^{j+} = m_1^{j-}$ for long and short positions in the limit:

Proposition 3 (destabilizing margins). *When the financiers are uninformed about the fundamental value, then, as $a \to 0$, the margins on long and short positions approach*

$$m_1^j = \bar{\sigma}^j + \bar{\theta}^j |\Delta p_1^j| = \bar{\sigma}^j + \bar{\theta}^j |\Delta v_1^j + \Delta \Lambda_1^j|. \tag{23}$$

Margins are increasing in price volatility and market illiquidity can increase margins.

Intuitively, since liquidity risk tends to increase price volatility, and since uninformed financiers may interpret price volatility as fundamental volatility, this increases margins.[7] Equation (23) corresponds closely to real-world margin setting, which is primarily based on volatility estimates from past price movements. This introduces a procyclicality that amplifies funding shocks – a major criticism of the Basel II capital regulation. (See Appendix A.2 for how banks' capital requirements relate to our funding constraint.) Equation (23) shows that illiquidity increases margins when the liquidity shock $\Delta \Lambda_1^j$ has the same sign as the fundamental shock Δv_1^j (or is greater in magnitude), for example, when bad news and selling pressure happen at the same time. On the other hand, margins are reduced if the nonfundamental z-shock counterbalances a fundamental move. We denote the phenomenon that margins can increase as illiquidity rises by *destabilizing margins*. As we will see next, the information available to the financiers (i.e., whether margins are stabilizing or destabilizing) has important implications for the equilibrium.

3. Fragility and Liquidity Spirals (Time 1)

We next show how speculators' funding problems can lead to liquidity spirals and fragility – the property that a small change in fundamentals can lead to a large jump in illiquidity. We show that funding problems are especially escalating with uninformed financiers (i.e., destabilizing margins). For simplicity, we illustrate this with a single security $J = 1$.

3.1. Fragility

To set the stage for the main fragility proposition below, we make a few brief definitions. Liquidity is said to be *fragile* if the equilibrium price $p_t(\eta_t, v_t)$ cannot be chosen to be continuous in the exogenous shocks, namely η_t and Δv_t. Fragility arises when the excess demand for shares $x_t + \sum_{k=0}^{1} y_1^k$ be non-monotonic in the price. While under "normal" circumstances, a high price leads to a low total demand (i.e., excess demand is decreasing), binding funding constraints along with destabilizing margins (margin effect) or speculators' losses (loss effect) can lead to an increasing demand curve. Further, it is natural to focus on *stable* equilibria in which a small negative (positive) price perturbation leads to excess demand (supply), which, intuitively, "pushes" the price back up (down) to its equilibrium level.

---

[7] In the analysis of time 0, we shall see that margins can also be destabilizing when price volatility signals future liquidity risk (not necessarily fundamental risk).

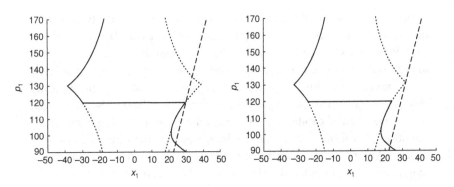

Figure 6.3. Speculator demand and customer supply. This figure illustrates how margins can be destabilizing when financiers are uninformed and the fundamentals have volatility clustering. The solid curve is the speculators' optimal demand for $a = 1\%$. The upward sloping dashed line is the customers' supply, that is, the negative of their demand. In panel A, the speculators experience a zero wealth shock, $\eta_1 = 0$, while in panel B they face a negative wealth shock of $\eta_1 = -150$, otherwise everything is the same. In panel A, perfect liquidity $p_1 = v_1 = 120$ is one of two stable equilibria, while in panel B the unique equilibrium is illiquid.

Proposition 4 (fragility). *There exist $\underline{x}, \underline{\theta}, \underline{a} > 0$ such that:*

(i) With informed financiers, the market is fragile at time 1 if speculators' position $|x_0|$ is larger than $\underline{x}$ and of the same sign as the demand shock Z_1.

(ii) With uninformed financiers the market is fragile as in (i) and additionally if the ARCH parameter θ is larger than $\underline{\theta}$ and the probability, a, of sequential arrival of customers is smaller than $\underline{a}$.

Numerical example. We illustrate how fragility arises due to destabilizing margins or dealer losses by way of a numerical example. We consider the more interesting (and arguably more realistic) case in which the financiers are uninformed, and we choose parameters as follows.

The fundamental value has ARCH volatility parameters $\underline{\sigma} = 10$ and $\theta = 0.3$, which implies clustering of volatility. The initial price is $p_0 = 130$, the aggregate demand shock of the customers who have arrived at time 1 is $Z_1 = z_0 + z_1 = 30$, and the customers' risk aversion coefficient is $\gamma = 0.05$. The speculators have an initial position of $x_0 = 0$ and a cash wealth of $W_1 = 900$. Finally, the financiers use a VaR with $\pi = 1\%$ and customers learn their endowment shocks sequentially with probability $a = 1\%$.

Panel A of Figure 6.3 illustrates how the speculators' demand x_1 and the customers' supply (i.e., the negative of the customers' demand as per Equation (12)) depend on the price p_1 when the fundamental value is

$v_1 = 120$ and the speculators' wealth shock is $\eta_1 = 0$. Customers' supply is given by the upward sloping dashed line since, naturally, their supply is greater when the price is higher. Customers supply $Z_1 = 30$ shares, namely the shares that they anticipate receiving at time $t = 3$, when the market is perfectly liquid, $p_1 = v_1 = 120$ (i.e., illiquidity is $|\Lambda_1| = 0$). For lower prices, they supply fewer shares.

The speculators' demand, x_1, must satisfy the margin constraints. It is instructive to consider first the simpler limiting case $a \to 0$ for which the margin requirement is simply $m = \bar{\sigma} + \bar{\theta}|\Delta p_1| = 2.326(10 + 0.3|\Delta p_1|)$. This implies that speculators demand $|x_1| \leq W_1/(\bar{\sigma} + \bar{\theta}|\Delta p_1|)$. Graphically, this means that their demand must be inside the "hyperbolic star" defined by the four (dotted) hyperbolas (that are partially overlaid by a solid demand curve in Figure 6.3). At the price $p_1 = p_0 = 130$, the margin is smallest and hence the constraint is most relaxed. As p_1 departs from $p_0 = 130$, margins increase and speculators become more constrained – the horizontal distance between two hyperbolas shrinks.

After establishing the hyperbolic star, it is easy to derive the demand curve for $a \to 0$: For $p_1 = v_1 = 120$, the security's expected return is zero and each speculator is indifferent between all his possible positions on the horizontal line. For price levels $p_1 > v_1$ above this line, the risk-neutral speculators want to short-sell the asset, $x_1 < 0$, and their demand is constrained by the upper-left side of the star. Similarly, for prices below v_1 speculators buy the asset, $x_1 > 0$, and their demand is limited by the margin constraint. Interestingly, the speculators' demand is upward sloping for prices below 120. As the price declines, the financiers' estimate of fundamental volatility, and consequently of margins, increase.

We now generalize the analysis to the case where $a > 0$. The margin setting becomes more complicated since uninformed financiers must filter out to what extent the equilibrium price change is caused by a movement in fundamentals Δv_1 and/or an occurrence of a liquidity event with an order imbalance caused by the presence of customers 0 and 1, but not customer 2. Since customers 0 and 1 want to sell ($Z_1 = 30$), a price increase or modest price decline is most likely due to a change in fundamentals, and hence the margin setting is similar to the case of $a = 0$. This is why speculators' demand curve for prices above 100 almost perfectly overlays the relevant part of the hyperbolic star in Figure 6.3. However, for a large price drop, say below 100, financiers assign a larger conditional probability that a liquidity event has occurred. Hence, they are willing to set a lower margin (relative to the one implying the hyperbolic star) because they expect the

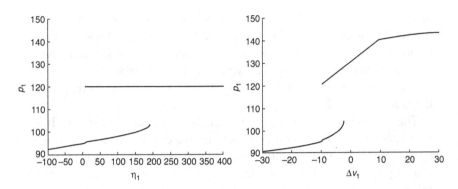

Figure 6.4. Fragility due to destabilizing margins. The figure shows the equilibrium price as a function of the speculators' wealth shock η_1 (panel A) and of fundamental shocks Δv_1 (panel B). This is drawn for the equilibrium with the highest market liquidity (light line) and the equilibrium with the lowest market liquidity (dark line). The margins are destabilizing since financiers are uninformed and fundamentals exhibit volatility clustering. The equilibrium prices are discontinuous, which reflects *fragility* in liquidity since a small shock can lead to a disproportionately large price effect.

speculator to profit as the price rebounds in period 2 – hence, the cushioning effect discussed above reappears in the extreme here. This explains why the speculators' demand curve is backward bending only in a limited price range and becomes downward sloping for p_1 below roughly 100.[8]

Panel A of Figure 6.3 shows that there are two stable equilibria: a perfect liquidity equilibrium with price $p_1 = v_1 = 120$ and an illiquid equilibrium with a price of about 94 (and an uninteresting unstable equilibrium with p_1 just below 120).

Panel B of Figure 6.3 shows the same plot as panel A, but with a negative wealth shock to speculators of $\eta_1 = -150$ instead of $\eta_1 = 0$. In this case, perfect liquidity with $p_1 = v_1$ is no longer an equilibrium since the speculators cannot fund a large enough position. The unique equilibrium is highly illiquid because of the speculators' lower wealth and, importantly, because of endogenously higher margins.

This "disconnect" between the perfect-liquidity equilibrium and the illiquid equilibrium and the resulting fragility is illustrated more directly in Figure 6.4. Panel A plots the equilibrium price correspondence for different

---

[8] We note that the cushioning effect relies on the financiers' knowledge that the market will become liquid in period $t = 2$. This is not the case in the earlier period 0, though. In an earlier version of the paper, we showed that the cushioning effect disappears in a stationary infinite horizon setting in which the "complementary" customers arrive in each period with a constant arrival probability.

exogenous funding shocks η_1 (with fixed An $\Delta v_1 = -10$) and shows that a marginal reduction in funding cannot always lead to a smooth reduction in market liquidity. Rather, there must be a level of funding such that an infinitesimal drop in funding leads to a discontinuous drop in market liquidity.

The dark line in Figure 6.4 shows the equilibrium with the highest market liquidity and the light line shows the equilibrium with the lowest market liquidity. We note that the financiers' filtering problem and, hence, the margin function depend on the equilibrium selection. Since the margin affects the speculators' trades, the equilibrium selection affects the equilibrium outcome everywhere – prices are slightly affected even outside the η region (v_1 region) with fragility.

Panel B of Figure 6.4 plots the equilibrium price correspondence for different realizations of the fundamental shock Δv_1 (with fixed $\eta_1 = 0$) and shows the same form of discontinuity for adverse fundamental shocks to v_1. The discontinuity with respect to Δv_1 is most easily understood in conjunction with panel A of Figure 6.3. As Δv_1 falls, the horizontal line of speculator demand shifts downward, and the customer supply line moves downward. As a result, the perfect liquidity equilibrium vanishes. Panel B of Figure 6.4 also reveals the interesting asymmetry that negative fundamental shocks lead to larger price movements than corresponding positive shocks (for $Z_1 := z_0 + z_1 > 0$). This asymmetry arises even without a loss effect since $x_0 = 0$.

Fragility can also arise because of shocks to customer demand or volatility. Indeed, the market can also be suddenly pushed into an illiquid equilibrium with high margins due to an increase in demand and an increase in volatility. Paradoxically, a marginally larger demand for liquidity by customers can lead to a drastic reduction of liquidity supply by the speculators when it pushes the equilibrium over the edge.

While the example above has speculators with zero initial positions, $x_0 = 0$, it is also interesting to consider $x_0 > 0$. In this case, lower prices lead to losses for the speculators, and graphically this means that the constraints in the "hyperbolic star" tighten (i.e., the gap between the hyperbolas narrows) at low prices. Because of this "loss effect," the discontinuous price drop associated with the illiquid equilibrium is even larger.

In summary, this example shows how destabilizing margins and dealer losses give rise to a discontinuity in prices, which can help to explain the sudden market liquidity dry-ups observed in many markets. For example, Russia's default in 1998 was in itself only a trivial wealth shock relative to global arbitrage capital. Nevertheless, it had a large effect on liquidity in global financial markets, consistent with our fragility result that a small wealth shock can push the equilibrium over the edge.

3.2. Liquidity Spirals

To further emphasize the importance of speculators' funding liquidity, we now show how it can make market liquidity highly sensitive to shocks. We identify two amplification mechanisms: a "margin spiral" due to increasing margins as speculator financing worsens, and a "loss spiral" due to escalating speculator losses.

Figure 6.2 illustrates these "liquidity spirals." A shock to speculator capital ($\eta_1 < 0$) forces speculators to provide less market liquidity, which increases the price impact of the customer demand pressure. With uninformed financiers and ARCH effects, the resulting price swing increases financiers' estimate of the fundamental volatility and, hence, increases the margin, thereby worsening speculator funding problems even further, and so on, leading to a "margin spiral." Similarly, increased market illiquidity can lead to losses on speculators' existing positions, worsening their funding problem and so on, leading to a "loss spiral." Mathematically, the spirals can be expressed as follows:

Proposition 5. (i) *If speculators' capital constraint is slack, then the price p_1 is equal to v_1 and insensitive to local changes in speculator wealth.*
(ii) **(Liquidity spirals)** *In a stable illiquid equilibrium with selling pressure from customers, $Z_1, x_1 > 0$, the price sensitivity to speculator wealth shocks η_1 is*

$$\frac{\partial p_1}{\partial \eta_1} = \frac{1}{\frac{2}{\gamma(\sigma_2)^2} m_1^+ + \frac{\partial m_1^+}{\partial p_1} x_1 - x_0} \tag{24}$$

and with buying pressure from customers, $Z_1, x_1 < 0$,

$$\frac{\partial p_1}{\partial \eta_1} = \frac{-1}{\frac{2}{\gamma(\sigma_2)^2} m_1^- + \frac{\partial m_1^-}{\partial p_1} x_1 + x_0}. \tag{25}$$

*A **margin/haircut spiral** arises if $\frac{\partial m_1^+}{\partial p_1} < 0$ or $\frac{\partial m_1^-}{\partial p_1} > 0$, which happens with positive probability if financiers are uninformed and a is small enough. A **loss spiral** arises if speculators' previous position is in the opposite direction as the demand pressure, $x_0 Z_1$ 0.*

This proposition is intuitive. Imagine first what happens if speculators face a wealth shock of $1, margins are constant, and speculators have no inventory $x_0 = 0$. In this case, the speculator must reduce his position by $1/m_1$. Since the slope of each of the two customer demand curves is[9] $1/(\gamma(\sigma_2)^2)$, we got a total price effect of $1/(\frac{2}{\gamma(\sigma_2)^2}m_1)$.

The two additional terms in the denominator imply amplification or dampening effects due to changes in the margin requirement and to profit/losses on the speculators' existing positions. To see that, recall that for any $k > 0$ and l with $|l| < k$, it holds that $\frac{1}{k-l} = \frac{l}{k} + \frac{l}{k^2} + \frac{l}{k^3} + \cdots$; so with $k = \frac{2}{\gamma(\sigma_2)^2}m_1$ and $l = -\frac{\partial m_1^{\pm}}{\partial p_1}x_1 \pm x_0$, each term in this infinite series corresponds to one loop around the circle in Figure 6.2. The total effect of the changing margin and speculators' positions amplifies the effect if $l > 0$. Intuitively, with $Z_1 > 0$, then customer selling pressure is pushing down the price, and $\frac{\partial m_1^{+}}{\partial p_1} < 0$ means that as prices go down, margins increase, making speculators' funding tighter and thus destabilizing the system. Similarly, when customers are buying, $\frac{\partial m_1^{-}}{\partial p_1} > 0$ implies that increasing prices leads to increased margins, making it harder for speculators to short-sell, thus destabilizing the system. The system is also destabilized if speculators lose money on their previous position as prices move away from fundamentals.

Interestingly, the total effect of a margin spiral together with a loss spiral is greater than the sum of their separate effects. This can be seen mathematically by using simple convexity arguments, and it can be seen intuitively from the flow diagram of Figure 6.2.

Note that spirals can also be "started" by shocks to liquidity demand Z_1, fundamentals v_1, or volatility. It is straightforward to compute the price sensitivity with respect to such shocks. They are just multiples of $\frac{\partial p_1}{\partial \eta_1}$. For instance, a fundamental shock affects the price both because of its direct effect on the final payoff and because of its effect on customers' estimate of future volatility – and both of these effects are amplified by the liquidity spirals.

Our analysis sheds some new light on the 1987 stock market crash, complementing the standard culprit, portfolio insurance trading. In the 1987 stock market crash, numerous market makers hit (or violated) their funding constraint:

"By the end of trading on October 19, [1987] thirteen [NYSE specialist] units had no buying power," – SEC (1988, chap. 4, p. 58)

---

[9] See Equation (12).

While several of these firms managed to reduce their positions and continue their operations, others did not. For instance, Tompane was so illiquid that it was taken over by Merrill Lynch Specialists and Beauchamp was taken over by Spear, Leeds & Kellogg (Beauchamp's clearing broker). Also, market makers outside the NYSE experienced funding troubles: the Amex market makers Damm Frank and Santangelo were taken over; at least 12 OTC market makers ceased operations; and several trading firms went bankrupt.

These funding problems were due to (i) reductions in capital arising from trading losses and defaults on unsecured customer debt, (ii) an increased funding need stemming from increased inventory, and (iii) increased margins. One New York City bank, for instance, increased margins/haircuts from 20% to 25% for certain borrowers, and another bank increased margins from 25% to 30% for all specialists (SEC, 1988, pp. 5–27 and 5–28). Other banks reduced the funding period by making intraday margin calls, and at least two banks made intraday margin calls based on assumed 15% and 25% losses, thus effectively increasing the haircut by 15% and 25%. Also, some broker-dealers experienced a reduction in their line of credit and – as Figure 6.1 shows – margins at the futures exchanges also drastically increased (SEC 1988 and Wigmore 1998). Similarly, during the ongoing liquidity and credit crunch, the margins and haircuts across most asset classes widened significantly starting in the summer of 2007 (see IMF Global Stability Report, October 2007).

In summary, our results on fragility and liquidity spirals imply that during "bad" times, small changes in underlying funding conditions (or liquidity demand) can lead to sharp reductions in liquidity. The 1987 crash exhibited several of the predicted features, namely capital-constrained dealers, increased margins, and increased illiquidity.

4. Commonality and Flight to Quality (Time 1)

We now turn to the cross-sectional implications of illiquidity. Since speculators are risk-neutral, they optimally invest all their capital in securities that have the greatest expected profit $|\Lambda^j|$ per capital use, i.e., per dollar margin m^j, as expressed in Equation (14). That equation also introduces the shadow cost of capital ϕ_1 as the marginal value of an extra dollar. The speculators' shadow cost of capital ϕ_1 captures well the notion of funding liquidity: a high ϕ means that the available funding – from capital W_1 and from collateralized financing with margins m_1^j – is low relative to the needed funding, which depends on the investment opportunities deriving from demand shocks z^j.

The market liquidity of all assets depends on the speculators' funding liquidity, especially for high-margin assets, and this has several interesting implications:

Proposition 6. *There exists $c > 0$ such that, for $\theta^j < c$ for all j and either informed financiers or uninformed with $a < c$, we have:*

(i) **Commonality of market liquidity.** *The market illiquidities $|\Lambda|$ of any two securities, k and l, co-move,*

$$\text{Cov}_0\left(\left|\Lambda_1^k\right|, \left|\Lambda_1^l\right|\right) \geq 0, \tag{26}$$

and market illiquidity co-moves with funding illiquidity as measured by speculators' shadow cost of capital, ϕ_1,

$$\text{Cov}_0\left[|\Lambda_1^k|, \phi_1\right] \geq 0. \tag{27}$$

(ii) **Commonality of fragility.** *Jumps in market liquidity occur simultaneously for all assets for which speculators are marginal investors.*

(iii) **Quality and liquidity.** *If asset l has lower fundamental volatility than asset k, $\underline{\sigma}^l < \underline{\sigma}^k$, then l also has lower market illiquidity,*

$$\left|\Lambda_1^l\right| \leq \left|\Lambda_1^k\right|, \tag{28}$$

if $x_1^k \neq 0$ or $|Z_1^k| \geq |Z_1^l|$.

(iv) **Flight to quality.** *The market liquidity differential between high- and low-fundamental-volatility securities is bigger when speculator funding is tight, that is, $\underline{\sigma}^l < \underline{\sigma}^k$ implies that $\left|\Lambda_1^k\right|$ increases more with a negative wealth shock to the speculator,*

$$\frac{\partial|\Lambda_1^l|}{\partial(-\eta_1)} \leq \frac{\partial|\Lambda_1^k|}{\partial(-\eta_1)}, \tag{29}$$

if $x_1^k \neq 0$ or $|Z_1^k| \geq |Z_1^l|$. Hence, if $x_1^k \neq 0$ or $|Z_1^k| \geq |Z_1^l|$ a.s., then

$$\text{Cov}_0\left(\left|\Lambda_1^l\right|, \phi_1\right) \leq \text{Cov}_0\left(\left|\Lambda_1^k\right|, \phi_1\right). \tag{30}$$

Numerical example, continued. To illustrate these cross-sectional predictions, we extend the numerical example of Section 3 to two securities. The two securities only differ in their long-run fundamental volatility: $\bar{\sigma}^1 = 7.5$ and $\bar{\sigma}^2 = 10$. The other parameters are as before, except that we double W_1 to 1800 since the speculators now trade two securities, the financiers remain uninformed, and we focus on the simpler limited case with $a \to 0$.

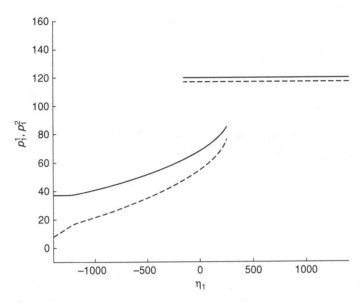

Figure 6.5. Flight to quality and commonality in liquidity. The figure plots the prices p_1^j of assets 1 and 2 as functions of speculators' funding shocks η_1. Asset I (solid curve) has lower long-run fundamental risk than asset 2 (dashed curve), $\bar{\sigma}^1 = 7.5 < 10 = \bar{\sigma}^2$.

Figure 6.5 depicts the assets' equilibrium prices for different values of the funding shock η_1. First, note that as speculator funding tightens and our funding illiquidity measure ϕ_1 rises, the market illiquidity measure $|\Lambda_1^j|$ rises for both assets. Hence, for random η_1, we see our commonality in liquidity result $\text{Cov}_0[|\Lambda_1^k|, |\Lambda_1^l|] > 0$.

The "commonality in fragility" cannot directly be seen from Figure 6.5, but it is suggestive that both assets have the same range of η_1 with two equilibrium prices p_1^j. The intuition for this result is the following. Whenever funding is unconstrained, there is perfect market liquidity provision for all assets. If funding is constrained, then it cannot be the case that speculators provide perfect liquidity for one asset but not for the other, since they would always have an incentive to shift funds towards the asset with non-perfect market liquidity. Hence, market illiquidity jumps for both assets at exactly the same funding level.

Our result relating fundamental volatility to market liquidity ("quality and liquidity") is reflected in p_1^2 being below p_1^1 for any given funding level. Hence, the high-fundamental-volatility asset 2 is always less liquid than the low-fundamental-volatility asset 1.

Figure 6.5 also illustrates our result on "flight to quality." To see this, consider the two securities' relative price sensitivity with respect to η_1.

For large wealth shocks, market liquidity is perfect for both assets, i.e., $p_1^1 = p_1^2 = v_1^1 = v_1^2 = 120$, so in this high range of funding, market liquidity is insensitive to marginal changes in funding. On the lower branch of the graph, market illiquidity of both assets increases as η_1 drops since speculators must take smaller stakes in both assets. Importantly, as funding decreases, p_1^2 decreases more steeply than p_1^1, that is, asset 2 is more sensitive to funding declines than asset 1. This is because speculators cut back more on the "funding-intensive" asset 2 with its high margin requirement. Speculators want to maximize their profit per dollar margin, $|\Lambda^j|/m^j$, and therefore $|\Lambda^2|$ must be higher than $|\Lambda^1|$ to compensate speculators for using more capital for margin.

Both price functions exhibit a kink around $\eta = -1210$, because, for sufficiently low funding levels, speculators put all their capital into asset 2. This is because the customers are more eager to sell the more volatile asset 2, leading to more attractive prices for the speculators.

5. Liquidity Risk (Time 0)

We now turn attention to the initial time period, $t = 0$, and demonstrate that (i) funding liquidity risk matters even before margin requirements actually bind; (ii) the pricing kernel depends on future funding liquidity, ϕ_{1+1}; (iii) the conditional distribution of prices p_1 is skewed due to the funding constraint (inducing fat tails *ex ante*); and (iv) margins m_0 and illiquidity Λ_0 can be positively related due to liquidity risk even if financiers are informed.

The speculators' trading activity at time 0 naturally depends on their expectations about the next period and, in particular, the time 1 illiquidity described in detail above. Further, speculators risk having negative wealth W_1 at time 1, in which case they have utility $\varphi_t W_t$. If speculators have no dis-utility associated with negative wealth levels ($\varphi_t = 0$), then they go to their limit already at time 0 and the analysis is similar to time 1.

We focus on the more realistic case in which the speculators have dis-utility in connection with $W_1 < 0$ and, therefore, choose not to trade to their constraint at time $t = 0$ when their wealth is large enough. To understand this, note that while most firms legally have limited liability, the capital W_t in our model refers to pledgable capital allocated to trading. For instance, Lehman Brothers' 2001 Annual Report (p. 46) states:

"The following must be funded with cash capital: Secured funding 'haircuts,' to reflect the estimated value of cash that would be advanced to the Company by counterparties against available inventory, Fixed assets and goodwill, [and] Operational cash ... "

Hence, if Lehman suffers a large loss on its pledgable capital such that $W_t < 0$, then it incurs monetary costs that must be covered with its unpledgable capital like operational cash (which could also hurt Lehman's other businesses). In addition, the firm incurs non-monetary cost, like loss in reputation and in goodwill, that reduces its ability to exploit future profitable investment opportunities. To capture these effects, we let a speculator's utility be $\phi_1 W_1$, where ϕ_1 is given by the right-hand side of Equation (14) both for positive and negative values of W_1. With this assumption, equilibrium prices at time $t = 0$ are such that the speculators do not trade to their constraint at time $t = 0$ when their wealth is large enough. In fact, this is the weakest assumption that curbs the speculators' risk taking since it makes their objective function linear. Higher "bankruptcy costs" would lead to more cautious trading at time 0 and qualitatively similar results.[10]

If the speculator is not constrained at time $t = 0$, then the first-order condition for his position in security j is $E_0[\phi_1(p_1^j - p_0^j)] = 0$. (We leave the case of a constrained time-0 speculator for Appendix B.) Consequently, the funding liquidity, ϕ_1, determines the pricing kernel $\phi_1/E_0[\phi_1]$ for the cross section of securities:

$$p_0^j = \frac{E_0\left[\phi_1 p_1^j\right]}{E_0[\phi_1]} = E_0\left[p_1^j\right] + \frac{Cov_0\left[\phi_1, p_1^j\right]}{E_0[\phi_1]}. \tag{31}$$

Equation (31) shows that the price at time 0 is the expected time-1 price, which already depends on the liquidity shortage at time 1, further adjusted for liquidity risk in the form of a covariance term. The liquidity risk term is intuitive: The time-0 price is lower if the covariance is negative, that is, if the security has a low payoff during future funding liquidity crises when ϕ_1 is high.

An illustration of the importance of funding-liquidity management is the "LTCM crisis." The hedge fund Long Term Capital Management (LTCM) had been aware of funding liquidity risk. Indeed, they estimated that in

---

[10] We note that risk aversion also limits speculators' trading in the real world. Our model based on margin constraints differs from one driven purely by risk aversion in several ways. For example, an adverse shock that lowers speculator wealth at $t = 1$ creates a profitable investment opportunity that one might think partially offsets the loss – a natural "dynamic hedge." Because of this dynamic hedge, in a model driven by risk-aversion, speculators (with a relative-risk-aversion coefficient larger than one) increase their $t = 0$ hedging demand, which in turn, lowers illiquidity in $t = 0$. However, exactly the opposite occurs in a setting with capital constraints. Capital constraints prevent speculators from taking advantage of investment opportunities in $t = 1$ so they cannot exploit this "dynamic hedge." Hence, speculators are reluctant to trade away the illiquidity at $t = 0$.

times of severe stress, haircuts on AAA-rated commercial mortgages would increase from 2% to 10%, and similarly for other securities (HBS Case N9-200-007(A)). In response to this, LTCM had negotiated long-term financing with margins fixed for several weeks on many of their collateralized loans. Other firms with similar strategies, however, experienced increased margins. Due to an escalating liquidity spiral, LTCM could ultimately not fund its positions in spite of its numerous measures to control funding risk, it was taken over by fourteen banks in September 1998. Another recent example is the funding problems of the hedge fund Amaranth in September 2006, which reportedly ended with losses in excess of USD 6 billion. The ongoing liquidity crisis of 2007–2008, in which funding based on the asset-backed commercial paper market suddenly eroded and banks were reluctant to lend to each other out of fear of future funding shocks, provides a nice out-of-sample test of our theory.[11]

Numerical example, continued. To better understand funding liquidity risk, we return to our numerical example with one security, $\eta_1 = 0$ and $a \to 0$. We first consider the setting with uninformed financiers and later turn to the case with informed financiers.

Figure 6.6 depicts the price p_0 and expected time-1 price $E_0[p_1]$ for different initial wealth levels, W_0, for which the speculators' funding constraint is not binding at $t = 0$. The figure shows that even though the speculators are unconstrained at time 0, market liquidity provision is limited with prices below the fundamental value of $E_0[v] = 130$. The price is below the fundamental for two reasons: First, the expected time-1 price is below the fundamental value because of the risk that speculators cannot accommodate the customer selling pressure at that time. Second, p_0 is even below $E_0[p_1]$, since speculators face liquidity risk: Holding the security leads to losses in the states of nature when speculators are constrained and investment opportunities are good, implying that $\mathrm{Cov}[\phi_1, p_1] < 0$. The additional compensation for liquidity risk is $\frac{Cov_0[\phi_1, p_1^j]}{E_0[\phi_1]}$, as seen in Equation (31), which is the difference between the solid line p_1 and the dashed $E_0[p_1]$.

The funding constraint not only affects the price level, it also introduces skewness in the p_1-distribution conditional on the sign of the demand pressure. For $Z_1 > 0$, speculators take long positions and, consequently, negative v_1-shocks lead to capital losses with resulting liquidity spirals. This amplification triggers a sharper price drop than the corresponding price

---

[11] See Brannermeier (2009) for a more complete treatment of the liquidity and credit crunch that started in 2007.

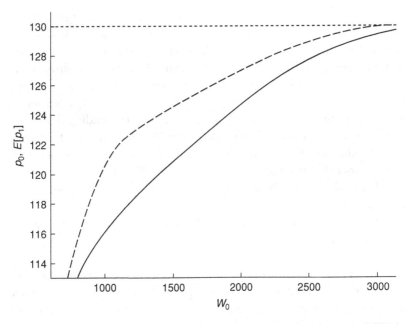

Figure 6.6. Illiquidity at time 0. This graph shows the price p_0 at time 0 (solid line), the expected time-1 price $E_0[p_1]$ (dashed line), and the fundamental value $E_0[v] = 130$ (dotted line) for different levels of speculator funding W_0. The price p_0 is below the fundamental value due to illiquidity, in particular, because of customer selling pressure and the risk that speculators will hit their capital constraints at time 1, even though speculators are not constrained at time 0 for the depicted wealth levels.

increase for positive v_1-shocks. Figure 6.7 shows this negative skewness for different funding levels W_0. The effect is not monotone – zero dealer wealth implies no skewness, for instance.

When customers want to buy (not sell as above), and funding constraints induce a positive skewness in the p_1-distribution. The speculator's return remains negatively skewed, as above, since it is still its losses that are amplified. This is consistent with the casual evidence that hedge fund return indexes are negatively skewed, and it can help explain why FX carry trade returns are negatively skewed (see Brunnermeier, Nagel, and Pedersen 2009). It also suggests that from an *ex ante* point of view (i.e., prior to the realization of Z_1), funding constraints lead to higher kurtosis of the price distribution (fat tails).

Finally, we can also show numerically that unlike at time $t = 1$, margins can be positively related to illiquidity at time 0, even when financiers are

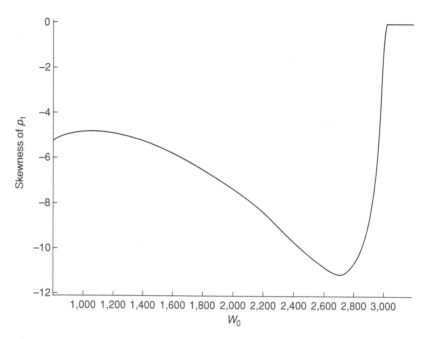

Figure 6.7. Conditional price skewness. The figure shows the conditional skewness of p_1 for different funding levels W_0. While the funding constraint is not binding at time 0, it can become binding at time 1, leading to large price drops due to liquidity spirals. Price increases are not amplified, and this asymmetry results in skewness.

fully informed.[12] This is because of the liquidity risk between time 0 and time 1. To see this, note that if we reduce the speculators' initial wealth W_0, then the market becomes less liquid in the sense that the price is further from the fundamental value. At the same time, the equilibrium price in $t = 1$ is more volatile and thus equilibrium margins at time 0 can actually increase.

6. New Testable Predictions

Our analysis provides a theoretical framework that delivers a unified explanation for a host of stylized empirical facts. Our analysis further suggests a novel line of empirical work that tests the model at a deeper level, namely, its prediction that speculator funding is a driving force underlying these market liquidity effects.

[12] The simulation results are available upon request from the authors.

First, it would be of interest to empirically study the determinants of margin requirements (e.g., using data from futures markets or from prime brokers). Our model suggests that both fundamental volatility and liquidity-driven volatility affect margins (Propositions 2 and 3). Empirically, fundamental volatility can be captured using price changes over a longer time period, while the sum of fundamental and liquidity-based volatility can be captured by short-term price changes as in the literature on variance ratios (see, for example, Campbell, Lo, and MacKinlay 1997). Our model predicts that, in markets where it is harder for financiers to be informed, margins depend on the total fundamental and liquidity-based volatility. In particular, in times of liquidity crises, margins increase in such markets, and, more generally, margins should co-move with illiquidity in the time series and in the cross section.[13]

Second, our model suggests that an exogenous shock to speculator capital should lead to a reduction in market liquidity (Proposition 5). Hence, a clean test of the model would be to identify exogenous capital shocks, such as an unconnected decision to close down a trading desk, a merger leading to reduced total trading capital, or a loss in one market unrelated to the fundamentals of another market, and then study the market liquidity and margin around such events.

Third, the model implies that the effect of speculator capital on market liquidity is highly nonlinear: a marginal change in capital has a small effect when speculators are far from their constraints, but a large effect when speculators are close to their constraints – illiquidity can suddenly jump (Propositions 4 and 5).

Fourth, the model suggests that a cause of the commonality in liquidity is that the speculators' shadow cost of capital is a driving state variable. Hence, a measure of speculator capital tightness should help explain the empirical co-movement of market liquidity. Further, our result "commonality of fragility" suggests that especially sharp liquidity reductions occur simultaneously across several assets (Proposition 6(i)–(ii)).

Fifth, the model predicts that the sensitivity of margins and market liquidity to speculator capital is larger for securities that are risky and illiquid on average. Hence, the model suggests that a shock to speculator capital would lead to a reduction in market liquidity through a spiral effect that is stronger for illiquid securities (Proposition 6(iv)).

---

[13] One must be cautious with the interpretation of the empirical results related to changes in Regulation T since this regulation may not affect speculators but affects the demanders of liquidity, namely the customers.

Sixth, speculators are predicted to have negatively skewed returns since, when they hit their constraints, they incur significant losses because of the endogenous liquidity spirals, and, in contrast, their gains are not amplified when prices return to fundamentals. This leads to conditional skewness and unconditional kurtosis of security prices (Section 5).

7. Conclusion

By linking funding and market liquidity, this paper provides a unified framework that explains the following stylized facts:

(1) Liquidity suddenly dries up; we argue that fragility in liquidity is in part due to destabilizing margins, which arise when financiers are imperfectly informed and the fundamental volatility varies.
(2) Market liquidity and fragility co-moves across assets since changes in funding conditions affects speculators' market liquidity provision of all assets.
(3) Market liquidity is correlated with volatility, since trading more volatile assets requires higher margin payments and speculators provide market liquidity across assets such that illiquidity per capital use, i.e., illiquidity per dollar margin, is constant.
(4) Flight to quality phenomena arise in our framework since when funding becomes scarce speculators cut back on the market liquidity provision especially for capital intensive, i.e., high margin, assets.
(5) Market liquidity moves with the market since funding conditions do.

In addition to explaining these stylized facts, the model also makes a number of specific testable predictions that could inspire further empirical research on margins. Importantly, our model links a security's market illiquidity and risk premium to its margin requirement (i.e., funding use) and the general shadow cost of funding.

Our analysis also suggests policy implications for central banks. Central banks can help mitigate market liquidity problems by controlling funding liquidity. If a central bank is better than the typical financiers of speculators at distinguishing liquidity shocks from fundamental shocks, then the central bank can convey this information and urge financiers to relax their funding requirements – as the Federal Reserve Bank of New York did during the 1987 stock market crash. Central banks can also improve market liquidity by boosting speculator funding conditions during a liquidity crisis, or by simply stating the intention to provide extra funding during times of crisis, which would loosen margin requirements as financiers' worst-case scenarios improve.

APPENDIX A: REAL-WORLD MARGIN CONSTRAINTS

A central element of our paper is the capital constraints that the main providers of market liquidity face. In this section, we review the institutional features that drive the funding constraints of securities firms such as hedge funds, banks' proprietary trading desks, and market makers.

A.1. Funding Requirements for Hedge Funds

We first consider the funding issues faced by hedge funds since they have relatively simple balance sheets and face little regulation. A hedge fund's capital consists of its equity capital supplied by the investors, and possible long-term debt financing that can be relied upon during a potential funding crisis. The investors can withdraw their capital at certain times so the equity is not locked into the firm indefinitely as in a corporation,[14] but, to ensure funding, the withdrawal is subject to initial lock-up periods and general redemption notice periods before specific redemption dates (typically at least a month, often several months or even years). Also, hedge funds use a variety of other contractual arrangements to manage their funding liquidity: "Side pocket" determines that a proportion of each investor's capital, for example, 10%, can only be redeemed when the designated assets (e.g., a privately held firm) are sold. A "gate" limits the fraction of the total capital that can leave the fund during any redemption period. Individual investors' redemptions are typically prorated in case of excess demand for outflows. "Withdrawal suspensions" (or *force majeure* terms) temporarily suspend withdrawals completely.

Hedge funds usually do not have access to unsecured debt financing, but a few large hedge funds have managed to obtain medium-term bank loans, a guaranteed line of credit,[15] or even issued bonds (see, for example, *The Economist* 1/27/2007, p. 75).

The main sources of leverage for hedge funds are (i) collateralized borrowing financed through the repo market; (ii) collateralized borrowing

---

[14] A few hedge funds have in fact raised some amount of permanent equity capital.
[15] A line of credit may have a "material adverse change" clause or other covenants subject to discretionary interpretation of the lender. Such covenants imply that the line of credit may not be a reliable source of funding during a crisis.

financed by the hedge fund's prime broker(s); and (iii) implicit leverage using derivatives, either exchange traded or over the counter (OTC). Real-world financing contracts are complex, opaque (i.e., negotiated privately and hence unobservable to an outsider), different across market partici-pants, and change over time, so our description is somewhat stylized and we discuss some caveats below. Nevertheless, all three forms of financing are based on the same general principle, which we describe first, and then we outline a few specific issues.

The guiding principle for margin setting on levered positions is that the hedge fund's counterparty should be relatively immune to the hedge fund's possible losses. In particular, if a hedge fund buys at time t a long position of $x_t^j > 0$ shares of a security j at price p_t^j, it has to come up with $x_t^j p_t^j$ dollars. The security can, however, be used as collateral for a new loan of, say, l_t^j dollars. The difference between the price of the security and the collateral value is denoted as the margin requirement $m_t^{j+} = p_t^j - l_t^j$. Hence, this position uses $x_t^j m_t^{j+}$ dollars of the fund's capital. The collateralized funding implies that the cash use depends on margins, not notional amounts. The margins are typically set so as to make the loan almost risk-free for the counterparty, that is, such that it covers the largest possible price drop with a certain degree of confidence (i.e., it covers the VaR).[16] Hence, if the price drops and the hedge fund defaults, the counterparty can still recover its loan by selling the security.

Similarly, if the hedge fund wants to sell short a security, $x^j < 0$, then the fund asks one of its brokers to locate a security that can be borrowed, and then the fund sells the borrowed security. Duffie, Gârleanu, and Pedersen (2002) describe in detail the institutional arrangements of shorting. The broker keeps the proceeds of the short sale and, additionally, requires that the hedge fund posts a margin m_t^{j-} that covers the largest possible price increase with a certain degree of confidence (in case the hedge fund defaults when the price increases, in which case the broker needs enough cash to buy the security back at a higher price).

This stylized description of collateralized financing portrays well the repo market for fixed-income securities (e.g., government and corporate bonds) and the prime brokerage that banks offer hedge funds for financing equities and convertible bonds, among other things. However, these forms

---

[16] An explicit equation for the margin is given by Equation (6) in Section 1. Often, brokers also take into account the delay between the time a failure by the hedge fund is noticed, and the time the security is actually sold. Hence, the margin of a one-day collateralized loan depends on the estimated risk of holding the asset over a time period that is often set as five to ten days.

of financing have different implementation. Prime brokerage is an ongoing service provided by banks in which they finance a whole portfolio of the hedge funds' securities on an ongoing basis (as well as providing other services), whereas in the repo market, a hedge fund will often get bids from multiple counterparties each time they make a new repo transaction. The portfolio nature of the prime brokerage business means that the prime broker can take diversification among securities into account and therefore lower the margin using so-called cross-margining, as we describe further below.

As an aside, margins on U.S. equities are in principle subject to Regulation T, which stipulates that non-brokers/dealers must put down an initial margin (down payment) of 50% of the market value of the underlying stock, both for new long and short positions. Hedge funds can, however, get around Regulation T in various ways and therefore face significantly lower stock margins. For example, their prime broker can organize the transaction offshore or as a total return swap, which is a derivative that is functionally equivalent to buying the stock.

With derivatives, the principle is similar, although the hedge fund does not "borrow against" the security, it must simply post margins to enter into the derivative contract in the first place. Suppose, for instance, that a hedge fund buys an OTC forward contract. The forward contract initially has a market value of zero (so in this sense the contract has leverage built in), but this does not mean that you can buy the forward without cash. To enter into the forward contract, which obviously has risk, the hedge fund must post margins corresponding to the largest adverse price move with a certain confidence. To ease netting long and short positions, unwinding, and other things, many OTC derivatives are structured using standardized swaps provided by the International Swaps and Derivatives Association (ISDA).

For exchange-traded derivatives such as futures and options, a hedge fund trades through a clearing broker (sometimes referred to as a futures clearing merchant). The exchange requires margins from the broker, and these margins are set using the same principle as described above, that is, the margin is set to make the exchange almost immune to losses and hence riskier contracts have larger margins. The broker, in turn, typically passes the margin requirement on to the hedge fund. Sometimes, the broker requires higher margins from the hedge fund or lower margins (the latter is considered granting the hedge fund a risky loan, usually at an interest rate spread). While the broker margins are opaque as mentioned above, the exchange margins are usually publicly available. Figure 6.1 depicts the exchange margins charged by the CME for the S&P 500 futures contract.

A hedge fund must finance all of its positions, that is, the sum of all the margin requirements on long and short positions cannot exceed the hedge fund's capital. In our model, this is captured by the key Equation (4) in Section 1.

At the end of the financing period, time $t + 1$, the position is "marked-to-market," which means that the hedge fund is credited any gains (or pays any losses) that have occurred between t and $t + 1$, that is, the fund receives $x_t^j(p_{t+1}^j - p_t^j)$ and pays interest on the loan at the funding rate. If the trade is kept on, the broker keeps the margin to protect against losses going forward from time $t + 1$. The margin can be adjusted if the risk of the collateral has changed, unless the counterparties have contractually fixed the margin for a certain period.

Instead of posting risk-free assets (cash), a hedge fund can also post other risky assets, say asset k, to cover its margin on position, say x^j. However, in this case, a "haircut," h_t^k, is subtracted from asset k's market value to account for the riskiness of the collateral. The funding constraint becomes $x_t^j m_t^j \leq W_t - x_t^k h_t^k$. Moving the haircut term to the left-hand side reveals that the haircut is equivalent to a margin, since the hedge fund could alternatively have used the risky security to raise cash and then used this cash to cover the margins for asset j. We therefore use the terms "margins" and "haircuts" interchangeably.

We have described how funding constraints work when margins and haircuts are set separately for each security position. As indicated earlier, it is, however, increasingly possible to "cross-margin" (i.e., to jointly finance several positions). This leads to a lower total margin if the risks of the various positions are partially offsetting. For instance, much of the interest rate risk is eliminated in a "spread trade" with a long position in one bond and a short position in a similar bond. Hence, the margin/haircut of a jointly financed spread trade is smaller than the sum of the margins of the long and short bonds. For a strategy that is financed jointly, we can reinterpret security j as such a strategy. Prime brokers compete (especially when credit is as loose as in early 2007) by, among other things, offering low margins and haircuts, a key consideration for hedge funds, which means that it has become increasingly easy to finance more and more strategies jointly. It is by now relatively standard to cross-margin an equity portfolio or a portfolio of convertible bonds, and so-called cross-product-margining, which attempts to give diversification benefits across asset classes, is becoming more common although it is associated with some issues that make some hedge funds avoid it.[17] In the extreme, one can imagine a joint financing of a hedge fund's total position such that the "portfolio margin" would be equal to the maximum portfolio loss with a certain confidence level. Currently, it is often not practical to jointly finance a large portfolio with all the benefits of diversification. This is because a large hedge fund finances its trades using several brokers; both a hedge fund and a broker can consist of several legal entities (possibly located in different jurisdictions); certain trades need separate margins paid to exchanges (e.g., futures and options) or to other counterparties of the prime broker (e.g., securities lenders); prime brokers may not have sufficiently sophisticated models to evaluate the diversification benefits (e.g., because they do not have enough data on the historical performance of newer products such as CDOs); and because of other practical difficulties in providing joint financing. Further, if the margin requirement relies on assumed stress scenarios in which the securities are perfectly correlated (e.g., due to predatory trading, as in Brunnermeier and Pedersen 2005), then the portfolio margin constraint coincides with posilion-by-position margins.

A.2. Funding Requirements for Commercial and Investment Banks

A bank's capital consists of equity capital plus its long-term borrowing (including credit lines secured from commercial banks, alone or in syndicates), reduced by assets that cannot be readily employed (e.g., goodwill, intangible assets, property, equipment, and capital needed for daily operations), and further reduced by uncollateralized loans extended by the bank to others (see, for example, Goldman Sachs's 2003 Annual Report). Banks also raise money using short-term uncollateralized loans, such as commercial paper and promissory notes, and, in the case of commercial banks, demand deposits. These sources of financing cannot, however, be relied on in times of funding crisis since lenders may be unwilling to continue lending, and therefore this short-term funding is often not included in measures of capital.

---

[17] For instance, cross-product margining means that the broker effectively can move extra cash from one margin account to cover a loss elsewhere, even if the hedge may dispute the loss. Also, collecting all positions with one broker may mean that the hedge fund cannot get a good pricing on the trades, e.g., on repos, and may expose the hedge fund to predatory trading.

The financing of a bank's trading activity is largely based on *collateralized* borrowing. Banks can finance long positions using collateralized borrowing from corporations, other banks, insurance companies, and the Federal Reserve Bank, and can borrow securities to short-sell from, for instance, mutual funds and pension funds. These transactions typically require margins that must be financed by the bank's capital, as captured by the funding constraint in Equation (4).

The financing of a bank's trading is more complicated than that of a hedge fund, however. For instance, banks may negotiate zero margins with certain counterparties, and banks can often sell short shares held in-house, that is, held in a customer's margin account (in "street name") such that the bank does not need to use capital to borrow the shares externally. Further, a bank receives margins when financing hedge funds (i.e., the margin is negative from the point of view of the bank). In spite of these caveats, in times of stress, banks face margin requirements and are ultimately subject to a funding constraint in the spirit of Equation (4). Bear Stearns's demise is a vivid reminder that banks' funding advantage from clients' margin accounts can quickly evaporate. In March of 2008, Bear Stearns's clients terminated their brokerage relationships and ran on the investment bank. Only an orchestrated merger with JPMorgan Chase avoided a bankruptcy.

Banks must also satisfy certain regulatory requirements. Commercial banks are subject to the Basel Accord, supervised by the Federal Reserve System for U.S. banks. In short, the Basel Accord of 1988 requires that a bank's "eligible capital" exceeds 8% of the "risk-weighted asset holdings," which is the sum of each asset holding multiplied by its risk weight. The risk weight is 0% for cash and government securities, 50% for mortgage-backed loans, and 100% for all other assets. The requirement posed by the 1988 Basel Accord corresponds to Equation (4) with margins of 0%, 4%, and 8%, respectively. In 1996, the accord was amended, allowing banks to measure market risk using an internal model based on portfolio VaRs rather than using standardized risk weights. To outmaneuver the Basel Accord, banks created a shadow banking system, which allowed them to off-load assets to off-balance sheet vehicles like SIVs and conduits. For details, see Brunnermeier (2009).

Broker-speculators in the United States, including banks acting as such, are subject to the Securities and Exchange Commission's (SEC's) "net capital rule" (SEC Rule 15c3-1). This rule stipulates, among other things, that a broker must have a minimum "net capital," which is defined as equity capital plus approved subordinate liabilities minus "securities haircuts" and operational charges. The haircuts are set as security-dependent percentages of the market value. The standard rule requires that the net capital exceeds at least $6\frac{2}{3}$% (15:1 leverage) of aggregate indebtedness (broker's total money liabilities) or alternatively 2% of aggregate debit items arising from customer transactions. This constraint is similar in spirit to Equation (4).[18] As of August 20, 2004, SEC amended the net capital rule for Consolidated Supervised Entities (CSEs) such that CSEs may, under certain circumstances, use their internal risk models to determine whether they fulfill their capital requirement (SEC Release No. 34-49830).

A.3. Funding Requirements for Market Makers

There are various types of market-making firms. Some are small partnerships, whereas others are parts of large investment banks. The small firms are financed in a similar way to hedge funds in that they rely primarily on collateralized financing; the funding of banks was described in Section A2.

Certain market makers, such as NYSE specialists, have an obligation to make a market; and a binding funding constraint means that they cannot fulfill this requirement. Hence, avoiding the funding constraint is especially crucial for such market makers.

Market makers are in principle subject to the SEC's net capital rule (described in Section A2), but this rule has special exceptions for market makers. Hence, market makers' main regulatory requirements are those imposed by the exchange on which they operate. These constraints are often similar in spirit to Equation (4).

APPENDIX B: PROOFS

Proof of Propositions 1–3

These results follow from the calculations in the text.

Proof of Proposition 4

We prove the proposition for $Z_1 > 0$, implying $p_1 \leq v_1$ and $x_1 \geq 0$. The complementary case is analogous. To see how the equilibrium depends on

---

[18] Let L be the lower of $6\frac{2}{3}$% of total indebtedness or 2% of debit items and h^j the haircut for security j; then the rale requires that $L \leq W - \sum_j h^j x^j$, that is, $\sum_j h^j x^j \leq W - L$.

the exogenous shocks, we first combine the equilibrium condition $x_1 = -\sum_{k=0}^{1} y_1^k$ with the speculator funding constraint to get

$$m_1^+ \left(Z_1 - \frac{2}{\gamma(\sigma_2)^2}(v_1 - p_1) \right) \le b_0 + p_1 x_0 + \eta_1, \tag{B1}$$

that is,

$$G(p_1) := m_1^+ \left(Z_1 - \frac{2}{\gamma(\sigma_2)^2}(v_1 - p_1) \right) - p_1 x_0 - b_0 \le \eta_1. \tag{B2}$$

For η_1 large enough, this inequality is satisfied for $p_1 = v_1$, that is, it is a stable equilibrium that the market is perfectly liquid. For η_1 low enough, the inequality is violated for $p_1 = \frac{2v_1}{\gamma(\sigma_2)^2} - Z_1$, that is, it is an equilibrium that the speculator is in default. We are interested in intermediate values of η_1. If the left-hand side G of (B2) is increasing in p_1, then p_1 is a continuously increasing function of η_1, implying no fragility with respect to η_1.

Fragility arises if G can be decreasing in p_1. Intuitively, this expression measures speculator funding needs at the equilibrium position, and fragility arises if the funding need is greater when prices are lower, that is, further from fundamentals. (This can be shown to be equivalent to a non-monotonic excess demand function.)

When the financiers are informed, the left-hand side G of (B2) is

$$(\bar{\sigma} + \bar{\theta}|\Delta v_1| + p_1 - v_1) \left(Z_1 + \frac{2}{\gamma(\sigma_2)^2}(p_1 - v_1) \right) - p_1 x_0 - b_0. \tag{B3}$$

The first product is a product of two positive increasing functions of p_1, but the second term, $-p_1 x_0$, is decreasing in p_1 if $x_0 > 0$. Since the first term does not depend on x_0, here exists $\underline{x}$ such that, for $x_0 > \underline{x}$, the whole expression is decreasing.

When the financier is uninformed, we first show that there is fragility for $a = 0$. In this case, the left-hand side of (B2) is

$$G^0(p_1) := (\bar{\sigma} + \bar{\theta}|\Delta p_1|) \left(Z_1 + \frac{2}{\gamma(\sigma_2)^2}(p_1 - v_1) \right) - p_1 x_0 - b_0. \tag{B4}$$

When $p_1 < p_0$, $\bar{\theta}|\Delta p_1|\theta(p_0 - p_1)$ decreases in p_1 and, if $\bar{\theta}$ is large enough, this can make the entire expression decreasing. (Since $\bar{\theta}$ is proportional to θ, this clearly translates directly to θ.) Also, the expression is decreasing if x_0 is large enough.

Finally, on any compact set of prices, the margin function converges uniformly to (23) as a approaches 0. Hence, G converges uniformly to G^0. Since the limit function G^0 has a decreasing part, choose $p_1^a < p_1^b$ such that

$\varepsilon := G^0(p_1^a) - G^0(p_1^b) > 0$. By uniform convergence, choose $\underline{a} > 0$ such that for $a < \underline{a}$, G differs from G^0 by at most $\varepsilon/3$. Then, we have

$$G(p_1^a) - G(p_1^b) = G^0(p_1^a) - G^0(p_1^b) + [G(p_1^a) - G^0(p_1^a)]$$
$$- [G(p_1^b) - G^0(p_1^b)] \tag{B5}$$

$$\geq \varepsilon - \frac{\varepsilon}{3} - \frac{\varepsilon}{3} = \frac{\varepsilon}{3} > 0, \tag{B6}$$

which proves that G has a decreasing pan.

It can be shown that the price cannot be chosen continuously in η_1 when the left-hand side of (B2) can be decreasing.

Proof of Proposition 5

When the funding constraint binds, we use the implicit function theorem to compute the derivatives. As above, we have

$$m_1^+ \left(Z_1 - \frac{2}{\gamma(\sigma_2)^2}(\nu_1 - p_1) \right) = b_0 + p_1 x_0 + \eta_1. \tag{B7}$$

We differentiate this expression to get

$$\frac{\partial m_1^+}{\partial p_1} \frac{\partial p_1}{\partial \eta_1} \left(Z_1 - \frac{2}{\gamma(\sigma)_2^2}(\nu_1 - p_1) \right) + m_1^+ \frac{2}{\gamma(\sigma_2)^2} \frac{\partial p_1}{\partial \eta_1} = \frac{\partial p_1}{\partial \eta_1} x_0 + 1, \tag{B8}$$

which leads to Equation (24) after rearranging. The case of $Z_1 < 0$ (i.e., Equation (25)) is analogous.

Finally, spiral effects happen if one of the last two terms in the denominator of the right-hand side of Equations (24) and (25) is negative. (The total value of the denominator is positive by definition of a stable equilibrium.) When the speculator is informed, $\frac{\partial m_1^+}{\partial p_1} = 1$ and $\frac{\partial m_1^-}{\partial p_1} = -1$ using Proposition 2. Hence, in this case, margins are stabilizing.

If the speculators are uninformed and a approaches 0, then using Proposition 3, we find that $\frac{\partial m_1^+}{\partial p_1} = \frac{\partial m_1^+}{\partial \Lambda_1}$ approaches $-\bar{\theta} < 0$ for $\nu_1 - \nu_0 + \Lambda_1 - \Lambda_0$ and $\frac{\partial m_1^-}{\partial p_1} = \frac{\partial m_1^-}{\partial \Lambda_1}$ approaches $\bar{\theta} > 0$ for $\nu_1 - \nu_0 + \Lambda_1 - \Lambda_0 > 0$. This means that there is a margin spiral with positive probability. The case of a loss spiral is immediately seen to depend on the sign on x_0.

Proof of Proposition 6

We first consider the equation that characterizes a constrained equilibrium. When there is selling pressure from customers, $Z_1^j > 0$, it holds that

$$\left|\Lambda_1^j\right| = -\Lambda_1^j = v_1^j - p_1^j = \min\left\{(\phi_1 - 1)m_1^{j+}, \frac{\gamma\left(\sigma_2^j\right)^2}{2}Z_1^j\right\}, \quad \text{(B9)}$$

and if customers are buying, $Z_1^j < 0$, we have

$$\left|\Lambda_1^j\right| = \Lambda_1^j = p_1^j - v_1^j = \min\left\{(\phi_1 - 1)m_1^{j-}, \frac{\gamma\left(\sigma_2^j\right)^2}{2}\left(-Z_1^j\right)\right\}. \quad \text{(B10)}$$

We insert the equilibrium condition $x_1^j = -\sum_k y_1^{j,k}$ and Equation (12) for $y_1^{j,k}$ into the speculators' funding condition to get

$$\sum_{Z_1^j > \frac{2(\phi_1-1)m_1^{j+}}{\gamma(\sigma_2^j)^2}} m_1^{j+}\left(Z_1^j - \frac{2(\phi_1 - 1)m_1^{j+}}{\gamma(\sigma_2^j)^2}\right)$$

$$+ \sum_{-Z_1^j > \frac{2(\phi_1-1)m_1^{j-}}{\gamma(\sigma_2^j)^2}} m_1^{j-}\left(-Z_1^j - \frac{2(\phi_1 - 1)m_1^{j-}}{\gamma(\sigma_2^j)^2}\right)$$

$$= \sum_j x_0^j p_1^j + b_0 + \eta_1, \quad \text{(B11)}$$

where the margins are evaluated at the prices solving Equations (B9)–(B10). When ϕ_1 approaches infinity, the left-hand side of Equation (B11) becomes zero, and when ϕ_1 approaches one, the left-hand side approaches the capital needed to make the market perfectly liquid. As in the case of one security, there can be multiple equilibria and fragility (Proposition 4). On a stable equilibrium branch, ϕ_1 increases as η_1 decreases. Of course, the equilibrium shadow cost of capital ($\phi_1 - 1$) is random since $\eta_1, \Delta v_1^1, \ldots, \Delta v_1^j$ are random. To see the commonality in liquidity, we note that $|\Lambda^j|$ is increasing in ϕ_1 for each $j = k, l$. To see this, consider first the case $Z_1^j > 0$. When the financiers are uninformed, $a = 0$, and $\theta^j = 0$, then, $m_1^{j+} = \bar{\sigma}^k$, and, therefore, Equation (B9) shows directly that $|\Lambda_1^j|$ increases in ϕ_1 (since the minimum of increasing functions is increasing). When financiers are informed and $\theta^j = 0$ then $m_1^{j+} = \bar{\sigma}^k + \Lambda_1^j$, and, therefore, Equation (B9) can be solved to be $|\Lambda_1^j| = \min\{\frac{\phi_1-1}{\phi_1}\bar{\sigma}^j, \frac{\gamma(\sigma_2^k)^2}{2}Z_1^k\}$, which increases in ϕ_1. Similarly, Equation (B10) shows that $|\Lambda^j|$ is increasing in ϕ_1 when $Z_1^j < 0$.

Now, since $|\Lambda^j|$ is increasing in ϕ_1 and does not depend on other state variables under these conditions, $\text{Cov}(|\Lambda^k(\phi)|, |\Lambda^l(\phi)|) > 0$ because any two functions that are both increasing in the same random variable are positively correlated (the proof of this is similar to that of Lemma 1 below). Since $|\Lambda^j|$ is bounded, we can use dominated convergence to establish the existence of $c > 0$ such that part (i) of the proposition applies for any θ^j, $a < c$.

To see part (ii) of the proposition, note that, for all j, $|\Lambda^j|$ is a continuous function of ϕ_1, which is locally insensitive to ϕ_1 if and only if the speculator is not marginal on security j (i.e., if the second term in Equation (B9) or (B10) attains the minimum). Hence, $|\Lambda^j|$ jumps if and only if ϕ_1 jumps.

To see part (iii), we write illiquidity using Equations (B9)–(B10) as

$$|\Lambda_1^j| = \min\left\{(\phi_1 - 1)m_1^{j,\,sign(Z_1^j)}, \frac{\gamma(\sigma_2^j)^2}{2}|Z_1^j|\right\}. \tag{B12}$$

Hence, using the expression for the margin, if the financier is uninformed and $\theta^j = a = 0$, then

$$|\Lambda_1^j| = \min\left\{(\phi_1 - 1)\bar{\sigma}_1^j, \frac{\gamma(\sigma_2^j)^2}{2}|Z_1^j|\right\} \tag{B13}$$

and, if the financiers are informed and $\theta^j = 0$, then

$$|\Lambda_1^j| = \min\left\{\frac{\phi_1 - 1}{\phi_1}\bar{\sigma}_1^j, \frac{\gamma(\sigma_2^j)^2}{2}|Z_1^j|\right\}. \tag{B14}$$

In the case of uninformed financiers as in Equation (B13), we see that, if $x_1^k \neq 0$,

$$|\Lambda_1^j| = (\phi_1 - 1)\bar{\sigma}_1^k > (\phi_1 - 1)\bar{\sigma}_1^t \geq |\Lambda_1^t| \tag{B15}$$

and, $|Z_1^k| \geq |Z_1^l|$,

$$|\Lambda_1^k| = \min\left\{(\phi_1 - 1)\bar{\sigma}_1^k, \frac{\gamma(\sigma_2^k)^2}{2}|Z_1^k|\right\}$$

$$> \min\left\{(\phi_1 - 1)\bar{\sigma}_1^l, \frac{\gamma(\sigma_2^l)^2}{2}|Z_1^l|\right\} = |\Lambda_1^l|. \tag{B16}$$

Since Λ^k and Λ^l converge to these values as θ^j, a approach zero, we can choose c so that inequality holds for θ^j, a below c. With informed financiers, it is seen that $|\Lambda_1^k| \geq |\Lambda_1^l|$ using similar arguments.

For part (iv) of the proposition, we use that

$$\frac{\partial |\Lambda_1^j|}{\partial(-\eta_1)} = \frac{\partial |\Lambda_1^j|}{\partial \phi_1} \frac{\partial \phi_1}{\partial(-\eta_1)}. \tag{B17}$$

Further, $\frac{\partial \phi_1}{\partial(-\eta_1)} \geq 0$ and, from Equations (B13)–(B14), we see that $\frac{\partial |\Lambda_1^k|}{\partial \phi_1} \geq \frac{\partial |\Lambda_1^l|}{\partial \phi_1}$. The result that $\mathrm{Cov}(\Lambda^k, \phi) \geq \mathrm{Cov}(\Lambda^l, \phi)$ now follows from Lemma 1 below.

Lemma 1. *Lei X be a random variable and g_i, $i = 1, 2$, be weakly increasing functions of X, where g_1 has a larger derivative than g_2, that is, $g_1'(x) \geq g_2'(x)$ for all x and $g_1'(x) > g_2'(x)$ on a set with nonzero measure. Then,*

$$\mathrm{Cov}[X, g_1(X)] > \mathrm{Cov}[X, g_2(X)]. \tag{B18}$$

Proof: For $i = 1, 2$ we have

$$\mathrm{Cov}[X, g_i(X)] = E[(X - E[X])g_i(X)] \tag{B19}$$

$$= E\left[(X - E[X])\left(\int_{E[X]}^{X} g_i^t(y)dy\right)\right]. \tag{B20}$$

The latter expression is a product of two terms that always have the same sign. Hence, this is higher if g_i' is larger. ∎

Liquidity Risk (Time 0). Section 5 focuses on the case of speculators who are unconstrained at $t = 0$. When a speculator's problem is linear and he is constrained at time 0, then he invests only in securities with the highest expected profit per capital use, where profit is calculated using the pricing kernel $\phi_1^i / E_0[\phi_1^i]$. In this case, his time-0 shadow cost of capital is

$$\phi_0^i = E_0[\phi_1^i]\left\{1 + \max_j \left(\frac{E_0\left[\frac{\phi_1^i}{E_0[\phi_1^i]}p_1^j\right] - p_0^j}{m_0^+}, -\frac{E_0\left[\frac{\phi_1^i}{E_0[\phi_1^i]}p_1^j\right] - p_0^j}{m_0^-}\right)\right\}. \tag{B21}$$

References

Abreu, D., and M. K. Brunnermeier. 2002. Synchronization Risk and Delayed Arbitrage. *Journal of Financial Economics* 66:341–60.

Acharya, V. V., and L. H. Pedersen. 2005. Asset Pricing with Liquidity Risk. *Journal of Financial Economics* 77:375–410.

Acharya, V. V., S. Schaefer, and Y. Zhang. 2008. Liquidity Risk and Correlation Risk: A Clinical Study of the General Motors and Ford Downgrade of 2005. Working Paper, London Business School.

Adrian, T., and H. S. Shin. 2009. Liquidity and Leverage. *Journal of Financial Intermediation*.

Aiyagari, S. R., and M. Gertler. 1999. "Overreaction" of Asset Prices in General Equilibrium. *Review of Economic Dynamics* 2:3–35.

Allen, F., and D. Gale. 1998. Optimal Financial Crisis. *Journal of Finance* 53:1245–84.

Allen, F., and D. Gale. 2004. Financial Intermediaries and Markets. *Econometrica* 72:1023–61.

Allen, F., and D. Gale. 2005. Financial Fragility, Liquidity, and Asset Prices. *Journal of the European Economic Association* 2:1015–48.

Allen, F., and D. Gale. 2007. *Understanding Financial Crises.* Clarendon Lectures in Economics. Oxford, UK: Oxford University Press.

Amihud, Y., and H. Mendelson. 1989. The Effects of Beta, Bid-Ask Spread, Residual Risk, and Size on Stock Returns. *Journal of Finance* 44:479–86.

Attari, M., A. S. Mello, and M. E. Ruckes. 2005. Arbitraging Arbitrageurs. *Journal of Finance* 60:2471–511.

Benston, G. J., and R. L. Hagerman. 1974. Determinants of the Bid-Ask Spread in the Over-the-Counter Market. *Journal of Financial Economics* 1:353–64.

Bernanke, B., and M. Gertler. 1989. Agency Costs, Net Worth, and Business Fluctuations. *American Economic Review* 79:14–31.

Bernardo, A. E., and I. Welch. 2004. Liquidity and Financial Markets Run. *Quarterly Journal of Economics* 119:135–58.

Brunnermeier, M. K. 2009. Deciphering the Liquidity and Credit Crunch 2007–08. *Journal of Economic Perspectives.* 2009, Issue 1.

Brunnermeier, M. K., S. Nagel, and L. H. Pedersen. 2009. Carry Trades and Currency Crashes, in Daron Acemoglu, Kenneth Rogoff, and Michael Woodford (eds.), *NBER Macroeconomics Annual 2008*, vol. 23. Cambridge, MA: MIT Press.

Brunnermeier, M. K., and L. H. Pedersen. 2005. Predatory Trading. *Journal of Finance* 60:1825–63.

Bryant, J. 1980. A Model of Reserves, Bank Runs, and Deposit Insurance. *Journal of Banking and Finance* 4:335–44.

Campbell, J. Y., A. W. Lo, and A. C. MacKinlay. 1997. *The Econometrics of Financial Markets.* Princeton, NJ: Princeton University Press.

Chordia, T., R. Roll, and A. Subrahmanyam. 2000. Commonality in Liquidity. *Journal of Financial Economics* 56:3–28.

Chordia, T., A. Sarkar, and A. Subrahmanyam. 2005. An Empirical Analysis of Stock and Bond Market Liquidity. *Review of Financial Studies* 18:85–129.

Chowdhry, B., and V. Nanda. 1998. Leverage and Market Stability: The Role of Margin Rules and Price Limits. *Journal of Business* 71:179–210.

Comerton-Forde, C., T. Hendershott, C. M. Jones, P. C. Moulton, and M. S. Seasholes. 2008. Time Variation in Liquidity: The Role of Market Maker Inventories and Revenues. Working Paper, Columbia University.

Coughenour, J. R., and M. M. Saad. 2004. Common Market Makers and Commonality in Liquidity. *Journal of Financial Economics* 73:37–69.

DeLong, J. B., A. Shleifer, L. H. Summers, and R. J. Waldmann. 1990. Noise Trader Risk in Financial Markets. *Journal of Political Economy* 98:703–38.

Diamond, D., and P. Dybvig. 1983. Bank Runs, Deposit Insurance, and Liquidity. *Journal of Political Economy* 91:401–19.

Duffie, D., N. Gârleanu, and L. H. Pedersen. 2002. Securities Lending, Shorting, and Pricing. *Journal of Financial Economics* 66:307–39.

Eisfeldt, A. 2004. Endogenous Liquidity in Asset Markets. *Journal of Finance* 59:1–30.

Fisher, I. 1933. The Debt-Deflation Theory of Great Depression. *Econometrica* 1:337–57.

Fostel, A., and J. Geanakoplos, 2008. Leverage Cycles and The Anxious Economy. *American Economic Review* 98:1211–44.

Garleanu, N., and L. H. Pedersen. 2007. Liquidity and Risk Management. *The American Economic Review* (Papers & Proceedings) 97:193–97.

Garleanu, N., L. H. Pedersen, and A. Poteshman. 2008. Demand-Based Option Pricing. *Review of Financial Studies*.

Geanakoplos, J. 1997. Promises, Promises in W.B. Arthur, S. Durlauf and D. Lane (eds.), *The Economy as an Evolving Complex System II* 1997: 285–320. Addison-Wesley, Reading MA.

Geanakoplos, J. 2003. Liquidity, Default and Crashes: Endogenous Contracts in General Equilibrium, in Mathias Dewatripont, Lars Peter Hansen, and Stephen J. Turnovsky (eds.), *Advances in Economics and Econometrics: Theory and Applications II, Eighth World Congress*, vol. 2, pp. 170–205. Econometric Society Monographs. Cambridge, UK: Cambridge University Press.

Gennotte, G., and H. Leland. 1990. Market Liquidity, Hedging, and Crashes. *American Economic Review* 80:999–1021.

Glosten, L. R., and P. R. Milgrom. 1985. Bid, Ask, and Transaction Prices in a Specialist Market with Heterogeneously Informed Traders. *Journal of Financial Economics* 14:71–100.

Gromb, D., and D. Vayanos. 2002. Equilibrium and Welfare in Markets with Financially Constrained Arbitrageurs. *Journal of Financial Economics* 66:361–407.

Grossman, S. J. 1988. An Analysis of the Implications for Stock and Futures Price Volatility of Program Trading and Dynamic Hedging Strategies. *Journal of Business* 61:275–98.

Grossman, S. J., and M. H. Miller. 1988. Liquidity and Market Structure. *Journal of Finance* 43:617–33.

Grossman, S. J., and J.-L. Vila. 1992. Optimal Dynamic Trading with Leverage Constraints. *Journal of Financial and Quantitative Analysis* 27:151–68.

Hameed, A., W. Kang, and S. Viswanathan. 2005. Asymmetric Comovement in Liquidity. Mimeo, Duke University.

Hasbrouck, J., and D. Seppi. 2001. Common Factors in Prices, Order Flows, and Liquidity. *Journal of Financial Economics* 59:383–411.

Ho, T. S. Y., and H. R. Stoll. 1981. Optimal Dealer Pricing under Transactions and Return Uncertainty. *Journal of Financial Economics* 9:47–73.

Ho, T. S. Y., and H. R. Stoll. 1983. The Dynamics of Dealer Markets under Competition. *Journal of Finance* 38:1053–74.

Holmström, B., and J. Tirole. 1998. Private and Public Supply of Liquidity. *Journal of Political Economy* 106:1–39.

Holmström, B., and J. Tirole. 2001. LAPM: A Liquidity-Based Asset Pricing Model. *Journal of Finance* 56:1837–67.

Huberman, G., and D. Halka. 2001. Systematic Liquidity. *Journal of Financial Research* 24:161–78.

Ibbotson. 1999. *Cost of Capital Quarterly, 1999 Yearbook*, 2nd ed. Chicago: Ibbotson Associates, 1976.

International Monetary Fund. 2007. *Global Financial Stability Report.* October.

Kiyotaki, N., and J. Moore. 1997. Credit Cycles. *Journal of Political Economy* 105:211–48.

Kyle, A. S. 1985. Continuous Auctions and Insider Trading. *Econometrica* 53:1315–35.

Kyle, A. S., and W. Xiong. 2001. Contagion as a Wealth Effect. *Journal of Finance* 56:1401–40.

Liu, J., and F. A. Longstaff. 2004. Losing Money on Arbitrages: Optimal Dynamic Portfolio Choice in Markets with Arbitrage Opportunities. *Review of Financial Studies* 17:611–41.

Lustig H., and Y. Chien. 2005. The Market Price of Aggregate Risk and Wealth Distribution. NBER Working Paper 11132.

Mitchell, M., L. H. Pedersen, and T. Pulvino. 2007. Slow Moving Capital. *American Economic Review (Papers & Proceedings)* 97:215–20.

Morris, S., and H. Shin. 2004. Liquidity Black Holes. *Review of Finance* 8:1–18.

Pastor, L., and R. F. Stambaugh. 2003. Liquidity Risk and Expected Stock Returns. *Journal of Political Economy* 111:642–85.

Plantin, G., H. Sapra, and H. S. Shin. 2005. Marking-to-Market: Panacea or Pandora's Box? *Journal of Accounting Research* 46:435–60.

Shleifer, A., and R. W. Vishny. 1992. Liquidation Values and Debt Capacity: A Market Equilibrium Approach. *Journal of Finance* 47:1343–66.

Shleifer, A., and R. W. Vishny. 1997. The Limits of Arbitrage. *Journal of Finance* 52:35–55.

Stiglitz, J. E., and A. Weiss. 1981. Credit Rationing in Markets with Imperfect Information. *American Economic Review* 71:393–410.

Stoll, H. R. 1978. The Supply of Dealer Services in Securities Markets. *Journal of Finance* 33:1133–51.

Vayanos, D. 2004. Flight to Quality, Flight to Liquidity, and the Pricing of Risk. Working Paper, London School of Economics.

Weill, P.-O. 2007. Leaning Against the Wind. *Review of Economic Studies* 74:1329–54.

Wigmore, B. 1998. Revisiting the October 1987 Crash. *Financial Analysis Journal* 54:36–48.

Xiong, W. 2001. Convergence Trading with Wealth Effects: An Amplification Mechanism in Financial Markets. *Journal of Financial Economics* 62(2):247–92.

CHAPTER 7

Liquidity and the 1987 Stock Market Crash

Summary and Implications

This article establishes the relation between stock market crashes and liquidity shocks, presenting evidence from the October 19, 1987 stock market crash. It argues that the crash was due in part to a realization that financial markets were not as liquid as had been previously assumed, and that liquidity can suddenly dry up. The paper proposes that the price decline reflected in part a reevaluation of stocks in light of the realization that their liquidity was lower. In fact, stocks whose liquidity deteriorated more also suffered greater price decline.

Leading into the crash, there were a number of days of negative news and sharp price declines, which triggered sell-off by program traders that employed strategies of portfolio insurance and dynamic hedging, which exacerbated the declines.[1] The financial markets then became less liquid in the United States and globally. The average bid–ask spread doubled and the quoted market depth – measured by the number of shares that dealers and traders are willing to trade at the quoted bid and ask prices – fell substantially. Trading was also hampered by technical difficulties related to handling the transaction volumes, stocks opened late, market makers who normally provided liquidity faced severe funding problems, and there were even rumors that the NYSE would shut down. The lack of liquidity and liquidity risk became scarily apparent and made investors incorporate greater liquidity discount into stock prices.

To test the liquidity shock explanation of the crash, this article examines the liquidity-return relation of NYSE stocks that were included in the S&P 500 index. The evidence is that stocks which suffered greater decline in

---

[1] Before the crash, there were also economic news, captured by the bond-stock earnings yield differential that could forecast the crash. See Berge, Consigli, and Ziemba (2008).

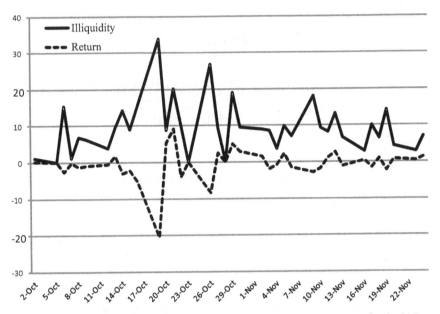

Figure PIII.5. Illiquidity and stock returns during October–November 1987 for the S&P 500 stock index. Illiquidity is measured here by the daily ratio of absolute return to share volume (properly scaled to match the scale of returns).

their liquidity also experienced greater price decline. A doubling of a stock's bid–ask spread can explain a drop in its price of approximately 11% over and above a stock with no change in liquidity, and a decline in the quoted depth (the quantity that market makers are willing to trade at the quoted prices) implied additional significant price decline.

Following the crash, liquidity improved as investors realized that the NYSE and many of the market makers were surviving and that their funding would ultimately recover. However, liquidity remained significantly worse than its pre-crash levels for the rest of 1987. Stocks whose liquidity recovered more following the crash also saw their prices recover more, consistent with the pricing of liquidity. A stock that experienced a drop in its bid–ask spread by half would see its price recover 4% more than a stock with no liquidity improvement.

The illiquidity-price relation for the period surrounding the crash is shown in Figure PIII.5. For the S&P 500 index, it plots the illiquidity of the index against the index return for the months of October and November 1987. (Illiquidity here is the index price impact, the ratio of absolute return to the share volume, properly scaled.) Illiquidity was very low early in October, then started rising as some price declines and subsequent reaction by traders caused great price impact. Illiquidity climbed before October 19, the day of the crash, and as traders realized that, prices declined. On the day of the crash, there is a sharp rise in illiquidity together with a sharp price decline. This pattern of negative illiquidity-price relation repeated on October 26 and a few times during the month of November, during which illiquidity slowly declined. Altogether, the data on the 1987 stock market crash highlight the negative relation between market illiquidity and stock prices.

Liquidity and the 1987 Stock Market Crash

Yakov Amihud, Haim Mendelson, and Robert Wood

Journal of Portfolio Management, 1990

The Crash of October 1987 was a puzzling event – puzzling not only for what happened on October 19, but also for what subsequently did not happen. In spite of the magnitude and momentum of the crash, its effect was limited primarily to the financial markets, while the economy as a whole did not change its course. And, although the "bad news" that was supposed to be predicted by the crash has apparently not materialized, the market suffered a lasting decline after October of 1987.

This article advances a liquidity theory of the crash, proposing that the price decline in October 1987 reflects, at least in part, a revision of investors' expectations about the liquidity of the equity markets. Amihud and Mendelson [1986a, 1986b, 1989] have shown that the market price of stocks is positively associated with their liquidity (after controlling for risk). Given this relationship, when the liquidity of assets turns out to be less than had been expected, their price should decline.

We suggest that the main news that caused the prolonged decline in stock prices was the crash itself – that is, the realization that financial markets are not as liquid as previously assumed. Investors recognized that stock prices should reflect a larger discount for the costs of illiquidity, which turned out to be much higher than had been expected before the crash. Partial recovery following the crash reflects an upward reevaluation of the liquidity of the markets – that is, investors recognized that while the markets are not as liquid as had been assumed prior to the crash, they are also not as illiquid as when there was the possibility of closing the markets altogether.

These illiquidity problems, reflected in wider spreads between the quoted bid and ask prices, have persisted long after the crash, and market impact estimates have stayed significantly larger than they had been prior to the crash.[1] Thus, the crash and subsequent events have produced new information about the markets themselves rather than fundamental news about the economy.

Part of the liquidity-related price decline on October 19, 1987, was temporary. Unexpected sale pressure, even absent any negative information, can generate a temporary negative price impact, as we sometimes observe in block sales. But much of the effect was permanent. Investors realized that they may well have to pay a larger discount when they wish to sell stocks in a hurry. These illiquidity costs result in a stream of future cash outflows that translate into a loss of value.[2]

In general, illiquidity reflects the difficulty of converting cash into assets and assets into cash, or the costs of trading an asset in the market. Some of the costs of illiquidity are explicit and easy to measure, while others are more subtle. These costs include the bid–ask spread, market-impact costs, delay and search costs, and brokerage commissions and fees. These components of illiquidity cost are highly correlated: Stocks that have high bid–ask spreads also have high transaction fees and high search and market-impact costs, and are thinly traded (McInish and Wood [1989]). When the bid–ask spread widens, it signals that immediacy of execution is more costly, that is, asset liquidity is lower.

The 1987 Crash

We suggest that recognition that the market is less liquid than had been previously thought contributed to the decline of stock prices. Before that time, investors believed that the market was extremely liquid. Portfolio insurers assumed that in the event of a decline the market would absorb large sale quantities with only a minimal price impact.[3] Investors believed that when orders (buy or sell) arrived on the trading floor, the market

---

[1] More recently, market liquidity has increased – and so have stock prices.

[2] An important attribute of the costs of illiquidity is that they are incurred *repeatedly* throughout the life of the stock. Hence, an apparently small increase in illiquidity costs may have a sizable impact on value. See Amihud and Mendelson [1988a].

[3] See Treynor [1988]. Recognizing this problem, Ferguson and O'Brien [1988] propose stabilizing forward contracts for portfolio insurers to help resolve the liquidity issue and "discourage excessive growth based on unrealistically optimistic estimates of liquidity."

would provide the needed liquidity to execute them without a significant price change.[4] This turned out not to be the case.

The crash was preceded by a few days of unusual price declines that culminated in a large selling pressure on Monday, October 19. This selling pressure was a test of the assumptions of unlimited liquidity. As we know, the markets failed this test: The price impact triggered by the sale orders was much larger than had been anticipated. To some extent, the reason was technological – the arrival of orders on one side of the market was faster than on the other. Normally, rational, value-motivated traders would step in to buy when large unexpected sell orders reach the market. The technology of market operation, however, made this impossible (Amihud and Mendelson [1988b]).

A number of operational problems exacerbated market illiquidity. Orders could not be executed, and information on market conditions and on order execution was delayed. Consequently, much of the burden of responding to the unexpected order flow fell on the exchange specialists, market makers, and other traders with immediate access to the trading floor. Such access was largely infeasible for outside investors who could have entered the market and traded against the mechanically-generated sell orders.

Those with immediate access to trading could not, however, provide the necessary liquidity because the capital that they could commit at short notice was small relative to market volume. Market depth was reduced, and quoted bid–ask spreads increased to unprecedented levels. All this meant lower liquidity.

The opening transaction, which is usually the largest of the day (Amihud and Mendelson [1987]), was delayed (in some large stocks – for two hours), meaning these stocks became virtually illiquid. There were even worse indications of illiquidity: "As the 19th wore on, investors witnessed symptoms of market failure and were frightened by the rumors that the NYSE would close" (Leland and Rubinstein [1988, p. 46]). The closing of the stock exchange is the ultimate in illiquidity!

After the crash, the decline in liquidity linfered continuous liquidity problems: "Blocks of 25,000 shares can now move prices as much as 100,000-share blocks did before the crash" (Wallace [1987]). Seven months after the crash, liquidity indicators that measure price impact showed that the order

---

[4] The liquidity of the market increased continually in the 1980s. Looking at market "depth," the average stock showed no price change or a $1/8 change in 1,000 shares of volume 89.2% of the rime, up from 80.4% in 1980. Gammill and Perold [1989, p. 13] point out that the liquidity of the market had peaked before the crash: "Stock market volume was never greater and spreads never narrower, at least until October 1987."

quantity needed to effect a given change in stock prices had declined by about a third compared to the 1986 level, which was, in turn, four to six times higher than the 1981 level. According to Wallace (1988):

In reaction to these conditions, some money managers and traders now calculate a "liquidity discount" for their portfolios; that is, the extra amount it would cost to bail out of their stocks in such a thin market.... The discount on a $2 million portfolio has jumped to 3 percent or 4 percent of its total value, from 1 percent before October.

Applying the Amihud–Mendelson theory of the liquidity–price relationship, investors' expectations about market liquidity imply a certain level of prices for any given state of the fundamental values. If the liquidity of the market turns out to be substantially lower, we should expect a significant decline in stock prices even without any change in the fundamentals – or, put differently, liquidity is another fundamental factor that must be taken into account in stock pricing. We suggest that, in essence, what happened was a revision in investors' assessment of the liquidity of the market, and subsequently the market experienced a decline in value.

Empirical Test

This section presents evidence linking the decline in stock prices to increased illiquidity. Our sample consists of 451 stocks included in the S&P 500 index and traded on the New York Stock Exchange for which we had complete data over the test periods. The sample data, every trade and quote for these stocks during the test periods, were provided by the Institute for the Study of Securities Markets.

We compare three periods:

Period I: The week of October 5–October 9, 1987.
Period II: October 19, 1987.
Period III: October 30, 1987.

Period I, before the crash, is taken as the "normal" benchmark, before the unusual price declines that preceded the crash. Period II is the crash day, and Period III is an arbitrary postcrash date.

For each stock, we calculated the return and the quoted bid–ask spreads, as presented in Table 7.1. The summary statistics show a sizable increase in the dollar bid–ask spread between Periods I and II; even in Period III, about two weeks after the crash, the spreads remained high. The relative (percentage) bid–on average compared to the relative spreads of Period I.

Table 7.1. *Summary statistics for the variables studied*

Variable	Mean	Standard deviation
$R_{21} = P1019/P1009 - 1$	−0.2688	0.0825
$R_{32} = P1030/P1019 - 1$	0.0545	0.1450
SP1	0.2710	0.0849
SP2	0.4422	0.2164
SP3	0.3757	0.1797
SP1/P1009	0.788%	0.5510
SP2/P1019	1.715%	1.2090
SP3/P1030	1.405%	0.9630

Note: P1009, P1019, and P1030 are the closing prices for October 9, 19, and 30, respectively. The ratios are calculated for each stock. SP1, SP2, and SP3 are the average quoted bid–ask spreads in dollars during Periods I, II, and III, respectively. All prices are closing. The average spreads are calculated from all quotes during the period.

In Period III it still remained substantially higher than in Period I. These data suggest a sizable decrease in market liquidity on the day of the crash, which prevailed even after the unusual price shocks had subsided.

Table 7.1 shows that increases in the bid–ask spread, which measure an increase in illiquidity, were associated with a decline in prices, so that when the spread increased, prices fell. If illiquidity indeed contributed to the crash, we should observe a greater price decline for stocks that suffered from greater liquidity problems. That is, across stocks there should be greater price declines for stocks whose bid–ask spread increased more relative to its pre-crash level. Our estimation model is

$$R_{21}^i - \beta^i \cdot R_{21}^m = \alpha_0 + \alpha_1 \cdot DSP_{21}^i + \alpha_2 \cdot PERSPT^i + \epsilon^i,$$

where $DSP_{21}^i = SP2^i/SP1^i - 1$ is the percentage change in the dollar spread for stock i, and PERSPI is the relative (percent) spread for stock i in period I; stocks with lower PERSPI can be considered as more liquid.

The left-hand side of the equation is the "abnormal" price change for stock i, obtained by subtracting from the actual stock return the expected return for that stock given the market return between Periods I and II. The beta coefficients β^i were obtained from Standard & Poor's estimates, which use sixty months of return data up to the end of 1986, and R_{21}^m is the average return on the sample between Periods I and II. (The beta coefficients were adjusted to average 1.0 for the sample.)

On the right-hand side of the equation, the explanatory variables are the relative change in the dollar bid–ask spread for each stock i and the initial

Table 7.2. *Estimation of the effects of changes in the bid–ask spread (α_1), the initial spread (α_2), and the change in quote size (α_3) on the change in stock prices*

	"Crash" (Period II vs. I)			"Recovery" (Period III vs. II)		
	A-1	B-1	C-1	A-2	B-2	C-2
α_0	0.0376	0.0247	0.0011	−0.0104	0.0323	0.0339
	(5.12)	(1.73)	(0.07)	(1.40)	(2.04)	(1.92)
α_1	−0.0599	−0.0555	−0.0470	−0.0828	−0.0804	−0.0836
	(5.12)	(6.21)	(5.09)	(2.62)	(2.61)	(2.59)
α_2		1.3160	1.4694		−5.5361	−5.5049
		(0.95)	(1.08)		(2.94)	(2.93)
α_3			0.0283			−0.0010
			(3.13)			(0.19)

stock spread in the "benchmark" period. We use the change in the dollar spread rather than in the relative spread, because the change in relative spread includes the change in relative prices, which is the dependent (left-hand side) variable. The economically meaningful variable is the relative spread, so the equation actually is biased against our hypothesis.

We also estimated the equation with the period subscript 21 replaced by 32, that is, comparing Period III to Period II. Between these periods, there was a modest recovery in prices (5.45% on average); bid–ask spreads declined from their highs during the crash, but still stayed above their pre-crash levels (see Table 7.1). Again, we expect that the greater the decline in the bid–ask spread from Period II to Period III, the greater the associated increase in price.

We first estimated the equation by setting $\alpha_2 = 0$ (i.e., ignoring the dependence of the price change on the initial level of liquidity), correcting the standard errors to obtain heteroscedastic-consistent estimates. The results, presented in Table 7.2, columns A-1 and A-2, strongly support our hypothesis on the cross-sectional relationship between liquidity differentials and price differentials during the crash. Stocks that experienced a greater increase in their bid–ask spread suffered a greater price decline during the crash, after controlling for the market effect. Column A-2 of Table 7.2 shows the results for the "recovery" period. Again, α_1 is negative and significant, i.e., stocks whose bid–ask spreads shrunk relative to their crash levels enjoyed a greater recovery than stocks that remained illiquid.

Next, we examined whether the *initial* level of liquidity (in addition to *changes* in liquidity) of the sample stocks played a role in the crash and in the subsequent recovery, by estimating α_2 in the equation. The results appear in Table 7.2, columns B-1 and B-2. The variable PERSPI is insignificant in the crash, but has a negative and significant coefficient in the postcrash period. This captures the so-called flight to quality, which we suggest should be interpreted as a flight to liquidity. Investors fearing another liquidity-related crash reallocated assets towards high-liquidity stocks, which explains the greater price recovery of these stocks. As the October 19–October 30 period provided no news to indicate a forthcoming change in the cash flows that these firms generate, the relative increase in the price of high-liquidity stocks implies a decline in their expected returns relative to those of low-liquidity (high PERSPI) stocks, consistent with Amihud and Mendelson [1986a, 1986b].

Our hypothesis on illiquidity as a factor in the crash is corroborated by the report of the Quality of Markets Committee of the International Stock Exchange (ISE) in London: "A key test of the effectiveness of a market is how well liquidity is maintained under pressure. We have commented . . . on the improvement in liquidity . . . over the past year" (Kamphuis et al. [1989], p. 281).

On the crash day (October 20), however, there was a dramatic increase in measures of illiquidity: the relative (percentage) bid–ask spreads for the group of most liquid stocks, which averaged 1.2% before the crash, rose and peaked at 3.4%, remaining at about 3% through early November 1987. The bid–ask spreads of the second most liquid group of stocks rose from 2.5% to 5.5% on the crash day and to 6.5% through early November. As the average price decline on the day of the crash was 22%, the increase in the relative bid–ask spread reflects mostly an increase in the spread in pence.

The data for three stocks analyzed by the market quality committee show this clearly: For Shell T&T, the spread increased from 6 pence to 20 pence on the day of the crash; for Amstrad, it increased from 4.5 to 9.5 pence; and for Jaguar, it rose from 5 to 15 pence on the crash day. By the end of 1987, the committee found that the spreads had narrowed somewhat, but still remained higher than before October. Correspondingly, the London market remained depressed.

Another measure of illiquidity that the committee analyzed is market depth, that is, the size of market makers' quotes. Quote size is usually reduced under extreme market conditions, implying an increased impact of a given size order on price. The maximum quote size for the group of the most liquid ISE stocks fell from 64,000 (average per stock) to 34,000. For the second liquidity group, the maximum quote size had fallen from 50,000 to 12,000 shares per stock. Although by year-end, the quote size had recovered, it made up hardly half of the decline.

We tested the effect of the quote size on price changes across stocks in our sample. As for the ISE, the quote size fell substantially on the crash day, but it quickly recovered. We reestimated our model, adding a new variable, DQTSZ, the change in quote size (the number of shares for which the quote applies). We defined our depth variables $MQTSZ_i$ as the sum of the median quantities quoted on the bid and the III).[5] Then, we formed the depth ratios $DQTSZ_{21} = MQTSZ_2/MQTSZ_1$ and $DQTSZ_{32} = MQTSZ_3/MQTSZ_2$.

Adding DQTSZ to the equation, and denoting its coefficient by α_3, we obtained the results in Table 7.2, columns C-l and C-2. They show that the change in quote size had a significant effect on the crash day. Across stocks, the greater the decline in the quote size, the greater the decline in the stock price relative to the expected decline (given the market decline). By October 30, 1987, however, the increase in the quote size did not play a significant role across stocks.

Concluding Remarks

We have suggested that the stock market crash of October 1987 can be interpreted in light of the relationship between liquidity and stock prices. Our theory is that the problems in stock trading and the sharp decline in liquidity, hitherto unexpected, contributed significantly to the decline in stock prices. Although the illiquidity problem prevailed only during the crash and for a number of months afterward, it had a lasting impact on stock prices because investors factor into the price the expected additional concessions they will incur when selling their stocks. Thus, the main news that led to the prolonged decline in stock prices was the crash itself, which changed investor perceptions of the liquidity of the market.[6]

Naturally, our measures of illiquidity cannot capture the fact that trading in some stocks was infeasible either because of extreme imbalances (e.g., they opened hours late) or because the trading floor was practically inaccessible to many traders. Nor can we directly capture the effect of the rumors about possible trading halts or market closing, which imply sharply lower liquidity. Ex post, we know that trading was not halted (except for a brief period on October 20) and, with the benefit of hindsight, trader assessment of the illiquidity of the market on October 19 and 20 was probably exaggerated just as judgments that preceded October 19, 1987, were too optimistic.

---

[5] As the Exchange reports 999 round lots (of 100 shares) as the highest number of shares quoted, we used the medians of quote sizes.

[6] Indeed, Shiller [1988] found in a survey that immediately after the crash, investors indicated that they responded to the news of the crash itself rather than to specific economic fundamentals.

These conclusions are consistent with the patterns of price behavior over these periods.[7]

The illiquidity problem encountered during the crash was international in nature. In Britain, for example, all measures of illiquidity soared on October 20, 1987, while prices declined. In the Tokyo Stock Exchange, the morning trading session did not take place. In general, the news of the liquidity failure of the United States markets made investors reassess the liquidity of markets around the world. Indeed, Roll (1988) found that price declines in the world's leading stock markets were associated with the trading mechanism employed in those markets. This corroborates our position on the relationship between market microstructure and the crash.

Taking a liquidity perspective toward the events of October 1987 suggests a simple criterion for the evaluation of policy options: They are beneficial if, and only if, they enhance market liquidity. From this perspective, proposed solutions such as circuit breakers resulting in lengthy trading halts, an increase in margin requirements, or institution of a sales tax on stocks are unsound because they are likely to reduce market liquidity and hence depress stock prices. Malkiel (1988) studies the recommendations of the Brady Commission in this spirit. See also Ferguson (1988).

We suggest elsewhere that improvements in trading mechanisms and the proper use of information technology have a greater potential than regulation.[8] The challenge is to find solutions that increase the liquidity of the market without hampering its efficiency (Bernstein (1987)).

References

Amihud, Yakov, and Haim Mendelson. "Asset Pricing and the Bid–Ask Spread." *Journal of Financial Economics*, 17, 1986a, pp. 223–49.

_____. "The Effects of Beta, Bid–Ask Spread, Residual Risk and Size on Stock Returns." *Journal of Finance*, Vol. 44, June 1989, pp. 479–86.

_____. "An Integrated Computerized Trading System." In Yakov Amihud, Thomas S.Y. Ho, and Robert A. Schwartz, eds. *Market Making and the Changing Structure of the Securities Industry*. Lexington: Lexington Books, 1985, pp. 217–35.

_____. "Liquidity, and Asset Prices: Financial Management Implications." *Financial Management*, Spring 1988a, pp. 5–15.

_____. "Liquidity and Stock Returns." *Financial Analysts Journal*, 42, May/June 1986b, pp. 43–8.

[7] Another factor that contributed to the crash was volatility (see Wood [1989]). Shiller [1988] argues that the increase in volatility during the crash was due not to fundamental factors, but rather to market psychology, and that it did not persist.

[8] Amihud and Mendelson [1985, 1988b] propose an integrated computerized trading system (ICTS) to increase market liquidity.

———. "Liquidity, Volatility and Exchange Automation." *Journal of Accounting, Auditing and Finance,* 3, Fall 1988b, pp. 389–95.

———. "Trading Mechanisms and Stock Returns: An Empirical Investigation." *Journal of Finance,* Vol. 42, No. 3, July 1987, pp. 533–53.

Bernstein, Peter. "Liquidity, Stock Markets and Market-Making." *Financial Management,* 16, Summer 1987, pp. 54–62.

Ferguson, Robert. "What to Do, or Not Do, About The Markets." *Journal of Portfolio Management,* Summer 1988, pp. 14–9.

Ferguson, Robert, and John O'Brien. "Stabilizing Forwards: For a More Stable Market." *Journal of Portfolio Management,* Summer 1988, p. 4.

Gammill, James F., Jr., and Andre F. Perold. "The Changing Character of Stock Market Liquidity." *Journal of Portfolio Management,* Spring 1989, pp. 13–8.

Kamphuis, R.W., R.C. Kormendi, and J.W. Henry Watson, eds. *Black Monday and the Future of Financial Markets.* Homewood, IL: Irwin, 1989.

Leland, Hayne, and Mark Rubinstein. "Comments on the Market Crash: Six Months After." *Journal of Economic Perspectives,* Vol. 2, No. 3, Summer 1988, pp. 45–50.

McInish, Thomas H., and Robert A. Wood. "An Analysis of Intraday Patterns in Bids, Asks and Spreads for NYSE Stocks." Working Paper, Department of Finance, University of Texas, 1989.

Malkiel, Burton G. "The Brady Commission Report: A Critique." *Journal of Portfolio Management,* Summer 1988, pp. 9–13.

Mendelson, Haim. "Random Competitive Exchange: Price Distributions and Gains From Trade." *Journal of Economic Theory,* Vol. 37, 1985, pp. 254–80.

The Quality of Markets Report, Winter 1987/1988. Quality of Markets Committee, The International Stock Exchange of Great Britain. Summary of key points is found in Kamphuis et al.

Roll, Richard. "The International Crash of October 1987." *Financial Analysts Journal,* September/October 1988, pp. 19–35.

Shiller, Robert. "Causes of Changing Financial Market Volatility." Paper presented at the Symposium on Financial Market Volatility, Federal Reserve Bank of Kansas City, August 1988.

Treynor, Jack L. "Portfolio Insurance and Market Volatility." *Financial Analysts Journal,* November-December 1988, pp. 71–3.

Wallace, Anice. "Pullback at Block Trading Desks." *New York Times,* December 25, 1987.

———. "Volume Cut Worrying Wall Street." *New York Times,* May 23, 1988.

Wood, Robert A. "The Volatility of the S&P 500: An Intraday Examination." Working Paper, The Pennsylvania State University, 1989.

CHAPTER 8

Slow Moving Capital

Summary and Implications

This article illustrates empirically how liquidity spirals affect prices during liquidity crises, namely, those of the convertible bond market in 2005 and 1998, and of the merger market in 1987. Convertible bonds are illiquid, and convertible bond hedge funds seek to earn the associated liquidity premium. When these hedge funds face funding problems, liquidity spirals cause significant sell-offs and price drops.

An example of this occurred in the first quarter of 2005, when more than 20% of the capital was redeemed from convertible bond hedge funds, which were therefore forced to sell large parts of their levered convertible bond holdings. The sell-offs led to price drops, requiring further sell-offs by the funds and increasing illiquidity. Convertible bonds ultimately cheapened 3% relative to their theoretical full-liquidity value, which can be estimated, because convertible bonds are derivatives. This was a large move, given the relatively low risk of these instruments and their close ties to the underlying stocks that were not affected. Levered convertible bond arbitrage lost about 7% and, as the situation stabilized and recovered, the strategy made back 15%.

Similarly, in 1998, the hedge fund Long Term Capital Management (LTCM) was forced to liquidate a sizable convertible bond portfolio due to losses in other markets. Convertible bonds cheapened 4% relative to the theoretical full-liquidity value due to the liquidity issues related to the selling pressure.

This article also documents liquidity spirals in the merger market in 1987. Market liquidity clearly deteriorated during the 1987 crash, especially in the merger arbitrage space that was dominated by proprietary traders in a few banks that experienced severe funding liquidity problems. Due to this illiquidity and the fear of deal failure, the spread between the offer price for a merger target and its current stock price widened from 3% to about 20%.

In summary, this paper shows how liquidity spirals make prices drop and rebound, because new capital arrives slowly. Due to illiquidity, the speed of arbitrage is not instantaneous, as in typical textbooks. Arbitrage spreads can take months to converge.

Slow Moving Capital

Mark Mitchell, Lasse Heje Pedersen, and Todd Pulvino[*]

American Economic Review, 2007

Unlike textbook arbitrageurs who instantaneously trade when prices deviate from fundamental values, real world arbitrageurs must overcome various frictions. For example, they often invest other people's money, resulting in a principal/agent problem that is exacerbated in market downturns. Rather than increasing investment levels when prices dip below fundamental values, arbitrageurs may, in the face of capital constraints, sell cheap securities causing prices to decline further. As a result, mispricings can be large and can extend for long periods of time.

We first study the convertible bond market in 2005 when convertible hedge funds faced large redemptions of capital from investors. These redemptions led to binding capital constraints for many funds, resulting in massive bond sales and, in many cases, fund liquidations. These sales reduced prices of convertibles relative to fundamental values, especially around redemption dates. While the group of multistrategy hedge funds that were not capital constrained increased their overall position, about half of these hedge funds actually acted as net sellers, consistent with the view that information barriers within a firm (not just relative to outside investors) can lead to capital constraints for trading desks with mark-to-market losses. We document similar patterns in the convertible bond market around the collapse of Long Term Capital Management (LTCM) in 1998. When LTCM

* Mitchell: CNH Partners, 2 Greenwich Plaza, 1st Floor, Greenwich, CT 06830 (e-mail: mmitchell@cnhpartners.com); Pedersen: Stern School of Business, New York University, 44 West Fourth Street, Suite 9-190, New York, NY 10012-1126, Centre for Economic Policy Research and National Bureau of Economic Research (e-mail: lpederse@stern. nyu.edu); Pulvino: CNH Partners, 2 Greenwich Plaza, 1st Floor, Greenwich, CT 06830 (e-mail: tpulvino@cnhpartners.com). We are grateful for helpful conversations with Lars N. Nielsen and research assistance from Rachel Perez and Linda Rabel.

incurred large losses on macroeconomic bets, the firm was forced to liquidate large convertible bond positions. These sales led to depressed valuations of convertible bonds despite the fact that there was little change in overall fundamentals. As a result, other hedge funds incurred large losses and were also forced to sell their convertible bond holdings. In both cases, it took several months for traders to increase their capital or for better-capitalized traders to enter.

We also study merger targets during the 1987 market crash. Merger arbitrageurs buy shares of target firms following merger announcements, providing liquidity to shareholders who choose to sell. The market crash and concurrently proposed antitakeover legislation caused merger spreads (the difference between the acquirer's offer and the target price) to widen substantially, inflicting large losses on arbitrageurs. Data from Wall Street proprietary arbitrage desks show that Wall Street firms reduced their exposure by selling target stocks. Furthermore, numerous arbitrage funds and Wall Street trading desks were forced to cease operations. Even though the market rebounded and the proposed legislation was dropped, spreads remained wide for several months, arguably caused by capital withdrawals from the market as natural liquidity providers became short-term liquidity demanders.

Our findings do not support the frictionless economic paradigm. Under this paradigm, a shock to the capital of a relatively small subset of agents should have a trivial effect on security prices, since new capital would immediately flow into the market and prices would be bid up to fundamental values. Rather, the findings support an alternate view that market frictions are of first-order importance. Shocks to capital matter if arbitrageurs with losses face the prospect of investor redemptions (Andrei Shleifer and Robert W. Vishny 1997), particularly when margin constraints tighten during liquidity crises (Markus K. Brunnermeier and Pedersen 2006), when other agents lack both infrastructure and information to trade the affected securities (Robert C. Merton 1987), and when agents require a return premium to compensate for liquidity risk (Viral V. Acharya and Pedersen 2005).

I. Convertible Bond Arbitrage: Capital Redemptions in 2005

Convertible bonds (corporate bonds with a call option on the underlying shares) are a capital source for many firms. Corporate capital needs are often immediate, and are facilitated by convertible arbitrage and other hedge funds, which account for up to 75% of the convertible market. Because the payoff of a convertible bond can nearly be replicated using other traded securities, its fundamental value can be inferred from the prices of those other securities. Convertible arbitrageurs transform the convertible bond into a security with much lower risk by short selling the underlying stock,[1] thereby reducing information asymmetries and allowing the firm to quickly issue the convertible.[2] In exchange for providing liquidity to issuing firms, convertible bonds are often issued at prices below fundamental value.

Post issuance, convertibles are illiquid and, likely for this reason, often continue to trade below fundamental values. Assuming correct hedging, convertible arbitrage has minimal fundamental risk, and thus leverage is often used to enhance returns. The primary risk is that short-run losses can arise if the bond becomes even cheaper, a problem which is exacerbated by the risk of forced liquidation at such an inopportune time.

In early 2005, large institutional investors in convertible arbitrage funds began to withdraw capital, purportedly because of low returns generated in 2004. According to the Barclay Group, more than 20% of capital was redeemed from convertible arbitrage funds in the first quarter of 2005. To meet investor redemptions, hedge funds began to sell convertible bonds causing their prices to fall relative to their fundamental values. As a result, convertible arbitrage funds experienced negative returns, which caused further investor redemptions and more selling. The Barclay Group reported that by the first quarter of 2006 assets managed by convertible arbitrage funds had fallen by half.

Figure 8.1 displays the market value of convertible bond holdings, obtained from quarterly SEC 13-F filings, by convertible arbitrage funds during the first quarter of 2004 through the third quarter of 2006.[3] We consider the reporting entity to specialize in convertible arbitrage if it is a hedge fund, and if more than 50% of its SEC13-F reported assets are held in convertible securities at the end of 2004. We include only those funds that have at least $100 million in convertibles at the end of 2004. The final sample contains twenty-eight convertible arbitrage funds. These twenty-eight

---

[1] The arbitrageur also may sell short risk-free bonds to hedge interest rate risk, sell short nonconvertible bonds or buy credit default swaps to hedge credit risk, and sell stock options to hedge volatility risk.

[2] In 1990, SEC Rule 144A became effective allowing firms to issue securities to qualified institutional buyers (QIBs) without having to register these securities, thereby accelerating the capital raising process. QIBs are allowed to resell the securities in the secondary market to other QIBs, prior to their subsequent registration. In recent years, nearly all convertible bonds have been issued via the 144A market. The transaction time is usually one to two days from announcement to closing, and is often less than 24 hours. Issuing a convertible bond via the public market would take at least a month.

[3] The SEC requires institutions with greater than $100 million in equity or equity-linked securities to report their holdings within 15 days of the end of each calendar quarter.

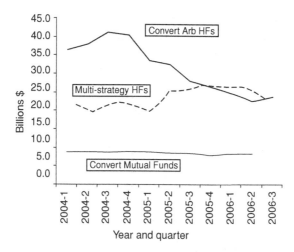

Figure 8.1. Adjusted holdings of convertible bonds in billions of dollars.

funds owned approximately $40 billion of convertible bonds at the end of 2004, roughly 15% of the total U.S. convertible market.[4]

To estimate changes in the value of holdings caused by selling activity, we removed the effect of changes in individual bond values using returns from the Merrill Lynch All US Convertibles Index. The data confirm the steep decline in convertibles held by hedge funds. By the end of 2005, the sample of twenty-eight funds had sold 35% (t-statistic = −2.75 under the null hypothesis of no change in holdings) of their convertible bonds, and by the third quarter of 2006, they had sold 41% (t-statistic = −3.02).[5] These data understate the true decline in holdings as we are not able to locate 13-F filings for several funds which are known to have liquidated.[6]

---

[4] Note that there are numerous small (e.g., less than $100 million in assets) and foreign convertible arbitrage funds that are not required to report holdings to the SEC and are therefore missing from the sample. Furthermore, although holdings by Wall Street trading desks must be reported to the SEC, they are commingled with the firms' other holdings, and it is therefore difficult to ascertain the trading desks' positions. Anecdotal evidence suggests that, like the typical convertible fund, the largest trading desks significantly reduced inventories during 2005. Of course, for every seller there is a buyer, so the net selling that we observe must correspond to net buying by investors whose holdings we do not observe. These funds may not specialize in convertibles.

[5] Interestingly, the large hedge fund Amaranth Advisors sold more than half of its convertible book after convertibles reached their cheapest level in 2005, and instead expanded its energy trading which had been profitable. Amaranth lost $6 billion from energy bets in September 2006 and had to shut down as a result.

[6] Funds often report their holdings to the SEC under a different entity name than the fund name, thereby making it difficult to locate all of the funds, especially those that have liquidated and are no longer in business.

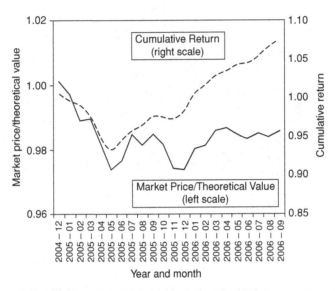

Figure 8.2. Price-to-theoretical-value of convertible bonds, and return of convertible bond hedge funds (2004/12–2006/09).

The massive selling of convertibles caused prices to decline relative to theoretical values. To determine the impact of the sell-off, we analyze a dataset of 550 U.S. convertible bonds during the period 2005–2006. For each bond, the market price (obtained from various Wall Street bank trading desks) is compared to the theoretical value calculated using a finite difference model that incorporates the terms of each bond and the following inputs: (a) issuer stock price; (b) volatility estimates derived from historical volatility and implied volatility from the options market; (c) credit spread estimates based on credit default swaps, straight debt yields, investment bank estimates, and bond ratings; and (d) the term structure of interest rates. To mitigate the impact of outliers, we focus on the median discount of market price to theoretical value. We also limit the sample to convertible securities where the underlying stock price is at least 65% of the bond's conversion price, since focusing on the more equity-sensitive part of the convertible universe mitigates errors associated with inaccurate credit spread estimates.

Figure 8.2 displays the median market price divided by the theoretical value from January 2005 through September 2006. Bond prices deviated significantly from theoretical values, reaching a maximum discount of 2.7% in mid-May 2005. Based on the historical distribution calculated over the 1985–2004 period, this is roughly 2.5 standard deviations from the average. It was the largest deviation from theoretical value since LTCM began liquidating its convertible portfolio in August 1998. As shown, the discount to theoretical value reaches maxima around the deadlines for investor redemption notices, namely 45 days before the end of June and 45 days before the end of December (which we confirm using daily data, not reported).

Figure 8.2 also shows that convertible hedge funds had returns of −7.2% during January–May 2005, as reported by the hedge fund indices. This negative return is roughly what would be expected by a 2.7% cheapening of bonds, assuming a typical fund leverage of 3:1. The loss could be caused in part by imperfect hedging, but we estimate that this effect is small since volatility and credit spreads changed little over the period. The fact that bond prices dropped significantly without changes in fundamentals is consistent with the view that the price drop was driven by redemptions from convertible funds. Moreover, convertible prices rebounded in 2006, providing further evidence that 2005 losses were driven by capital flows and not by deteriorating fundamentals.

The deviation of convertible bond prices from theoretical values provided a seemingly profitable opportunity for multistrategy hedge funds, for which the stated advantage is their ability to quickly allocate capital across strategies depending on attractiveness. To determine whether multistrategy funds increased their exposure to convertible bonds in 2005, we examined funds that invested in convertible bonds, but where convertible bonds represented less than 50% of their portfolios at the end of 2004. Requiring some ownership of convertible bonds was intended to identify those funds that have the necessary infrastructure to provide liquidity to the selling funds on a timely basis.

As shown in Figure 8.1, multistrategy funds eventually began to invest in convertible arbitrage, but not until well after the first quarter 2005 sell-off. In fact, in response to negative returns, two large multistrategy funds reportedly replaced their convertible trading staffs. Other multistrategy hedge funds may have been waiting for bonds to cheapen further before increasing investment levels, especially in light of numerous reports at the time of entire portfolio liquidations. For the sample of twenty-seven multistrategy funds that have convertible holdings, we show that they increased their holdings by 36% and 18% by the end of 2005 and the third quarter 2006, respectively.[7] This increase is largely driven by one of the

---

[7] We also examined the holdings of large multistrategy funds that did not have any convertible holdings as of the end of 2004 and found that these funds did not purchase material quantities of convertible bonds in 2005.

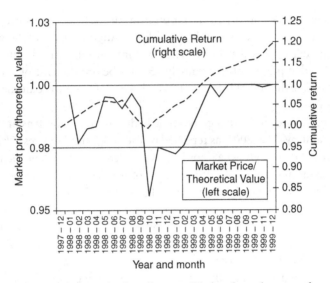

Figure 8.3. Price-to-theoretical-value of convertible bonds, and return of convertible bond hedge funds (1997/12–1999/12).

twenty-seven multistrategy funds, however. More than half of the funds actually reduced their exposure between the end of 2004 and the third quarter of 2006.

Other natural buyers of convertibles are convertible mutual funds. From the CRSP Mutual Funds Database, we examined sixteen convertible mutual funds that had at least $100 million in net asset value (NAV) at the end of 2004. As shown in Figure 8.1, these funds experienced minor investor redemptions in 2005 and, since they are unable to employ leverage, mutual funds became forced sellers rather than natural liquidity providers.

A phenomenon similar to that of 2005 occurred in 1998 following the LTCM crisis. When LTCM experienced large losses on macroeconomic bets, it was forced to liquidate investments across markets, even those in which fundamentals had not changed. As shown in Figure 8.3, LTCM's liquidation of its convertible bond portfolio caused bond prices to fall, which in turn caused other hedge funds to sell their convertible holdings. Using a proprietary dataset, we examine a large portfolio of convertible bonds during the LTCM crisis. Employing a methodology similar to that used to examine the 2005 episode, we document that convertible bond prices fell dramatically, eventually reaching a discount to theoretical value of more than 4% (nearly four standard deviations from the historical distribution's average). As in 2005, it took several months before bond prices returned to more normal levels and equilibrium was restored.

II. Merger Arbitrage and the Stock Market Crash of 1987

Merger arbitrage is a strategy which seeks to capture the difference (deal spread) between the stock price of a target firm and the offer price made by the acquirer. After a merger announcement, the target's stock price usually appreciates considerably (20–30%), but then trades at a small discount to the offer price until the deal is complete. Many mutual funds and other investors that hold the target stock sell their shares soon after the announcement. By selling, they insure against losses in case the deal is not consummated. While the probability of failure is usually small, losses conditional on failure can be large. Investors often lose the entire merger premium realized at the deal announcement, and can suffer additional losses if, following deal cancellation, the target stock trades below its preannouncement price. By purchasing target shares after merger announcements, merger arbitrageurs provide insurance against deal failure.

In a cash merger, the arbitrageur buys the target stock and holds it until merger consummation with the expectation of realizing the difference between the offer price and the current price. In a stock merger, the arbitrageur sells short the acquirer stock to eliminate market risk. Given that the return can be locked in by the arbitrageur, and since the deal failure risk is typically idiosyncratic and thus diversifiable, merger arbitrage is viewed as a market neutral strategy. However, Mitchell and Pulvino (2001) find that mergers are more likely to fail in the event of severe market downturns and propose a nonlinear asset pricing model to estimate the risk and return to merger arbitrage. They create a portfolio of merger arbitrage investments and document that in most months the merger arbitrage portfolio exhibits systematic risk close to zero, but in severely declining markets, the market beta of merger arbitrage increases to 0.50.

Figure 8.4 displays daily merger arbitrage median spreads and returns for a portfolio of merger deals involving US publicly traded targets during the crash of 1987. On October 1, 1987, the median spread for the sample of 107 ongoing merger deals was 3.3%. During the period October 14–16, the US House Ways and Means Committee proposed legislation to ban leveraged buyouts and hostile mergers as analyzed by Mitchell and Jeffry M. Netter (1989). By October 16, in response to the proposed legislation, the median deal spread had increased to 5.4%. During the stock market crash on October 19, 1987, and October 20, 1987, the median spread increased to 9.7% and 15.1%, respectively, as the arbitrage community expected the termination or revision of many of the ongoing merger transactions.[8]

---

[8] Many NASDAQ stocks did not trade on October 19, 1987 and thus the October 20, 1987, spread better reflects the impact of the market crash on merger arbitrage.

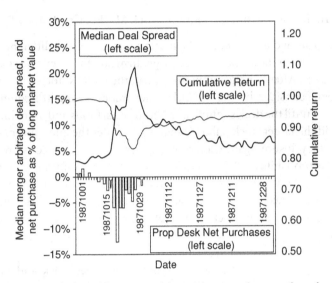

Figure 8.4. Merger deal spreads, merger arbitrage returns, and net purchases by merger-arb proprietary traders.

As shown in Figure 8.4, this dramatic increase in deal spreads caused severely negative returns to merger arbitrage portfolios.

Figure 8.4 also displays the trading activity of 18 anonymous merger arbitrage desks from major Wall Street firms.[9] For the month of October 1987 (the only month for which the data were provided), we display net purchases as a percentage of the total long portfolio value aggregated across the eighteen trading desks. These desks owned more than 10% of the total value of takeover targets as of the beginning of October and thus were influential in setting deal spreads. During the October 1–13 period, the eighteen desks were net purchasers of target shares. Beginning October 14, contemporaneous with the proposed antitakeover legislation, the desks began to reduce their positions. They accelerated their selling on October 19, reducing their holdings by 6%, and then sold more than 12% of their positions on October 20. Interestingly, these desks continued as net sellers every day during the remainder of the month, despite a 5% stock market rebound and an indication by Congress that the antitakeover legislation

[9] The data were collected at the request of Mitchell and Netter (1989) while at the SEC. · The data are deemed by the New York Stock Exchange (NYSE) to be confidential in their entirety, and confidential treatment has been requested by the NYSE in a letter dated February 10, 1988, which has been filed pursuant to 17 CRF 200.83(e) with the Freedom of Information Act Officer at the Securities and Exchange Commission (SEC).

proposal would be withdrawn. We believe that the continued selling pressure from the proprietary desks was caused by internal capital constraints that were likely imposed as a result of the large losses. Indeed, many proprietary merger arbitrage trading desks shuttered operations in the aftermath of the crash and several arbitrage funds also shut down.

Whereas merger arbitrageurs typically serve a function of providing liquidity to target shareholders, they instead became liquidity demanders, resulting in a substantial dislocation in merger targets' stock prices. Because merger activity continued to be robust following the crash, there was an opportunity for surviving desks and a few well-capitalized entrants to invest in merger target stocks at very attractive spreads (for example, Warren Buffet entered the merger arbitrage market for a brief period after the crash). These investors realized stellar returns over the next year, until capital flowed back into the market and deal spreads returned to more normal levels.

III. Discussion: The Speed of Arbitrage

We document what appear to be major and persistent price deviations from fundamental value, suggesting that while arbitrage is reasonably fast when market participants are not capital constrained, it can be slow following major capital dislocations. Convertible arbitrageurs provide immediate liquidity to firms unable to raise cash efficiently via the equity or straight debt markets. In return, these arbitrageurs receive a premium for holding a security that is highly illiquid. Likewise, merger arbitrageurs provide immediate liquidity to investors seeking to sell target shares after a merger announcement and, in return, receive a premium for bearing deal failure risk. However, in situations where external capital shocks force liquidity providers to reverse order and become liquidity demanders, it can take months to restore equilibrium to the dislocated market. This is because (a) information barriers separate investors from money managers; (b) it is costly to maintain dormant capital, infrastructure, and talent for long periods of time, while waiting for profitable opportunities; and (c) markets become highly illiquid when liquidity providers are constrained and traders demand higher expected returns as compensation for this lack of liquidity. The result is that profit opportunities for unconstrained firms can persist for months. Given the relative ease of estimating deviations from fundamentals in the convertible and merger markets, the time required to restore equilibrium is likely to be longer in other markets. We view our results as evidence that real world frictions impede arbitrage capital.

References

Acharya, Viral V., and Lasse H. Pedersen. 2005. "Asset Pricing with Liquidity Risk." *Journal of Financial Economics*, 77(2): 375–410.

Brunnermeier, Markus K., and Lasse H. Pedersen. 2005. "Market Liquidity and Funding Liquidity." Unpublished.

Merton, Robert C. 1987. "A Simple Model of Capital Market Equilibrium with Incomplete Information." *Journal of Finance*, 42(3): 483–510.

Mitchell, Mark L., and Jeffry M. Netter. 1989. "Triggering the 1987 Stock Market Crash: Antitakeover Provisions in the Proposed House Ways and Means Tax Bill?" *Journal of Financial Economics*, 24(1): 37–68.

Mitchell, Mark, and Todd Pulvino. 2001. "Characteristics of Risk and Return in Risk Arbitrage." *Journal of Finance*, 56(6): 2135–75.

Shleifer, Andrei, and Robert W. Vishny. 1997. "The Limits of Arbitrage." *Journal of Finance*, 52(1): 35–55.

References for Introductions and Summaries

Acharya, Viral V., Yakov Amihud, and Sreedhar Bharath. 2010. Liquidity risk of corporate bond returns. Working paper, New York University, Stern School of Business.

Acharya, Viral V., and S. Viswanathan. 2011. Leverage, moral hazard and liquidity. *Journal of Finance* 66, 99–138.

Amihud, Yakov, Allaudeen Hameed, Wenjin Kang, and Huiping Zhang. 2011. The liquidity premium: International evidence. Working paper, New York University, Stern School of Business.

Amihud, Yakov, and Haim Mendelson. 1980. Market making with inventory. *Journal of Financial Economics* 8, 31–53.

Amihud, Yakov, and Haim Mendelson. 1986a. Liquidity and stock returns. *Financial Analysts Journal* 42 (May/June), 43–8.

Amihud, Yakov, and Haim Mendelson, 1987. Trading mechanisms and stock returns: An empirical investigation. *Journal of Finance* 42, 533–53.

Amihud, Yakov, and Haim Mendelson. 1987a. Are trading rule profits feasible? *Journal of Portfolio Management* 14 (1), 77–8.

Amihud, Yakov, and Haim Mendelson. 1988. Liquidity and asset prices: Financial management implications. *Financial Management* 17 (1), 5–15.

Amihud, Yakov, and Haim Mendelson. 2012. Liquidity, the value of the firm, and corporate finance. *Journal of Applied Corporate Finance* 24 (1), 17–32.

Amihud, Yakov, Haim Mendelson, and Ruslan Goyenko. 2010. The excess return on illiquid stocks. Working paper, New York University, Stanford University, McGill University.

Amihud, Yakov, Haim Mendelson, and Lasse Heje Pedersen. 2005. Liquidity and asset prices. *Foundations and Trends in Finance* 1, 269–364.

Aragon, George O., and Philip E. Strahan. 2010. Hedge funds as liquidity providers: evidence from the Lehman bankruptcy. *Journal of Financial Economics*, forthcoming.

Anginer, Deniz. 2010. Liquidity clienteles. Working paper, The World Bank.

Ashcraft, Adam, Nicolae Garleanu, and Lasse Heje Pedersen. 2010. Two monetary tools: Interest rates and haircuts. *NBER Macroeconomics Annual*, forthcoming.

Asness, Cliff, Andrea Frazzini, and Lasse Heje Pedersen. 2012. Leverage aversion and risk parity. *Financial Analysts Journal* 68 (1), 47–59.

Atkins, Allen B., and Edward A. Dyl. 1997. Transaction costs and holding periods for common stocks. *Journal of Finance* 52, 309–25.

271

Bekaert, Geert, Campbell R. Harvey, and Christian Lundblad. 2007. Liquidity and expected returns: Lessons from emerging markets. *Review of Financial Studies* 20, 1781–831.

Berge, Klaus, Giorgio Consigli, and William T. Ziemba. 2008. The predictive ability of the bond-stock earnings yield differential model. *Journal of Portfolio Management* 34 (3), 63–80.

Bowen, David, Mark C. Hutchison, and Niall O'Sulliva., 2010. High frequency equity pairs trading: Transaction costs, speed of execution and patterns of returns. Working paper.

Brennan, Michael J., and Avanidhar Subrahmanyam. 1996. Market microstructure and asset pricing: On the compensation for illiquidity in stock returns. *Journal of Financial Economics* 41, 441–64.

Brunnermeier, Markus, and Lasse Heje Pedersen. 2005. Predatory trading. *Journal of Finance* 60, 1825-63.

Carhart, Mark M. 1997. On persistence in mutual fund performance. *Journal of Finance* 52, 57–82.

Chen, Long, David A. Lesmond, and Jason Z. Wei. 2007. Corporate yield spreads and bond liquidity. *Journal of Finance* 62, 119–49.

Chordia, Tarun, Richard Roll, and Avanidhar Subrahmanyam. 2000. Commonality in liquidity. *Journal of Financial Economics* 56, 3–28.

CFTC-SEC, 2010. *Findings Regarding the Market Events of May 6, 2010.* Report of the Staffs of the CFTC and SEC to the joint advisory committee on emerging regulatory issues.

Comerton-Forde, Carol, Terrence Hendershott, Charles M. Jones, Pamela C. Moulton, and Mark S. Seasholes. 2010. Time variation in liquidity: The role of market-maker inventories and revenues. *Journal of Finance* 65, 295–332.

Datar, Vinay T., Narayan Y. Naik, and Robert Radcliffe. 1998. Liquidity and stock returns: An alternative test. *Journal of Financial Markets* 1, 203–19.

DeJong, Frank, and Joost Driessen. 2007. Liquidity risk premia in corporate bond markets. Working paper, Tilburg University and University of Amsterdam.

Dias, Jorge D., and Miguel A. Ferreira. 2005. Timing and holding periods for common stocks: A duration-based analysis. Working paper, ISCTE Business School.

Dick-Nielsen, Jens, Peter Feldhutter, and David Lando. 2011. Corporate bond liquidity before and after the onset of the subprime crisis. *Journal of Financial Economics*, forthcoming.

Duarte, Jefferson, and Lance Young. 2009. Why is *PIN* priced? *Journal of Financial Economics* 91, 119–38.

Duffie, Darrell. 2010. Asset price dynamics with slow-moving capital. *Journal of Finance* 65, 1238–68.

Duffie, Darrell, Nicolae Garleanu, and Lasse Heje Pedersen. 2005. Over-the-counter markets. *Econometrica* 73, 1815–47.

Duffie, Darrell, Nicolae Garleanu, and Lasse Heje Pedersen. 2007. Valuation in over-the-counter markets. *Review of Financial Studies* 20, 1865–900.

Easley, David, Soeren Hvidkjaer, and Maureen O'Hara. 2002. Is information risk a determinant of asset returns? *Journal of Finance* 57, 2185–222.

Easley, David and Maureen O'Hara. 2004. Information and the cost of capital. *Journal of Finance* 59, 1553–83.

Fama, Eugene F., and Kenneth R. French. 1993. Common risk factors in the returns on stocks and bonds. *Journal of Financial Economics* 33, 3–56.

Fang, Vivian W., Thomas H. Noe, and Sheri Tice. 2009. Stock market liquidity and firm value. *Journal of Financial Economics* 94, 150–69.

Frazzini, Andrea, and Lasse Heje Pedersen. 2010. Betting against beta. Working paper, NYU.

Frazzini, Andrea, and Lasse Heje Pedersen. 2011. Embedded leverage. Working paper, NYU.

Garleanu, Nicolae and Lasse Heje Pedersen. 2004. Adverse selection and the required return. *Review of Financial Studies* 17, 643–65.

Garleanu, Nicolae, and Lasse Heje Pedersen. 2011. Margin-based asset pricing and deviations from the law of one price. *Review of Financial Studies* 24, 1980–2022.

Geyer, Alois and William T. Ziemba. 2008. The Innovest Austrian pension fund financial planning model InnoALM. *Operations Research* 56, 797–810.

Glosten, Lawrence R., and Paul R. Milgrom. 1985. Bid, ask and transaction prices in a specialist market with heterogeneously informed traders. *Journal of Financial Economics* 14, 71–100.

Hasbrouck, Joel. 2009. Trading costs and returns for U.S. equities: Estimating effective costs from daily data. *Journal of Finance* 64, 1445–77.

Hund, John, and David A. Lesmond. 2008. Liquidity and credit risk in emerging debt markets. Working paper, Tulane University.

Ivashina, Victoria, and David S. Scharfstein. 2010. Bank lending during the financial crisis of 2008. *Journal of Financial Economics* 97, 319–38.

Jain, Pankaj K. 2005. Financial market design and the equity premium: Electronic versus floor trading. *Journal of Finance* 60, 2955–85.

Kessler, Stephan, and Bernd Scherer. 2011. Hedge fund return sensitivity to global liquidity. *Journal of Financial Markets* 14, 301–22.

Kirilenko, Andrei, Albert S. Kyle, Mekrdad Samadi and Tugkan Tuzum. 2011. The Flash Crash: The impact of high frequency trading on an electronic market. *Working paper.*

Kyle, Albert S. 1985. Continuous auctions and insider trading. *Econometrica* 53, 1315–35.

Lesmond, David A., Joseph P. Ogden, and Charles A. Trzcinka. 1999. A new estimate of transaction costs. *Review of Financial Studies* 12, 1113–41.

Lin, Hai, Junbo Wang, and Chunchi Wu. 2011. Liquidity risk and expected corporate bond returns. *Journal of Financial Economics* 99, 628–50.

Liu, Weimin. 2006. A liquidity-augmented capital asset pricing model. *Journal of Financial Economics* 82, 631–71.

Loderer, Claudio, and Lukas Roth. 2005. The pricing discount for limited liquidity: Evidence from SWX Swiss Exchange and the Nasdaq. *Journal of Empirical Finance* 12, 239–68.

Longstaff, Francis A. 1995. How much can marketability affect security values? *Journal of Finance* 50, 1767–74.

Longstaff, Francis A., Sanjay Mithal, and Eric Neid. 2005. Corporate yield spreads: Default risk or liquidity? New evidence from the credit default swap market. *Journal of Finance* 60, 2213–53.

Malaby, Sebastian. 2010. More Money Than God. The Penguin Press, New York.

Menselson, Haim, 1982. Market behavior in a clearing house. *Econometrica* 50, 1505–24.

Mendelson, Haim. 1985. Random competitive exchange: Price distributions and gains from trade. *Journal of Economic Theory* 37, 254–80.

Muscarella, Chris J., and Michael S. Piwowar. 2001. Market microstructure and securities values: Evidence from the Paris Bourse. *Journal of Financial Markets* 4, 209–29.

Naes, Randi, and Bernt Arne Odegaard. 2009. Liquidity and Asset Pricing: Evidence on the role of investor holding period. *Working paper.*

Nashikkar, Amrut, Marti Subrahmanyam, and Sriketan Mahanti. 2011. Liquidity and arbitrage in the market for credit risk. *Journal of Financial and Quantitative Analysis* 46, 627–56.

Pastor, Lubos, and Robert F. Stambaugh. 2003. Liquidity risk and expected stock returns. *Journal of Political Economy* 111, 642–85.

Pedersen, Lasse Heje. 2009. When everyone runs for the exit. *International Journal of Central Banking* 5, 177–99.

Reinhart, Carmen M., and Kenneth S. Rogoff. 2009. This Time Is Different: Eight Centuries of Financial Folly. Princeton University Press, Princeton, NJ.

Sadka, Ronnie. 2011. Hedge-fund performance and liquidity risk. *Journal of Investment Management*, forthcoming.

Silber, William L. 1991. Discounts on restricted stocks: The impact of illiquidity on stock prices. *Financial Analysts Journal* 47(4), 60–4.

Watanabe, Akiko, and Masahiro Watanabe. 2008. Time-varying liquidity risk and the cross section of stock returns. *Review of Financial Studies* 21, 2449–86.

Ziemba, Rachel E.S., and William T. Ziemba. 2007. Scenarios for Risk Management and Global Investment Strategies. England: John Wiley & Sons.

Index

Printed in the United States
By Bookmasters